D1475252

Practice to Deceive

Other Works by Joseph Rosenblum

Shakespeare: An Annotated Bibliography

A Bibliographic History of the Book:
An Annotated Guide to the Literature

Thomas Holcroft: Literature and Politics in England
in the Age of the French Revolution

Prince of Forgers

Edited works

The Plays of Thomas Holcroft

Lives of Mississippi Authors, 1817–1967
(with James B. Lloyd and Robert Linder)

American Book Collectors and Bibliographers,
First and Second Series

Sir Walter Wilson Greg: A Selection of His Writings

Shakespeare

The Amazing Stories of Literary Forgery's Most Notorious Practitioners

Joseph Rosenblum

Mundus vult decipi, ergo decipiatur

Oak Knoll Press
New Castle, Delaware
2000

First Edition

Published by Oak Knoll Press
310 Delaware Street, New Castle DE 19720

ISBN: 1-58456-010-X

Title: Practice to Deceive
Author: Joseph Rosenblum
Editor: Mary Hallwachs
Typographer: MidAtlantic Books & Journals, Inc.
Publication Director: J. Lewis von Hoelle
Cover Design: M. Hohner J. von Hoelle

Copyright: ©1999 Joseph Rosenblum

Library of Congress Cataloging-in-Publication Data

Rosenblum, Joseph
    Practice to deceive: the incredible story of literary forgery's most
notorious practitioners/Joseph Rosenblum
        p. cm.
    Includes bibliographical references (p.) and index.
    ISBN 1-58456-010-X
        1. Literary forgeries and mystifications--History. I. Title.

PN171.F6 R67 2000
098'.3--dc21
                                                                99-048636

ALL RIGHTS RESERVED:
No part of this book may be reproduced in any manner without the
express written consent of the publisher, except in the
case of brief excerpts in critical reviews and articles. All inquiries should
be addressed to: Oak Knoll Press, 310 Delaware Street,
New Castle, DE 19720

Printed in the United States of America on 60# natural smooth
archival, acid-free paper.

For Fluff, Hodge, Lily, Sir Lynxalot,
and Black Cat, O.F.C.

and

For Pam, Laurie, Ida, and Suzanne

si qua est ea gloria

List of Illustrations

Table of Contents

Acknowledgments

"On the earth the broken arcs; in the heaven, the perfect round." The arcs of this book would be still less perfect than they are without the assistance of many people whose generosity with their time and knowledge I am delighted to acknowledge here. John von Hoelle and Robert Fleck of Oak Knoll Press provided encouragement and useful suggestions. The careful reading of the typescript by Professor Mark Smith-Soto of the University of North Carolina at Greensboro, Mary Hallwachs, and Suzanne Rosenblum greatly improved the text. Arthur Freeman and Janet Ing Freeman, who know more about John Payne Collier than anyone else, kindly agreed to read my chapter on this forger and thus saved me from numerous errors. Vivien Griffiths and Mrs. Chris Hay of the Birmingham Central Library uncovered information about the fate of the William-Henry Ireland papers donated to the Birmingham Public Library by Clement Ingleby. For assistance with the William Canynge inscription I am grateful to Mrs. Jane Bradley, Local Studies Librarian, Bristol. David L. Langenberg, Associate Librarian, University of Delaware, tracked down the authorship of an article on George Gordon Byron. Gregory Gilbert of Justin G. Schiller, Ltd. and Leo Biondi of Heritage Book Shop kindly supplied me with information about the manuscript of Charles Dickens' *The Haunted Man,* which Mark William Hofmann used in one of his fraudulent schemes. Paul Husbands of the Research Department, Rare Books, Manuscript and Special Collections Library, Duke University, generously consulted Duke's copy of Emanuel Bowen's *A Complete System of Geography* to determine George Psalmanazar's contributions thereto. The staff of the Walter Clinton Jackson Library, University of North Carolina at Greensboro, was, as always, most helpful. Gale Research of Detroit kindly has allowed me to reprint my article on Thomas James Wise that appeared in somewhat different form in the *Dictionary of Literary Biography,* vol. 184, edited by William Baker and Kenneth Womack, Copyright 1997 Gale Research. All rights reserved. Reproduced by permission.

Picture Credits

Portraits of James McPherson and William-Henry Ireland, courtesy of the National Portrait Gallery.

Painting of Thomas Chatterton by Henry Wallis, courtesy of the Tate Gallery, London, and Art Resource, New York.

Portrait of John Payne Collier, by permission of Oxford University Press.

Portrait of Mark William Hofmann, courtesy of Ana Durban and the Salt Lake Tribune.

Vrain Lucas Fascimile, courtesy of the University of Delaware Library, Newark, Delaware.

Foreword

Like dark shadows over the wide vistas of Western literature, the subtle arts of the literary forger have always been found fascinating. Professor Rosenblum's scholarship and research brings to life nine of these infamous scoundrels and their incredible stories. Each story not only enlightens the reader about the cunning, skill and techniques of the chosen forgers, but explores their personalities and varied motives. In *Practice to Deceive* we are offered a unique window into their world, their everyday habits and maybe even a glimpse into their minds. What compulsion drove these men to risk their good names, their professions, and for some, their freedom? What triggered the will to create their spurious literature and the audacity required to swindle or dupe their unsuspecting buyers?

The reader will find many motives in these stories. For most forgers, it was simply a quick way to easy money, with the added benefits of momentary fame, admiration or status among peers. However, with some of these fallen gentlemen, more subtle motives lurk just below the surface. The more discerning reader will find that some of the sinister forgeries of Mark Hofmann were designed to attack the very foundations of the Mormon Church. Did religious demagoguery have some part in Hofmann's deadly crimes? Most of the 27,000 plus forgeries of the Frenchman Vrain-Denis Lucas (Prince of Forgers) had a strong patriotic theme to them as he tried to influence the course of French history while making his millions. Yet who could stay angry at a Frenchman who had the impudence to create letters in modern French between Cleopatra and Caesar about sending their son to France for, "*Its good air and the things taught there.*" And what was really behind the chicanery of the eighteen-year old William-Henry Ireland who found a "lost" Shakespearean play and pulled off one of the greatest hoaxes in British theatrical history?

It's probably the sheer audacity of these literary rouges and the gullibility of so-called "experts" and collectors that we find most interesting. As in the medieval passion plays and American Western dramas, truth and reason ultimately win out. Most of our colorful villains are discovered and exposed when they meet their match among literature's great defenders. Usually through their technical carelessness, disdain for credibility, or their vanity, they seemed to plant the seeds of their own exposure.

In this intriguing work, Professor Rosenblum gives his readers a profound look into the ingenious, if not a bit melodramatic world of the literary forger, and captures all the frailties of the human condition with humor, suspense and well-written prose.

John Lewis
Accomac, Va.

Introduction
Forgery from Antiquity to 1700

Of the making of books there is no end, saith the preacher, and some of those books have proved not to be what they appear. The nine forgers examined in this book are among the most notorious, and fascinating, practitioners of the art in the past three centuries. They were, however, working in a tradition that is as old as literature itself. Already in the 5th century B.C., the Greek historian Thucydides maintained that written records were not to be trusted because they could so easily be manufactured.

A millennium later, David the Armenian listed five reasons for forgery. Chief among these was the delight the creators took in passing off their own works as those of others. Western literature begins with Homer, and so does forgery. The Greek historian Herodotus commented in the 5th century B.C. that the so-called Homeric Hymns and *Margites*, attributed to Homer, were thought to be by someone else (Book II, 117; Book IV, 32). The scholars at the Alexandrian Museum divided the works of Aeschylus into "Aitnaiai gnesoi" and "Aitnaiai nothoi," the legitimate and the spurious. Even Aeschylus' authentic works, though, were subject to contamination. At the end of Aeschylus' *Seven against Thebes* (467 B.C.), the herald announces that Eteocles is to be buried, but the body of his brother, Polynices, is to be left for birds and dogs to consume. Antigone, sister to the dead men, resolves to bury Polynices despite the decree. It is likely that this section of Aeschylus' play is a later addition taken from Sophocles' *Antigone* (441 B.C.), rather than part of the original.

The anonymous authors of the Homeric hymns and of the addition to *Seven against Thebes* apparently did not flaunt their activities. In the 4th century B.C., Dionysius "the Renegade" was less discreet. He composed a play, *Parthenopaeus,* which he claimed was a lost work by the 5th-century B.C. Athenian tragedian Sophocles.[1] Dionysius then showed his "discovery" to the critic Heraclides, who had himself indulged in the occasional fabrication. After Heraclides accepted the Sophoclean attribution, Dionysius declared himself the author. Heraclides responded with the Greek equivalent of "Piffle." Whereupon Dionysius showed Heraclides certain acrostics concealed in the text. One of them read, "An old monkey isn't caught by a trap. Oh yes, he's caught at last, but it takes time." Even more biting was another: "Heraclides is ignorant of letters."[2]

The 2nd-century A.D. physician Galen was prompted to compile a bibliography of his works when he discovered a spurious title being sold as his at a Roman bookstore.[3] Perhaps Galen took some comfort from the knowledge that the Hippocratic corpus had been emended by later additions attributed to the founder of medicine. Galen's edition of Hippocrates sought to distinguish these accretions from the authentic originals.

This delight in passing off one's own work as that of another's infected the greatest of Renaissance scholars and clerics. The 1998 *Encyclopaedia Britannica* called Joseph Justus Scaliger (1540–1609) "the most eminent scholar of his time."[4] He used his extensive knowledge of classical history to produce a spurious Greek chronicle, and his fluency in that language allowed him to manufacture a collection of poetry that he attributed to Astrampsychus. In 1529 Antoine Guevara, archbishop of Montenedo (Spain), published the *Libro aureo de Marco Aurelio emperador* (the golden book of the emperor Marcus Aurelius), supposedly consisting of the letters of this stoical ruler. Accepted as genuine and translated into English as *The Dial of Princes* (1557) by Sir Thomas North, it contributed to the vogue of ornate Euphuistic writing epitomized by the Elizabethan John Lyly. The 16th-century historian Carlo Sigonio was arguably the greatest Ciceronian scholar of his day. In the 1580s

---

1   Parthenopaeus, whose name means maiden-one or maiden-faced, was one of the seven generals leading the attack against Thebes in Aeschylus' play on this subject. Parthenopaeus is killed in the battle.
2   Anthony Grafton, *Forgers and Critics: Creativity and Duplicity in Western Scholarship* (Princeton: Princeton University Press, 1990), 3–4.
3   *De libris propriis* (of his own books).
4   10:497.

he published the complete text of Cicero's *Consolatio,* written by the 1st-century B.C. Roman rhetorician on the death of Cicero's daughter, Tullia. The *Consolation* had been known since antiquity and had been preserved in fragments; Sigonio's text was a brilliant recreation, but it was not genuine. The style was, however, so convincingly Ciceronian that the fabrication was accepted for two centuries.

As a second motive for forgery David the Armenian listed money. Even in the classical era, age bestowed value. In the 1st century A.D., Juba II, ruler of Mauritania, is known to have paid a premium for manuscripts of Pythagorus that had been artificially antiqued. That greed can prompt forgery in unlikely places is evidenced by the monks of Crowland, Lincolnshire. They created charters to hold on to their lands and privileges, and in 1393 Richard II confirmed two of these documents, one supposedly granted by Ethelbald of Mercia in 716, the other by Edred, king of England, in 948. Some twenty years later, facing a legal challenge from the monastery at Spalding, the monks of Crowland produced a whole series of fictitious charters, which they embedded in a history they attributed to Ingulf (d. 1109) and Peter of Blois. Despite occasional doubters such as Edward Gibbon, the deception continued to be accepted well into the 19th century.[5] The fabrication of legal documents was widespread in the Middle Ages. Giles Constable found that "of 164 known charters attributed to Edward the Confessor, 44 (27%) are spurious, 56 (34%) are uncertain, and 64 (39%) are authentic."[6]

David noted that collectors desiring rare books were tempted to manufacture what they could not find. In the 6th century B.C., the historian Acusilaus of Argos claimed that he had discovered in his garden ancient bronze plates inscribed with genealogical information. Pliny the Elder in the 1st century A.D. reported in his *Natural History* (XIII, 13) that a temple in Lycia possessed a letter on papyrus written by its native son Sarpedon, who was killed by Patroclus in the tenth year of the Trojan War.[7]

---

5   T.F. Tout, "Mediaeval Forgers and Forgeries," *Bulletin of the John Rylands Library* 5 (April–November 1919): 208–234, 222–224.

6   "Forgery and Plagiarism in the Middle Ages," *Archiv für Diplomatik, Schriftgeschichte, Siegel- und Wappenkunde* 29 (1983): 1–14, 11.

7   See *Iliad,* Book XVI.

A motive that escaped David's list, but that may have been responsible for more forgeries than any others in the Middle Ages, was religion.[8] Two of the best known of these are the Donation of Constantine (8th century) and the False Decretals (9th century). Pope Adrian I first referred to the Donation of Constantine in 777. According to this document, Pope Sylvester had cured the Roman Emperor Constantine of leprosy. In gratitude, Constantine retired to Asia Minor, where he built a capital city named for himself, and ceded the Lateran Palace and the entire Western Roman Empire to the pope. Constantine granted Sylvester religious authority over all other Christian churches. Because the Donation gave popes temporal authority over all the islands of the sea, the only English pope, Adrian IV (1154–1159), awarded Ireland to Henry II, king of England. The consequences of that gift have troubled both countries ever since. Not until the 15th century did the humanist Lorenzo Valla and Cardinal Nicholas of Cusa demonstrate that the Donation was fraudulent.

The Donation was included in the False Decretals that appeared in the 9th century. These were attributed to the encyclopedist Isidore of Seville (d. 636). Some of the material here was authentic, such as the "Hispana collectio," a gathering of the decisions of Greek, African, Gallic, and Spanish councils to 683. However, sixty papal rulings in the first part of the Decretals are spurious. Part III includes genuine letters from the 4th to the 8th centuries, but thirty-five forgeries are intermingled with them. One purpose of these fabrications was to protect the clergy from lay authority. Thus, Pope Eusebius is made to say, "It has hitherto been observed and ruled that the laity should not accuse the bishops, because they are not of the same mode of life." Similarly, Pope Felix declares, "It has been decreed by the rulers of the synods that no one should accuse a bishop before secular judges."[9]

---

8   David's final two explanations for the existence of forgeries relate to inadvertent confusion: editors mistaken for authors, or two people of the same name being mistaken for each other.

9   Quoted in James Anson Farrer, *Literary Forgeries* (London: Longman, Green, 1907), 135.

Sectarian prejudice also underlies the fabrications of Robert Ware. Robert's father, Sir James Ware (1594–1666), was a scrupulous Irish antiquarian. Robert was less addicted to the truth. In 1705 he published *The Antiquities and History of Ireland by the Right Hon. Sir J.*[ames] *W.*[are] *Now First Published in English, and the Life of Sir James Ware Prefixed.* Historians from the early 18th to the 20th century accepted the work as authentic, but Robert had interspersed various of his own creations, such as the correspondence between Sir James Croft, Lord Deputy of Ireland, and George Dowdall, Archbishop of Armagh. Robert held strongly anti-Catholic views, which he promulgated through his forgeries. In 1678, for example, he published *Strange and Remarkable Prophecies and Predictions,* which he attributed to another archbishop of Armagh, James Usher. Usher predicted dire consequences for Ireland for failing to enforce anti-Popery laws.

Three years later Robert Ware brought out *Historical Collections of the Church of Ireland during the Reigns of Henry VIII, Edward VI and Mary.* In one of Ware's stories here, Elizabeth Edmunds, a Protestant maid at an inn at Chester, stole a commission issued by the Catholic Queen Mary and carried by Dr. Cole, dean of St. Paul's, ordering the Lord Deputy of Ireland to prosecute Protestants. For her theft, the maid was rewarded by Queen Elizabeth with a pension of forty pounds a year. Ware claimed that he had found this account among his father's papers. He may have done so, but only if he placed the story there first, since it was his own invention. Another anecdote that Robert Ware published supposedly derived from William Cecil's memoirs. In August 1559, a Catholic canon of the cathedral of Christ Church, Dublin, sought to disrupt the reading of the reformed liturgy by placing a blood-soaked sponge on the crucifix at the altar. As blood began to trickle down, one of the canon's cohorts declared, "Behold, our Savior's image sweats blood," and another replied, "How can he choose but sweat blood when heresy is come into His Church?" An examination of the crucifix revealed the hoax, which led to Queen Elizabeth's decision to remove crucifixes from Anglican churches. Robert had created this tale, too.[10]

---

10   Philip Wilson, "The Writings of Sir James Ware and the Forgeries of Robert Ware," *Transactions of the Bibliographical Society* 15 (1920): 83–94, 91.

Politics must rank with religion as a leading begetter of fabrications. The Athenian lawgiver Solon in the early 6th century B.C. and the Athenian tyrant Peisistratus later in that century were accused of inserting references to Athens into Homer's *Iliad* to demonstrate that their city had been important as far back as the Bronze Age. Modern scholars suspect that many of the place-names mentioned in the catalogue of Greek forces in the second book of the *Iliad* were introduced by traveling bards seeking to flatter their royal hosts. The "Royal Diaries" were composed in the late 4th century or early 3rd century B.C. to blacken the reputation of the recently deceased Alexander the Great by making him appear to be almost constantly drunk. Philo of Byblos (c. 70-c. 160 A.D.) produced a Phoenician history that he claimed was a Greek translation of the Phoenician Sanchuniathon (c. 1400–1200 B.C.). According to Philo, Hesiod and other Greeks had drawn on Sanchuniathon to produce their mythology. The *Phoenician History* also attacked contemporary Greek historians, particularly Plutarch, for their allegorizing tendencies. Philo's "translation" was accepted well until the 20th century; only in 1981 did Albert Irwin Baumgarten demonstrate that Philo had manufactured his account as an attack on the dominant Greco-Roman culture, and an attempt to establish the primacy of Semitic civilization.[11]

Mary, Queen of Scots, was the victim of forgeries designed to blacken her reputation and eventually bring about her execution. In 1567, her political enemies in Scotland "discovered" a casket containing eight letters from Mary to James Hepburn, 4th Earl of Bothwell, 158 lines of poetry, and two contracts for the marriage of Bothwell and Mary. According to these "Casket Letters," Mary and Bothwell planned the murder of Mary's husband Henry Stewart, Lord Darnley, and the two conspirators were contracted to marry before Bothwell had divorced his wife. The letters were produced as evidence against Mary in her first trial in England in the winter of 1568–1569 and may have contributed to Queen Elizabeth's decision to keep Mary a prisoner. Nearly twenty years later, in October 1586, Mary was tried again, this time for conspiring to kill

---

11   Albert Irwin Baumgarten, *The Phoenician History of Philo of Byblos: A Commentary* (Leiden, E. J. Brill, 1981).

Elizabeth and take over the English throne. That Mary, after twenty years a prisoner, had been involved in plots to escape, is true. However, some of the letters produced in evidence against her were probably altered, if not written entirely, under the direction of Sir Francis Walsingham, director of what might be styled Her Majesty's Secret Service. Mary was beheaded on 8 February 1587.

Such forgeries were undertaken in deadly earnest. *The Travels of Sir John Mandeville* (1356?) offers an example of fabricating for fun. The author claimed that he had been born and raised at Saint Albans, that he began his travels on Saint Michael's Day in 1322, and recorded his adventures from memory in 1356. Sir John's journey took him to Egypt, Palestine, Armenia, Persia, the land of the Amazons, India, and China. In the course of his narrative, the author described the customs of the natives, the landscape, and monsters he had encountered. The English Sir John probably was the Frenchman Jean de Bourgogne, who never left Europe. He manufactured his travels by combining his reading with a vivid imagination.

Another author who delighted in fabrication is Thomas Dangerfield (1650?–1685). Dangerfield dabbled in various types of counterfeiting, including coining. He also helped manufacture evidence of a Presbyterian plot against King Charles II. A more lighthearted manifestation of his penchant for falsification is his *Don Tomazo* (1680), his supposed autobiography. Like Sir John Mandeville he claimed to have traveled widely, serving as a soldier in Spain; leading a life of dissipation in Cairo, where he disguised himself as a Turk; spying for both the Dutch and the French back in Europe.

The following nine chapters will reveal a mixture of these six motives. For some, money was the primary incentive; others were prompted by religious or patriotic impulses. Whatever the reasons that led these men to weave their tangled webs, all nine confirm James Anson Farrer's assessment of the breed of forgers: "Audacious, designing, but interesting figures, who, in revolt against the world's conventional standards, employed letters, as other men freely and without censure employ politics."[12]

12 *Literary Forgeries,* 281.

Mr George Psalmanazar.

I

George Psalmanazar, Formosan

n 1704 there appeared a volume with the imposing title of *An Historical and Geographical Description of Formosa, an Island subject to the Emperor of Japan. Giving an Account of the Religion, Customs, Manners, &c. of the Inhabitants. Together with a Relation of what happen'd to the Author in his Travels, particularly his Conferences with the Jesuits, and others, in several Parts of Europe. Also the History and Reasons of his Conversion to Christianity, with his Objections against it (in defence of Paganism) and their Answers. To which is prefix'd, A PREFACE in Vindication of himself from the Reflections of a Jesuit lately come from China, with an Account of what passed between them* (London: Printed for Dan. Brown [et al.], 1704). In the epistle dedicatory, addressed to Henry Compton, Bishop of London, the author, who called himself George Psalmanazar, claimed that he wrote this book for two reasons:

> The Europeans *have such obscure and various Notions of* Japan, and especially of our Island Formosa, *that they can believe nothing for Truth that has been said of it.* But *the prevailing Reason for this my Undertaking was, because the* Jesuits *I found have impos'd so many stories, and such gross Fallacies upon the Public, that they might the better excuse themselves from those base Actions, which deservedly brought upon them that fierce Persecution in* Japan: *I thought therefore it would not be unacceptable if I publish'd a short Description of the Island* Formosa, *and told the Reasons why this wicked Society,*[1] *and at last all that profess'd Christianity, were, with them, expell'd that Country.*

---

1 The Jesuits.

Psalmanazar began his book with a highly imaginative account of himself. About 1694 a Father de Rode of Avignon came to Formosa in the guise of a native of Japan. De Rode advertised himself as a tutor of Latin, and Psalmanazar's rich father engaged de Rode to teach the young man the language. For four years de Rode lived with Psalmanazar's family at Xternetsa, the capital of Formosa. Then de Rode was recalled to Europe, but he concealed his destination by claiming that he wished to travel through Asia, Africa, and Europe before returning to Japan. De Rode particularly praised Christian countries, inspiring in the nineteen-year-old Psalmanazar a desire to accompany his tutor. De Rode feigned reluctance to take the young man but finally agreed, at the same time urging Psalmanazar to bring with him as much of his father's money as possible.

At the port of Khadzey, de Rode and his young companion found a ship belonging to Psalmanazar's father. Psalmanazar ordered the crew to take them to Luconia in the Phillippines. From there the two made their way back to Avignon, and only then did Psalmanazar discover that de Rode was a Christian. De Rode offered to send Psalmanazar back to Formosa or to educate him as a Catholic. Fearing that the offer of returning to Formosa was false, Psalmanazar agreed to convert if the Jesuits could convince him that their religion was superior to paganism. They could not: in particular Psalmanazar pointed out the absurdity of the Catholic belief in transubstantiation, i.e., that the communion wine and wafer actually, not just symbolically, become the blood and body of Christ. This passage, like the epistle dedicatory and the title of Psalmanazar's book, indicates that Psalmanazar was appealing to anti-Catholic prejudices in England, then at war with Catholic France: the doctrine of transubstantiation was rejected by the Anglican Church.

Unable to convince Psalmanazar to convert, the Jesuits next tried to bribe him. "But I *knew so well their Insincerity and cheating Tricks,* by their counterfeiting themselves to be Heathens in *Formosa,* and by breaking their Promise of allowing me Liberty of Conscience, that I could put no Confidence in any Promises they made me."[2] So the Jesuits resorted to threats. Psalmanazar

2   *Historical and Geographical Description of Formosa,* 20.

had been in Avignon for fifteen months, six in a monastery and nine elsewhere. Now he was told that he had ten days to convert or be thrown into prison by the Inquisition. He gained a few extra days because this conversation occurred on 1 August, and the Jesuits wanted him to convert on the Feast of the Assumption of the Virgin Mary, August 15.[3] On 10 August Psalmanazar escaped from Avignon by bribing a sentinel.

His flight was interrupted when he was captured by soldiers belonging to the Elector of Cologne. The captain took Psalmanazar to the colonel, who also wanted to convert the young man. To that end he sent Psalmanazar to another group of Jesuits. Their arguments were no more persuasive than those of the first group, nor would Psalmanazar yield to their bribes. The colonel now threatened to imprison Psalmanazar and allow him only bread and water until he converted. Luckily for Psalmanazar, the captain not only rescued the young man from this fate but also secured his release from the army.

Psalmanazar's freedom was, however, short-lived. At Cologne he was seized by soldiers of the Prince of Mecklenburg serving under Dutch command. Now the Lutherans tried to convert Psalmanazar, but again he overcame their arguments. A Calvinist almost persuaded him to become a Christian, but Psalmanazar could not accept the extreme view of predestination presented to him. Then at Sluys in the Netherlands he met the Anglican priest Alexander Innes, "who proposed to me the Christian Religion in its Purity, without those Monstrous Doctrines of Transubstantiation, Consubstantiation and absolute Predestination: A Religion that was not embarrassed with any of those absurdities which are maintained by the many various Sects in *Christendom*,"[4] and Psalmanazar was converted.

Psalmanazar's actual biography was colorful enough. He was born to a Catholic family in the south of France sometime between 1679 and 1684. When he was about five his parents separated, and he remained with his mother, while his father went to Germany.

---

3   The Anglicans reject the Catholic belief that Mary, like Jesus, was assumed bodily into heaven. Psalmanazar is thus again mocking the Catholics here for what he expected his readers to regard as Papist superstitions.

4   *An Historical and Geographical Description of Formosa*, 36–37.

The first school he attended was run by two Franciscan monks. When Psalmanazar was nine his tutor was transferred to a new post twenty-four miles away; Psalmanazar accompanied him and attended the local Jesuit college. Then a Dominican started a class in philosophy in Psalmanazar's native town, and Psalmanazar returned home to study with him. The man proved to be a poor scholar, and after a year Psalmanazar left for another Dominican school, where he studied theology.

He now neglected his schoolwork, though, and left the Dominicans to become a tutor to the nephew of a rich man at Avignon. He subsequently held other teaching posts, but none paid well, and he decided to return home. He said that he was an Irish theological student who had fled his native land to escape religious persecution and was embarked on a pilgrimage to Rome. He secured a certificate so identifying him, and to lend credibility to his claim he stole a pilgrim's staff and cloak from a church. Making his way by begging, he visited his mother and then traveled to Germany to see his father and to secure a teaching post. Psalmanazar was proficient in Latin—he wrote his account of Formosa in that language and it was translated into English by a Mr. Oswald—and he apparently knew some Greek as well. But he spoke no German, and he claimed that his Latin and Greek pronunciation differed from that approved in Germany, so he could not find a job.

He therefore resumed his travels, now claiming to be a Japanese convert to Christianity, drawing on what he had learned from the Jesuits about the Far East and supplementing fact with imagination. As proof of his origins, he created a new certificate to replace the one he had received at Avignon and affixed the old seal to his fabrication. For a time he worked in a coffeehouse at Aix-la-Chapelle before joining a regiment of the Elector of Cologne. Here he underwent another metamorphosis, into a heathen Japanese. At Bonn his colonel dismissed him as unsuited to the soldier's life, but at Cologne the young man, still in the guise of a heathen Japanese, enlisted in a regiment of the Duke of Mecklenburg. He then took the name of Salmanazar, from *2 Kings* 17:3, and later changed the spelling to Psalmanaazaar before settling on the final form. To lend credibility to his assumed identity he made a book with pictures of the sun, the moon, and stars, along with a text in characters he invented, and from this text he chanted his supposed prayers.

In late 1702 the regiment came to Sluys, where Alexander Innes was chaplain to the Scottish regiment stationed there.[5] The governor of the town, Brigadier George Lauder, invited Psalmanazar to his house, where Psalmanazar debated theology with Isaac d'Amalvi, the minister of the French church. Innes, who was also present, asked Psalmanazar to visit him to discuss religion. Innes, not persuaded by Psalmanazar's heathen pretense, gave the young man a passage from Cicero's *De natura deorum* (on the nature of the gods) to translate into Japanese, took that version, and then asked for a second translation of the same passage. The two efforts were sufficiently different to expose Psalmanazar, but Innes decided to use Psalmanazar for his own advancement. Innes invented yet another identity for the supposed Oriental, the one included in the *Historical and Geographical Description of Formosa* and presented at the beginning of this chapter. Innes wrote to Henry Compton, Bishop of London, about Psalmanazar, who had agreed to convert to Anglicanism. Innes baptized the "heathen," with George Lauder standing godfather. Psalmanazar took the brigadier's name but soon dropped the surname, retaining only George.

The Bishop of London invited Innes and his convert to London. Bishop Compton hoped that Psalmanazar could teach missionaries the Formosan language, so they could travel to the island to convert the natives. Innes secured Psalmanazar's release from the army, and at the end of 1703 the two men traveled to England by way of Rotterdam. To maintain his disguise, Psalmanazar lived on a diet of raw meat, roots, and herbs. Even so, he encountered skepticism. Why was he so fair-skinned? He replied that as a member of the privileged class—eventually he claimed to be the son of the king—he did not venture out into the sun. Could he offer any proof of his statements, Bishop Gilbert Burnet asked. "The manner of my flight," Psalmanazar replied, "did not allow me to bring credentials. But suppose your Lordship

---

5   The Dutch and English were allied against France in the War of the Spanish Succession.

were at Formosa and should say you were an Englishman, might not the Formosan as justly reply, 'You say you are an Englishman, but what proof can you give that you are not of any other country, for you look as like a Dutchman as any that ever traded to Formosa.' "[6] The bishop said no more.

A more dangerous opponent was the Jesuit Father Fontenay, who had spent eighteen years in China. On Wednesday, 2 February 1704, the two debated before the Royal Society. Fontenay stated, correctly, that Formosa belonged to China, not Japan, but Psalmanazar insisted on his version. Psalmanazar asked Fontenay how else Formosa was called, and the Jesuit replied, "Tyowan" (i.e., Taiwan). Again he was right, but Psalmanazar said that Tyowan was a different island, a Dutch colony. According to Psalmanazar the Chinese called Formosa Pak-Ando, and the natives called their island Gad-Avia. Fontenay denied that "Pak" was even a Chinese word.

The two met again a week later (9 February) when they dined with Hans Sloane, Secretary of the Royal Society, and they met a third time in the Temple Coffeehouse in Devereux Court in the Strand, near Temple Bar. Fontenay asked about Psalmanazar's leaving Formosa and denied any knowledge of a Father de Rode, but the Jesuit did not attempt to contradict any of Psalmanazar's statements, apparently realizing that the young man's inventions were more credible that his own truths.

Psalmanazar's success derived not only from his skill at invention but also from his manner of living. As he wrote in his *Memoirs,*

> The plainness of my dress and diet, the little trouble I gave myself about worldly wealth, preferment, or even acquiring or securing a base competency, a good-natured and charitable disposition, visibly natural to me, my averseness to drinking, lewd women, &c. and a great reservedness to such of the fair sex as had either lost their reputation, though they lived still in credit and splendor, and even to those who betrayed too small a regard for their character . . ., these,

---

6   Quoted in Philip W. Sergeant, *Liars and Fakers* (London: Hutchinson & Co., 1925), 212.

together with the warmth I naturally expressed for religion, and the real delight I took in the publick offices of it, appeared such convincing proofs of my sincerity, that those of my friends to whom I was most intimately known, were the most impatient and displeased to have it called in question; for who could imagine, as they often urged, that a youth of so much sense and learning for his years, so seemingly free from ambition and other vices, could be abandoned enough to be guilty of such abominable an imposture and impiety, for the sake of a little plain, homely food and rayment?[7]

During this time Psalmanazar was living with Innes in Pall Mall and working on his version of the Formosan language. At Innes' urging he "translated" the Anglican catechism into Formosan and presented a copy to the Bishop of London. Innes then persuaded Psalmanazar to write a history of Formosa. Innes secured for him Bernhard Varen's *Descriptio regni Iaponiae* (description of the kingdom of Japan), first published at Amsterdam by Ludovico Elzevir in 1649 and reprinted at Cambridge in 1673, and Georgius Candidius' *A Short Account of the Island of Formosa,* which had appeared at Frankfurt in 1649. Psalmanazar worked quickly, completing the book in two months.

The result conformed to the intention that Psalmanazar set out in his *Memoirs:* "I . . . resolved with myself to give such a description of [Formosa] as should be wholly new and surprising and should in most particulars clash with all accounts other writers had given of it."[8] Candidius, a Dutch missionary, had written that begging was widespread on the island. Psalmanazar wrote that each village had a poorhouse and that begging was forbidden. Candidius denied the existence of a central government; Psalmanazar created one. Candidius claimed that laws were virtually non-existent, that robbery was scarcely punished, that murder and adultery were compensated for by a few hogs. Psalmanazar invented a harsh penal code according to which robbers and murderers were hanged upside down and shot to death with arrows. Nor were these the most serious offenses:

---

7   *Memoirs* (London: Printed for the Executrix, 1764; 2d ed., London: R. Davis [et al], 1765), 168–169. All references to the *Memoirs* come from the second edition.
8   *Memoirs,* 182.

> If a Son or a Daughter shall strike their Father or Mother, or one of their Kindred that is Ancient, or one that is superior to them in Power, their Arms and Legs shall be cut off, and a Stone being tied about their Neck, they shall be thrown into the Sea, or a River. But if any one shall strike a Priest, their Arms shall be burnt off, and then their Body shall be buried alive.[9]

Psalmanazar devoted a lengthy section of his account to the religion of Formosa. Initially the inhabitants had worshiped the sun, moon, and ten stars. About nine hundred years earlier, however, Zeroaboabel[10] and Chorche Matchin had taught the Formosans to worship a supreme god greater than these celestial bodies. These two philosophers had told the people to build a temple and annually offer as a sacrifice the hearts of 20,000 children under the age of nine. The people objected to such cruelty and drove away the two men. Earthquakes and plagues ensued, and wild animals entered the people's houses and devoured their children.[11] The prophet Psalmanaazaar promised peace between the supreme deity and the inhabitants, but they were to build a temple and sacrifice a hundred oxen, a hundred rams, and a hundred goats, in addition to the hearts of 20,000 children under the age of nine.

Psalmanaazaar taught the Formosans to divide the year into ten months, each named for one of the ten stars: Dig, Damen, Analmen, Anioul, Dattibes, Dabes, Anaber, Nechem, Koriam, and Turbam. The third, fifth, seventh, and ninth months have thirty-seven days, the rest thirty-six. The last day of each of the longer months is a fast day. The year begins with a ten-day festival in Dig, in which 18,000 boys under the age of nine are sacrificed. Each of the other nine months begins with the sacrifice of a thousand animals.

The Formosans have a High Priest (Gnotoy Bonzo), who is forbidden to marry. He appoints the other priests, who are allowed

---

9 *An Historical and Geographical Description of Formosa*, 165–166.

10 Like Psalmanazar's own, this name derives from the Bible. See Ezra 3:2, 8; 5:2; *Nehemiah* 12:1; *Haggai* 1:1, 12, 14; 2:2, 23.

11 Here again Psalmanazar draws on the Bible, in this case the plagues visited on the Egyptians in *Exodus*.

to marry, "Except they be Regulars; and then they are oblig'd to continue unmarried, and to live in Convents with their Brethren under one Supervisor, who shall admit them to the Priestly Office." The Regulars, whose task is teaching, "are to shave their Head, but not to cut their Beard. They are to wear a Gown that does not open before or behind, and a Hood upon their Heads."[12] Regulars are called Bonzos Roches, and their supervisor is known as Bonzo Soulleto. While the Regulars might appear to resemble Catholic monks, Psalmanazar makes clear that their vow of celibacy is conditional only: they are free to leave their monastery to marry. Moreover, "They make no Vows of a blind Obedience to their Superiors, of an affected Poverty, and Humility, and of renouncing the Riches of this World."[13] While revering a supreme god, the Formosans continue to worship the sun, moon, and ten stars, praying to the sun and five stars each morning, to the moon and the other five stars at night.

To maintain the population, given the extensive annual slaughter of children, a man may marry as many wives as he can afford, but if he marries beyond his means he is beheaded. Women marry between the ages of ten and fifteen; they may not remarry after their husbands' death.

Addressing the question of his own light complexion, Pslamanazar explained:

> Altho' the Country be very hot, yet the Men in all Formosa are very fair, at least those who can live upon their Means; but the Country People, Servants, and others, who are expos'd to the heat of the Sun, and are forc'd to work in the open Air all Day, are very much tawn'd by the burning Heat. The Men of Estates, but especially the Women, are very fair; for they during the hot season live under Ground in Places that are very cold.[14]

Once more differing from Candidius, who reported neither gold nor silver mines, Psalmanazar stated that both were found in

---

12   *An Historical and Geographical Description of Formosa*, 185.
13   Ibid., 188–189.
14   Ibid., 221.

the country. So, too, are elephants, "rhinocerots,"[15] camels, sea-horses, apes, crocodiles, and wild bulls. The first four "are tame, and very useful for the service of Man."[16] The Formosans keep toads in their houses "to attract all the Venom that may happen to be there," and they keep weasels to kill mice.[17] They also keep a lizard-like creature called "*Varchiero,* i.e. the Persecutor of Flies; its Skin is smooth and clear like Glass, and appears in various colors according to the Situation of its Body."[18]

As for diet, Formosans "commonly eat the Flesh of Venison and of Fowl, raw: And, which may seem strange here in *England,* they eat Serpents also, which they look upon as very good Meat and very savoury, being broil'd upon the Coals: But before they eat them, they take care to extract all the Poison out of them."[19] This process involves beating the serpents to make them angry; all the poison then supposedly rises to the head, which is then cut off.

Psalmanazar had devoted a hundred pages of his book to the-ological questions even before he began discussing Formosa, and at the end of his book he returned to an overt attack on both Jesuits and the Dutch.[20] He claimed that the Jesuits had planned to betray Japan to Spain and to persuade the Emperor to kill all non-Christians, which led instead to a massacre of Christians in the country. Psalmanazar linked these schemes to the Gunpowder Plot of 1605, in which dissident Catholics had planned to blow up Parliament and the royal family. He then accused the Dutch of securing trading rights in Japan by pretending not to be Christians, going so far as to trample on the Cross.[21]

---

15   Ibid., 264.
16   Ibid.
17   Ibid., 265.
18   Ibid.
19   Ibid., 263.
20   Although the English and Dutch were at the moment allied, they were traditional maritime rivals. Anti-Dutch sentiment was strong in England in the 17th and 18th centuries. See, for example, Andrew Marvell's "The Character of Holland" (1653), John Dryden's "Annus Mirabilis" (1667), and Book III of *Gulliver's Travels* (1726).
21   This charge of mercenary sacrilege was often leveled against the Dutch by the English. At the end of Book III of *Gulliver's Travels,* when Gulliver asks the emperor of Japan to excuse him from the ceremony of trampling on the crucifix, the emperor doubts whether Gulliver is "a real Hollander or no." The emperor assures Gulliver that if any Dutchman learns of Gulliver's scruples, that Dutchman will cut Gulliver's throat. (Jonathan Swift, *Gulliver's Travels,* ed. Peter Dixon and John Chalker [London: Penguin, 1967], 262.

At the end of his book Psalmanazar once more attacked the Jesuits:

> From what has been said of the Causes of the great Persecution of the Christians in Japan, we may clearly understand how great a Prejudice the Jesuits have done to Christianity, and what a Reproach they have brought upon the Christian Name, by imposing their Popish Errors upon the People as necessary Articles of Faith, and by contriving that barbarous and bloody Massacre which they intended against all the poor Pagans: Whereas if they had propos'd the Christian Religion in its Purity and Simplicity, and behaved themselves towards their Proselytes with that Meekness, Charity, and Sincerity, which became their Apostolical Office, I dare be confident to affirm, that in all Probability the whole Empire of *Japan* had now been Christian.[22]

Here, then, was a text to appeal to Anglican orthodoxy, anti-Dutch sentiment, and the vogue for travel literature. Psalmanazar embellished his text with illustrations of his own devising, showing the buildings, costumes, and ceremonies of the island, such as the grill on which the hearts of the boys were annually burnt. He included a chart of the twenty letters of the Formosan alphabet, a curious farrago of Hebrew (e.g., Mem, Nen, Kaphi), Greek (Lamdo, Epsi), and nonsense (Hamno, Pedlo, Dam, Raw).

For his efforts Psalmanazar received ten guineas (£10 10s.), and he was sent to Christ Church, Oxford to study, though he did little more than revise his book for a second edition that appeared in 1705, and for which he received another twelve guineas. To create the illusion that he was hard at work, he left a candle burning in his window, and he would sleep in an easy chair so that his bed would appear untouched. He even walked with a limp to suggest that his studying had brought on an attack of the gout.

At Oxford he was asked about Formosa, and these conversations led to changes in the second edition. Thus, Psalmanazar originally wrote that a man could behead his wife and eat her. A woman protested that the practice was barbarous. Psalmanazar

---

22 Ibid., 322–323.

conceded that the beheading was unpleasant, but that eating human flesh was not a sin, though he allowed that it might not represent the best of manners. In the second edition he added human flesh to the Formosan diet, though only of enemies slain in battle or executed criminals; he wrote nothing about consuming wives. He claimed that his grandfather maintained his vigor to the age of 117 by sucking the blood of a viper each morning. He related that Formosans had "bosom-snakes" that protected them and also kept them cool when traveling.[23]

While Psalmanazar was at Oxford, Innes was rewarded for converting the Formosan by being appointed chaplain-general to the British forces in Portugal. After spending six months at Oxford, Psalmanazar returned to Innes' house in Pall Mall to finish work on the second edition of his book, which began with a new thirty-four page preface addressing objections that had been raised against the first edition. He also wrote *A Dialogue between a Japonese and a Formosan about Some Points of Religion* (London: Bernard Lintot, 1707), written to "vindicate the Japonese from that unjust Character this part of the World is pleased to give them, viz. of being a people much given to Superstition."[24]

Psalmanazar is probably also the author of *An Enquiry into the Objections against George Psalmanazar* (London: Lintot, n.d.).[25] The frontispiece, a map of Formosa supplied by a "Captain Bowery," shows that Formosa consists of two islands, as Psalmanazar asserted. The pamphlet explains that Psalmanazar's version of the Lord's Prayer in Formosan differed from that given in another work because those living along the coast speak a different dialect from those who live inland. Also included is a letter in French by someone who some five years earlier had heard of a Chinaman recently arrived at Avignon. The letter-writer claimed that he had tried to find this immigrant. Unsuccessful at the time, he later met the man in London and discovered that he was a Japanese person from Formosa. Since the pamphlet claimed that this letter was in the hands of the bookseller, Psalmanazar must have manufactured it.

---

23   Sergeant, 219.
24   Ibid., 222–223.
25   The *National Union Catalogue* suggests 1710 as the date of publication.

Like *An Historical and Geographical Description of Formosa,* the pamphlet concluded with an attack on the Jesuits. In 1706 Isaac d'Amalvi, having read a French translation of Psalmanazar's book on Formosa with its account of the young man's conversion, attacked that story in *Eclaircissemen[t]s* (clarifications; The Hague; Pierre Husson, 1706). Psalmanazar included in his pamphlet a response entitled *L'Eclercisseur Eclercy;*[26] *or an Answer to a Book entitled Eclercissements sur ce que, &c.*

That Psalmanazar remained a celebrity for years after the appearance of his book on Formosa is indicated by the following mock-advertisement in *The Spectator* for 16 March 1711. Alluding to Psalmanazar's discussion of cannibalism in the second edition of his book, Joseph Addison wrote, "*On the first of April will be performed at the Play-house in the* Hay-market *an Opera call'd* The Cruelty of Atreus. N.B. *The Scene wherein* Thyestes *eats his own Children, is to be performed by the famous Mr* Psalmanazar, *lately arrived from* Formosa: *The whole Supper being set to Kettle-drums.*[27]

By this time Psalmanazar had abandoned his Oriental writing, though not his Oriental identity. Sometime around 1710 a Mr. Pattenden developed a technique for creating porcelain dishes, a popular import from China and Japan, but was unable to secure financial backing for producing these in England. Pattenden asked Psalmanazar to claim that the latter had learned the technique in Formosa, and Psalmanazar agreed, not only because Pattenden offered to share the profits but "much more so as it would yield a kind of convincing proof to the fabulous account I had given of myself."[28] The dishes were advertised as "White Formosa Work," but the enterprise failed, perhaps because Pattenden charged too much for his plates.

Psalmanazar next returned to tutoring before becoming clerk to a British regiment in 1715. He remained in this post for two years, until the soldiers were posted to Ireland. A stint at fan-painting led to Psalmanazar's acquaintance with a clergyman who raised

---

26 The clarifier clarified.
27 *The Spectator,* ed. Donald F. Bond (Oxford: Clarendon Press, 1965), I, 65.
28 *Memoirs,* 197.

a subscription to allow Psalmanazar to become an Anglican priest, but Psalmanazar chose instead to become a hack writer, working as a translator and author.

About this time (c. 1720) a clergyman from Braintree, Essex, introduced Psalmanazar to Robert Nelson's *The Practice of True Devotion* (1698) and another work entitled *Reformed Devotion*. These works effected a transformation in Psalmanazar's life, and he began to study Hebrew so that he could read the Old Testament in the original. He even contemplated a translation of the Psalms. Though this work did not materialize, Psalmanazar undertook many other projects.

From 7:00 A.M. to 7:00 P.M. each day Psalmanazar wrote, sustaining himself with ten or twelve drops of opium each day taken in a pint of punch. Among Psalmanazar's projects over the next decades was *A General History of Printing* (London: Printed for the Author , 1732) begun by Samuel Palmer but largely written by Psalmanazar under the patronage of the Earl of Pembroke. Palmer, who died in 1732, had also asked Psalmanazar to contribute to a *Universal History* (London: J. Batley [et al.], 1736-1744). For the first edition he wrote about the early history of the Jews, the Celts and Scythians, ancient Greece, the empires of Nice and Trebizon, the ancient Spaniards, Gauls, and Germans. For the second edition he added to the histories of Thebes and Corinth, wrote about Xenophon's retreat from Persia as recounted in the *Anabasis,* and extended the history of the Jews from the destruction of the Temple to the 18th century, though this last piece was not included. Psalmanazar also assisted in preparing the index for the second edition.

In 1747 there appeared Emanuel Bowen's *Complete System of Geography* (London: E, Bowen). Psalmanazar wrote the chapters on Spain and its islands off the coast; Portugal; Savoy; Italy, with sections on the Principality of Piedmont, Sicily, Sardinia, Corsica, and the islands near Sicily, Sardinia, and the Italian coast; Muscovy; Turkey; China, Japan, Jetzo, and the islands off their coasts, including Formosa. To the chapter on Africa he contributed the units dealing with Egypt, Abyssinia, Libya, Barbary, "Barca, Tripoli, Tunis," Morocco, Fez, the river of Sanaga, Madagascar, Cape Verde Islands, the Canary Islands, and the Azores; and for the America chapter he wrote about Brazil, Tierra del Fuego and the straits of Magellan, Canada, the French province of Louisiana, the Bahamas, and Bermuda. In the section dealing with Formosa he recanted his famous book, writing of it:

> Psalmanazar . . . hath long since ingenuously owned the contrary, though not in so public a manner as he might perhaps have done, had not such an avowment been likely to have affected some few persons who for private ends took advantage of his youthful vanity to encourage him in an imposture which he might otherwise never have had the thought, much less the confidence, to have carried out. These persons being now dead, and out of all danger of being hurt by it, he now gives us leave to assure the world that the greatest part of that account was fabulous.[29]

Another of Psalmanazar's works appeared in 1753 as *Essays on the Following Subjects: I. On the Reality and Evidence of Miracle . . . II. On the Extraordinary Adventure of Balaam . . . III. On the Surprising March and Final Victory . . . IV. On the Religious War of the Israelitish Tribes . . . V. On the Amazing Speedy Relief which Saul Brought to the Besieged Inhabitants of Jabesh-Gilead* (London: A. Millar) by "An obscure layman in town."

In his old age Psalmanazar lived in Ironmonger Row, Old Street, Clerkenwell, where he frequented the parish church of St. Luke and an alehouse patronized by Samuel Johnson. Johnson became a great admirer of Psalmanazar, both because of the latter's piety and because of their shared experiences as struggling Grub Street writers. In his diary Johnson recorded,

"I never yet saw a regular family unless it were that of Mrs. [Elizabeth] Harriots, nor a regular man except Mr. Campbel [i.e., Dr. John Campbell] whose exactness I know only by his own report, and Psalmanazar whose life was I think, uniform."[30] Johnson told Boswell on 18 April 1778, "I never sought much after any body. . . . But I sought after George Psalmanazar the

---

29 Quoted in Sergeant, 230.
30 Samuel Johnson, *Diaries, Prayers, and Annals,* ed. E. L. McAdam, Jr., with Donald and Mary Hyde (New Haven: Yale University Press, 1958), 134.

most. I used to go and sit with him at an alehouse in the city."[31] Johnson also told Boswell, "I should as soon think of contradicting a BISHOP" as contradicting Psalmanazar.[32]

Two of Johnson's other biographers attested to the admiration the old Psalmanazar commanded. Sir John Hawkins claimed in his *Life of Samuel Johnson* (London: J. Buckland [et al.], 1787), that Psalmanazar "was so well known and esteemed, that . . . scarce any person, even children, passed him without shewing him the usual signs of respect" (546), and Hester Thrale wrote of Psalmanazar in her *Anecdotes* (London: T. Cadell, 1786): "His pious and patient endurance of a tedious illness, ending in an exemplary death, confirmed the strong impression his merit had made upon the mind of Mr. Johnson. 'It is so *very* difficult (said he always) for a sick man not to be a scoundrel'" (175). For Tobias Smollett, Psalmanazar was an emblem of the ills the hack writer suffered. In *Humphrey Clinker* (London: W. Johnston and B. Collins, 1671 [i.e., 1771]) Smollett has Jeremy Melford describe Psalmanazar as one "who, after having drudged half a century in the literary mill, in all the simplicity and abstinence of an Asiatic, subsists upon the charity of a few booksellers, just sufficient to keep him from the parish" (II, 35).

By the time Smollett's novel appeared, Psalamanazar had been dead for several years, having died at his house in Ironmonger's Row on 3 May 1763, leaving his property to his housekeeper and friend Sarah Rewalling. Included in this legacy was the manuscript of Psalmanazar's *Memoirs,* which the author instructed Rewalling to sell to whichever publisher offered the most money for it. He claimed that he had begun this account in 1728, when illness forced him to retire to the country. About this time he probably read William Law's just published *A Serious Call to a Devout and Holy Life.* This reading, combined with his sickness, prompted him to provide

---

31   James Boswell, *Life of Johnson,* ed. George Birkbeck Hill and L. F. Powell (Oxford: Clarendon Press, 1934), III, 314.
32   Ibid., IV, 274.

a faithful narrative of my education, and the sallies of my wretched youthful years, and the various ways by which I was in some measure unavoidably led into the base and shameful imposture of passing upon the world for a native of Formosa, and a convert to Christianity, and backing it with a fictitious account of that island, and of my own travels, conversion, &c., all or most of it hatched in my own brain, without regard to truth and honesty.[33]

He acknowledged that his account of Formosa "was no other than a mere forgery of my own devising, a scandalous imposition on the public, and such, as I think myself bound to beg God and the world pardon for writing, and have been long since, as I am to this day, and shall be as long as I live, heartily sorry for, and ashamed of."[34]

The press of business did not allow him to make much progress with his autobiography until the end of his life. In this memoir he concealed the names of his parents and the date and place of his birth, though he confessed that he never left Europe. As Huckleberry Finn said regarding Mark Twain's account of Tom Sawyer, Psalmanazar here told the truth, mainly, and he provided the fullest account available about his activities. If the *Memoirs* reveals a misspent youth, it was nonetheless a youth that caused little harm and provided merriment to future generations, and it was followed by half a century's atonement of drudgery and piety. Hence, one would be inclined to place Psalmanazar in the Purgatory rather than the Inferno of literary vagabonds.

---

33 *Memoirs*, 5.
34 Ibid., 7.

James Macpherson, by George Romney, 1779–1780

II

"Ossian" James Macpherson

meeting between the Reverend John Home and James Macpherson in the early autumn of 1759 at the Scottish resort of Moffat led to one of the most controversial and influential forgeries in the history of 18th-century letters. Frank Brady, biographer of James Boswell, went so far as to call it "the most startling phenomenon in the history of British literature."[1] The unwitting instigator of the deception was the thirty-four year old playwright John Home, whose *Douglas* (1756) had earned him the title of the Scottish Shakespeare, though only north of the Tweed. David Garrick, London's leading actor, had refused to allow the piece to be performed at his theater in Drury Lane. When *Douglas* was performed at London's other playhouse, Covent Garden, it enjoyed some success. London's Scots flocked to support it, and they taunted the English in the audience with cries of "Whaur's yer Wullie Shakespeare noo?" But that Great Cham of literature, Samuel Johnson, claimed "that there were not ten good lines in the whole play."[2] Similar English indifference or hostility greeted William Wilkie's *Epigoniad* (Edinburgh: Hamilton, Balfour, & Neill, 1757), which, according to Home, put Scotland "in raptures."[3]

Home was interested in collecting and disseminating Scottish literature, especially its older poetry. His conversations on this topic with the English poet William Collins at the home of Thomas Barrow of Winchester in 1749 had prompted Collins' writing "An

1 *James Boswell: The Later Years* (New York: McGraw-Hill, 1984), 71.
2 James Boswell, *Boswell's Life of Johnson*, ed. George Birkbeck Hill and L. F. Powell (Oxford: Clarendon Press, 1950), V, 360.
3 Quoted in Richard B. Sher, "'Those Scotch Impostors and Their Cabal': Ossian and the Scottish Enlightenment," in *Man and Nature: Proceedings of the Canadian Society for Eighteenth-Century Studies* (London, Ontario: Published for the Society by the Faculty of Education, the University of Western Ontario, 1982), 55-63, 56.

Ode on the Popular Superstitions of the Highlands of Scotland, Considered as the Subject of Poetry." In this work Collins imagines Home's hearing "strange lays" that have been "taught by the father to his list'ning son." The poem continues:

> Old Runic bards shall seem to rise around,
> With uncouth lyres, in many-coloured vest,
>   Their matted hair with boughs fantastic crown'd:
> Whether thou bid'st the well-taught hind repeat
>   The choral dirge that mourns some chieftain brave,
>
>   * * *
>
> Or whether, sitting in the shepherd's shiel [hut],
>   Thou hear'st some sounding tale of war's alarms
> When, at the bugle's call, with fire and steel,
>   The sturdy clans pour'd forth their bony [bonnie]
>   swarms,
> And hostile brothers met to prove each other's arms.
>   (ll. 38–45, 47–52)

Collins' descriptions resemble the plots of many of the poems Macpherson would soon publish.

Home's enthusiasm for Scottish poetry was shared not only by Collins but also by, among others, Alexander Pope, not the famous English poet but rather the minister of Rea in Caithness; by Alexander MacDonald, who in 1751 published a collection of his own Gaelic verse, *Ais-eiridh na Sean Chánoin Albannaich* (revival of the old Alban tongue); Adam Ferguson, professor of Moral Philosophy at Edinburgh University; and Jerome Stone, who for five years served as minister at Dunkeld in Perthshire. In 1756 Stone published a translation from the Gaelic in the *Scots Magazine,* 18 (January 1756): 15–17, rendering "Bas Fhraoch," (the death of Fraoch) into 18th-century ballad meter and taking some liberties with the original to make it more pleasing to a genteel English-speaking audience. The opening two stanzas of the original read, in English,

> A friend's sigh comes from the Meadow of Fraoch,
> The sigh of a hero dying a bloody death;

That is the sigh which makes a man sad,
And which causes a young woman to weep heavily.

Over to the west is the cairn which encloses
Fraoch, son of Faidheach, of the soft locks;
The man who gladdened Meadhbh
Carn Fraoich takes its name from him.

Stone's version reads,

WHENCE come these dismal sounds that fill our ears!
    Why do the groves such lamentations send!
Why sit the virgins on the hill of tears,
    While heavy sighs their tender bosoms rend!
They weep for Albin with the flowing hair,
    Who perish'd by the cruelty of Mey;
A blameless hero, blooming, young, and fair;
    Because he scorn'd her passions to obey.
See on yon western hill the heap of stones,
Which mourning friends have raised o'er his bones!

Stone has added the language of 18th-century sentimental poetry, such as the virgins with their tender bosoms and flowing hair, he has changed the characters' names to make them more euphonious to an English ear, and "the man who gladdened" Mey now scorns "her passions to obey."[4] Stone, who died shortly after publishing this piece, accompanied his translation with a letter urging others to recover such works:

> Those who have any tolerable acquaintance with the Irish language must know that there are a great number of poetical compositions in it, and some of them of very great antiquity, whose merit entitles them to an exemption from the unfortunate neglect, or rather abhorrence, to which ignorance has subjected that emphatic language in which they were composed. Several of these performances are to be met with,

---

4   Quoted in Howard Gaskill, "'Ossian' Macpherson: Towards a Rehabilitation," *Comparative Criticism* 8 (1986): 113–146, 122–123.

which for sublimity of sentiment, nervousness of expression, and high-spirited metaphor, are hardly to be equalled among the chief productions of the most cultivated nations. Others of them breathe such tenderness and simplicity, as must be affecting to every mind that is in the least tinctured with the softer passions of pity and humanity. . . . It is hoped that the uncommon turn of several expressions, and the seeming extravagance there is in some of the comparisons I have preserved in the translation, will give no offence to such persons as can form a just notion of those compositions, which are the productions of simple and unassisted genius, in which energy is always more sought after than neatness, and the strictness of connexion less adverted to than the design of moving the passions and affecting the heart.[5]

Among the readers of this letter and poem was almost certainly James Macpherson, who was contributing poetry to the *Scots Magazine*. Macpherson was born on a small farm at Invertromie near Ruthven, Inverness-shire, on 27 October 1736. For six years he attended the nearby Badenoch parochial school, and in February 1753 he matriculated at King's College, Aberdeen. In 1755 he was forced to leave this school because he could no longer afford the tuition, but he was able to continue his studies at Marischal College in the same city. He also studied at Edinburgh University, but he never received a degree. While still a student he published his first poem, "To a Friend Mourning the Death of Miss . . . " (*Scots Magazine* 17 [May 1755]: 249), based on Horace's Ode 24 of Book I on the death of Virgil's friend Quintillius.

In 1756 Macpherson returned to Ruthven, where he taught at the local charity school. Here he began to collect Highland poetry. Two years later he was back in Edinburgh, working as copy-editor and hack writer for the publisher John Balfour. In this year he published "On the Death of Marshall Keith" in the *Scots Magazine* (20 [October 1758]: 550) and *The Highlander* (Edinburgh: Ruddiman, Jr. and Company, 1758), which attracted little atten-

---

5   *Scots Magazine* 18 (January 1756): 15.

tion. *The Highlander* draws on traditional Gaelic material. The hero, Duffus, like Finn MacCumhail (or Fingal, a traditional Gaelic warrior) grows up in obscurity and defends Scotland against a Danish invasion. Despite his literary origins in old Highland ballads, Duffus exhibits the generosity and sensitivity of an 18th-century gentleman. This combination of modernity and antiquity would characterize Macpherson's later productions as well.

In 1758, too, Macpherson became tutor to Thomas Graham of Balgowan, son of the laird of Balgowan. While traveling with Graham in 1759, Macpherson met Adam Ferguson, who gave him a letter of introduction to Home. Later that year, traveling with Graham to Moffat, Macpherson encountered Home on the bowling green of the resort, where they talked about their mutual interest in the poetry of the Highlands. Despite Collins' vision of Home's listening to Gaelic verse, Home in fact had no cognisance of the tongue. Macpherson, on the other hand, had grown up hearing and speaking Gaelic, though he read it only with difficulty because of its lack of spelling rules. Home asked for an English translation of one of the many poems Macpherson claimed he had gathered. Having apparently boasted of both his collection and his knowledge of Gaelic verse, Macpherson found himself in a difficult position. To admit that he could not satisfy Home would have been embarrassing, but he could not honestly give the playwright what he wanted. Macpherson therefore tried to free himself from the request, or at least excuse in advance what he feared might prove a disappointing offering, by protesting that "the Genius of the Gaelic language was so different from the English that a Translation of the former into the latter, would prove merely a simple inanimated tale, when stript of that energetic gracefulness, and harmonious phraseology which so strongly mark the originals."[6] Home insisted, and Macpherson then produced "The Death of Oscur," based on two authentic Gaelic ballads; but in the form presented it was essentially an original work by Macpherson. In this short piece, supposedly composed by the 3rd-century blind bard Ossian, his son, Oscur, kills his (Oscur's) best friend, Dermid,

---

6   Cited in Fiona J. Stafford, *The Sublime Savage: A Study of James Macpherson and the Poems of Ossian* (Edinburgh: Edinburgh University Press, 1988), 81.

in a duel over Dargo's daughter. Distraught, Oscur then tricks her into killing him, and when she recognizes what she has done, she kills herself. The poem's emphasis on heroism, sacrifice, and doomed love would underlie Macpherson's other Ossian poems. The portrait of Ossian in this poem derives in part from Thomas Gray's "The Bard" (1757). Such borrowings would also reappear in Macpherson's later writings.

Home was ecstatic and asked for more such pieces, and Macpherson provided these as well. When two of Home's literary friends from Edinburgh, George Laurie and Alexander Carlyle, visited Moffat on 2 October, Home showed them the verses. They, too, were delighted. Carlyle later recalled, "I was perfectly astonished by the poetical genius displayed in them. We agreed that it was a precious discovery, and that as soon as possible, it should be published to the world."[7] Macpherson had opened the sluices, and no further struggles could prevent his being swept away by the flood of enthusiasm he had released.

Home took his translations back to Edinburgh, where he showed them to other literati. Hugh Blair was especially impressed and sent for Macpherson, who at first declined the invitation. Blair persisted, and Macpherson relented. When Blair asked for more poems, Macpherson reluctantly complied. Blair and Sir David Dalrymple sent two samples south to the English poets Thomas Gray and William Shenstone and to the antiquarian Horace Walpole. One of the pieces they sent tells of the deaths of Daura, her brother Arindel, and her lover Armor. The other contains six descriptions of an autumn night as sung by five bards and their chief.

On 3 February 1760 Walpole wrote to thank Dalrymple:

> I am much obliged to you, Sir, for the Irish poetry; they are poetry, and resemble that of the East; that is, they contain natural images and natural sentiment elevated, before rules were invented to make poetry difficult and dull. The transitions are as sudden as those in Pindar, but not so libertine, for they start into new thoughts on the subject without wander-

---

7   Ibid., 78.

ing from it. I like particularly the expression of calling Echo,
Son of the Rock. The monody is much the best.[8]

On 4 April 1760 Walpole once more wrote to Dalrymple to
express his appreciation. He added that Gray, William Mason,
George Lyttleton, and others who had seen the samples "are in
love with your Erse elegies."[9]

In that same month Gray wrote to Walpole:

> I am so charmed with the two specimens of Erse poetry, that
> I cannot help giving you the trouble to inquire a little
> farther about them, and should wish to see a few lines of the
> original that I may form some slight idea of the language, the
> measures and the rhythm. . . .
>
> I make this inquiry in quality of an antiquary, and am not
> otherwise concerned about it: for if I were sure that any one
> now living in Scotland had written them to divert himself and
> laugh at the credulity of the world, I would undertake a
> journey into the Highlands only for the pleasure of seeing
> him.[10]

In June or July 1760 Gray wrote to Thomas Wharton, again
declaring his admiration for the poetry, whether ancient or not:

> I am gone mad about them. they are said to be translations (lit-
> eral & in prose) from the Erse-tongue, done by one
> Macpherson, a young clergyman in the High-lands. he means
> to publish a Collection he has of these specimens of antiquity,
> if it be antiquity: but what plagues me is, I can not come to any
> certainty on that head. I was so struck, so *extasié* with their
> infinite beauty, that I writ into Scotland to make a thousand
> enquiries, the letters I have in return are ill-wrote, ill-reason'd,
> unsatisfactory, calculated (one would imagine) to deceive one,

---

8 *Horace Walpole's Correspondence with David Dalrymple,* ed. Wilmarth Sheldon
   Lewis, Charles H. Bennett, and Andrew G. Hoover (New Haven: Yale University
   Press, 1951), in *The Correspondence of Horace Walpole,* XV, 61. The reference to
   Echo is to the line, "She went; and she called on Armor. Nought answered, but the
   son of the rock."

9 Ibid., 65.

10 *Horace Walpole's Correspondence with Thomas Gray,* ed. W. S. Lewis, George L. Lam,
   and Charles H. Bennett (New Haven: Yale University Press, 1948), *The
   Correspondence of Horace Walpole,* XIV, 106.

& yet not cunning enough to do it cleverly. in short, the whole external evidence would make one believe these fragments (for so he calls them, tho' nothing can be more entire) counterfeit: but the internal is so strong on the other side, that I am resolved to believe them genuine, spite of the Devil & the Kirk. . . . this Man is the very Demon of Poetry, or he has lighted on a treasure hid for ages.[11]

On 14 June 1760 a seventy-page pamphlet entitled *Fragments of Ancient Poetry, Collected in the Highlands of Scotland, and Translated from the Galic or Erse Language* was published anonymously at Edinburgh. The work contained fifteen fragments, including the piece about Daura that Walpole had seen ("Fragment XI"). The other sample that had been sent to England was published in 1765 as a footnote to "Croma." A second edition of *Fragments* followed later that year with a sixteenth poem added. Of these, only two, "Fragment VI, The Maid of Caraca," and "Fragment XIII" (XIV in the second edition) could be called translations. The others were Macpherson's adaptations and inventions, though Hugh Blair, who knew no Gaelic, in his anonymous preface called them "genuine remains of ancient Scottish poetry."[12] Macpherson had considered presenting the pieces in rhyme, but Blair convinced him to use a rhythmic prose that contributed to their sense of antiquity and hence their popularity.

After receiving a copy of the *Fragments,* Gray wrote to William Mason on 7 August 1760, "I continue to think them genuine, tho' my reasons for believing the contrary are rather stronger than ever: but I will have them antique, for I never knew Scotchman of my time, that could read, much less write, poetry; & such poetry too!"[13] William Shenstone was similarly impressed. He urged the antiquarian Bishop Thomas Percy to buy the pamphlet, and Shenstone wrote to John MacGowan, who had sent him a

11   *Correspondence of Thomas Gray,* ed. Paget Toynbee and Leonard Whibley, with corrections and additions by H. W. Stam (Oxford: Clarendon Press, 1970), II, 679–680. Gray errs in calling Macpherson a clergyman. He studied divinity at Edinburgh but was never ordained.

12   James Macpherson, *The Poems of Ossian and Related Works,* ed. Howard Gaskill, with an introduction by Fiona Stafford (Edinburgh: Edinburgh University Press, 1996), 5.

13   *Correspondence of Thomas Gray,* II, 690.

copy of the *Fragments,* "Here is indeed pure original genius! The very quintessence of poetry; a few drops of which, properly managed, are enough to give a flavour to quart-bottles." Shenstone suspected that Macpherson had taken "pretty considerable freedoms" in adapting the poems, but Shenstone added, "I do not in the least disapprove of this; knowing by experience, that trivial amendments in these old compositions often render them highly striking, which would be otherwise quite neglected. And surely, under all the infirmities of age, they may be said to have an absolute claim to some indulgencies of this kind."[14]

Gray had questioned the word "fragments" of the title, since the poems presented seemed complete in themselves. For the 18th-century, though, the epic was the highest form of poetry, and in the preface to *Fragments* Hugh Blair had written,

> It is believed, that, by a careful inquiry, many more remains of ancient genius, no less valuable than those now given to the world, might be found in the same country where these have been collected. In particular there is reason to hope that one work of considerable length, and which deserves to be styled an heroic poem [i.e., epic], might be recovered and translated, if encouragement were given to such an undertaking.[15]

Blair even described the subject of the missing epic: the invasion of Ireland by the Danish Swaran and his defeat by Fingal, king of Scotland, a subject not far removed from that of Macpherson's *The Highlander.* Macpherson had told Blair that he knew of such an epic, and the subject, as already noted, was traditional, recounted in two Gaelic ballads that Macpherson knew, "Garbh Macstairn" and "Magnus," and in the prose "The Battle of Vestry," dealing with a Viking raid on Ireland. Macpherson's task was to turn these and other shorter poems into a long one, of which the last three pieces in the first edition of *Fragments* were a sample.

Once more Macpherson tried to back out of the project, claiming that he could not afford the Highland expedition that

---

14   *The Letters of William Shenstone,* ed. Marjorie Williams (Oxford: Basil Blackwell, 1939), 596–597.

15   *The Poems of Ossian and Related Works,* 6.

would be necessary for him to hunt for manuscripts and listen to recitations. Blair, however, was not to be denied. While the literary world might ignore Home's plays or Wilkie's modern epic, a long poem from the 3rd century would gain recognition for Scotland. Blair therefore instructed Macpherson to write a letter that would encourage contributions for an extended trip into the Highlands. On 16 June 1760 Macpherson complied:

> Revd Sir
>
> None would be more willing to undertake the work you and others, my friends, recommend, did it suit with my interests[,] than I. I certainly admire the poetry of my country much; and would with eagerness seise on every opportunity to make its beauties known.
>
> But, Sir, a journey thro' the Highlands and Isles is attended with risque and Expence that are not proper for me to incur on my own bottom.
>
> I would be obliged to throw up the business I pursue [of tutor]; devote myself for twelve month, at least, to that work, and, besides my travelling expences, be obliged to gratify some persons who are in possession of the original poems.
>
> All which put together makes it too great a venture for me to go on such a design without assistance and encouragement.
>
> Did all things answer I could make a large, and I hope a valuable, collection of our ancient poetry; but as I cannot well spare the expence and time I must give over all thoughts of the matter.
>
> It were to be wished however that these remains of genius were not lost, And I am extreamly sorry it does not suit with my present circumstances to have the pleasure of preserving them. With great Respect I am
>
> Revd Sir
Your most Obedient
Humble Servant

James Macpherson[16]

---

16 Quoted in Robert Hay Carnie, "Macpherson's *Fragments of Ancient Poetry* and Lord Hailes," *English Studies* 41 (1960):17–26, 23. Lord Hailes is Sir David Dalrymple.

Robert Hay Carnie, who first published the letter, called it "a striking example of literary impudence,"[17] though one might more generously interpret it as an effort to frighten away the Edinburgh literati without confessing to previous chicanery. Macpherson was asking for not only traveling expenses but also money to buy manuscripts and to reward those who would recite poetry from memory, and, in addition, a year's salary. His request would either liberate him from the project or richly reward him for undertaking it.

If the letter was a bid for freedom from Ossian, it failed. Blair sent a copy to Sir David Dalrymple, who raised over £20. Robert Chalmers raised another £60, and Elizabeth Montagu may have donated £100. In August 1760 Macpherson set off to find the missing epic. Richard B. Sher observed that the poems that Macpherson "found" were his productions, but responsibility for their composition must be shared by "a 'cabal' of Edinburgh literary men who provided the necessary inspiration, incentive, financial support, editorial assistance, publishing connections, and emotional encouragement."[18]

Macpherson took far less than the year he had mentioned in his letter. For six weeks he traveled through Inverness-shire, the Isle of Skye, and the Outer Hebrides, returning to his home at Ruthven in October. A second journey took him along the Argyleshire coast and to the Island of Mull. He heard Gaelic ballads, which he transcribed, and he acquired some manuscripts. The most important of these was *The Book of the Dean of Lismore,* compiled by Sir James Macgregor and his brother Duncan in Perthshire between 1512 and 1542.[19] The volume, which probably owes its preservation to Macpherson, contains 311 quarto pages in phonetic Gaelic. Of the 11,000 lines of poetry, about 2,500 are Ossianic; these comprise the oldest part of the collection and include twenty-seven ballads, one ballad fragment, and some quatrains. Macpherson incorporated four of these poems into his epic. He also secured the *Little Book of Clanranald,* with some

---

17   Ibid.
18   "Those Scotch Impostors and Their Cabal," in *Ossian Revisted,* 55.
19   Howard Gaskill suggested that Macpherson may have secured *The Book of the Dean* in 1759. See his article "What Did James Macpherson Really Leave on Display at His Publisher's Shop in 1762?" *Scottish Gaelic Studies* 16 (1990): 67–89.

thirty pages of Ossianic verse. The Reverend James Maclagan of Amulree sent Macpherson some thirteen ballads, including the "Lay of Garbh" and the "Great Strait of the Finns," both of which Macpherson adapted. To help him interpret the manuscripts Macpherson engaged two Gaelic scholars, his kinsman Lachlan Macpherson of Strathmashie and the Reverend Andrew Gallie. By January 1761 Macpherson was back in Edinburgh, and in mid-February he was in London with Robert Chalmers looking for a publisher. By April he had completed a 19,000 word epic about the battle of Fingal and Swaran, just as Blair had predicted.

Sir David Dalrymple sent a copy of the manuscript to Horace Walpole. After seeing *Fragments* in print Walpole had questioned Blair's claim that some of the poems included were parts of a larger work, and he even entertained reservations about the poems' antiquity. The new verses temporarily converted him. On 14 April 1761 he wrote to Dalrymple of *Fingal,* "There are most beautiful images in it, and it surprises one how the bard could strike out so many shining ideas from a few so very simple objects, as the moon, the storm, the sea and the heath, from whence he borrows almost all his allusions. . . . My doubts of the genuineness are all vanished."[20]

On 1 December 1761 *Fingal. An Ancient Poem, in Six Books; Together with Several Other Poems, Composed by Ossian, the Son of Fingal. Translated from the Galic Language, by James Macpherson* was published, followed in March 1763 by *Temora, an Ancient Epic Poem, in Eight Books; Together with Several Other Poems, Composed by Ossian, the Son of Fingal. Translated from the Galic Language, by James Macpherson.* In his "Dissertation Concerning the Antiquity, &c. of the Poems of Ossian, the Son of Fingal" that appeared with *Fingal,* Macpherson wrote, "All that can be said of the translation is that it is literal, and that simplicity is studied. The arrangement of the words in the original is imitated, and the inversions of the style observed."[21] In fact, Derick S. Thomson, who made a thorough study of Macpherson's originals, concluded that Fingal incorporates some fourteen or fifteen ballads. In some cases

20   *The Correspondence of Horace Walpole,* XV, 71–72.
21   *The Poems of Ossian and Related Works,* 52.

Macpherson followed his sources closely; elsewhere he adapted freely. *Temora,* except for Book I, is virtually all Macpherson's invention. Thomson summarized, "Although much has been found in common between Macpherson's work and the ballads, essentially they are profoundly different. The ballads are thoroughly native; Macpherson's work is a blend—and seldom a happy one—of several different cultures."[22]

Editorial practices of the time allowed great liberties. Both Alexander Pope in his edition of Shakespeare and the much more scholarly Richard Bentley in his edition of Milton sought to "restore" their respective authors' texts by eliminating what they regarded as corruptions. Thomas Percy's *Reliques of Ancient English Poetry* (London: J. Dodsley, 1765) and Sir Walter Scott's *Minstrelsy of the Scottish Border* (Kelso: J. Ballantine, for T. Cadell, Jun. and W. Davies, London, 1802) presented their older poetry in modern dress, as did Stone in his 1756 translation cited earlier in this chapter. Macpherson may have believed that he, too, was purging the text of corruptions and restoring connections that had been lost over the centuries. Andrew Gallie recalled that in 1760 as Macpherson was reading the Clanranald manuscript he would denounce "the bard who dictated to the amanuensis, saying, 'D--n the scoundrel, it is he himself that now speaks, and not Ossian.'"[23] In the "Dissertation" preceding *Temora* Macpherson declared,

> The opening of the poem of Temora made its appearance in the first collection of Ossian's works [*Fingal*]. The second book, and several other episodes, have only fallen into my hands lately. The story of the poem, with which I had been long acquainted, enabled me to reduce the broken members of the piece into the order in which they now appear. For the ease of the reader, I have divided it myself into books, as I had done before with the poem of *Fingal*.[24]

---

22 *The Gaelic Sources of Macpherson's "Ossian"* (Edinburgh: Oliver and Boyd for the University of Aberdeen, 1952), 84.

23 *Report of the Committee of the Highland Society of Scotland* (Edinburgh, 1805), 44.

24 *The Poems of Ossian and Related Works,* 215.

Among Macpherson's tutors at Aberdeen had been Thomas Blackwell, whose *Enquiry into the Writings of Homer* (1735) suggested that Homer may have created his epic by combining and adapting various extant fragments, just as Macpherson was doing.

Whether or not Macpherson thought that he was rescuing ancient Highland poetry from corruption and oblivion—and the excitement that his Ossianic verses generated did lead to genuine research into this material—he infused 18th-century sensibilities into these works. These contemporary attitudes, more than any anti-quarian value that the poems of Ossian may have possessed, guaranteed their popularity by appealing to the values of Macpherson's readers.

Foremost among these modern sensibilities was a Rousseauesque love of the primitive. Macpherson wrote in the preface to *Temora* that the poem presented Highlanders who "lived in a country only fit for pasture[;] they were free of that toil and business, which engrosses the attention of a commercial people."[25] Such fondness for an earlier, uncorrupted age resonated with particular power in Scotland, where the defeat of the 1745 attempt to overthrow the Hanoverians had been followed by puni-tive measures against the Highlanders and had provoked English suspicions against the entire country. Tartans and bagpipes were banned; clan leaders were stripped of their weapons and their authority. In "A Dissertation Concerning the Antiquity, &c. of the Poems of Ossian" Macpherson described the transformation he had witnessed in his lifetime:

> The communication with the rest of the island is open, and the introduction of trade and manufactures has destroyed that leisure which was formerly dedicated to hearing and repeating the poems of ancient times. Many have now learned to leave their mountains, and seek their fortunes in a milder climate; and though a certain *amor patriae* [love of country] may sometimes bring them back, they have, during their absence, imbibed enough of foreign manners to despise the customs of their ancestors. . . . Men begin to be less devoted to their

---

25   Ibid., 206.

chiefs, and consanguinity is not so much regarded. When property is established, the human mind confines its views to the pleasure it procures.[26]

Neither commerce nor materialism divides the heroes of Ossian. Uwe Böker observed that Goethe in *Götz von Berlichingen* (1773) and *Die Leiden des jungen Werthers* (the sorrows of young Werther, 1774) reflects the values of the Ossian poems, which the young Goethe admired. In these early works Goethe contrasts "those imbued with an almost pantheistic awareness of nature and an independence of self and spirit [with] the regulated, materialistic, rational world."[27]

At the same time that Macpherson celebrates a primitive golden age, his poems acknowledge that this age has ended. Osssian laments,

> I have seen the walls of Balclutha, but they were desolate. The fire had resounded in the halls: and the voice of the people is heard no more. The stream of Clutha was removed from its place, by the fall of the walls. —The thistle shook, there, its lonely head: the moss whistled to the wind. The fox looked out, from the windows, the rank grass of the wall waved round his head. Desolate is the dwelling of Moina, silence is in the house of her fathers.[28]

Ossian's father, Fingal, is dead, as is his son, Oscur. Ossian remains the last of his race, and with his own imminent death both heroes and bards will be no more. As the poet sings in "Berrathon,"

> The life of Ossian fails. I begin to vanish on Cona; and my steps are not seen in Selma. Beside the stone of Mora I shall fall asleep. The winds whistling in my grey hair shall not waken me. . . .

---

26 Ibid., 51.
27 "The Marketing of Macpherson: The International Book Trade and the First Phase of German Ossian Reception," in *Ossian Revisited*, ed. Howard Gaskill (Edinburgh: Edinburgh University Press, 1991), 73-93, 87.
28 From "Carthon: A Poem," in *The Poems of Ossian and Related Works*, 128.

> The chiefs of other times are departed; they have gone without their fame. The sons of future years shall pass away; and another race arise. The people are like the waves of ocean: like the leaves of woody Morven, they pass away in the rustling blast, and other leaves lift their green heads.[29]

Hugh Blair commented on this air of sadness that pervades the poetry of Ossian, which "breathes nothing of the gay and chearful kind; an air of solemnity and seriousness is diffused over the whole. . . . His poetry, more perhaps than that of any other writer, deserves to be stiled, *The Poetry of the Heart*."[30] Macpherson was echoing sentiments expressed in such grave-yard poems as Edward Young's *The Complaint, or Night Thoughts on Life, Death, and Immortality* (1742-1746), Robert Blair's "The Grave" (1743) and Thomas Gray's *Elegy Wrote in a Country Church-Yard* (1751) and that would soon resound in novels like Laurence Sterne's *A Sentimental Journey* (1768) and Henry Mackenzie's *The Man of Feeling* (1771). John Dwyer has called Ossian "an eighteenth-century ideal type—the 'man of feeling.'"[31]

For the 18th century, primitivism and melancholy were not merely admirable in themselves. From their differing perspectives, Rousseau and the Scottish Enlightenment believed that these were keys to virtue. Rousseau celebrated the noble savage, and John Dwyer cites Henry Mackenzie's claim that "the stimulation of melancholy feelings" will lead to "social sympathy" and a sense of "the duties of humanity."[32] Only villains like Starno, Swaran, and Annir delight in fighting. Fingal prefers peace; Cathmor and Brauno befriend the stranger. Seven paths lead guests to the hall of Cathmor, though he himself "dwelt in the wood to avoid the voice of praise."[33] In Book III of *Fingal* the eponymous hero speaks as a noble savage or Enlightenment gentleman when he tells his

---

29 *The Poems of Ossian and Related Works*, 198.

30 *In Critical Dissertation on the Poems of Ossian, the Son of Fingal*, included in *The Poems of Ossian and Related Works*, 356.

31 "The Melancholy Savage: Text and Context in the *Poems of Ossian*," in *Ossian Revisited*, 164–206, 187.

32 Ibid., 188.

33 *Temora*, Book I, in *The Poems of Ossian and Related Works*, 229

grandson, "O Oscar! Bend the strong in arms: but spare the feeble hand. Be thou a stream of many tides against the foes of thy people; but like the gale that moves the grass to those who seek thine aid."[34] Such magnanimity is extended even to the enemy. Because Fingal loved the sister of Swaran, he spares the invader's life and allows Swaran to depart in peace. Swaran then praises his foe: "In peace thou art the gale of spring. In war the mountain-storm."[35]

Macpherson's Ossianic poems owed much of their initial popularity to their underlying 18th-century attitudes. They also appealed to audiences by echoing the period's favorite authors. The hymn to the sun that concludes "Carthon," one of the most admired of Ossian's works, combines Satan's address to the sun in Book IV of *Paradise Lost* and Milton's lines on his blindness in Book III of that epic. Ossian, like Milton and Homer, is presented as a blind bard. The passage on the ruined hall of Balclutha derives from chapter 13 of *Isaiah*. The comparison of humanity to leaves and blades of grass is both biblical and Homeric (*Iliad*, Book VI). In "Comála" the eponymous heroine exclaims to the Roman Caracalla, "Confusion pursue thee over the plains; and destruction overtake thee, thou king of the world."[36] The passage is barely modified from the opening lines of Thomas Gray's "The Bard" (1757), from which Macpherson had drawn for his first Ossianic fragment on the death of Oscur: "Ruin seize thee, ruthless king!/Confusion on thy banners wait." In "Fragment XI" Armyn shouts, "Rise, winds of autumn, rise; blow upon the dark heath! Streams of the mountains, roar! Howl, ye tempests, in the top of the oak!"[37] Here the 3rd-century bard is virtually quoting Shakespeare's *King Lear*, III, ii, 1–3: "Blow, winds, and crack your cheeks. Rage, blow!/You cataracts and hurricanoes, spout/Till you have drenched our steeples, drowned the cocks." "Fragment X" is a *Romeo and Juliet*-like tale of lovers separated by a family feud. When the heroine learns that her lover and brother have killed each other, she buries herself with them. Vinvella in the first

---

34   Ibid., 77.
35   *Fingal*, Book VI, in *The Poems of Ossian and Related Works,* 101.
36   Ibid., 107.
37   Ibid., 22.

"Fragment" speaks of her lover in lines reminiscent of the *Song of Songs*. "My love is a son of the hill. He pursues the flying deer. His gray dogs are panting around him; his bow-string sounds in the wind. Whether by the fount of the rock, or by the stream of the mountain thou liest; when the rushes are nodding with the wind, and the mist is flying over thee, let me approach my love unperceived, and see him from the rock."[38] The rhythmic prose of the Ossian poems also derives from the King James Bible.

Macpherson's poems are rooted in the 18th century, but they heralded the Romantic rebellion to follow and, indeed, gave impetus to that movement. As Fiona Stafford noted, Macpherson's "Celtic world was remote and mysterious, its heroes ideal, magnificent and yet intangible. The dark scenery and the supernatural elements appealed strongly to Gothic tastes, as well as to those readers seeking the Sublime. . . . Unlike the urban society of Western Europe, Macpherson's Celts almost seemed part of the natural world."[39] Yet if Macpherson had presented this poetry as his own work, which it essentially is, the works of Ossian would not have enjoyed the warm reception they received. An air of antiquity was an essential ingredient; when it was joined with contemporary attitudes and allusions, the result proved the perfect combination to seize the imagination of the literary world.

The praise lavished on *Fragments* continued for *Fingal*. Tobias Smollett in the *Critical Review* for December 1761 (12:412) ranked Ossian above Homer and Virgil. Edmund Burke, author of A *Philosophical Enquiry into the Origin of Our Ideas of the Sublime and Beautiful* (1757), was not as flattering in his review published in the *Annual Register* for 1761 (4:277-282), but he did like *Fingal*. *The Monthly Review,* which earlier had dissented from the chorus of enthusiasm for *Fragments,* praised the epic. "The cast of obscurity that envelopes the whole, will excite in us a kind of veneration which precise ideas, correct imagery, and perfect similitude of allusion could never inspire" (26 [January 1762]: 44-50, 44). Hugh Blair, who could be expected to praise

---

38   Ibid., 7.
39   *The Sublime Savage,* 177–178.

what he had labored so zealously to bring to light, concurred, writing in his *Critical Dissertation,*

> Accuracy and correctness; artfully connected narration; exact method and proportion of parts, we may look for in polished times. The gay and the beautiful, will appear to more advantage in the midst of smiling scenery and pleasurable themes. But amidst the rude scenes of nature, amidst rocks and torrents and whirlwinds and battles, dwells the sublime. It is the thunder and the lightning of genius. It is the offspring of nature, not of art. . . . Hence the concise and simple style of Ossian, gives great advantage to his sublime conceptions; and assists them in seizing the imagination with full power.[40]

In his *London Journal* for 8 February 1763 James Boswell, who had contributed money for Macpherson's Highland expedition in 1760, recorded that Thomas Sheridan

> preferred [Ossian] to all the poets in the world, and thought he excelled Homer in the Sublime and Virgil in the Pathetic. He [Sheridan] said Mrs. Sheridan and he had fixed it as the standard of feeling, made it like a thermometer by which they could judge of the warmth of everybody's heart; and that they calculated before hand in what degrees all their acquaintances would feel them, which answered exactly. "To be sure," said he, "except people have genuine feelings of poetry, they cannot relish these poems."[41]

Boswell himself, who later changed his mind about Ossian, probably under the influence of Samuel Johnson, wrote to Andrew Erskine on 17 December 1761 warmly recommending *Fingal.* Declaring that he preferred Ossian to Homer, Virgil, and Milton, Boswell concluded, "Take my word for it; [Ossian] will make you feel you have a soul."[42]

---

40   *The Poems of Ossian and Related Works,* 394–395.
41   *Boswell's London Journal,* 1762-1763, ed. Frederick A. Pottle (New York: McGraw-Hill, 1950), 182.
42   Cited in Bailey Saunders, *The Life and Letters of James Macpherson* (London: S. Sonnenschein; New York: Macmillan, 1894), 173.

Erskine followed his friend's advice, and on 10 January 1762 he wrote back to Boswell, "It is quite impossible to express my admiration for [Ossian's] Poems; at particular passages I felt my whole frame trembling with ecstacy; but if I was to describe all my thoughts, you would think me absolutely mad. The beautiful wildness of his fancy is inexpressibly agreeable to the imagination."[43]

Appreciation for Macpherson's poetry persisted for decades. In a letter to the London schoolmaster John Murdoch (15 January 1783) Robert Burns wrote that Ossian was one of "the glorious models after which I endeavor to form my conduct."[44] In 1796 Samuel Taylor Coleridge published "Imitated from Ossian" and "The Complaint of Ninathoma," another Ossianic poem. Despite William Wordsworth's dismissal of Ossian in his "Essay Supplementary to the Preface" of the 1815 edition of his poetry, such pieces as "Glen Almain," "Effusion in the Pleasure-ground on the Banks of the Bran," "The Earl of Breadalbane's Ruined Mansion," and the Staffa sonnets show that he was influenced by Macpherson's poems.[45] In *The Wild Irish Girl* (London: R. Phillips, 1806) by Lady Sydney Owenson Morgan, the heroine, Princess Glorvina, declares, "When my spirits are sunk, I fly to my English Ossian, and then my sufferings are soothed and every desponding spirit softens into a sweet melancholy, more delicious than joy itself" (II, 95). Ormsby Bethel in Charles Maturin's *The Wild Irish Boy* (1808) takes Ossian's poems with him when he moves to the Lake District. Of 130 English libraries sold between 1771 and 1800, 37 contained copies of Ossian, and on 17 July 1805 the Scottish antiquarian and historian George Chalmers wrote to the publisher Archibald Constable, "Except the Bible and Shakespeare, there is not any book sells better than Ossian. This sale seems to me to arise from the intrinsic merit of the book, and not from the talk about it."[46] In his 1818 *Lectures on the English*

---

43   Quoted in *The Sublime Savage*, 1.

44   *The Letters of Robert Burns*, 2nd ed., ed. G. Ross Roy (Oxford: Clarendon Press, 1984), I, 17.

45   For a discussion of Macpherson's influence on Wordsworth, see Fiona J. Stafford, "'Dangerous Success': Ossian, Wordsworth, and English Romantic Literature," in *Ossian Revisited*, 49–72, and J. R. Moore, "Wordsworth's Unacknowledged Debt to Macpherson." *Publications of the Modern Language Association* 40 (1925): 362–378.

46   Cited in John Valdimir Price, "Ossian and the Canon in the Scottish Enlightenment," in *Ossian Revisited*, 108–128, 124.

Poets the critic William Hazlitt linked Ossian with Homer, the Bible, and Dante as "four of the principal works of poetry in the world," and he went on to say that Ossian "is a feeling and a name that can never be destroyed in the minds of his readers."[47]

Macpherson's poetry remained popular well into the 19th century. Matthew Arnold, speaking to students at Oxford in 1866, declared,

> I am not going to criticise Macpherson's Ossian here. Make the part of what is forged, modern, tawdry, spurious, in the book, as large as you please; strip Scotland, if you like, of every feather of borrowed plumes which on the strength of Macpherson's Ossian she may have stolen from . . . the true home of the Ossianic poetry, Ireland; I make no objection. But there will still be left . . . a residue with the very soul of the Celtic genius in it, and which has the proud distinction of having brought this soul of the Celtic genius into contact with the genius of the nations of modern Europe, and enriched all our poetry by it. Woody Morven, and echoing Lora, and Selma with its silent halls! —we owe them a debt of gratitude, and when we are unjust enough to forget it, may the Muse forget us![48]

In November 1854 Lady Jane Wilde wrote to friends that her second son would be named Oscar Fingal Wilde, adding, "Is not that grand, misty, and Ossianic?"[49]

Enthusiasm for Ossian was hardly limited to the British Isles. When Thomas Jefferson's cousin Robert Skipworth requested a reading list, Jefferson included the poetry of Ossian and Hugh Blair's *Critical Dissertation*. In February 1773 Jefferson himself wrote to Macpherson, by way of Charles Macpherson, of the Ossianic works, "These peices [sic] have been, and will I think during my lifetime continue to be to me, the source of daily and exalted pleasure. The tender, and the sublime emotions of the mind

---

[47] *The Complete Works of William Hazlitt,* ed. P.P. Howe (London: Dent, 1930), V, 15, 18.

[48] *Lectures and Essays in Criticism,* ed. R. H. Super, with the assistance of Sister Thomas Marion Hoctor (Ann Arbor: University of Michigan Press, 1962), in *The Complete Prose Works of Matthew Arnold,* III, 370-371.

[49] Quoted in Fiona J. Stafford's introduction to *The Poems of Ossian and Related Works,* v.

were never before so finely wrought up by human hand. I am not ashamed to own that I think this rude bard of the North the greatest Poet that has ever existed."[50] Jefferson requested a copy of the Gaelic originals, but Macpherson declined to send one, claiming that transcribing the poems would require too much work. John Trumbull's satire *M'Fingal* (1775) assumes that American readers would know the Ossianic original. Before 1800 the American writers Josius Arnold, Joseph Ladd, John Linn, William Mumford, and Jonathan Sewall all had imitated or parodied the Scottish bard. Paul J. DeGategno draws parallels between James Fenimore Cooper's Indians and Ossian's Highland heroes. He likens the death of Uncas in *The Last of the Mohicans* (1826) to that of Oscur, son of Ossian, in *Temora*. In *A Week on the Concord and Merrimack Rivers* (1849) Henry David Thoreau, who believed Macpherson's Ossianic poems to be authentic translations, praised these works, and in the January 1844 issue of the Transcendental organ the *Dial* he wrote, "Ossian reminds us of the most refined and rudest eras, of Homer, Pindar, Isaiah, and the American Indians. In his poetry, as in Homer's, only the simplest and most enduring features of humanity are seen, such essential parts of a man as Stonehenge exhibits of a temple."[51] Walt Whitman called them "the stanchest [sic] friends of my other soul, my poems."[52] Whitman was not always so enthusiastic: he wrote on the margin of a paragraph by Margaret Fuller, "Don't fall into the Ossianic, *by any chance*," but he went on to add, "Is [Ossian] not Isaiah, Job, the Psalms, and so forth, transferred to the Scotch Highlands?"[53] Whitman's long lines of rhythmic free verse derive primarily from the King James Bible, but they probably also owe something to Macpherson's prose poetry. Professor H. T. Kirby-Smith goes so far as to claim that "the chief secular model for American nineteenth-century poets of a greatly loosened—even prosaic—metric remained 'Ossian.'"[54]

---

50 Quoted in Paul J. DeGategno, "'The Source of Daily and Exalted Pleasure': Jefferson Reads the Poems of Ossian," in *Ossian Revisited*, 94–108, 98–99.
51 Cited in H. T. Kirby-Smith, *The Origins of Free Verse* (Ann Arbor: The University of Michigan Press, 1996), 153.
52 Quoted in Paul J. DeGategno, *James Macpherson* (Boston: Twayne, 1989), 134.
53 H. T. Kirby-Smith, 154.
54 Ibid., 152.

On the Continent Ossian was even more popular and influential. By 1800 at least some of Macpherson's Ossianic verse had been translated into ten languages (French, Italian, German, Spanish, Dutch, Danish, Swedish, Polish, Hungarian, and Russian), and by 1860 the figure had risen to twenty-six. In Italy Melchiorre Cesarotti, who translated the poems, was called Father Ossian, and he gave the name of Oscar to his favorite disciple, Giuseppe Barbieri. Jean Baptiste Bernadotte, king of Sweden, named his heir Oscar for Ossian's son. German enthusiasts took Ossianic names like Ryno and Cronnan, and at banquets they crowned themselves with oak leaves; the oak looms large in Ossian's work. Rudolf Tombo, Jr.'s *Ossian in Germany* (New York: Columbia University Press, 1901) includes a list of German translations, imitations, critical essays, and reviews of Ossian that extends to more than sixty pages. Tombo concludes,

> There was scarcely a writer of note [in Germany] who did not at some time or other fall under the spell [of Macpherson's poetry]. Schiller's earliest dramas show traces of Ossian's influence. . . . The *Storm and Stress* writers found nourishment in the writings of a genius who observed no rules. . . . Jacob Grimm was extremely anxious to appear as their champion. The melancholy of Novalis sought consolation in the Ossianic "joy of grief." Tieck produced several imitations in his youth. Hölderlin also read the poems with ardor. (67)

In 1771 Johann Gottfried Herder wrote to his fiancée, Caroline Flachsland, "But love in the songs of the Scottish bard! It is only in those that one finds all the tenderness, the gentleness, the grace, the nobility, the power and the delicate moral purity that seduces us completely and yet leaves us human."[55] A year earlier Herder had written to Johann Heinrich Merck, "Should I ever reach the coasts of Britain, I will only hurry through, see some theatre and Garrick, and say hello to [Scottish philosopher David] Hume, and then it will be up to Wales and Scotland, and

---

55   Quoted in Paul van Tieghem, *Le préromantisme: Études d'histoire littéraire européenne* (Paris: Félix Alcan, 1924), 282.

to the Western Isles, on one of which Macpherson sits, Ossian's youngest son."[56]

Probably no one in Germany, perhaps in Europe, exceeded the young Goethe in admiration for Ossian. At the age of twenty-two he translated Ossian for his beloved Friederike Brion, as his hero Werther translates Ossian for Charlotte. Though Goethe later said that Werther's abandoning Homer for Ossian signals the young man's mental disintegration, the praise that Werther bestows on the poet in *The Sorrows of Young Werther* reveals Goethe's feelings in the 1770s. Under the date of 12 October 1772 Werther writes of Ossian, "What a world this sublime poet has opened to me! . . . I see past ages glow into life in the soul of the hero when the friendly beam shone on the adventures of the brave, and the moonlight illuminated their ships, homeward bound and hung with wreaths of victory."[57] Herder had read Ossian in Italian and German. About 1780 Goethe offered him his copy in English. "But," Goethe added, "I must have it back. Send me an answer quickly, since I cannot bear to see you deprived of such pleasure as I have experienced. For there is nothing to surpass it."[58]

In France, too, Ossian enjoyed great popularity. The first translations of some of the *Fragments* appeared there only months after their initial publication, and, as in Germany, a river of translations and adaptations followed. Paul van Tieghem found that of 640 private French libraries catalogued between 1760 and 1800, 178 owned copies of Ossian in some form; in the 19th century the figure was 174 copies in 631 French libraries. With the rise to power of Napolean, the Ossianic vogue received still greater impetus because Napoleon greatly admired the Scottish bard. The French writer Antoine Vincent Arnault claimed that *Temora* was Napoleon's favorite poem. Ossian was part of the 350-volume traveling library that accompanied the dictator on his campaigns, and it was among the books he took with him to Saint Helena. In

---

56   Quoted in "The Marketing of Macpherson," 87.

57   Johann Wolfgang von Goethe, *The Sorrows of Young Werther and Novella*, trans. Elizabeth Mayer and Louise Bogan (New York: Random House, 1971), 110.

58   Quoted in "The Marketing of Ossian," 79.

1804 his administration prepared a list of 526 titles to be sent to all French lycées. Only twenty-two were by foreigners, and of these, ten were English. Shakespeare was not included; Ossian was.

As in Germany, the major writers, as well as many minor ones, fell under Ossian's spell. François Auguste René, le Vicomte de Chateaubriand translated three poems from the Reverend John Smith's *Galic Antiquities* (1780), a spurious collection of Ossianic verse prompted by Macpherson's poems and often published with them in France. In 1802 René, the hero of Chateaubriand's eponymous novel, goes to the Highlands and hears a bard chanting amidst the Ossianic landscape. Stendhal read Ossian in 1811 while traveling in Italy. On 1 June 1809 Alphonse Marie Louis de Lamartine wrote to Aymon de Virieu that he, Lamartine, dreamed of spending some winter months in the Scottish Highlands near the ghosts of Ossian and Fingal. In his *Confidences* (1849) Lamartine named Ossian as one of his chief influences. He called Ossian the Homer of his early years, the poet who taught him imagery and emotion. John Semple Smart quoted Lamartine's statement that "the harp of Morven is the emblem of my soul."[59] As late as 1868 Lamartine devoted two of his "Conversations" in his *Cours familier de littérature* to Ossian.

Alfred de Vigny and the young Victor Hugo read and admired Macpherson's work. Alfred de Musset's *La coupe et les lèvres* (1832), though set in the Tyrol, recreated Ossian's misty lakes and clouds, and in *Le Saule* (1830) he offered his version of the beginning of the "Songs of Selma." Prosper Mérimée learned English by reading Ossian, and Alexandre Dumas memorized hundreds of lines of this poetry.

Macpherson's influence extended to other art forms. Franz Schubert, Felix Mendelssohn, and Johannes Brahms composed music based on his poems. François Gérard painted Ossian invoking the spirits on the shore of Lorna (1801) for Napoleon's residence, Malmaison, and Anne-Louis Girodet executed *Ossian and the French Generals* (1801) and *The Death of Malvina* (1802).

---

59 *James Macpherson: An Episode in Literature* (London: David Nutt, 1905), 16.

Jean-Auguste-Dominique Ingres' *Dream of Ossian* was completed in 1813.

Such admiration was not, however, universal; even some of those who liked the poetry, such as Thomas Gray, questioned its antiquity. To some extent the debate about Ossian was territorial. Ireland and Scotland shared a Gaelic heritage, and most of the action in *Fingal* and *Temora* takes place in Ireland. The heroes in Macpherson's poems, however, are Scottish. Charles O'Connor's *Dissertaions on the History of Ireland* (1766) criticized Macpherson's geography and chronology in claiming that Ossian and his poems belonged to Ireland.

Anticipating objections to the antiquity of his poems, Macpherson in the Advertisement to the first edition of *Fingal* promised to publish the Gaelic works or at least deposit them in a public library, though in fact he did neither. He also left with his London publisher, Thomas Becket, a copy of the "originals," though exactly what he left remains a matter of speculation. When the poems were published in Gaelic in 1807, one of the editors, John McArthur, claimed that Macpherson had left Becket these pieces, as well as the manuscripts he had collected.[60] Howard Gaskill has suggested that Macpherson created a Gaelic version of at least part of *Fingal*, and deposited this, since an inspection of the genuine manuscripts would have revealed the liberties Macpherson had taken.[61] Macpherson even included a Gaelic version of Book VII of *Temora* along with the English in 1763. This specimen had been translated into Gaelic from the English, probably by Macpherson himself, though Lachlan Macpherson of Strathmashie has been implicated, probably unjustly, in its production.[62] Such measures were insufficient for David Hume even during his period of belief in Ossian's authenticity. In 1763 he urged Hugh Blair to gather "positive testimony from many different hands, that such poems are vulgarly recited in the Highlands, and have there been

---

60   *The Poems of Ossian, in the Original Gaelic, with a Literal Translation into Latin* (London: Highland Society of London, 1807), III, 347.

61   "What Did James Macpherson Really Leave on Display at His Publisher's Shop in 1762?"

62   Ibid., 82, and note 63.

long the entertainment of the people."[63] The proofs that Blair included in an "Appendix" to his *Critical Dissertation* published in 1765 satisfied Hume, though a decade later Hume wrote, but did not publish, an essay rejecting the antiquity and authenticity of Macpherson's "translations."

Bishop Thomas Percy had initially been skeptical of Macpherson's poetry. However, in October 1765 he accompanied his kinsman Lord Algernon Percy to Edinburgh University, where the young lord was to matriculate. Hugh Blair was to be Lord Percy's tutor, and Blair introduced the bishop to Adam Ferguson, who taught moral philosophy at the school. During this visit to Edinburgh, John Macpherson, a young Highland student, recited some poetry in Gaelic; according to Thomas Percy, Ferguson assured him that this poetry was the original for part of *Fingal.* Percy thereupon abandoned his earlier doubts, writing to the Welsh antiquarian Evan Evans, "When I was in Scotland I made great inquiry into the Authenticity of Ossian's Poetry; and could not resist the Evidence that poured in upon me; so that I am forced to believe them, as to the main, genuine in spite of my teeth."[64] At Blair's request Percy then added the following note to the second edition of his *Reliques of Ancient English Poetry* (London: J. Dodsley, 1767):

> But no pieces of [the Irish bards'] poetry have been translated, unless their claim may be allowed to those beautiful pieces of ERSE POESY, which were lately given to the world in an English dress by Mr. MACPHERSON: Several fragments of which the editor of this book has heard sung in the original language, and translated viva voce, by a native of the Highlands, who had, at the time, no opportunity of consulting Mr. Macpherson's book. (I, xlv)

After conversing with Sir John Elliot(t), who claimed that Macpherson had told him that he, Macpherson, was the author of

---

63   *The Letters of David Hume*, ed. John Young Thomson Greig (Oxford: Clarendon Press, 1932), I, 400.

64   *The Correspondence of Thomas Percy and Evan Evans*, ed. Aneirin Lewis (Baton Rouge: Louisiana State University Press, 1957), 117.

the Ossianic poems, Percy again changed his mind and omitted the reference to Macpherson in the 1775 (third) edition of his *Reliques.*[65]

In chapter six of Book I of *The Decline and Fall of the Roman Empire* (London: W. Strahan, 1776) Edward Gibbon cited Ossian's account of the Caledonian War between the Romans, led by the emperor Severus, and the Scots early in the third century. Gibbon remarked that "Something of a doubtful mist still hangs over these Highland traditions, nor can it be entirely dispelled by the most ingenious researches of modern criticism."[66] In a footnote to this passage Gibbon further questioned the poetry by noting that the use of the nickname Caracalla for Severus's son Antoninus was highly suspicious.

The most famous doubter, and the person who probably did most to damage the credibility of Macpherson's poems, was Samuel Johnson. Unlike his biographer James Boswell, Johnson never was impressed with the quality of the verse. He called Ossian's poetry "a mere unconnected rhapsody, a tiresome repetition of the same images."[67] When Hugh Blair asked Johnson whether the latter thought that any 18th-century man could have written the poems of Ossian, Johnson, unaware of Blair's involvement with the work, replied, "Yes, Sir, many men, many women, and many children."[68] Nor did he believe in their authenticity. When he met Macpherson in 1764, Johnson asked several questions about the poetry but received no satisfactory answers. Nearly a decade later, while traveling in the Highlands with Boswell in 1773, Johnson repeatedly inquired about the poems of Ossian in an effort to learn the truth. Like so many others involved with the poetry, from John Home and Hugh Blair onward, Johnson knew no Gaelic; but he satisfied himself that the works were Macpherson's own creations. Hence, in his *A Journey to the*

---

65 For a full discussion of Percy's sense of betrayal by Blair and Ferguson, see Richard B. Sher, "Percy, Shaw, and the Ferguson 'Cheat': National Prejudice in the Ossian Wars," in *Ossian Revisited*, 207–245.

66 *The Decline and Fall of the Roman Empire,* ed. David Womersley (London: Allen Lane, 1994), I, 52.

67 *Boswell's Life of Johnson,* II, 126.

68 Ibid., I, 396.

Western Islands of Scotland (London: W. Strahan and T. Cadell, 1775), Johnson denounced them in the strongest possible language:

> I suppose my opinion of the poems of Ossian is already discovered. I believe they never existed in any other form than that which we have seen. The editor, or author, never could shew the original; nor can it be shewn by any other; to revenge reasonable incredulity, by refusing evidence, is a degree of insolence, with which the world is not yet acquainted; and stubborn audacity is the last refuge of guilt. It would be easy to shew it if he had it; but whence could it be had? It is too long to be remembered, and the language formerly had nothing written. He has doubtless inserted names that circulate in popular stories, and may have translated some wandering ballads, if any can be found; and the names and some of the images being recollected, make an inaccurate auditor imagine, by the help of Caledonian bigotry, that he formerly heard the whole. (273–274)

Macpherson was about to bring out two historical works for William Strahan, Johnson's publisher, and Macpherson feared that Johnson's attack on his credibility would hurt sales. On 13 January 1775 the first edition of Johnson's *Journey* was distributed to booksellers. Macpherson saw a copy, and two days later he wrote to Strahan to protest the tone of the criticism. Johnson did not reply, so Macpherson wrote again, requesting a public apology and the removal of the offending passage from all subsequent editions. Macpherson even drafted the apology he wanted published:

> The Author of the *Journey to the Western Islands of Scotland* finding, when it was too late to make any alterations, that some expressions in page   and   have given offence to the gentleman alluded to, he takes this method of informing the public, that he meant no personal reflection; and that, should this work come to a second impression, he will take care to expunge such words as seem, though undesignedly, to convey an affront. This is a piece of justice, which the author owes to himself as well as to that gentleman.

Macpherson's accompanying letter to Strahan stated,

As I am *very serious* upon this business I insist, that you will keep it to yourself; for were it not [for] the present circumstances of an affair, in which you (as well as I) are concerned [the histories about to be published], I should before this time have traced out the author of this journey, in a very *effectual* manner. Unless I have a satisfactory answer, I am determined (indeed it is necessary) to bring that business to a *conclusion* before I *begin* any other.[69]

Macpherson also had Thomas Becket, the publisher of *Fingal* and *Temora,* insert an announcement in the newspapers asserting that, as already noted, Macpherson had left manuscripts in his shop, had advertised their accessibility at the time, and had even proposed publishing the Gaelic "originals" if enough people had subscribed.

On 17 January Strahan, who also could lose money as a result of Johnson's criticism of Macpherson, wrote to reassure him that he would "do every thing in my Power to obtain you some kind of Satisfaction, and such as may be agreeable to you." The next day Strahan again wrote to Macpherson:

I have seen Dr. Johnson. He declares under his Hand to me, that he meant no *personal affront* to you, and we shall take care that exceptionable Words shall be left out in all future Editions, the present ones being already too much dispersed to admit of Alteration. . . . I think this is sufficient, especially as you declare yourself indifferent to a Want of Belief in others.[70]

Strahan had used the word "ones" to refer to the copies in print because the second edition was already too far advanced to delete the offending passage without great cost. When this second edition appeared with the wording unchanged, Macpherson believed that Johnson had reneged on his promise. Macpherson thereupon sent an insolent letter, now lost, apparently calling

---

69   *Boswell's Life of Johnson*, II, 512.
70   Quoted in Fiona Stafford, "Dr. Johnson and the Ruffian: New Evidence in the Dispute between Samuel Johnson and James Macpherson," *Notes and Queries* 234 (March 1989): 71-77, 73–74.

Johnson "an infamous liar and traducer" and stating that "neither his age nor infirmity should protect him if he came in his way." The letter may even have included a challenge to a duel.[71]

Taking Macpherson's threat seriously, Johnson bought a large walking stick for protection. Sir John Hawkins described it as

> an oak-plant of tremendous size, a plant, I say, and not a shoot or branch, for it had had a root, which being trimmed to the size of a large orange, became the head of it. Its height was upwards of six feet, and from about an inch in diameter at the lower end, increased to near three: this he kept in his bed-chamber, so near the chair in which he constantly sat, as to be within reach.[72]

But Johnson was not intimidated. On 20 January 1775 he replied to Macpherson's threats in one of his most famous letters:

> Mr. James Macpherson—I received your foolish and impudent note. Whatever insult is offered me I will do my best to repel, and what I cannot do for myself the law will do for me. I will not desist from detecting what I think a cheat, from any fear of the menaces of a Ruffian.
>
> You want me to retract? What shall I retract? I thought your book an imposture from the beginning, I think it upon yet surer reasons an imposture still. For this opinion I give the publick my reasons which I here dare you to refute.
>
> But however I may despise you, I reverence truth and if you can prove the genuineness of the work I will confess it. Your rage I defy, your abilities since your Homer are not so formidable, and what I have heard of your morals disposes me to pay regard not to what you shall say, but to what you can prove.
>
> You may print this if you will.
>
> Sam. Johnson[73]

---

71 *Boswell's Life of Johnson*, II, 512.
72 *The Life of Samuel Johnson, LL.D.* (London: J. Buckland [et al.], 1787), 491.
73 *The Letters of Samuel Johnson,* ed. Bruce Redford (Princeton: Princeton University Press, 1992), II, 168–169. In 1773 Macpherson published a translation of the *Iliad* in Ossianic rhythmic prose. The edition was not a success with critics or the public. The reference to Macpherson's morals is equally apt; Macpherson, who never married, fathered five children.

Though Macpherson did not publish the letter, excerpts appeared in the *St. James Chronicle* for 28–31 January and in the *Morning Post* for 1 February, hardly achieving the effect Macpherson had sought.

The controversy over the authenticity of Macpherson's poetry persisted throughout the 18th century in Britain, though on the Continent the majority of readers accepted the works as genuine. In 1797, a year after Macpherson's death, the Highland Society of Scotland appointed a committee, headed by the author Henry Mackenzie, to examine the matter. The committee sent six detailed questions to clergyman and antiquaries in the Highlands. The first question, for example, asked,

> Have you ever heard repeated or sung, any of the poems ascribed to Ossian, translated and published by Mr. Macpherson? By whom have you heard them so repeated, and at what time or times? Did you ever commit any of them to writing, or can you remember them so well as now to set them down? In either of these cases, be so good as to send the Gaelic original to the Committee.[74]

While the committee was still collecting evidence, Malcolm Laing in 1800 published a *History of Scotland*. In an appendix he accused Macpherson of assembling his poems from some hundred sources, ancient and modern. In 1805 Laing published an edition of Macpherson's poetry, in which he ascribed virtually every line to one of eighty-eight authors. Laing equated similarity with plagiarism, and while, as already noted, Macpherson was not above borrowing from popular authors, his work was in fact more than a pastiche of literary allusions.

In that year the committee also published its findings in a 155-page report with two hundred pages of appendices that contained the supporting documentation. If Laing was too harsh, one might argue that the Highland Society report erred in the other direction, accusing Macpherson only of careless editing. Bailey Saunders summarized the committee's findings:

---

74   Quoted in DeGategno, *James Macpherson*, 110.

(1.) That a great legend of Fingal, and Ossian, his son and songster, had immemorially existed in Scotland; and that Ossianic poetry, of an impressive and striking character, was to be found generally and in great abundance in the Highlands; and that there were still, or until lately, many persons who could repeat large fragments of it.

(ii.) That while fragments had been found giving the substance and sometimes the literal expression of parts of Macpherson's work, no one poem was discoverable the same in title or tenor with his publications.

(iii.) That while the committee inclined to believe that he supplied chasms and gave connections by inserting passages of his own, and that he added to the dignity and delicacy of the work by omitting or shortening certain incidents and refining the language, its members recognized that it was now impossible to determine how far these liberties extended; for Macpherson had enjoyed advantages which they did not possess, in that they made their investigations forty years later, when a search for Ossianic poetry was likely to be impeded or defeated by the change which had come over the Highlands during that period.[75]

Two years later the Highland Society of London published the Gaelic "originals." As stated above, Macpherson had translated part of *Temora* from English into Gaelic in 1763, and he may have translated part of *Fingal* to leave with Thomas Becket in 1762. About 1784 a group of Scotsmen in India raised £1,000 to publish the poems in Gaelic, and Macpherson then renewed his efforts, in a desultory manner, to produce the originals. He even toyed with the idea of using Greek characters rather than the Latin alphabet for his transcriptions. When Macpherson died in 1796, John Mackenzie, Secretary to the Highland Society of London, became Macpherson's literary executor and assumed the task of preparing the Gaelic edition. He, too, died before the edition appeared. The Reverend Thomas Ross transcribed what was available—eleven of the shorter Ossianic poems were never translated

---

75 *The Life and Letters of James Macpherson,* 311–312.

back into Gaelic—and the edition appeared, giving evidence of authenticity to those who wished to believe. Not until 1952, when Derick Thomson published *The Gaelic Sources of Macpherson's "Ossian"* (Edinburgh: Edinburgh University Press) was the relationship between Macpherson's poetry and the authentic verses of Ossian established. In effect, Johnson had been correct when he told the Reverend Donald Macqueen, minister of Kilmuir, Skye, that Macpherson "found names, and stories, and phrases, nay passages in old songs, and with them has blended his own compositions, and so made what he gives to the world as the translation of an ancient poem."[76]

Such restoration or chicanery, however one wishes to view it, nonetheless merits admiration. As Sir Walter Scott observed in his review of the *Report of the Committee of the Highland Society of Scotland,*

> While we are compelled to renounce the pleasing idea, "that Fingal lived, and that Ossian sung," our national vanity may be equally flattered by the fact, that a remote, and almost barbarous corner of Scotland, produced, in the 18th century, a bard, capable not only of making an enthusiastic impression on every mind susceptible of poetical beauty, but of giving a new tone to poetry throughout all Europe.[77]

By any measurement, Macpherson's poems were successful. Sales earned Macpherson £1,200, and they launched him on a highly lucrative literary career. The Advertisement to the first edition of *Fingal* particularly thanked "a certain noble person,"[78] identified in *Temora* as John Stuart, Earl of Bute, then prime minister. Bute sent Macpherson £300 a year for some years, and in 1764 he named Macpherson provincial secretary to George Johnstone, governor of West Florida. After fifteen months Macpherson returned to England, where he served as a pro-ministerial writer for a succession of Whig governments. Like his antagonist Samuel Johnson, he supported Lord North's policies, includ-

---

76 *Boswell's Life of Johnson*, V, 242.
77 *Edinburgh Review* 6 (July 1805): 462. The words Scott quoted come from Gibbon's *Decline and Fall*, Book I, ch. 6.
78 *The Poems of Ossian and Related Works*, 33.

ing the efforts to suppress the American Revolution, though Macpherson was more richly rewarded that Johnson: North paid Macpherson as much as £800 a year. Macpherson also produced popular historical works: *Introduction to the History of Great Britain and Ireland* (1771), *Original Papers Containing the Secret History of Great Britain, from the Restoration to the Accession of the House of Hanover* (1775), and *History of Great Britain from the Restoration to the Accession of the House of Hanover* (1775), this last a continuation of David Hume's work. Hume had not wanted Macpherson to act as his successor, but the public was so taken with the work that Strahan paid Macpherson £3,000 for the copyright. As for Ossian, Macpherson had published a collected edition in 1765 and a drastically revised version in 1773, after which he turned to history and politics, except when forced, as he was by Johnson in 1775, to revisit the poetry.

Macpherson's income grew even greater in 1778 when he became agent to Mohammed Ali, Nabob of Arcot, India. In 1780 Macpherson entered Parliament as member for Camelford, Cornwall, paying £4,000 for his seat. He was re-elected in 1784 and 1790, and he died in office. In 1783 the British government, grateful for his services, offered him the lands of his clan chieftain, Ewen Macpherson of Cluny, who had lost his property because of his support for the Stuart pretender "Bonnie" Prince Charles in 1745. Macpherson refused this offer, but he bought land at Badenoch, near his birthplace, and commissioned Robert Adam, the leading British architect of the time, to design his house, Belleville. According to Ann Grant from Laggan, who knew Macpherson at the end of his life, "He was a very good-natured man; and now that he had got all his schemes of interest and ambition fulfilled, he seemed to reflect and grow domestic, and showed, of late, a great inclination to be an indulgent landlord, and very liberal to the poor.[79]

Macpherson died at Belleville on 17 February 1796. In his will he left money for his five illegitimate children; his namesake, James, the eldest, inherited his property. To John Home, who had

---

79 *James Macpherson: An Episode in Literature,* 161.

inadvertently redirected Macpherson's life, the will bequeathed £2,000. Macpherson also left money for the construction of a monument to himself at Kingussie, and for burial in Poet's Corner, Westminster Abbey, where he lies close to his one-time opponent Samuel Johnson. Perhaps on his deathbed Macpherson recalled the last lines he gave to Ossian, which might have served as his own epitaph.

> Did thy beauty last, O Ryno? Stood the strength of car-borne Oscar? Fingal himself passed away; and the halls of his fathers forgot his steps.—And shalt thou remain, aged bard! when the mighty have failed?—But my fame shall remain, and grow like the oak of Morven; which lifts its broad head to the storm, and rejoices in the course of the wind.[80]

---

80 "Berrathon: A Poem," in *The Poems of Ossian and Related Works*, 198. "Berrathon" was published with *Fingal* in 1761. When Macpherson revised his Ossianic works in 1773 he placed it last, as Ossian's death song.

Thomas Chatterton

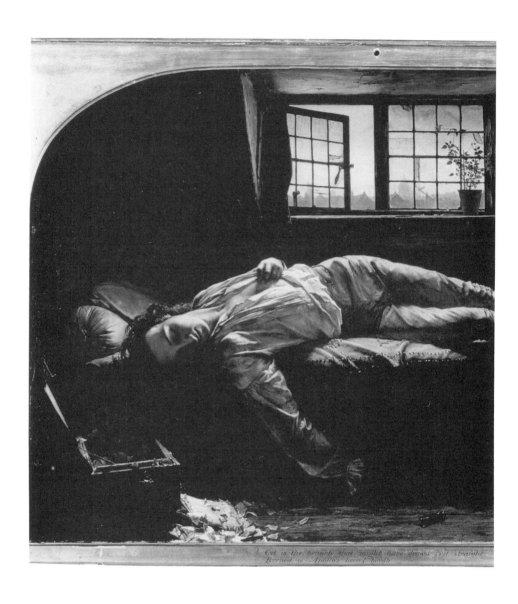

Thomas Chatterton by Henry Wallis

III

The Marvelous Thomas Chatterton

O̸n mid-September, 1768, a new bridge across the Avon at Bristol was opened to foot traffic, and on Michaelmas Day, 29 September, Bristol's mayor, George Weare, became the first person to drive across the bridge in a coach. Two days later the local newspaper, *Felix Farley's Bristol Journal,* carried an account by Dunhelmus Bristoliensis (the Durham man from Bristol) of a similar event that had taken place in 1247, when the city's first stone bridge had been opened.

> On Fridaie was the time fixed for passing the newe Brydge; aboute the time of the tollynge the tenth Clock, Master Greggorie Dalbenye, mounted on a Fergreyne [red or gray] Horse enformed Master Mayor all thyngs were prepared. . . . Master Maior bare in his Hande, a gouldin Rodde, and a Congeon [dwarf] Squier bare in his Hande, his Helmet: waulking by the Syde of the Horse; than came the Eldermen and Cittie Broders mounted on Sable Horses, dyght [adorned] with white trappynges and Plumes, and Scarlet Copes, and Chapeaus, having thereon Sable Plumes; after them the Preests, and Friars Parysh, Mendicaunt, and Seculor, some syngyng Saincte Warburghs Song, others soundyng Clarions thereto, and otherssome Citrialles [stringed musical instruments]. In thilk manner reechyng the Brydge the Manne with the Anlace [dagger], stode on the fyrst Top of a Mound, yreed [raised] in the midst of the Bridge; then want [went] up the Manne with the Sheelde, after him the Minstrels, and Clarions. And then the preestes and Freeres, all in white Albs makyng a most goodlie Shewe; the Maior and Eldermen standyng round theie sang, with the sound of Clarions, the Song of Saincte Baldwyn; which beyng done the Manne on the Top threwe with greet myght his Anlace into the See, and the Clarions, sounded an auntiant Charge, and

Forloyn [retreat]. Then theie sang again the Songe of Saincte Warburgh, and proceeded up Chrysts Hill, to the Cross where a Latin Sermon was preeched—by Ralph de Blundeville. And with sound of Clarion theie agayne went to the Brydge, and there dined, spendyng the rest of the daie, in Sportes and Plaies, the Freers of Saincte Augustine doeyng the Plaie of the Knyghtes of Brystowe, makynge a greete Fire at night on Kynwulph Hyll[.][1]

This account was supposedly a translation by the 15th-century secular priest Thomas Rowley from an earlier version. In fact, the piece was the invention of the fifteen-year-old Thomas Chatterton.

Chatterton's father, Thomas Chatterton, Sr., was a schoolmaster at the Redcliff and St. Thomas Charity School, which was established in 1733 at Chipping Sudbury and which moved to Pile Street, Bristol, in 1739. On 25 April 1748, at the age of thirty-five, Thomas, Sr., married the sixteen-year-old Sarah Young. Their first child, Mary, was born on 14 February 1749. On 12 December 1750 Sarah gave birth to a son, whom his parents named Giles Malpas Chatterton in honor of the man who in 1749 had given the money to add four rooms onto the Pile Street school as a residence. The child lived only four months and was buried on 17 April 1751. He therefore presumably died on 15 April, a date that would have some significance in the life of Thomas Chatterton, Jr., born on Monday evening, 20 November 1752, three months after his father's death at the age of thirty-nine (7 August 1752).

The elder Thomas was an antiquarian with a particular interest in the Roman coins found in and around Bristol, and he collected books; at his death he owned about 150 volumes. He also brought home old parchment manuscripts from the muniment room of St. Mary Redcliff Church across the street from his school. A chest containing these manuscripts had been opened about 1727 in a search for important documents. Those had been removed and the rest left, unlocked, for anyone to take. Thomas,

---

1   In *The Complete Works of Thomas Chatterton: A Bicentenary Edition,* ed. Donald S. Taylor in association with Benjamin B. Hoover, 2 vols. (Oxford: Clarendon Press, 1971), 56–57.

Sr., collected the parchments not for any antiquarian interest, but rather to provide coverings for his students' books. For £30 a year he was not only to teach but also to find "pens[,] ink and paper" for the boys.[2] His wife, a dressmaker, used the parchments for patterns and pinholders.

Young Thomas briefly attended the Pile Street school but was soon dismissed by the schoolmaster, Stephen Love, as "incapable of improvement."[3] Thomas' sister later recalled that the boy objected to reading in a small book. However, a large French vellum manuscript with decorated capitals caught his attention, and, having mastered his alphabet from this text, he went on to learn to read from a Bible in Gothic type. According to Herbert Croft, who went to Bristol after Chatterton's death to learn as much as he could about the young man, "C. became his own teacher, and his own schoolmaster, before other children are subjects for instruction."[4]

On 3 August 1760 Thomas matriculated at Colston's Hospital, a charity school established by Edward Colston in 1710, which Thomas Chatterton, Sr., had attended. Thomas, Jr. could have gone to the local free grammar school, but Colston's provided clothing, room, and board, and it paid the fee for an apprenticeship when students graduated. Financially, then, Colston's was ideal for Sarah, who thus had one less child to care for. Intellectually the choice was less satisfactory. At the grammar school Thomas would have studied the classics, whereas Colston's was designed to prepare its boys for careers in business.

Bristol was Britain's second largest city in the 18th century and a major trading center. Richard Holmes described the Bristol of the 1760s as possessing a "raw mercantile spirit, seething with new commercial enterprises; it was a city dominated by the power of local trading interests." The poet Richard Savage, who died in Bristol in 1743, denounced the city as "Thou blank of Sciences, thou dearth of Arts!"[5] Thomas, too, had no sympathy for this world of trade. In "The Whore of Babylon" he would write,

---

2   Quoted in Edward Harry William Meyerstein, *A Life of Thomas Chatterton* (New York: Scribner's, 1930), 7.
3   Meyerstein, 22.
4   In Meyerstein, 23.
5   Richard Holmes, "Thomas Chatterton: The Case Re-opened," *Cornhill Magazine* 178 (Autumn 1970), 203–251, 227–228.

> But bred in Bristol's mercenary Cell
> Compell'd in Scenes of Avarice to dwell
> What generous Passion can refine my Breast[?]
>   ***
> Bristol may keep her prudent Maxims still
> But know my saving Friends I never will
> The Composition of my Soul is made
> Too great for Servile avaricious Trade[.]
> (ll. 57–59, 533–536)[6]

Hence the curriculum of Colston's, consisting of reading, writing, and accounting, did not excite Thomas. The monastic aspects of the school probably did appeal to him, though. The rules required that the boys be tonsured, like priests and monks, and that they wear a blue gown of medieval cut. The school had been erected on the site of a former Carmelite priory, the ruins of which still stood in 1760.

Though classes ran from 7:00 A.M. to 11:00 A.M. and 1:00 P.M. to 5:00 P.M., Thomas was not overworked. In his free time he wandered about the church and cemetery of St. Mary Redcliff, studying the old graves and their inscriptions. Here he saw the two monuments to William Canynge, five times mayor of Bristol in the fifteenth century and restorer of the church where he was buried. Here, too, lay Thomas Rowley, Bristol bailiff and sheriff. Chatterton would create a fictional 15th-century Bristol around these two historical figures. He could also indulge his budding anti-quarian tastes by taking home manuscripts that remained in the church's muniment room. At about the age of ten, Thomas joined Fisher's circulating library in St. James parish, and he haunted the local bookshops, borrowing such volumes as he could not afford to buy. The largest of these stores was Samuel Green's of St. Michael's Hill, which in 1768 would move to Wine Street at the corner of Dolphin Lane. On Green's shelves was a copy of the works of Geoffrey Chaucer, edited by Thomas Speght, which Thomas read. Thomas's favorite shop, however, was that of a Mr. Goodall in Tower Lane. In 1824 John Evans reported that Thomas "was

---

6 *The Complete Works of Thomas Chatterton*, 453, 467.

particularly attached to one book, on Saxon manners and customs,"[7] perhaps Richard Verstegen's *A Restitvtion of Decayed
Intelligence, in Antiquities,* first published in 1605. The 1655 edition (London: Printed by T. Newcomb for Joshua Kirton) mentions both Aella and Bertha on page 110; these are the hero and
heroine of Chatterton's play *Ælla.* Thomas kept a list of books that
he read between his eleventh and twelfth years. Among the seven-
ty titles, history and divinity predominated, but his tastes were
eclectic. According to the not always reliable Bristol poet and sta-
tioner James Thistlethwaite,

> In the course of the year 1768 and 1769—Chatterton being
> between 15 and 16 years old—wherein I frequently saw and
> conversed with C., the eccentricity of his mind, and the ver-
> satility of his disposition, seem to have been singularly dis-
> played. One day he might be found busily employed in the
> study of Heraldry and English Antiquities, both of which are
> numbered amongst the most favourite of his pursuits; the
> next, discovered him deeply engaged, confounded, and per-
> plexed, amidst the subtleties of metaphysical disquisition, or
> lost and bewildered in the abstruse labyrinth of mathematical
> researches; and these in an instant again neglected and thrown
> aside to make room for astronomy and music, of both of
> which sciences his knowledge was entirely confined to theory.
> Even physic [medicine] was not without a charm to allure his
> imagination, and he would talk of Galen, Hippocrates, and
> Paracelsus, with all the confidence and familiarity of a modern
> empirick.[8]

Thomas also had begun to write poetry. On 8 January 1763
Felix Farley's Bristol Journal ran the sixteen-line "On the Last
Epiphany, or Christ Coming to Judgment," which William Tyson
attributed to Chatterton in 1842. According to Thomas' sister,
Mary,

> At 12 years old [Thomas] was confirmed by the Bishop, he
> made very senciable [sic] serious remarks on the awfulness of

---

7 In Meyerstein, 48.
8 In Holmes, 232; Meyerstein, 75.

the ceremony and his own feelings and convictions during it. Soon after this in the week he was doorkeeper he made some verses on the last day, I think about 18 lines, paraphrased 9 chapter of Job and not long after some chapters in Isaiah. He had been gloomy from the time he began to learn, but we remark'd he was more chearful after he began to write poetry. Some saterical peices [sic] we saw soon after.[9]

In his edition of Chatterton's works Donald S. Taylor argues against Tyson's attribution because Thomas was not confirmed until he was twelve, and in 1763 he was only ten. Certainly by the next year he was making verses. On 1 January 1764, Mary gave Thomas a small notebook for his poetry. When he returned the notebook to her at the end of the year, it was nearly full. Under the date of 14 April 1764 was "Apostate Will," a fifty-four line satire on a Methodist who changes his faith to suit his purse. In 1764 Thomas also composed the unfinished "Sly Dick," another satire on greed, and "A Hymn for Christmas Day." Tyson attributed to Chatterton three other satires, two in poetry and one in prose, that appeared in *Felix Farley's Bristol Journal* for 7 January 1764. Again the theme is "the pleasing Hope of Gain."[10]

All of these pieces are written in the standard idiom of the time, but James Thistlethwaite assigns to this year the pseudo-medieval "Elinoure and Juga" by Thomas Rowley. Supposedly in 1764 Thomas Phillips, who entered Colston's on 14 December 1758 and became usher (assistant teacher) in 1765, showed Thistlethwaite a parchment with this poem. Phillips did organize a poetry-writing group at the school, but there is no evidence that Chatterton participated, and Donald S. Taylor assigns "Elinoure and Juga" to 1769. Still, Phillips and Chatterton were friends, and when the latter learned of Phillips' death, he composed three versions of an elegy, in which he called the usher "Master of the boundless Lyre."[11]

---

9   Quoted in *The Complete Works of Thomas Chatterton,* 1138.
10 "The Churchwarden and the Apparition, A Fable," l. 5, in *Complete Works,* 689. Taylor lists the three pieces under "Works of Doubtful Authenticity."

On 1 July 1767 Chatterton graduated from Colston's, and on that same day he was apprenticed to John Lambert, a Bristol lawyer, to learn to become a scrivener (copier of legal documents), Colston's paying the £10 apprenticeship fee. Chatterton was supposed to work twelve hours a day, six days a week. The terms of his seven-years' indentureship dictated that "Taverns he shall not frequent, at Dice he shall not play, Fornication he shall not commit, Matrimony he shall not contract." In return for Thomas' labor and good behavior, Lambert would feed, house, and clothe him, and at the end of seven years Lambert would give Thomas four shillings and sixpence and two suits of clothes.[12] Chatterton resented being treated as a servant, but his duties were not onerous. Lambert rarely had more than two or three hours of copying for his apprentice each day, leaving Thomas time to indulge his penchant for reading and writing. Sometime during this period Chatterton invented Thomas Rowley, priest and poet. Richard Holmes called this creation "one of the most extraordinary acts in English literature."[13]

Chatterton's literary reputation rests on his poetry, which is indeed remarkable, particularly for one who died before his eighteenth birthday. What other writer in any language created such a body of work, and such good work, at that age? But Chatterton's achievement goes beyond the composition of pseudo-medieval verse. He imagined an entire world, for which he created a language, a history, and a geography, giving, as Theseus in act V of *A Midsummer Night's Dream* says poets do, to airy nothings a local habitation and a name.

At the center of Chatterton's 15th-century Bristol were Rowley and Canynge. Their biographies evolved, but in the final version Rowley was born at Norton Mal-reward, Somersetshire, five miles southeast of Bristol, and educated first at the (fictional) convent of St. Kenna at Keynsham.[14] He and William Canynge were classmates at the Carmelite priory located on the future site

---

11   "Elegy to the Memory of Mr. Thomas Phillips, of Fairford," first version, l. 9, *Complete Works*, 383.

12   Meyerstein, 63.

13   Holmes, 214.

of Colston's Hospital. Rowley took holy orders about 1430 and served as parish priest of St. John's. He was also Canynge's confessor. Rowley, a Yorkist in the Wars of the Roses, traveled around Britain to secure antiquities for Canynge and was well rewarded for his efforts, as he was for the poetry he wrote for his patron. After one successful search for drawings, Canynge gave Rowley £200, an astonishing sum, and for the "Bristowe Tragedie" Canynge paid him £20. Rowley retired to Westbury, where he died in 1478.[15]

Canynge was a younger son of a successful merchant, and the death of his father and older brother left him rich. Chatterton created differing accounts of Canynge's marital history. In "Canynge's Will" he was married to Johanna Hathwaie, probably a Shakespearean borrowing, but she died childless. However, the will also mentions three sons (whose names are not consistent). In the "Lyfe of W: Canynge—by Rowlie" Canynge married Johanna Young in 1431, but she died that same year. According to "The Storie of Wyllyam Canynge," he married Johanna earlier, so she could have been the mother of these children. In 1432 Canynge opened a freemason's lodge at his home and began rebuilding St. Mary Redcliff. Canynge's generosity was most evident in his gifts to Rowley and in his restoration of the church. In 1461 Edward IV ordered the widowed Canynge to remarry. Instead, Canynge took holy orders and retired to Westbury, paying Edward 3,000 marks to make peace with the king. In 1467 Canynge invited Rowley to join him at Westbury. Canynge died there in 1474. Rowley described Canynge as "talle and statelie. His Eyes and Haire are jeat blacke hys Aspecte sweete and Skynne blanche [white] han he not soe moche nobilnesse yn hys Fygure he woulde bee Wommanysh, or ne so moch swotiness [sweetness], proud and dyscorteous[.] yn Looke hys Lyppes are rudde [red] and hys Lymbes albeytte large are honge ne lyke a Stronge Pole."[16] At the end of a series of letters

---

14   Chatterton did not assign Rowley a place of birth until the final Rowley piece, "An Excelente Balade of Charitie," where he mentions Norton Mal-reward in a footnote. Though the place is real, Chatterton almost certainly chose it for its literal meaning, since by the time he wrote this piece, some time between May of 1769 and July 1770, he had become convinced that he would gain neither wealth nor fame from his Rowley poems, only one of which was published in his lifetime.

15   Chatterton does not mention Rowley's death, but the historical Rowley died in 1478.

from Canynge, Rowley described his patron as not just a great merchant. "As a Leorned Wyseager [philosopher] he excelled ynne alle thynges. as a Poette and Peyncter he was greete[.]"[17]

Around Rowley and Canynge gathered a coterie of like-minded literary and benevolent men; Chatterton's world was exclusively masculine. One of the most important of these figures was John a Iscam (whose name came from William Camden's *Britannia*). He helped Rowley create the play "The Parlyamente of Sprytes" for the dedication of the new St. Mary Redcliff in 1435, and John himself composed another interlude, "The Merrie Tales of Laymyngetowne." He also acted in Rowley's *Ælla*. The freemason's lodge that Canynge established at his home dedicated itself to intellectual and civic improvement.

Though this world was Chatterton's own invention, it was based on extensive study. His version of Canynge's life, for example, while embroidered, had some basis in fact. In the south transept of St. Mary Redcliff Chatterton would have read the following text on a painted wooden panel enclosed in a black wooden frame:

> Mr. William Canings, Ye Richest Marchant of ye towne of Bristow Afterwards chosen 5 times Mayor of ye said towne for ye good of ye Comon Wealth of ye same. He was in order of Priesthod 7 yeares afterwards Deane of Westbury & died ye 7th of Novem 1474 which said William did build within ye said towne of Westbury a Colledge which his canons & ye said William did maintaine by space of 8 yeares 800 handy craftsmen, besides Carpenters & masons every day 100 men Besides King Edward ye 4th had of ye said William 3000 marks for his peace to be had in 2470 tonnes of shiping.[18]

The historical Canynge had a wife named Joan and two sons, and he was a benefactor to both St. Mary Redcliff and Westbury, as Chatterton claimed.

---

16 *Complete Works,* 134.
17 Ibid., 233.
18 This version of the inscription was kindly supplied me by Jane Bradley of the Bristol Central Library. She received the transcript through the good offices of St. Mary Redcliff.

Donald S. Taylor quotes R. C. Collingwood's observation that "as works of imagination, the historian's work and the novelist's do not differ. Where they do differ is that the historian's picture is meant to be true. The novelist has a single task only: to construct a coherent picture, one that makes sense."[19] As medieval documents, the Rowley pieces are forgeries; as imaginative recreations they form a fascinating fiction.

Chatterton's knowledge of the medieval world now seems limited, but he sought to learn as much as he could. His medieval vocabulary contains some 1,800 words, all of them drawn from some legitimate source. Most of his archaisms he derived from Nathaniel Bailey's *Universal Etymological English Dictionary* (London: D. Midwinter, 1737) and John Kersey's *Dictionarium Anglo-Britannicum*, 3rd edition (London: J. Phillips [et al.], 1721).[20] These he supplemented with such works as Thomas Benson's *Vocabularium Anglo-Saxonicum* (Oxford: S. Smith and B. Walford, 1701), Elisha Coles' *An English Dictionary* (London: J. Walthoe [et al.], 1732), Edward Phillips' *New World of Words* edited by Kersey, 6th edition (London: J. Phillips, 1706), and Stephen Skinner's *Etymologicon Linguae Anglicanae* edited by Thomas Kenshaw (London: T. Roycroft for H. Brome, 1671). To assist 18th- century readers, the 1710 edition of Gavin Douglas' medieval Scottish translation of Virgil's *Aeneid*, edited by Thomas Ruddiman, noted forty-four ways in which Douglas' language differed from contemporary English. According to Taylor, "Of the forty-four rules listed, all but nine . . . can also be illustrated from Rowley." Chatterton was, of course, at the mercy of his sources. Kersey defined "heck" as a rock, a misprint for rick. Hence, in the "Song of Saincte Werburgh" Chatterton imagines the saint walking on water "Till he gaynd the distant Heck"(l. 13).[22]

Chatterton's spelling is erratic because he thought that no spelling rules existed in the 15th century. Any form of a word that was not modern therefore could be medieval. According to the

---

19   In *Complete Works*, 1176.
20   The editions cited here are those given in Donald S. Taylor's *Complete Works*.
21   *Complete Works*, 1180.
22   Ibid., 58.

Irish poet Austin Clarke, the exotic orthography carried its own significance: "To Chatterton, these bristling consonants and double vowels were like the harness and martial gear of medieval days. Plain words, mailed in strange spellings, might move like knights in full armour amid the resounding panoply of war."[23]

In the "Letter to the Dygne [worthy] Mastre Canynge" preceding *Ælla*, Rowley wrote,

> Pardon, yee Graiebarbes [graybeards], gyff [if] I saie, onwise
> Yee are, to stycke so close and bysmarelie [curiously]
> To hystorie; you doe ytte tooe moche pryze,
> Whyche amenused [lessened] thoughtes of poesie;
>
> ***
>
> Cannynge and I from common course dyssente;
> Wee ryde the stede, botte yev [give] to hym the reene;
> Ne wylle betwene crased [old] molterynge [moldering]
>   bookes be pente,
> Botte soare on hyghe, and yn the sonne-bemes sheene[.]
> (ll.73-76, 81-84)[24]

Chatterton, like Rowley, could stray from fact. Sometimes, as in the case of the biographies of Rowley and Canynge or the bridge narrative, he willfully embroidered the past. Elsewhere, he revealed his ignorance and later had to invent other accounts to explain his mistakes. He apparently did not know, for example, that Saint Werburgh was a woman, so in his song he made the saint male. He then created a story of two saints with the same name, the female version of Bristol having been converted by and taken the name of the male saint from Redcliff. Chatterton's "Bristowe Tragedie" tells of the execution of a Yorkist who attempted to assassinate the Earl of Warwick but was himself executed at Bristol in 1461, with Edward IV in attendance. The execution had in fact occurred, but Chatterton's first hero was misnamed Sir Charles Brandon. After discovering that Brandon lived too late to figure in

---

23   Quoted in Holmes, 230
24   *Complete Works,* 177–178.

the poem, Chatterton changed the name to Bawdin. The man beheaded was actually named Sir Baldwin Fulford; but even after learning the truth, Chatterton refused to make any further alterations in his poem. In the first version of "The Battle of Hastings," Chatteron assigned the poem to "Turgot a Saxon Monk in the *Tenth* [sic] Century";[25] the battle was fought, of course, in the eleventh.

As with his language, though, Chatterton did not merely invent people and events. Greggorie Dalbenye in the bridge narrative is based on George Daubeny, sheriff of Bristol in 1769, and Ralph de Blundeville is a composite of Thomas de Blundeville, Bishop of Norwich (d. 1236) and Randolph Blondeville, a 12th-century Earl of Chester. For his description of Bristol Castle, only the ruins of which were standing in the mid 18th century, Chatterton turned to the accounts of the 15th-century William Wyrcestre and 16th-century John Leland. Among the historical works that Chatterton read were William Camden's *Britannia*, translated from the Latin and edited by Edmund Gibson (London: Printed by F. Collins for A. Swalle [et al.], 1695) and his *Remains Concerning Britain* (London: Charles Harper and John Amery, 1674); Thomas Fuller's *The Church-History of Britain* (London: J. Williams, 1655); John Guillim, *A Display of Heraldrie* (London: Printed by Thomas Cotes, for Jacob Blome, 1638); Peter Heylyn, *A Help to English History* (London: Printed by B. Motte, for C. Harper, 1709); Raphael Holinshed, *The Chronicles of England, Scotland, and Ireland*, 2 volumes (London: s.n., 1587); John Speed, *The Historie of Great Britain*, 3rd edition (London: Printed by I. Dawson, for G. Humble, 1632); Edward Stillingfleet, *Origines Britannicae, or, the Antiquities of the British Churches* (London: Printed by M. Flesher for Henry Mortlock, 1685); John Stow, *The Annales of England* (London: G. Bishop and T. Adams, 1605); and John Weever's *Ancient Fvnerall Monvments* (London: Printed by T. Harper, 1631). His literary models were similarly wide-ranging. Rowley's poems contain echoes of Shakespeare, John Dryden, John Gay, Edmund Spenser, Nicholas

---

25   Ibid., 26.

Rowe, Thomas Otway, Alexander Pope, Nathaniel Lee, John Milton, Thomas Percy's *Reliques of Ancient English Poetry*, and Michael Drayton.

Chatterton's forgeries invite comparison with Macpherson's, which appeared in the early 1760s and that Chatterton read and imitated, producing seven Ossianic prose poems. Both Macpherson and Chatterton were attempting to break away from the classical models of the Augustan age to find sources of inspiration in Britain's own past. Both were also reacting against what they regarded as the mercantile world of 18th-century Britain, creating in its place a society linked by bonds of friendship rather than money. Canynge's older brother, Robert, "was a Manne after his Fadre's owne Harte, greedie of Gayne, and sparynge of Almes Deedes; but Mastere William was mickle Courteous, and gave me manie Markes in my neede," Rowlie reports in "A Brief Account of William Cannings."[26] Canynge writes to Rowlie that his fellow members of the town council "doe notte bethynke me a Manne to advyse them bicaus I wulde not have them doe meane thynges for Gayne."[27] In "An Excelente Balade of Charitie," Chatterton's retelling of the story of the Good Samaritan, the good priest gives alms to the beggar and tells him, "Here take this silver, it maie eathe [ease] thie care;/We are Goddes stewards all, nete [nothing] of our owne we bare" (ll. 83-84).[28] Dissatisfied with the brazen world in which they found themselves, each sought to create a golden age.

Yet the differences are equally telling. Macpherson's Ossian belongs to an oral culture; when a monk suggests writing down Ossian's songs, the bard rebuffs the offer. Macpherson never attempted to produce antique manuscripts of his own, though he claimed to have more than he actually possessed. Chatterton's society is decidedly literate. For some of the Rowley works Chatterton created parchment manuscripts, rubbing them with yellow ochre or dirt, or holding them over a flame, to make them seem antique. He used an ink that looked old, and he developed a

---

26 Ibid., 51.
27 Ibid., 121.
28 Ibid., 648.

generic 15th-century hand. He was not especially careful with his penmanship, though. On 30 December 1813 John Rickman reported to Charles and Mary Lamb and William Hazlitt that he, Rickman, had seen one of Chatterton's forgeries, in which there were seventeen kinds of "e's" in various shapes. Lamb replied, "Oh, that must have been modern—written by one of the 'mob of gentlemen who write with ease.' "[29] When Chatterton did not manufacture a parchment, he said that one existed. In what is either a very clever spoof, a possible hoax by Chatterton himself, or a piece intended to show Rowley's ingenuity, the poet-priest writes,

> I mervaile moche, our *scriveynes* [scriveners] and *amanuenses* doe not gette lytel letters cutt in wood, or caste in yron, and thanne followynge by the eye, or with a fescue, everyche letter of the boke thei meane to copie, fix the sayde wooden or yron letters meetelie disposed in a frame or chase; thanne daube the same over with somme atramentous [inky] stuffe, and layinge a thynne piece of moistened parchment or paper on these letters, presse it doune with somme smoothe stone or other heavie weight: by the whiche goodlye devyce a manie hundreth copies of eche boke might be wroughte off in a few daies, instead of employing the eyen and hondes of poor clerkes for several monthes with greate attentyon and travaile.[30]

Crediting Rowley with inventing the process of printing with movable type seems extreme, but Chatterton (or his imitator) must have recognized that Rowley's life spanned the age of manuscript and print.

Rowley's world, again unlike Macpherson's, is urban rather than rustic. It is also in many ways an 18th-century world, with Canynge acting as a dilettante collecting antiquities, and Canynge's masonic lodge as a kind of club or society for improvement. Canynge wrote to Rowley that he hoped to bring together

29 *Henry Crabb Robinson on Books and Their Writers,* ed. Edith J. Morley, 3 vols. (London: Dent, 1938), I, 134. Lamb is punning on Alexander Pope's description of Restoration authors in "The First Epistle of the Second Book of Horace," as "The Mob of Gentlemen who wrote with Ease" (l. 108).

30 *Complete Works,* 60.

"menne of counynge Wytte to advaunce the Glorie of thys oure Towne. Whatte wee shalle unkeven [uncover] that wylle benefytte Menne shalle be knowen, whatte wylle harme, unknowen, . . . botte wee wylle streve to advaunce auntyaunt Accountes Glorie and Profytte, with the Helpe of Godde."[31] Westbury is as much a country house retreat as it is a medieval monastic establishment, the interludes performed for Canynge amateur theatricals, not guild-sponsored mystery plays.

Macpherson may have imagined himself as a latter-day Ossian; Chatterton certainly saw himself as Rowley, for whom Canynge served as both patron and father. Both Macpherson and Chatterton hoped to better their unpleasant circumstances by their pens: Macpherson disliked being a tutor, and Chatterton hated his apprenticeship. In their visions of escape, though, Macpherson was the more modern, seeking to appeal to booksellers and the book-buying public. Chatterton, perhaps because he was younger, perhaps because he never knew his father, perhaps because he was psychologically rooted in the Middle Ages, repeatedly sought for someone who would appreciate and reward his talents as Canynge did Rowley's. Later writers recreated Chatterton as the model of the other-worldly poet, and Chatterton himself denounced mercenary motives; but money was never far from his mind. He hoped to publish his Rowley pieces, and after he abandoned his medieval world as an unprofitable proposition and turned to political writing, he was still searching for a Maecenas. Much of the bitterness in his satires can be attributed to his repeated disappointments.

The bridge narrative seemed to bring forth Canynge-like patrons in the guise of George Symmes Catcott and William Barrett. Catcott was a Bristol pewterer and antiquarian who boasted that he owned no book less than a hundred years old. Barrett had come to Bristol in 1745, where he became an apothecary and, in 1760, a surgeon at St. Peter's Hospital. In that year he began a history of Bristol, which would eventually appear in 1789. In part the long delay in publication resulted from a paucity of documents.

---

31   Ibid., 231.

After reading the bridge narrative, Catcott (whom Chatterton insisted on calling "Catgut") sought out Chatterton and introduced him to Barrett. Chatterton said that he had found the bridge narrative in a manuscript his father had taken from the chest in the muniment room of St. Mary Redcliff, and there were more parchments where that had come from. The first poem that Chatterton showed them was "Bristowe Tragedie," which introduces Canynge as a loyal but compassionate subject who seeks to save the life of the condemned Bawdin. Shortly thereafter Chatterton produced the first version of the "Battle of Hastynges," which he claimed as his own. Barrett and Catcott refused to believe him, and he later gave them a second version that he attributed to Rowley.

Another early piece was "Craishes Herauldry," in which Chatterton gave pedigrees to some of his Bristol acquaintances. Chatterton was writing poetry for John Baker, a young man about his own age, to send to Baker's girl-friend, Eleanor Hoyland; ten of these poems survive. "Craishes Heraldry" describes the Baker crest as "a Goats head Couped holding in his Mouth a Rose barbd proper,"[32] alluding to Baker's amorous (and libidinous) propensities. Thomas Broughton was vicar of St. Mary Redcliff, and John Broughton would edit Chatterton's *Miscellanies* in 1778. The Broughton family is traced back to 1241. Henry Burgum, who was eager for noble ancestors, was George Catcott's business partner; Chatterton included a "Burgh." Since neither Barrett not Catcott is included, "Craishes Heraldry" probably predates Chatterton's introduction to these men. Canynge's grandfather is listed, followed by the second-longest entry, for the Chattertons, who have a pedigree going back to Normandy in 1034. The list ends in the C's, except for the Rumsey family, which has the longest listing. Chatterton was in love with Polly (Maria) Rumsey, daughter of a cooper in Redcliff Street, and he retained his fondness for her until his death.

Rowley's lament in *Ælla* that history is preferred to poetry reflects Chatterton's experience in Bristol. He had included two

---

32   *Complete Works,* 45.

poems with his bridge narrative, the two songs supposedly sung when the bridge was dedicated in 1247. Only the prose account was published. Barrett and Catcott wanted historical documents; of the forty-two parchments that went to the British Museum from Barrett's collection, only two contain poetry. Despite his disappointment with these prosaic preferences, Chatterton gave the men what they wanted, and despite his hostility to his native city, he attempted to present it with a glorious past. William Camden claimed that Bristol was insignificant before the middle of the 11th century; Chatterton set out to prove him wrong. "Of the Auntiaunt Forme of Monies" in the "Yellow Roll" and the "Explayneals" in the accompanying "Purple Roll," all but one of the coins found around Bristol are pre-Norman, indicating that Bristol had been a major trading center in Roman and Saxon times. Chatterton-Rowley gave Bristol a mayor before any other British city. Canynge had asked Rowley to compile a history of Bristol, just as Barrett and Catcott urged Chatterton to gather documents relating to the city's past, and Rowley had turned to the account of Turgot, an authentic monk-historian of Durham who died in 1115. Chatterton's "D.B." signature derives from Turgot, though the Bristol connection for Turgot is Chatterton's invention. The walls around Redcliff probably were built in the 12th century, but the Turgot account places them in the 8th. In another account Rowley claimed that men from Bristol were the first to trade with Ireland, and the earliest of these merchants came from Redcliff. In "The Merrie Tricks of Laymyngetowne," Lamington's London creditors send his goods to Bristol to be sold, indicating that in the Middle Ages Bristol offered a better market than the English capital. "The Rolle of Seyncte Bartlemeweis Priorie" describes the priory's library as containing a wealth of manuscripts, giving Bristol a rich literary heritage, and Rowley's "Heraldic Account of Bristol Artists and Writers" enhances that sense of cultural riches.

In return for this wealth of material that included over 300 drawings, as well as genealogies, letters, five maps, descriptions of churches (about half of them Chatterton's inventions), catalogues and histories, Chatterton was given access to the libraries of Barrett and Catcott. George Catcott's brother, Alexander, a local vicar, also opened his library to him. Of the three, Alexander was at once the most admiring and the most suspicious of the young man, thinking him a genius and capable of writing anything that was attributed to Rowley. The extent of Barrett's gullibility is uncertain. As an antiquarian, he should have recognized that the writing did not correspond to any known 15th-century hand, and mistakes like the dating of the Battle of Hastings should have given him pause. Unlike Alexander Catcott, though, Barrett and George Catcott did not believe, or chose not to believe, that a poorly educated teenager could produce the Rowley material on his own. Barrett, moreover, wanted the documents to be authentic so he could use them in his history, which he did in 1789, long after serious doubts had been cast on the authenticity of the Rowley material.

Whenever possible, Chatterton insinuated his medieval poetry into his accounts, but he recognized that Bristol offered no market for verse. Even his prose was not well rewarded. For Henry Burgum, Chatterton created an elaborate pedigree from the time of the Norman Conquest to the mid-15th century. Chatterton must have worked hard, ruling each page into sections and writing in black and red inks to create an air of authenticity. For his efforts he received a crown (five shillings); and for a continuation, which included a poem supposedly written about 1320 by Henry's ancestor John de Burgham, "one of the Greatest Ornaments of the age in which he lived," according to Chatterton,[33] Burgum gave Chatterton another crown.

Chatterton therefore began looking beyond Bristol for an audience. On 21 December 1768 he wrote to London publisher James Dodsley,

> I take this Method to acquaint you, that I can procure Copys of several ancient Poems; and an Interlude, perhaps the oldest dramatic Piece extant; wrote by one Rowley, a Priest in Bristol, who lived in the Reigns of Henry 6th. and Edward 4th:—If these Pieces will be of any Service to you, at your Command, Copys shall be sent to you by

---

33   *Complete Works,* 330.

Your most obedient Servant
De Be.
Bristol, Decr. 21.68

Please direct for D.B.[34] to be
left with Mr. Thos. Chatterton
Redclift Hill   Bristol[35]

When Dodsley did not reply, Chatterton wrote to him again on 15 February 1769.

Sir

Having intelligence that the Tragedy of Ælle, was in being, after a long and laborious Search, I was so happy, as to attain a Sight of it. Struck with the beautys of it, I endeavoured to obtain a Copy . . . to send to you; but the Present Possessor absolutely denies, to give me one, unless I give him a Guinea for a Consideration. As I am unable to procure such a sum, I made search for another Copy, but unsuccessfully—Unwilling such a beauteous Piece, should be losst, I have made bold to apply to you; several Gentn. of Learning who have seen it join with me in praising it—I am far from having any mercenary Views for myself in this Affair, And, was I able, would print it on my own Risque. It is a perfect Tragedy, the Plot, clear, the Language, spirited, and the Songs interspersed in it, are flowing, poetical and Elegantly Simple. The Similes judiciously applied and tho' wrote in the reign of Henry 6th., not inferior to many of the present Age. If I can procure a Copy with or without the Gratification, it shall immediately be sent to you—The Motive that actuates me to do this, is, to convince the World that the Monks (of whom some have so despicable an Opinion) were not such Blockheads, as generally thought and that good Poetry might be wrote, in the dark days of Superstition as well as in these more inlightened Ages. an immediate Answer will oblige me. I shall not receive your Favor as for myself but as your Agent I am Sir

Your Most obedient Servant:

---

34   Chatterton was adopting the name Dunhelmus Bristoliensis, which he had used for the bridge narrative.
35   *Complete Works,* 157.

T: Chatterton

P.S.

My reason for concealing
my Name, was, lest my Master   Bristol
(who is now out of Town)   February 15.69
should see my Letters and think
I neglected his Business—
Direct for me on Redclift Hill—[36]

Perhaps as early as December 1768, certainly by mid-February 1769, Chatterton had completed the play he was offering Dodsley. *Ælla,* the longest piece Chatterton composed, was supposedly commissioned by Canynge to celebrate the laying of the foundation for the new St. Mary Redcliff. The hero of the piece, Ælla Saxon, ward of Bristol Castle, has just married Birtha, also loved by the wicked Celmonde. In the midst of the wedding celebration Ælla must set off to fight the Danes. He defeats them but is mortally wounded. When he returns to Bristol Castle he learns that Birtha has run off with Celmonde, who in fact tricked her into accompanying him by promising to take her to Ælla. Ælla, thinking he has been abandoned, stabs himself. Before he dies, Birtha is brought back safely to the castle by Hurra, a Dane, who rescued Birtha from Celmonde and killed the villain. Birtha explains to her lover what has happened before they both die.

The story combines Shakespeare's *Othello* and *Romeo and Juliet,* with some borrowings from James Thomson's *Gondibert and Birtha;* but, as Donald S. Taylor observes, "The whole feeling of the play . . . is one of predominant freshness and originality."[37] The poetry is beautiful and contains what is probably Chatterton's best known verses, the minstrel's song presented by Birtha, her maid (Egwina), and the minstrels. Modeled on the "Willow" song that Desdemona sings to Emilia just before Desdemona dies in *Othello,* it nonetheless has a original poignancy.

---

36   *Complete Works,* 171–172.
37   *Complete Works,* 925.

O! synge untoe mie roundelaie,
O! droppe the brynie teare wythe mee,
Daunce ne moe atte hallie daie,
Lycke a reynynge ryver bee;
   Mie love ys dedde,
   Gon to hys death-bedde,
   All under the wyllowe tree.

***

Heere, uponne mie true loves grave,
Schalle the baren fleurs be layde,
Nee one hallie Seyncte to save
Al the celness [chastity] of a mayde.
   Mie love ys dedde.
   Gonne to hys death-bedde,
   Alle under the wyllowe tree.

***

Comme, wythe acorne-coppe and thorne,
Drayne mie hartys blodde awaie;
Lyfe and all yttes goode I scorne,
Daunce bie nete, or feaste by daie.
   Mie love ys dedde,
   Gon to hys death-bedde,
   Al under the wyllowe tree.
(ll. 961-967, 996-1002, 1010-1016)[38]

The third minstrel's description of autumn deserves to be equally well-known:

Whanne Autumpne blake [naked] and sonne-brente doe appere
With hys goulde honde guylteynge [gilding] the falleynge
   lefe,
   Bryngeynge oppe Wynterr to folfylle the yere,
   Beerybge uponne hys backe the riped shefe;
   Whan al the hyls wythe woddie sede ys whyte;

---

38   *Complete Works*, 210–211.

> Whanne levynne-fyres [lightning] and lemes [rays of light]
> do mete from far the syghte;
>
>> Whann the fayre apple, rudde [red] as even [evening] skie,
>> Do bende the tree unto the fructyle [fruitful] grounde;
>> When joicie [juicy] peres, and berries of black die,
>> Doe daunce yn ayre, and call the eyne arounde;
>> Thann, bee the even foule, or even fayre,
> Meethynckes mie hartys joie ys steynced [stained] wyth
> somme care. (ll. 296–307)[39]

Dodsley did not respond to Chatterton, who now sought another patron in the antiquarian Horace Walpole, in whom the young man probably sensed a kindred spirit. In 1751 Walpole had built a pseudo-Gothic house, Strawberry-Hill, at Twickenham, and the title-page of the first edition of *The Castle of Otranto* (London: Tho. Lownds, 1765; actually published 24 December 1764) stated that this first Gothic novel had been "Translated by/WILLIAM MARSHALL, Gent./From the Original ITALIAN of/ONUPHRIO MURALTO,/Canon of the Church of St. NICHOLAS/at OTRANTO." In the preface to that first edition Walpole had claimed,

> The following work was found in the library of an ancient
> catholic family in the north of England. It was printed at
> Naples, in the black letter [Gothic type], in the year 1529. . . .
> The style is the purest Italian. If the story was written near the
> time when it is supposed to have happened, it must have been
> between 1095, the æra of the first crusade, and 1243, the date
> of the last, or not long afterwards. . . . The beauty of the dic-
> tion, and the zeal of the author, [moderated however by sin-
> gular judgment] concur to make me think that the date of the
> composition was little antecedent to that of the impression.[40]

In the second edition (1765) Walpole admitted authorship. Here, then, was someone interested in the Middle Ages, a period dismissed by the 18th-century Enlightenment as barbaric, and a lit-

---

39   *Complete Works,* 186.

40   Horace Walpole, *The Castle of Otranto: A Gothic Story,* ed. Wilmarth Sheldon Lewis (London: Oxford University Press, 1969), 3.

erary hoaxer as well. Moreover, despite the Italian provenance that Walpole gave to his story, he was, unlike most of his contemporaries, particularly interested in British antiquities. Instead of collecting Italian art, he focused on English works, and he had compiled *A Catalogue of the Royal and Noble Authors of England* (1758) as well as *Anecdotes of Painting in England,* the first two volumes of which appeared in 1762. These works, which provided the model for Chatterton's "Heraldic Account of Bristol Artists and Writers," had been printed on Walpole's private press. Walpole thus could not only reward but also publish Chatterton. Walpole even had demonstrated an interest in William Canynge. In the *Anecdotes of Painting* Walpole referred to a manuscript dealing with a gift that Canynge had given to St. Mary Redcliff in 1470.

Chatterton carefully planned his campaign. Walpole had suggested that oil painting predated Jan van Eyck (1395–1441), and that this artist had learned this art form in England. Walpole had named no artists before the reign of King John, and he had little information about early stained glass and murals. On 25 March 1769 Chatterton wrote to Walpole in care of his (Walpole's) bookseller William Bathoe, who handled the sale of the *Anecdotes of Painting:*

> Sir
>
> Being versed a little in antiquitys, I have met with several Curious Manuscripts among which the following may be of Service to you, in any future Edition of your truly entertaining Anecdotes of Painting —In correcting the Mistakes (if any) in the Notes you will greatly oblige
>
> Your most humble Servant
>
> *Thomas Chatterton*[41]

Enclosed with the letter was Rowley's "The Ryse of Peynctenge, yn Englande, wroten bie T. Rowleie. 1469 for Mastre Canynge."

---

41 *Complete Works,* 258.

For Rowley, painting begins in England with the Britons'
painting themselves. The Saxons introduced heraldry, which in
turn led to more conventional painting. Chatterton included information about Saxon wall-paintings, sculpture, stained glass, and
embroidery from the 8th century onward. As Walpole had suspected, oil painting did predate Jan van Eyck: "Johne Seconde Abbate
of Seyncte Austyns Mynsterre was the fyrste Englyshe Paynctere yn
Oyles. . . . Chatelion a Frenshmane leorned Oyle Paynteynge of
Abbat Johne."[42] Oil painting thus originated not just in England,
but in Bristol. Chatterton used this opportunity to introduce
Walpole to Canynge and Rowley, to suggest the wealth of material
that was available by and about them, and to hint at what he hoped
from his correspondent. In the first footnote to "The Ryse of
Peynteynge" Chatterton identified Rowley as "a Secular Priest of
St. John's, in this City. his Merit as a Biographer, Historiographer is
great, as a Poet still greater: some of his Pieces would do honor to
Pope; and the Person under whose Patronage they may appear to
the World, will lay the Englishman, the Antiquary, and the Poet,
under an eternal Obligation[.]"[43] The second footnote, about
Canynge, implied what role Chatterton hoped Walpole would play:
Canynge was "The Founder of that noble Gothic Pile, Saint Mary
Redcliff Church in this City: the Mecenas of his time: one who could
happily blend the Poet, the Painter, the Priest, and the Christian—
perfect in each: a Friend to all in distress, an honor to Bristol, and a
Glory to the Church."[44] Chatterton also used this opportunity to
insert a specimen of his poetry, supposedly by John, second abbot,
who was "the greatest Poet of the Age, in which he lived."[45]

Chatterton had chosen the ideal fish and the perfect bait.
Three days later an excited Walpole wrote back:

> Sir
>
> I cannot but think myself singularly obliged by a
> Gentleman with whom I have not the pleasure of being

---

42   Ibid., 261.
43   Ibid., 259.
44   Ibid.
45   Ibid., 261.

acquainted, when I read your very curious and kind letter, which I have this minute received. I give you a thousand thanks for it, and for the very obliging offer you make me of communicating your MSS to me. What you have already sent me is very valuable and full of Information; but instead of correcting you, Sir; you are far more able to correct me. I have not the happiness of understanding the Saxon language, and without your learned notes, should not have been able to comprehend Rowley's text. . . .

Give me leave to ask you where Rowley's poems are to be found. I should not be sorry to print them, or at least a specimen of them, if they have never been printed.

The Abbot John's verses, that you have given me, are wonderfull for their harmony and spirit, tho there are some words I do not understand. you do not point out exactly the time when he lived, which I wish to know, as I suppose it was long before John ab Eyck's discovery of oil-painting. If so, it confirms what I had guessed, and have hinted in my Anecdotes, that oil-painting was known here much earlier than that Discovery or revival.[46]

On 30 March Chatterton responded with his "Historie of Peyncters yn Englande bie T. Rowley," which included more information about English sculptors and painters from the 6th to the 15th century and another poem by Abbot John, who was, according to Rowley, inducted as abbot in 1186 and remained in this post for twenty-nine years. Abbot John thus was painting in oils two centuries before van Eyck. Only a fragment of the accompanying letter has survived, but Chatterton apparently explained his circumstances and asked Walpole to use his interest to secure a more congenial and profitable post for him.

While Walpole was enthusiastic about these medieval documents that confirmed his conjectures and added to his limited information about early English art, he was also cautious. He had been tricked by Macpherson's fabrications and did not wish to appear foolish again. He therefore showed the "Ryse of Peyncteynge" to

---

46   Ibid., 262–263.

Thomas Gray and William Mason, two friends better versed in medieval history and literature than he. Both quickly identified the work as modern. Walpole's next letter to Chatterton is lost, but Walpole later summarized its contents:

> I undeceived him about my being a person of any interest, and urged to him that in duty and gratitude to his mother, who had straitened herself to breed him up to a profession, he ought to labour in it, that in her old age he might absolve his filial debt; and I told him, that when he should have made a fortune, he might unbend himself with the studies consonant to his inclinations. I told him also, that I had communicated his transcripts to much better judges, and that they were by no means satisfied with the authenticity of his supposed MSS.[47]

Stung by this rebuff, Chatterton wrote to Walpole on 8 April 1769,

> Sir,
>
>   I am not able to dispute with a person of your literary character. I have transcribed Rowley's poems, &c. &c. from a transcript in the possession of a gentleman who is assured of their authenticity. . . . The MSS. have long been in the hands of the present possessor, which is all I know of them.— Though I am but sixteen years of age, I have lived long enough to see that poverty attends literature. I am obliged to you, sir, for your advice, and will go a little beyond it, by destroying all my useless lumber of literature, and never using my pen again but in the law.[48]

Six days later Chatterton wrote to Walpole to ask him to return the manuscripts. The first draft of the letter was belligerent, and Barrett drafted a more moderate version. The third version of

---

47 Horace Walpole, *A Letter to the Editor of the "Miscellanies" of Thomas Chatterton* (Strawberry Hill: Printed by T. Kirgate, 1779), 35–36.

48 *Complete Works,* 271.

the letter, the one actually sent, merely restated Chatterton's assertion of the documents' authenticity and asked for their return. In the postscript Chatterton added, "If you will publish them yourself, they are at your service."[49] Walpole did not respond, and on 24 July Chatterton wrote to him, "I cannot reconcile your behaviour to me, with the notions I once entertained of you. I think myself injured, sir; and did not you know my circumstances, you would not dare to treat me thus. I have sent twice for a copy of the MS.:—No answer from you. An explanation or excuse for your silence would oblige

Thomas Chatterton."[50]

In a letter to a Mr. Stephens, a relative, Chatterton on 20 July 1769 calmly described the Walpole affair:

> Having some curious Anecdotes of Paintings and Painters I sent them to Mr. Walpole Author of the Anecdotes of Painting[,] Historic Doubts [on the Life and Reign of King Richard III,] and other Pieces well known in the learned World (His Answer I make bold to send you). Hence began a Literary Correspondence which ended as most such do. I differed from him in the age of a MS he insists upon his superior Talents, which is no proof of that Superiority: we possibly may publickly engage in one of the periodical Publications tho' I know not who will give the onsett.[51]

Chatterton's real feelings are expressed in a poem that he wrote sometime between 4 April and the end of July 1769.

> WALPOLE! I thought not I should ever see
> So mean a Heart as thine has proved to be;
> Thou, who in Luxury nurs'd behold'st with Scorn
> The Boy, who Friendless, Penniless, Forlorn,
> Asks thy high Favour,—thou mayst call me Cheat—
> Say, didst thou ne'er indulge in such Deceit?

---

49   Ibid., 274.
50   Ibid., 340.
51   Ibid., 338.

> Who wrote Otranto? But I will not chide,
> Scorn I will repay with Scorn, and Pride with Pride.
> Still, Walpole, still, thy Prosy Chapters write,
> And twaddling Letters to some Fair indite,
> Laud all above thee,—Fawn and Cringe to those
> Who, for thy Fame, were better Friends than Foes
> Still spurn the incautious Fool who dares— —
>
> Had I the Gifts of Wealth and Lux'ry shar'd
> Not poor and Mean—Walpole! Thou hadst not dared
> Thus to insult, But I shall live and Stand
> By Rowley's side—when Thou art dead and damned[.][52]

Chatterton intended to send this poem to Walpole, but Chatterton's sister dissuaded him, and it did not appear in print until 1871. Even after Walpole returned the manuscripts on 4 August 1769 Chatterton remained furious with him, and, as he suggested in his letter to Stephens, he engaged Walpole in various public journals. In "The Advice," published in the *Town and Country Magazine* Supplement for 1769 and addressed to Polly Rumsey, who was planning to marry Jack Fowler, Chatterton wrote, "To keep one lover's flame alive,/Requires the genius of a Clive,/With Walpole's mental taste (ll. 22-24).[53] The allusion is to Walpole's friendship with the actress Kitty Clive, to whom he rented "Little Strawberry Hill." Walpole was almost certainly homosexual, so his feelings for Clive were not romantic. Chatterton again referred to the Walpole-Clive relationship in *The Middlesex Journal* of 26 May 1770 in a supposed exhibition of sign paintings. Among the second day's exhibits is "*A Piece of Modern Antiquity, by Horace Walpole.*—This is no other than a striking portrait of the facetious Mrs. Clive. Horace, finding it too large to be introduced in his next edition of Virtû, has returned it on the town."[54] And in one of his last pieces, "Memoirs of a Sad Dog," published in the *Town and Country Magazine* for July and August 1770, Chatterton referred to "Baron Otranto, who has spent his whole

---

52 Ibid., 341.
53 Ibid., 427.
54 Ibid., 577.

life in conjectures," referring to a footnote on Jan van Eyck in the *Anecdotes of Painting* in which Walpole twice uses the word "conjecture." Chatterton goes on to write, "That his knowledge in antiquity equals his other accomplishments may be disputed."[55]

Unable to find a patron, Chatterton nonetheless was beginning to reach a larger audience. The *Town and Country Magazine* had begun in January 1769; in the second number, for February, Chatterton published a short piece on Saxon tinctures and perhaps one on Mr. Alcock, a Bristol miniaturist. In March he published the first of his seven Ossianics, "Ethelgar," followed in April by "Kenrick," and by "Cedrick" in May. The May issue of *Town and Country Magazine* also carried "Elinoure and Juga . . . by T. Rowley," the only Rowley poem to be published in Chatterton's lifetime.

By then Chatterton's Rowley phase was finished; his new poetic mode, as the piece on Walpole suggests, would be satire, his model the recently deceased Charles Churchill (1731–1764), who, along with John Wilkes, attacked the various Whig administrations. In a manic outburst of writing, between 27 and 30 October 1769 Chatterton produced 614 lines of verse, two-thirds of it critical of local and national figures. The other third consisted of three elegies to Thomas Phillips. Like so many other elegies, these poems are laments not only for the poet's friend but also for the poet himself.

---

55   Ibid., 658. The passage in *Anecdotes* (London: Swan Sonnenschein, Lowrey & Co., 1888), I, 27 n., reads, I cannot help hazarding a conjecture (though unsupported by any of the writers on painting). There is an old altar-table at Chiswick, representing the Lord Clifford and his lady kneeling.—Van Eyck's name is burnt in on the back of the board. If Van Eyck was ever in England, would it not be probable that he learned the secret of using oil here, and took the honour of the invention to himself, as we were then a country little known to the world of arts, nor at leisure enough, from the confusion of the times, to claim the discovery of a secret which soon made such fortune aboard? An additional presumption, though certainly not a proof, of Van Eyck's being in England, is a picture in the Duke of Devonshire's collection, painted by John ab Eyck in 1422, and representing the consecration of St. Thomas Becket. The tradition is, that it was a present to Henry V. from his uncle the Duke of Bedford, regent of France; but tradition is no proof; and two pictures of this author in England, one of them of an English family, and the other of an English story, are at least as good evidence for his having been here, as tradition for one of them being painted abroad. However, I pretend to nothing more in all this than mere conjecture.

In the first version of the work Chatterton wrote,

> Now rest my Muse, but only rest to weep,
> A Friend made dear by every Sacred tye:
> Unknown to me be Comfort, Peace, or Sleep,
> Phillips is dead, tis Pleasure then to die.
>
> Few are the Pleasures Chatteron e'er knew,
> Short were the moments of his transient Peace:
> But Melancholy rob'd him of those few,
> And this hath bid all future Comforts Cease.
>
> And can the Muse be silent! Phillips gone,
> And am I still alive? My Soul arise,
> The Robe of Immortality put on,
> And meet thy Phillips in his native Skys—(ll. 121-132)[56]

The satires continued, and though the attacks on local figures were not published, Chatterton did circulate them. When Alexander Catcott criticized some of Chatterton's poems, the young man replied with an "Epistle. To the Revd. Mr. Catcott," an attack on the vicar's *Treatise on the Deluge* (1761; 2d edition, 1768). Chatterton appended an apology:

> Mr. Catcott will be pleased to observe, that I admire many things in his learned Remarks: this Poem is an innocent Effort of Poetical Vengeance, as Mr. Catcott has done me the honor to criticise my Trifles. I have taken great Poetical Libertys and what I dislike in Verse possibly deserves my Approbation in the plain Prose of Truth—The many Admirers of Mr. Catcott may on Perusal of this rank me as an Enemy: but I am indifferent in all things. I value neither the Praise or Censure of the multitude.[57]

Alexander Catcott responded by barring Chatterton from his door.

London publishers reacted more favorably. In January 1770 Chatterton turned his "Constabiliad," a satire on Bristol figures,

---

56 *Complete Works*, 387.
57 Ibid., 419.

into "The Consuliad: An Heroic Poem," criticizing national offi-
cials. The anti-ministerial *Freeholder's Magazine* published by Isaac
Fell ran the piece in its January issue and paid Chatterton 10s. 6d.
for it. On 10 March 1770 Chatterton offered Fell "Resignation. A
Poem," on the Duke of Grafton's resignation as First Lord of the
Treasury, in effect Prime Minister (28 January 1770). On 13 March
Fell accepted the piece, and Fell wrote to Chatterton that as for
"the rest of your productions[,] you may rest assured. if you see
them in print you shall be made a Compliment equal to merrit[.]"[58]

Despite such encouragement, Chatterton found his circumstances increasingly unbearable. Sometime in early 1770 he wrote
to Michael Clayfield, a retired Bristol distiller or tobacconist who
had befriended Chatterton, that he was planning to commit suicide. John Lambert, Chatterton's employer, found the letter on
Chatterton's desk and sent it to Barrett, urging the antiquarian to
intervene. Barrett must have spoken to Chatterton, who wrote
back, "You must know that the 19/20th of my Composition is
Pride—I must either live a Slave, a Servant; to have no Will of my
own, no Sentiments of my own which I may freely declare as
such;—or Die—Perplexing Alternative! . . . I will endeavor to learn
Humility, but it cannot be here. What it may cost me in the Trial
Heaven knows!"[59] Was Chatterton serious about killing himself?
Was he hoping that such threats would free him from his inden-
tures so that he could seek his fortune as a political writer in
London?

On Saturday 14 April 1770 Chatterton left another suicide
note, in which he threatened to kill himself on Easter Sunday, 15
April, the anniversary of his infant brother's death. The note began
with a mock- poetic will, followed by one in prose, probably modeled on that of Samuel Derrick, Master of Ceremonies at Bath,
published in the *Town and Country Magazine* for April 1769,
which had carried two pieces by Chatterton. Chatterton used his
bequests to satirize his closest friends, Barrett, the Catcotts, and
Burgum, and Bristol in general, where "hardly twenty in the Town

58   Ibid., 493.
59   Ibid., 494.

can read" (l. 40).[60] Such mock-wills have a literary history. *The Tatler* for 23-26 April 1709 (no. 7) carried one by Richard Steele in which Isaac Bickerstaffe leaves his courage to "all who are ashamed of their distressed Friends, all Sneakers in Assemblies, and Men who shew Valour in Common Conversation," his wit "among such as think they have enough already," and his learning to "the Honourary Members of the Royal Society."[61] Similarly, Chatterton bequeathed "all my Vigor and Fire of Youth to Mr. George Catcott being sensible he is in most want of it." To Alexander Catcott he gave "some little of My freethinking that he may put on the Spectacles of reason and see how vilely he is duped in believing the Scripture literally."[62] Meyerstein located other examples of mock bequests in the *Universal Magazine* for July 1770 and the *General Evening Post* for 15 September 1770.[63]

Chatterton certainly intended for Lambert to find the "Will." Choosing "the feast of the resurrection,"[64] as he referred to Easter in the note, for his suicide may have been a satire on religion as well as an expression of the hope that on that day he would be freed from the tomb of Lambert's office. John Wilkes, whom Chatterton admired, was to be released from prison on 17 April; Chatterton requested a monument four feet five inches high, alluding to the famous number 45 of the *North Briton* that had led to Wilkes' prosecution in 1763. Perhaps Chatterton hoped that he, too, would be released about the same time as Wilkes.

Whatever the intent of the note, it did secure his freedom. Lambert canceled Chatterton's indentures, and Chatterton at once began preparing to leave Bristol for London. Despite his satires, he still had friends in the city who were willing to pay for his trip. Perhaps they were pleased to see his back; more probably, they liked him. Barrett contributed a guinea, and a subscription raised some £5. On Tuesday, 24 April 1770, at 9:00P.M., Chatterton boarded the "One Day Machine" to London. The cost

---

60   Ibid., 502.
61   *The Lucubrations of Isaac Bickerstaff Esq*, 4 vols. (London: Charles Lillie and John Morphew, 1710–1711), I, 57.
62   *Complete Works*, 504.
63   *A Life of Thomas Chatterton*, 344.
64   *Complete Works*, 503.

was £1 10s. to ride inside, half that to ride outside. Chatterton initially chose the less expensive fare, but at Bath rain began to fall, and he paid an extra seven shillings for a place within. Soon the rain turned to snow; by Wednesday morning the snow was a foot deep. The weather then turned fair, and he completed his journey on the box, arriving at Piccadilly, London at five o'clock that afternoon.

On 26 April he wrote to his mother to report his safe arrival in the capital. He noted that he had already called on William Edmunds, editor of *The Middesex Journal* at Shoe Lane; Isaac Fell of *The Freeholder's Magazine* at Paternoster Row; Archibald Hamilton, Jr. of the *Town and Country Magazine,* with offices at St. John's Gate, Clerkenwell; and James Dodsley at Pall Mall. The first three men all took the Patriot side against the ministry. Chatterton's tone was optimistic, as it would remain in all his letters home. He assured his mother that he had received "Great encouragement from them; all approved my design [of writing for them]; shall soon be settled."[65]

Chatterton moved into a house in Shoreditch that belonged to a Mr. Walmsley, a plasterer. Here for six weeks he shared a room with Walmsley's fourteen- or fifteen-year old nephew, who later reported that he suspected Chatterton of being a ghost. Chatterton ate little and rarely slept, and every morning the floor was strewn with bits of torn-up paper. Also living in the house was a relative of Chatterton, a Mrs. Ballance, who found him to be "as proud as Lucifer." She called him "Tommy" once, but only once, because he angrily "asked her if she ever heard of a poet's being called Tommy." When she suggested that he get a job, "He stormed about the room like a madman, and frightened her not a little, by telling her, he hoped . . . very soon to be sent prisoner to the Tower, which would make his fortune." He repeatedly asserted that "he should settle the nation before he had done."[66]

His writing career in London began auspiciously. The day after he arrived, *The Middlesex Journal* carried "The Hag," dated

---

65 *Complete Works,* 511.
66 Quoted in Meyerstein, 378.

from Bristol on 10 April, in which he attacked the Earl of Bute and the mother of George III as "an old stallion and a whore" (l. 66).[67] "The Candidates," dealing with the April 1770 election for Westminster, was published in *The Middlesex Journal* for 1 May 1770. On 2 May he composed the first of his two African eclogues, "Narva and Mored," which appeared in the *London Magazine* for that month.[68]

On 6 May he wrote home,

> I get four guineas a month by one magazine: shall engage to write a history of England and other pieces, which will more than double that sum. Occasional essays for the daily papers would more than support me. What a glorious prospect! . . . Bristol's mercenary walls were never destined to hold me—there, I was out of my element; now, I am in it—London! Good God! How superior is London to that despicable place Bristol— . . . The poverty of authors is a common observation, but not always a true one. No author can be poor who understands the arts of booksellers—Without this necessary knowledge, the greatest genius may starve; and, with it, the greatest dunce live in splendor. . . . I lodge in one of Mr. Walmsley's best rooms.[69]

To various acquaintances he wrote promising to secure publication of anything they sent him.

Chatterton actually was doing fairly well. He earned £4 15s. 9d. from his writing in May, and he was owed another £10 17s. 6d. for work accepted but not yet published. However, in May the government inadvertently dealt him a severe blow by cracking down on opposition publishers. Edmunds was sent to Newgate, and Isaac Fell was arrested for debt and sent to King's Bench prison. Chatterton's next letter to his mother is dated 14 May from King's Bench, no doubt to frighten her for a moment. The opening lines strike the usual jaunty note:

---

67   *Complete Works*, 500.
68   *London Magazine*, 39 (May 1770): 268.
69   *Complete Works*, 560-561.

Don't be surprized at the name of the place. I am not here as a prisoner. Matters go on swimmingly: Mr. Fell having offended certain persons, they have set his creditors upon him, and he is safe in the King's Bench. I have been bettered by this accident: His successors in the Freeholder's Magazine, knowing nothing of the matter, will be glad to engage me, on my own terms. Mr. Edmunds has been tried before the House of Lords, sentenced to pay a fine, and thrown into Newgate. His misfortunes will be to me of no little service.[70]

In fact, as Chatterton wrote more candidly in July in "Memoirs of a Sad Dog," "The late prosecutions against the booksellers having frightened them all out of their patriotism, I am necessitated either to write for the entertainment of the public, or in defence of the ministry. As I have some little remains of conscience, the latter is not very agreeable."[71]

He had had a bit of luck, though, as he went on to report:

Last week being in the pit of Drury-Lane Theatre, I contract-ed an immediate acquaintance (which you know is no hard task to me) with a young gentleman in Cheapside; partner in a music shop, the greatest in the city. Hearing I could write, he desired me to write a few songs for him: this I did the same night, and conveyed them to him the next morning. These he showed to a doctor in music, and I am invited to treat with this doctor, on the footing of a composer, for Ranelagh and the gardens [i.e., Vauxhall and Marybone Gardens. All three were popular places of amusement in London.]. *Bravo, hey boys, up we go!*[72]

The music shop was probably that of John Longman and Company, 26 Cheapside, established in 1767. The doctor in music may have been Thomas Arne but more likely was Samuel Arnold, co-owner of Marybone Gardens. Chatterton received a commission to write a burletta, *The Revenge,* for Marybone.

---

70 Ibid., 570.
71 Ibid., 661.
72 Ibid., 570.

Chatterton's thoughts then returned to "a place I am sickened to write of, Bristol. Tho', as an apprentice none had greater liberties, yet the thoughts of servitude killed me: now I have that for my labour, I always reckoned the first of my pleasures, and have still, my liberty."[73] He reported that London was filled with "pretty milliners."[74] However, he longed for a visit from the still unmarried Polly Rumsey. Two weeks later he again invited her to London.

Despite the government's actions against the Patriot cause, Chatterton was able to place a few pieces, signed "Decimus," in *The Middlesex Journal,* and on 25 May the periodical carried his praise of William Beckford, Lord Mayor of London, the richest man in England, and champion of the Patriot cause. Chatterton's letter, signed "Probus," earned him an introduction to Beckford, who might become the patron-father Chatterton had been seeking.

Chatterton's letter of 30 May to his sister sounded the standard optimistic note and was embellished with falsehoods. He was going to live with the brother of a Scottish lord. He was contributing to a history of London.[75] He was expecting to be introduced, or would introduce himself, to a leading figure in the ministry. "If money flowed as fast upon me as honours, I would give you a portion of 5000l."[76]

Chatterton composed a second "Probus" letter, but before it could be published, Beckford died (21 June 1770), and the piece, which had been accepted by *The Middlesex Journal,* did not appear. Chatterton wrote to his Bristol friend Thomas Cary that Beckford's death had cost him £1 11s. 6d., but elegies and essays had earned him five guineas, so that "Am glad he is dead by [£]3 13[s.] 6[d.]."[77] According to Ms. Ballance, Chatterton was hardly so callous or sanguine. She reported that "When Beckford died, he [Chatterton] was perfectly frantic, and out of his mind; and said he was ruined."[78] Apart from the loss of revenue from the canceled

---

73 Ibid., 570–571.
74 Ibid.
75 In 1773 John Noorthouk published *A New History of London.* Chatterton apparently had no hand in its composition.
76 *Complete Works,* 587.
77 Quoted in Meyerstein, 382.
78 In Meyerstein, 381.

Probus piece, Chatterton had lost a potential patron, precisely at a time when his fortunes were at a low point. Despite his statement that he profited from Beckford's death, there is no evidence that he published any elegies or essays. The *Public Advertiser* for 30 June announced an anonymous elegy published that morning, and it was included among Chatterton's works in the 1778 *Miscellanies;* but Donald S. Taylor includes it among "Works of Doubtful Authenticity." Chatterton's account book shows no income for June.

"The Death of Nicou, an African Eclogue,' is dated 12 June from Brooke Street, Holborn, one of London's least desirable addresses. Meyerstein quotes Sir William Jones's 1779 description of the house where Chatterton lived as "a dreary place [having] a miserable appearance."[79] Clergymen who visited there brought bodyguards. In "Memoirs of a Sad Dog" Chatterton described himself as "throned in a broken chair within an inch of a thunder-cloud,"[80] perhaps literary license, perhaps a description of his attic room. Chatterton's move from Shoreditch to Holborn suggests that he was in financial difficulties, though he may have wanted more privacy than he had at Walmsley's. The Brooke Street address also put Chatterton closer to Marybone Gardens and *The Middlesex Journal* offices at Shoe Lane. His Brooke Street landlady was a Mrs. Frederick Angel, a seamstress like his mother, though in Holborn such establishments could be fronts for houses of prostitution. Yet to Thomas Cary on 1 July he insisted that he was writing for "all the magazines," and, more truthfully, "A song of mine is a great favourite with the Town."[81] The song was "The Invitation," from Chatterton's burletta, then in rehearsal. On 6 July Chatterton received five guineas for *The Revenge*, almost all of which sum he spent on presents for his mother, grandmother, and sister. Two days earlier he had sent "An Excelente Balade of Charitie" to the *Town and Country Magazine,* his final effort to publish Rowley. The piece would linger with the publisher for weeks before being reject-ed.

---

79 Meyerstein, 391.
80 *Complete Works,* 652.
81 *Complete Works,* 641.

In his last surviving letter to his sister (20 July 1770) Chatterton wrote that he was working on an oratorio. As always he projected an image of popularity and success: "Almost all the next Town and Country Magazine is mine. I have an universal acquaintance: my company is courted every where. . . . I have a deal of business now and must therefore bid you adieu."[82] The part about the *Town and Country Magazine* was true; if his "Memoirs of a Sad Dog" had run in its entirety in the July 1770 issue instead of being divided in two, it would have occupied almost the entire issue.

In Bristol, rumor supported Chatterton's assertion of success. George Catcott wrote on 8 August 1770, "I am told you're employ'd sometimes as a political, and at other Times as a poetical Writer at a Salary of 2 Guineas a Week."[83] Chatterton received this letter on 11 August. Without contradicting Catcott, Chatterton wrote back that he hoped that with Barrett's help he could secure a post abroad as surgeon. Both Chatterton's landlady and Thomas Cross, the apothecary whose shop stood opposite Chatterton's garret, noted his pallor and tried to feed him. Except for once eating a large quantity of oysters that Cross offered him, Chatterton repeatedly declined their assistance.

In addition to the difficulty of making a living as a free-lance author, Chatterton faced another problem. In his letter to Catcott of 12 August he wrote,

> Angels, according to the Orthodox Doctrine, are creatures of the Epicene Gender, like the Temple Beaux: the Angel here [Mrs. Angel, his landlady], is of no such materials; for staggering home one Night from the Jelly house[84] I made bold to advance my hand under her covered way, and found her a very very Woman. She is not only an Angel, but an arch Angel; for finding I had Connections with one of her Assistants, she has advanced her demands from 6s. to 8s.6[d]. per Week, assured that I should rather comply than leave my Dulcinea, and her soft Embraces.[85]

---

82   Ibid., 650.
83   Ibid., 667.
84   Under the guise of selling confections, jelly houses were places for arranging assignations.
85   *Complete Works*, 670.

Like most adolescents, Chatterton wanted to appear sexually experienced, and he sometimes included sexual references in his writing. "The Rolle of Seyncte Bartlemeweis Priorie" lists four books about venereal disease among the priory's holdings, and "The Exhibition," dealing with indecent exposure, was considered too risqué to publish until the 20th century. In his "Will" Chatterton wrote that he was "sound of Body or it is the Fault of my last Surgeon,"[86] perhaps slyly suggesting that Barrett was treating him for a sexually transmitted disease. Chatterton had the reputation in Bristol of being a Lothario, and Mr. Walmsley's niece in Shoreditch, though she knew of no associations that Chatterton had with any females, regarded him as "a sad rake, and terribly fond of women."[87] To his sister Mary he wrote on 20 July 1770, "The ladies are not out of my acquaintance."[88] Chatterton's statement to Catcott about his Dulcinea might be idle boasting. The figure he cites for rent is high; it is high for sex and rent combined and may be meant to suggest prosperity.[89] The part about a Dulcinea may nonetheless be true. Michael Lort, the first person to gather materials about Chatterton after the writer's death, asserted that Thomas Cross told him that Chatterton "had the Foul Disease [syphilis] which he would cure himself and had calomel and vitriol of Cross for that purpose. [Cross] cautioned him *against the too free use* of these."[90]

Chatterton was taking opium, perhaps to ease the pangs of hunger, perhaps to ease the pain of venereal disease. On Friday, 24 August Chatterton bought arsenic from Cross; in the 18th century arsenic was used to treat venereal diseases. The next day Chatterton was found dead in his room, the floor strewn with pieces of paper. The coroner's verdict was suicide by reason of insanity, a judgment consistent with the poet's frequent threats to kill himself.

---

86   Ibid., 502.
87   In Meyerstein, 379-380.
88   *Complete Works,* 650.
89   Meyerstein, 391, cites figures showing that a room in a area such as Holborn would
       have cost about 2 and a half to three shillings a week.
90   Holmes, 244.

Two doubtful poems lend support to this finding. Published for the first time in the Bristol *Mercury* on the twenty-fifth anniversary of Chatterton's death, 24 August 1795, one begins, "Naked and friendless to the world expos'd/ Now every scene of happiness is closed;/My mind distress'd, and rack'd with anguish drear, /Adown my cheek oft rolls the falling tear." Later in the piece the writer finds "One comfort's left, and that's in speedy death" (1, 19).[91] Meyerstein thought the poem Chatterton's; Taylor is less certain. More dubious is a poem published for the first time in 1857 in a Boston edition of Chatterton's works. The piece was sent by John R. Dix, an unreliable source. It purports to be "The Last Verses Written by Chatterton" and is in effect a suicide note.

Chatterton may have killed himself intentionally, but he may instead have overdosed himself inadvertently in an effort to treat a venereal infection. He had learned some rudiments of medicine from Barrett, and a little learning is a dangerous thing. Even the physician-writer Oliver Goldsmith killed himself by taking James's Powder, an 18th-century panacea. On 28 August Chatterton, not yet eighteen years old, was buried in a pauper's grave in the cemetery attached to the workhouse in Shoe Lane. The grave was a common one, and in 1828 the workhouse and cemetery were demolished to make room for the new Fleet Market. The bodies were removed to St. Andrew's burial ground in Gray's Inn Road, and when that site was sold in 1892 the dead were interred in the City of London Cemetery at Little Ilford.

Even as the young man was being buried, Dr. Thomas Fry of St John's College, Oxford, having heard of the Rowley poems, was visiting Bristol in search of the verses and Chatterton. Learning of Chatterton's death, Fry borrowed some of the "transcripts" from Catcott and may have intended to edit them. In 1772 Chatterton's first Rowley poem, "Bristowe Tragedy," was published as *The Execution of Sir Charles Bawdin* (London: Newbery), edited by the Bristol literary figure and Chatterton acquaintance Thomas Eagles. Philologist and literary critic Thomas Tyrwhitt brought

---

91   *Complete Works,* 734–735.

out an edition of the Rowley poems in 1777, and it quickly went through two more editions over the next year. In 1778 John Broughton, a Bristol clergyman, supplemented Tyrwhitt's volume with a collection of *Miscellanies* (London: Fielding and Walker, 1778), which included a few pieces not by Chatterton.

Publication of the Rowley poems provoked two controversies. One involved Horace Walpole. Commenting on the Tyrwhitt edition in the *Monthly Review* for April, May, and June 1777, John Langbourne quoted George Catcott:

> In 1770, Chatterton went to London, and carried all this treasure with him, in hopes . . . of disposing of it to his advantage; he accordingly applied, as I have been informed, to that learned antiquary, Mr. Horace Walpole, but met with little or no encouragement from him; soon after *which*, in a fit of despair, as it is supposed, he put an end to his unhappy life. (56 [May 1777]: 332)

In the second volume of his *History of English Poetry* (1778) Thomas Warton similarly linked Walpole to Chatterton's death, though Warton later retracted the implied accusation. In fact, Walpole had heard nothing from Chatterton for more than a year before the young man's death and had learned of his death only on 23 April 1771, when Oliver Goldsmith informed him of it at the first annual banquet of the Royal Academy.

Walpole was reluctant to address these accusations and probably would not have responded had Broughton not attacked him in the preface to the *Miscellanies:*

> Although he [Chatterton] was of a profession [law] which might be said to accelerate his pursuit in antiquities, yet so averse was he to that profession, that he could never overcome it. One of his first efforts, to emerge from a situation so irksome to him, was an application to a gentleman well known in the republic of letters [Walpole]; which unfortunately for the public, and himself, met with a very cold reception; and which the disappointed author always spoke of with a high degree of acrimony, whenever it was mentioned to him. (xviii-xix)

Broughton went on to say that the reader might

> feel some indignation against the person to whom his
> [Chatterton's] first application was made, and by whom he
> was treated with neglect and contempt. It were to be wished
> that the public was fully informed of all the circumstances
> attending that unhappy application; the event of which
> deprived the world of works which might have contributed to
> the honour of the nation as well as the comfort and happiness
> of their unfortunate author. (xxi)

Walpole then published two hundred copies of *A Letter to the
Editor of the "Miscellanies of Thomas Chatterton"* (Strawberry Hill:
Printed by T. Kirgate, 1779; serialized in 1782 in the *Gentleman's
Magazine* for wider circulation), in which he wrote, "Is it not hard
that a man on whom a forgery has been tried unsuccessfully,
should for that single reason be held out to the world as the assas-
sin of genius?" (13). Walpole set out the facts, and he concluded
with an expression of admiration for the young writer: "I do not
believe that there ever existed so master a genius, except that of
Psalmanaazar,[92] who before twenty-two could create a language,
that all the learned of Europe, though they suspected, could not
detect" (40).

Not everyone could detect Chatterton's fabrications, either.
Tyrwhitt had believed the Rowley poems authentic when he began
to edit them, but in the third edition of the *Poems* he added an
appendix arguing that they were modern. Samuel Johnson, like
Walpole, was impressed with Chatterton: "This is the most
extraordinary young man that has encountered my knowledge. It
is wonderful how the whelp has written such things."[93] Still, he
recognized that it was the whelp who had composed them.
Thomas Warton and Edmond Malone also detected the modernity of the pieces, but Rowley had his supporters. In 1781 Jacob
Bryant argued their antiquity in *Observations upon the Poems of
Thomas Rowley,* as did Jeremiah Milles, Dean of Exeter and presi-

---

92   For George Psalmanazar see ch. 1.
93   *Boswell's Life of Johnson,* ed. George Birkbeck Hill and L. F. Powell
     (Oxford: Clarendon Press, 1934–1950), III, 51.

dent of the Society of Antiquities in his 1782 edition of the poems. Reyner Hickford's *Observations on the Poems Attributed to Rowley* (1782), Edward Burnaby Greene's *Strictures upon a Pamphlet Intitled "Cursory Observations on the Poems Attributed to Rowley"* (by Malone), and Thomas James Mathias' *An Essay on the Evidence, External and Internal, Relating to the Poems Attributed to Thomas Rowley* (1783) all maintained that Chatterton was the discoverer, not the author of the Rowley documents. As late as 1857 the antiquarian Samuel Roffey Maitland argued for the authenticity of the poems.

For most of Chatterton's admirers, though, authenticity was irrelevant. Whereas Macpherson's Ossian poems were admired primarily by those who believed them old, Chatterton's were appreciated as the brilliant products of a literary genius. For the Romantics, writing in their youth and meeting hostility from critics and indifference from the public, Chatterton became the very symbol of the poet. William Wordsworth gave him his most famous sobriquet when he described him in "Resolution and Independence" (1802) as "the marvellous Boy,/The sleepless Soul that perished in his pride" (ll. 43–44). Wordsworth's poem is written in the same meter as "An Excelente Balade of Charitie" and tells the same story, in which one person is rescued from despair by the intervention of another. Forty years later, when Henry Crabb Robinson asked Wordsworth "wherein Chatterton's excellence lay," the poet replied, "His genius was universal; he excelled in every species of composition; so remarkable an instance of precocious talent was quite unexampled. His prose was excellent; and his power of picturesque description and satire great."[94] Wordsworth subscribed to the 1803 edition of Chatterton's works edited by Robert Southey and Joseph Cottle, two Bristol literary figures, to raise money for Chatterton's widowed sister, Mary. The edition yielded her about £400. Southey, like Chatterton, spent many hours in St. Mary Redcliff, and often thought of Chatterton, imagining that he befriended the youth.

---

94 *Henry Crabb Robinson on Books and Their Writers*, 3 vols., ed. Edith J. Morley (London: Dent, 1938), II, 611.

Samuel Taylor Coleridge, who was married in St. Mary Redcliff, said that he began his "Monody on the Death of Chatterton" at the age of thirteen; he continued to revise it throughout his life. In the 1796 version, as Coleridge was contemplating the creation of an ideal society on the banks of the Susquehannah, he imagined Chatterton's joining this community:

> And we, at sober eve, would round thee throng,
> Hanging, enraptur'd, on that stately song,
> And greet with smiles the young-eyed Poesy
> All deftly mask'd as hoar antiquity![95]

Coleridge's "Rime of the Ancient Mariner" was originally spelled "Rime of the Ancyent Marinere," adopting Chatterton's archaic orthography, and the poem uses the same meter and rhyme scheme as the "Bristowe Tragedie." The opening of "Kubla Khan" recalls the beginning of "The Death of Nicou, an African Eclogue":

> On Tiber's banks, Tiber, whose waters glide
> In slow meanders down to Gaigra's side;
> And circling all the horrid mountain round,
> Rushes impetuous to the deep profound;
> Rolls o'er the ragged rocks with hideous yell;
> Collects its waves beneath the earth's vast shell:
> There for a while, in loud confusion hurl'd,
> It crumbles mountains down and shakes the world.
> Till born upon the pinions of the air,
> Through the rent earth, the bursting waves appear;
> Fiercely propell'd the whiten'd billows rise,
> Break from the cavern, and ascend the skies[.] (ll. 1-12)[96]

In 1815 John Keats addressed a sonnet to Chatterton:

> Oh Chatterton! How very sad thy fate!
> Dear child of sorrow! Son of misery!

---

95   Quoted in Meyerstein, 503.
96   *Complete Works,* 590.

How soon the film of death obscur'd that eye,
Whence genius wildly flashed, and high debate!
How soon that voice, majestic and elate,
    Melted in dying murmurs! O how nigh
    Was night to thy fair morning! Thou didst die
A half-blown flower, which cold blasts amate.
But this is past. Thou art among the stars
    Of highest heaven; to the rolling spheres
Thou sweetly singest—nought thy hymning mars
    Above the ingrate world and human fears.
On earth the good man base detraction bars
    From thy fair name, and waters it with tears![97]

Jack Stillinger, editor of the standard edition of Keats's poems, attributed the archaic "amate," meaning destroy, to the 16th-century poet Edmund Spenser, whom Keats admired; but the word may come instead from *Ælla,* in which the hero says, "Thou doest mie thoughtes of paying love amate" (l. 176).[98] Keats's first version of the dedication to *Endymion* (1818) read:

Inscribed
with every feeling of pride and regret,
and with "a bowed mind,"
To the memory of
The most english of Poets except Shakspeare,
Thomas Chatterton

John Hamilton Reynolds persuaded Keats to moderate the lines to read simply, "Inscribed to the memory of Thomas Chatterton."[99] The heroine in "The Eve of St. Mark" is named Bertha, as is the heroine of *Ælla.* On 21 September 1819 Keats wrote to John Hamilton Reynolds that Chatterton "is the purest writer in the English language. He has no French idiom, or particles like Chaucer—'tis genuine English idiom in English words." In his journal letter to his brother George and George's wife

97   *The Poems of John Keats,* ed. Jack Stillinger (Cambridge, Mass.: Belknap Press of Harvard University Press, 1978), 32.
98   *Complete Works,* 181.
99   *The Poems of John Keats,* 738, 102.

Georgiana in September 1819 Keats similarly wrote, "The purest english I think—or what ought to be the purest—is Chatterton's. . . . Chatterton's language is entirely northern. I prefer the native music of it to Milton's cut by feet."[100]

In the letter to Reynolds, Keats wrote, "I always associate Chatterton with autumn,"[101] and in the last and greatest of Keats's odes, "To Autumn," that association is evident. The bending apple trees derive from the third minstrel's song in *Ælla*, and line 25, "While barred clouds bloom the soft-dying day,"[102] originally read "While a gold cloud gilds the soft dying day," echoing the third minstrel's "Autumne . . ./ With hys goulde honde guylteynge the falleynge lefe" (ll. 1-2).[103]

Keats's friend Benjamin Bailey attested to Keats's knowledge of and admiration for the play:

> Methinks I now hear him recite, or chant, in his peculiar manner, the following stanza of the "Roundelay sung by the minstrels of Ella":

> > "Come with acorn cup & thorn
> > Drain my hertys blood away;
> > Life & all its goods I scorn;
> > Dance by night or feast by day."

> The first line to his ear possessed the great charm.[104]

In *Adonais* (1821) Percy Bysshe Shelley linked Chatterton, Sir Philip Sidney, Lucan, and Keats as great poets who had died young. Robert Browning used the occasion of reviewing Richard Henry Wilde's *Conjectures and Researches Concerning the Love, Madness, and Imprisonment of Torquato Tasso* (New York: A. V. Blake, 1842) for the *Foreign Language Review* of July 1842 to

---

100   *The Letters of John Keats,* 2 vols., ed. Maurice Buxton Forman (London: Oxford University Press, 1932), II, 419, 465.
101   Ibid., 419.
102   *The Poems of John Keats,* 477.
103   *Complete Works,* 186.
104   Quoted in Walter Jackson Bate, *John Keats* (Cambridge, Mass.: Belknap Press of Harvard University Press, 1964), 216.

write an essay on Chatterton, concluding, "There is fine, the finest poetry in Chatterton."[105] Ian Jack wrote that the form of Browning's "The Heretic's Tragedy: A Middle-Age Interlude," "Probably owes something to Chatterton, who always fascinated Browning,"[106] and the word "slug-horn" in "Childe Roland to the Dark Tower Came" (1855) appears several times in Chatterton's poetry.

To accompany Theodore Watts's 1880 essay on Chatterton, Dante Gabriel Rossetti, who had acquired a copy of the Rowley poems by the time he was twenty, wrote one of his finest sonnets:

> With Shakespeare's manhood at a boy's wild heart,—
> Through Hamlet's doubt to Shakespeare near allied,
> And kin to Milton through his Satan's pride,—
> At Death's sole door he stooped, and craved a dart;
> And to the dear new bower of England's art,—
> Even to that shrine Time else had deified,
> The unuttered heart that soared against his side,—
> Drove the fell point, and smote life's seals apart.
>
> Thy nested home-loves, noble Chatterton;
> The angel-trodden stair thy soul could trace
> Up Redcliffe's spire; and in the world's armed space
> Thy gallant sword play:—these to many an one
> Are sweet for ever; as thy grave unknown
> And love-dream of thine unrecorded face.[107]

Meyerstein quotes various comments from Rossetti's letters, in which appear such observation as "[Chatterton] was as great as any English poet whatever, and might absolutely, had he lived, have proved the only man in England's theatre of imagination who could have bandied parts with Shakespeare"; "Not to know Chatterton is to be ignorant of the true day-spring of modern

105 *The Complete Works of Robert Browning with Variant Readings & Annotations,* ed. Donald Smalley (Athens: Ohio University Press, 1971), III, 179.

106 *Browning's Major Poetry* (Oxford: Clarendon Press, 1973), 162.

107 *The Complete Poetical Works of Dante Gabriel Rossetti,* ed. William M. Rossetti (Boston: Roberts Brothers, 1896), Part II, 261.

romantic poetry"; "The finest of the Rowley poems, Eclogues, Ballad of Charity, &c., rank absolutely with the first poetry of the language."[108] At the age of seventeen, Vita Sackville-West composed a blank verse play about Chatterton. Peter Ackroyd's 1987 novel, *Chatterton*, attests to an abiding interest in the unfortunate author.

On the Continent Chatterton also served as a powerful icon of neglected genius. In France Henri Latouche wrote a 300-line elegy on the young poet (1825, published 1833). Alfred de Vigny's novel *Stello* (1832) depicted three poets destroyed by an unappreciative society: Nicolas Joseph Laurent Gilbert, who starved under the *ancien régime;* André Chenier, guillotined during the French Revolution; and Chatterton. In 1835 De Vigny returned to Chatterton in his eponymous last play. Queen Marie Amélie attended the opening performance, which received a twenty-minute standing ovation. In 1876 Ruggiero Leoncavallo saw a production of De Vigny's *Chatterton* and was prompted to compose an opera about the poet; it finally was performed in 1896. The German author Heinrich Blau wrote a tragedy about Chatterton (1887), and Ernst Penzoldt's novel *Der arme Chatterton: Geschichte eines Wunderkindes* (the poor Chatterton: the story of a genius) appeared in 1928.

As Rossetti's sonnet noted, no authentic portrait of Chatterton exists, but he was the subject of various romanticized paintings, beginning with the Chatterton handkerchiefs popular around 1781, showing a thin young man writing in a garret. Important examples of these portraits include R. Jeffrys Lewis' painting that shows Chatterton composing Rowley (1846), Henrietta Ward's *Chatterton, 1765* (1873, Bristol Art Gallery), John Joseph Barker's portrait at the Bath Art Gallery, and William Bright Morris' *Chatterton* (1869). The most famous of these pictures was executed by Henry Wallis, for which the young George Meredith served as model; it was painted in 1856 and hangs in the Tate Gallery, London.

---

108   Meyerstein, 516.

Like Macpherson, Chatterton was a herald of and influence on the Romantic poets of the 19th century. His medievalism and experimentation with metrical patterns helped free English poetry from its ties to classical models and conventional prosody. His early death, probably accidental, lent added power to his image of neglected talent, of the artist as outsider. As 15th-century literature his fabrications were clumsy, but as 18th-century poetry and as historical fiction, they reveal, as Horace Walpole wrote to William Cole on 19 June 1777, "astonishing genius."[109]

---

109 *Horace Walpole's Correspondence with the Reverend William Cole,* ed. W. S. Lewis and A. Dayle Wallace (New Haven: Yale University Press, 1937), *Horace Walpole's Correspondence,* II, 52.

W. H. Ireland

IV

Shakespearean Forgery 101:
William-Henry Ireland

*F*our forgers born in one prolific age
    Much critical acumen did engage:
      The first was soon by doughty Douglas scar'd
Tho' Johnson would have screened him had he dared;
The next had all the cunning of a Scot;
The third, invention, genius,—nay, what not?
Fraud, now exhausted, only could dispense
To her fourth son, their threefold impudence.

              William Mason, 1797[1]

Mason's poem, written in the last year of his life, refers to four famous 18th-century forgers. The first was William Lauder, who in the January 1747 issue of the *Gentleman's Magazine* claimed that John Milton's *Paradise Lost* (1667) was largely constructed from Jacobus Masenius' Latin poem *Sarcotis* (1654). In subsequent issues of the periodical Lauder showed further borrowings by Milton from Hugo Grotius' *Adamus Exsul* (Adam banished, 1601) and Andrew Ramsay's *Poemata Sacra* (sacred poems, 1633). Lauder proposed publishing the Grotius poem by subscription, and Samuel Johnson, no admirer of Milton, wrote the prospectus.

In 1750 Lauder published *An Essay on Milton's Use and Imitation of the Moderns in His "Paradise Lost,"* which included Johnson's prospectus for the Grotius project as preface as well as a postscript by Johnson. John Douglas, later to become bishop of Salisbury, was among those who recognized that Lauder had taken

---

1   *The Dictionary of National Biography* attributes the poem to Shakespeare scholar and prankster George Steevens.

all his examples of Milton's plagiarism from William Hog's Latin translation of *Paradise Lost* and had fraudulently ascribed the lines to others. Johnson dictated an apology that Lauder published on 20 December 1750, though Lauder later contended that he was merely playing a joke on Milton's admirers.

The second of the four forgers was the Scot James Macpherson, discussed above in chapter two, the third forger Thomas Chatterton (chapter three). The fourth forger, and, according to Mason the most impudent, was Samuel Ireland. In fact, the fourth forger was Samuel's son, William-Henry Ireland.

Samuel Ireland initially worked as a weaver in Spitalfields, a poor part of London. Apparently self-trained as an artist and engraver, he had honed his skills sufficiently by 1760 to receive a medal from the Society of Arts. In 1768 he was elected an Honorary Member of the Royal Academy of Arts, and in 1784 he exhibited a view of Oxford at the Royal Academy. By about 1782 he was living in the prosperous Arundel Street, the Strand, and in 1791 he moved to the still more prestigious address of 8 Norfolk Street.

Ireland was an antiquarian. By the time of his death in 1800 he owned part of Wycliffe's vestment, part of a cloak belonging to Charles I, a pinked leather shoe supposedly worn by Lady Lovelace in the 17th century, a garter worn by James II at his coronation, a red velvet purse given by Henry VIII to Anne Boleyn, a leather jacket that had belonged to Oliver Cromwell, a cloth jacket that had been Sir Philip Sidney's, Joseph Addison's fruit knife and a silver box, also Addison's, showing the ghost in *Hamlet,* a lock of Edward IV's hair, and another lock of hair with a gold ring that had belonged to Louis XVI. He also had more valuable items, such as paintings by Peter Paul Rubens, William Hogarth, and Anthony Van Dyck, and Inigo Jones's designs for Whitehall.

With Samuel and his antiquities lived a Mrs. Freeman, née Anna Maria de Burgh Coppinger, former mistress to John Montagu, 4th Earl of Sandwich. Supposedly Samuel's housekeeper and secretary, she was his mistress and mother of his four children: two daughters, Anna Maria and Jane, and two sons, Samuel, Jr. (born 15 June 1773) and William-Henry, born on 2 August 1775.[2] None of the children were baptized, a fact suggesting their illegitimacy. Nor is there any record of Samuel Ireland's marriage. Samuel, Jr. died young, and his father then took to addressing William-Henry as Samuel.

Another of Samuel's interests was the stage. He was a friend of Thomas Linley, part owner of the Drury Lane Theatre, so the Irelands often attended performances for free. William shared his father's love for drama. His favorite memory was acting in a production of Allan Ramsay's *The Gentle Shepherd* at the home of Richard Brinsley Sheridan in Burton Street. Ireland recalled, "My character, though of a trivial nature, did not diminish the zest I felt on that occasion; but, on the contrary, rendered my predilection for theatrical pursuits even more determined."[3]

Uncertain of his parentage—Samuel denied that Mrs. Freeman was the mother of his children and even gave William reason to suspect that he himself was not William's father—and addressed by the name of his dead sibling, William-Henry grew up feeling unwanted and unloved by the father he adored. A quiet child, William was regarded by both his parents as dull-witted if not an absolute idiot. William attended a school kept by a Mr. Harvest at the back of Kensington Square before being sent to an academy at Ealing run by a Mr. Shury. Shury, too, found the youth unpromising and sent him home after one term. For a year William studied at Dr. Barrow's academy in Soho Square, but the city air disagreed with him. In the fall of 1789 Samuel traveled to the Continent to make sketches for *A Picturesque Tour through Holland, Brabant and Part of France* (1790), the success of which made possible the move from Arundel Street to Norfolk Street. Samuel took his son with him and left him at a school at Amiens. Later William studied at Eu, Normandy.

Returning home in 1793 with an excellent command of French, William was apprenticed to the conveyancer William Bingley of the New Inn, a lawyer whose specialty was real estate. Like Thomas Chatterton, also apprenticed to a lawyer, William had little work to do, and again like Chatterton he became

---

2 These dates are taken from the Ireland family Bible.
3 *The Confessions of William-Henry Ireland* (London: Printed by Ellerton and Byworth for Thomas Goddard, 1805), 2.

I. Girtin sculp.

Facsimile of one of Ireland's Shakespearean forgery.

devoted to the Middle Ages. He bought pieces of armor and imagined himself living when these were new:

> I have often sighed to be the inmate of some gloomy castle; or that having lost my way upon a dreary heath, I might, like Sir Bertram, have been conducted to some enchanted mansion. Sometimes I have wished that by the distant chime of a bell I had found the hospitable porch of some old monastery, where, with the holy brotherhood, having shared at the board their homely fare, I might afterwards have enjoyed upon the pallet a sound repose, and with the abbots, blessing the ensuing morn, have hied me in pursuit of fresh adventures.[4]

He also composed pseudo-medieval poetry, such as the following acrostic "by thilke lerned clerke Dan Jan Lydgate, a monke of Burye, wrotten on his freynde and maisterr Geoffrey Chaucer":

> Con I yn rythms thilke clerke's fame make knowen
> Hondlynge so poorlee thys my quille
> As rathere makes me hys fame kille;
> Unlesse yt bene that gratefull minde alone
> Con trumpe hys praise; since butt for hym I owne
> Endlesse indeede had bene the travaile untoe mee
> Ryghte praisse and thankes to offerr thus yn poesie.[5]

William was particularly fond of Chaucer and remained so throughout his life.

In the evenings at the Ireland home Samuel would entertain the family by reading aloud. Among the books William heard was Herbert Croft's *Love and Madness* (1780). Its subject was James Hackman's murder of Martha Ray, who, like Mrs. Freeman, had been a mistress of the 4th Earl of Sandwich.[6] Given Mrs. Freeman's past, one can only imagine what her feelings were regarding Samuel's choice of reading matter. In 1778 Croft had gone to Bristol to gather facts about Thomas Chatterton, and he borrowed letters from the dead poet to his sister and mother. These he transcribed and shoe-horned into his novel. Croft argued that "forgery"

---

4   *Confessions,* 8–9.
5   *Confessions,* 9.
6   Martha Ray was murdered on 7 April 1779.

was the wrong word "to signify a crime for which a man suffers the most ignoble punishment, and the deception of ascribing a false antiquity of two or three centuries to compositions for which the author's name deserves to live for ever."[7] William identified himself with the dead forger: as he wrote in his *Confessions,* "The fate of Chatterton so strongly interested me, that I used frequently to envy his fate, and desire nothing so ardently as the termination of my existence in a similar cause."[8] William even composed an acrostic on Chatterton:

> Comfort and joy's for ever fled:
> He ne'er will warble more!
> Ah me! The sweetest youth is dead
> That e'er tun'd reed before.
> The hand of Mis'ry bow'd him low;
> E'en Hope forsook his brain:
> Relentless man contemn'd his woe:
> To you he sigh'd in vain.
> Oppress'd with want, in wild despair he cried
> "No more I'll live!" swallow'd the draught, and died.[9]

Samuel's favorite reading was Shakespeare, who had become divine in the 18th century. In 1769 the actor David Garrick had held a Shakespeare Jubilee at Stratford. Though the rainy weather had literally dampened the festivities, the event confirmed the bard's pre-eminence. On stage, between 1776 and 1800 the three most frequently produced tragedies at London's two theaters, Drury Lane and Covent Garden, were *Hamlet, Macbeth,* and *Romeo and Juliet.* Prices of Elizabethan books in general and of Shakespeare's works in particular began to rise as collectors sought these out. They also were willing to pay for Shakespearean artifacts. In 1790 the Princess Czartoryska gave twenty guineas for an old oak chair she found at the Shakespeare Birthplace. In 1786 London alderman, later Lord Mayor, John Boydell began his

---

7   Quoted in Bernard Grebanier, *The Great Shakespeare Forgery* (New York: Norton, 1965), 66–67.
8   *Confessions,* 11.
9   Ibid., 12.

gallery of illustrations of Shakespeare's plays, to which the leading artists of the day such as Sir Joshua Reynolds, Henry Fuseli, George Romney, Benjamin West, and Angelica Kauffmann contributed.

Discoveries of authentic Shakespearean material were also making news. In 1768 Albany Wallis, who became Samuel Ireland's lawyer and neighbor in Norfolk Street, found Shakespeare's mortgage deed for property the playwright had bought from Henry Walker in Blackfriars in 1613. The document had turned up among the papers of Reverend Featherstonehaugh of Oxted, Surrey. Wallis gave the mortgage to David Garrick, who bequeathed it to the British Museum. In 1795 Wallis found another deed relating to that property. In 1747 an authentic copy of Shakespeare's will had been discovered in the registry of the Prerogative Court of Canterbury in Somerset House, London. Surely other Shakespeare material lay waiting to be revealed.

Samuel hoped so. William remembered that his father often remarked, "that he would give all his curious books to become possessed of a single line of his [Shakespeare's] handwriting."[10] In 1793 Samuel was planning to follow his *Picturesque Views on the River Thames* (1791) and *Picturesque Views, on the River Medway* (1793) with *Picturesque Views on the Upper, or Warwickshire Avon* (1795). That summer Samuel, accompanied by his son, traveled to Stratford to make sketches and gather anecdotes for his book. While there Samuel sought out Shakespearean artifacts.

In 1756 the Reverend Francis Gastrell chopped down a mulberry tree supposedly planted by Shakespeare at his Stratford residence, New Place. Thomas Sharp had then used the wood to produce a quantity of cups and other items that would have required a forest of mulberry trees to manufacture. Samuel bought one of Sharp's cups. Nor was he alone in his enthusiasm. When Samuel's effects were sold at auction in 1801 the cup brought six guineas, more than any of his paintings by William Hogarth or Van Dyck. At Anne Hathaway's village of Shottery he bought a purse that the

---

10   William-Henry Ireland, *Authentic Account of the Shaksperian Manuscripts* (London: J. Debrett, 1796), 7.

playwright had given her and the oak chair in which Shakespeare had sat and held Anne on his knee while they were courting. The authenticity of both objects is open to question.

John Jordan, a wheelwright turned poet, Stratford tour guide, and manufacturer of Shakespearean anecdotes, regaled Samuel with stories of Shakespeare's drinking and provided a song that Shakespeare sang after he awoke under a crab apple tree following a night of revelry.[11] Samuel also heard the legend that after Gastrell had completed his sacrilege in 1759 by tearing down New Place itself, bundles of papers had been moved to Clopton House, about a mile from Stratford.[12] Samuel and William went there to inquire about Shakespeare manuscripts. The owner, Williams, had no doubt heard such queries before and had worked out an elaborate response. At least the exchange that William records in his *Confessions* sounds too obtuse—and too well rehearsed—to be factual. Williams told Samuel,

> By G-d I wish you had arrived a little sooner! Why, it isn't a fortnight since I destroyed several baskets-full of letters and papers, in order to clear a small chamber for some young partridges which I wish to bring up alive: and as to Shakspeare, why there were many bundles with his name wrote upon them. Why it was in this very fire-place I made a roaring bonfire of them.

Samuel exclaimed, "My G-d! Sir, you are not aware of the loss which the world has sustained. Would to heaven I had arrived sooner!" Williams called to his wife. When she entered the room he asked her, "My dear, don't you remember bringing me down those baskets of papers from the partridge-room? and that I told you there were some about Shakspeare the poet?" She then replied, "Yes, my dear; I do remember it perfectly well! and if you will call to mind my words, I told you not to burn the papers, as

---

11   Jordan was himself a minor Shakespearean forger. He sold a poem, supposedly by Shakespeare, to the scholar Edmond Malone, who included it in his 1790 edition of Shakespeare's works. The actual author was Jordan.

12   In another version of the story, the papers were moved to save them from a fire. Fires struck Stratford in 1614, 1641, and 1731.

they might be of consequence."[13] How many other gullible antiquarians must have experienced the same performance? Samuel
went up to the partridge room, where he found only partridges.
He also searched the rest of the house, but in vain.

The visit to Stratford intensified Samuel's desire for
Shakespearean manuscripts. William searched Bingley's office and
scoured the London bookstalls in an effort to oblige his father. He
found no manuscripts in Shakespeare's hand, but in the spring of
1794 he came upon a quarto tract dedicated to Queen Elizabeth.
It was bound in vellum and bore the queen's arms on the cover.
Ireland wrote in his *Confessions:* "As the work was dedicated to the
queen, and as from the appearance of the internal emblazoning,
covers, &c., it had probably once belonged to the library of that
queen, I determined on endeavouring to establish it as the presentation copy from the author."[14]

Ireland diluted ink with water and wrote a dedicatory epistle,
which he placed between the vellum cover and the loose front
pastedown. On his way home he stopped by the bookbinder
Laurie to show him the fabrication. One of Laurie's employees
suggested that he use a more antique-looking ink, which the jour-
neyman concocted from fluids used for marbling paper. The ink
was faint, but when held over a flame for a few seconds it became
dark brown. With his new ink, William rewrote the letter and gave
the book to his father, who did not question the authenticity of the
dedication. William later destroyed this letter so that the handwriting would not be compared with his later fabrications.

William next bought a modern bust of Cromwell. To it he
attached a piece of paper stating that Cromwell had given the
sculpture to John Bradshaw, president of the court that condemned Charles I. The recipient of Cromwell's gift was ill-chosen,
since Bradshaw and Cromwell were political opponents, but this
fact did not prevent various connoisseurs from identifying the bust
as the work of Abraham Simon, a leading Parliamentarian and arti-
san of the mid-1600s.

---

13 *Confessions,* 31–32.
14 Ibid., 38.

Late in 1794 William happened to see in a copy of Edmond Malone's edition of Shakespeare a reprint of the mortgage deed that Wallis had found and given to Garrick.[15] In his office he had an ample supply of parchment. When he had first become apprenticed to Bingley, the lawyer had another copyist and an errand-boy, Foster Powell. Bingley soon discharged the copyist, and when Powell died Bingley did not replace him, so William had the office to himself. To please his father he created a lease between Shakespeare and John Heminges on the one hand, and Michael and Elizabeth Fraser on the other.[16] The text was based on the Blackfriars mortgage deed. William used his antique-looking ink and traced Shakespeare's signature from a facsimile. He wrote Michael Fraser's signature with his left hand. Such deeds had wax seals attached with strips of parchment, but seals, like parchment, were plentiful in Bingley's office. Using a hot knife, William split a seal, hollowed it out and affixed it to his fabrication with new wax in the center. He then rubbed the seal with dirt to hide the seam.

On 2 December 1794 William told his father of his discovery. In one version of his story, on 22 November William had dined with Mr. Mitchell, a banker and family friend. Among the guests was a rich gentleman who, learning of William's interest in old books and manuscripts, invited the young man to examine his papers. William had delayed going, thinking that the invitation had in any case been merely polite conversation. Some days later, finding himself near the rich man's address, William had ventured to call on him, and there William had found a chest full of documents, including the lease. Chatterton, too, had claimed to have found his first fabrication, the "Bristowe Tragedie," in a chest in the muniment room of St. Mary Redcliff. At least in Chatterton's case the chest was real. When William showed the deed to the owner, the

---

15   Malone later led the attack on William's fabrications. Therefore, in his *Confessions,* William claimed that he saw the deed in the Samuel Johnson-George Steevens edition.

16   In his confessions of 1796, 1805, and 1832, William consistently maintained that he began his forgeries to make his father happy. Jeffrey Kahan argues in *Reforging Shakespeare: The Story of a Theatrical Scandal* (Bethlehem, Penn.: Lehigh University Press, 1998) that "William-Henry Ireland was not an innocent babe but a deliberate and calculating fraud" who acted for pecuniary gain (44).

rich man replied that he was welcome to it and anything else he found. To explain such generosity, William added that in rummaging through the chest he had found a document establishing the man's claim to a contested estate, so the Shakespeare documents were no more than just payment. As to the man's identity, William said he had been sworn to secrecy.

According to a later version of the discovery, dated 10 November 1795 and signed by William,

> I was at chambers, when [Montague] Talbot called in and shewed me a deed, signed Shakespeare. I was much astonished, and mentioned the pleasure my father would receive, could he but see it. Talbot then said I might shew it. I did not for two days: and at the end of that term he gave it me. I then pressed hard to know where it was found. After two or three days had elapsed, he introduced me to the party. He was with me in the room, but took little trouble in searching. I found a second deed, and a third, and two or three loose papers. We also discovered a deed, which ascertained to the party landed property, of which he had then no knowledge. In consequence of having found this, he told us we might keep every deed, every scrap of paper relative to Shakespeare. Little was discovered in town but what was above mentioned, but the rest came from the country; owing to the papers having been removed from London many years ago.[17]

The man wanted to make a copy of the Shakespeare deed, so William could not present the document to his father until 16 December. At last holding the parchment in his hand Samuel observed, "It is impossible for me to express the pleasure you have given me by the presentation of this deed: there are the keys of my bookcase; go and take from it whatsoever you please; I shall refuse

---

17   In Philip W. Sergeant, *Liars and Fakers* (London: Hutchinson, 1925), 251. Talbot was also apprenticed to a conveyancer nearby, and he soon discovered William's activities. He never exposed him, though, nor did the employee who supplied him with ink or the maid who cleaned Bingley's office and often saw William at work on his fabrications. Kahan's *Reforging Shakespeare* (pp. 96-101) suggests that Talbot may have kept silent not out of loyalty but in the expectation that he would share in the anticipated profits from the publication of the papers and the production of *Vortigern.*

you nothing."[18] For William his father's approval was reward rich enough; he replied that he wanted nothing in return. His father then went to his bookcase, unlocked the door, and presented his son with a copy of William Stokes's *The Vaulting Master* (1652), which Samuel valued at the substantial sum of three guineas.

Samuel was curious about the seal. On 18 December he took it to the Herald's Office to have it identified. No one there recognized it, so on 20 December Samuel consulted Sir Frederick Eden, chairman of the Globe Insurance Company and an antiquarian who prided himself on his knowledge of old seals. Eden thought that he detected a quintain, a target on a post used in training to joust with a lance and so related to shaking a spear. Sir Frederick even showed Samuel a picture of a quintain in John Stow's *Survey of London* (1598).

According to William, Samuel and others who saw the deed believed that the chest must contain more Shakespeare material, thus prompting William to continue with his fabrications. Samuel Ireland's diary entry for 26 December 1794 states that William himself was the first to suggest that other Shakespeare documents might be found where the first appeared.[19] On 17 December William presented his father with a promissory note from Shakespeare to John Heminges:

> One Moneth from the date hereat I doe promyse to paye to my good and Worthye Freynd John Hemynge the sume of five Pounds and five shillings English Monye as a recompense for hys greate trouble in setting and doinge much for me at the Globe Theatre as also for hys trouble in going downe for me to statford Witness my Hand.
>
> Wm Shakspere
>
> September the Nynth 1589[20]

---

18 *Confessions*, 51.
19 *Reforging Shakespeare*, 57.
20 *Miscellaneous Papers and Legal Instruments under the Hand and Seal of William Shakspeare . . . from the Original MSS. In the Possession of Samuel Ireland, of Norfolk Street* (London: Printed by Cooper and Graham [for] Mr. Egerton [et al.], 1796), A2^r.

Exactly one month later Heminges recorded payment of the debt, revealing Shakespeare's honesty. Shakespeare here misspells the name of his native city, and he refers to the Globe a decade before it was built.

William's next production, given to Samuel on 24 December, was a confession of faith. In 1757 Joseph Mosely, a master brick-layer, was retiling Shakespeare's birthplace in Henley Street. In the rafters he found John Shakespeare's "spiritual will," in which the playwright's father testified to his being a Catholic. The Shakespearean scholar Edmond Malone at first believed the document authentic; later he changed his mind. The reference to Purgatory in *Hamlet*, I, v, was also troubling to good Protestants. The questions of Shakespeare's religious beliefs and of the authen-ticity of the spiritual will, the original of which has disappeared, remain matters of debate.[21] These issues were even more trou-bling in the 18th century, and William was determined to make England's greatest writer a devout Anglican.

Ireland sought to copy Shakespeare's hand as closely as possible. As he later explained,

> In penning this profession of faith I formed the twelve differ-ent letters contained in the christian and sir names of Wm. Shakspeare as much as possible to resemble the tracings of his original autographs; and I was also particular in introducing as many capital *doubleyous* and *esses* as possible. The other letters were ideal, and written to correspond as nearly as might be with the general style of the twelve letters used in Shakspeare's names as written by himself.[22]

Samuel did not question the document's authenticity, but he wondered about the theology. He therefore invited Samuel Parr and Joseph Warton to read the confession. They visited on 1

---

21   The authenticity of the text itself is beyond question. In 1580 the Jesuits Edmund Campion and Father Parsons visited Stratford. They stayed at Clopton House and distributed printed copies of the spiritual will. Whether John Shakespeare put his mark to one of these is uncertain. If he did subscribe, he might well have hidden the document in the rafters to avoid detection, given the penalties imposed on Catholics under Elizabeth.

22   *Confessions*, 60.

February 1795. One of them gave his imprimatur, asserting, *Sir, we have very fine passages in our church service, and our litany abounds with beauties; but here, sir, here is a man who has distanced us all!*[23] William italicized these lines in his *Confessions* and recorded that upon hearing this praise accorded to his work he withdrew to the back dining room, adjacent to his father's study. There, "[I] reclined my head against the window frame, still ruminating on the words I had heard . . . fired with the idea of possessing genius to which I had never aspired." The young man dismissed as a fool by his father and teachers was hearing that he had exceptional abilities. William's joy was not all for himself, though. As he wrote, "Nor was my satisfaction a little heightened on finding that this effusion banished at once every idea of Shakspeare's catholicism from the minds of those whom I had frequently heard hazarding that opinion as to his religious tenets."[24]

William wrote the profession of faith on two blank half-sheets he had found with some accounts dating from the reign of Charles I. Encouraged by the praise his work had received, William resolved to forge ahead. He therefore visited a bookseller named Verey in Great May's Buildings, St. Martin's Lane, who for five shillings allowed the youth to take all the fly-leaves in the old folios and quartos he had in stock. To prevent precise dating of the papers, William at first used only those with no watermark. When he learned that a jug watermark had existed in the 16th century, he occasionally created his Shakespeareana on paper with that device as well.

A receipt intended to illustrate the early prominence of Shakespeare read,

In the Yeare o Chryste
Forre oure Trouble inne goynge toe Playe before the
Lorde Leycesterre ats house and oure greate
Expenneces thereuponne 19 poundes
Receyvedde ofs Grace the Summe o 50 Poundes[25]

---

23   *Confessions*, 68. After the fraud was exposed, Parr attributed the praise to Warton, and Warton denied ever seeing the papers.

24   Ibid., 61–60.

25   *Miscellaneous Papers*, A1$^\text{v}$.

William recognized that he was awarding Shakespeare an exorbitant sum of money, but he did not know when Leicester had died. He therefore dated the receipt "1590," two years after Leicester's death. When Samuel pointed out the error, William tore off the corner of the paper bearing the date.

Byng mentioned that no evidence existed of Henry Wriothesley, 3rd Earl of Southampton's patronage of Shakespeare, though a popular story, still widely believed, states that the earl, to whom Shakespeare dedicated both *Venus and Adonis* (1593) and *The Rape of Lucrece* (1594), gave Shakespeare the huge sum of £1000 that allowed the playwright to become a shareholder in the Lord Chamberlain's Men. In an afternoon William created an exchange of letters between the two. Shakespeare's letter read,

Mye Lorde

DOE notte esteeme me a sluggarde nor tardye for thus havynge delayed to answerre or rather toe thank you for youre greate Bountye I doe assure you my graciouse ande good Lorde that thryce I have essayed toe wryte and thryce mye efforts have benne fruitlesse I knowe notte what toe saye Prose Verse alle all is naughte gratitude is alle I have toe utter and that is tooe greate ande tooe sublyme a feeling for poore mortalls toe expresse O my Lord itte is a Budde which Bllossommes Bllooms butte never dyes itte cherishes sweete Nature ande lulls the calme Breaste toe softe softe repose Butte mye goode Lorde forgive thys mye departure fromme mye Subjecte which was toe retturne thankes and thankes I Doe retturne O excuse mee mye Lorde more at presente I cannotte

To which Southampton replied,

Deare Willam

I CANNOTTE doe lesse than thanke you forre youre kynde Letterre butte Whye dearest Freynd talke soe muche offe gratitude mye offerre was double the Somme butte you woulde accepte butte the halfe thereforre you neede notte speake soe much onn thatte Subjectte as I have beene thye Freynd soe

will I continue aughte thatte I canne doe forre thee praye
commande mee ande you shalle fynde mee

Yours
Southampton[26]

The letters show Shakespeare modest and grateful,
Southampton generous and familiar. John Mair writes that William
sought to present Shakespeare "as the possessor of all the personal and conventional virtues that to the eighteenth century seemed
nearly as important as genius. Shakespeare was already a great
poet; ideally, he must also be an eighteenth-century gentleman."[27]
William mentioned no specific sum in the letters, lest a later document surface to discredit his fabrication. He did not know that
samples of Southampton's neat, small handwriting existed; using
his left hand, William gave the earl an almost illegible scrawl.

William created a sketch of Shakespeare and filled in the
background with shields bearing Shakespeare's arms and with
other curious figures. This fabrication he presented to his father on
19 January 1795. Samuel dismissed the picture as worthless, but
the next day William "found" a letter to Richard Cowley to
accompany the drawing:

> HAVYNGE alwaye accountedde thee a Pleasaynte and wittye
> Personne ande oune whose Companye I doe muche esteeme
> I have sente thee inclosedde a whymsycalle conceyte which I
> doe suppose thou wilt easylye discoverre butte shoudst thou
> notte whye thenne I shalle sette thee onne mye table offe *log-
> gerre heades.*[28]

The drawing was thus authenticated; Samuel published it as
the frontispiece to his collection of the Shakespeare documents. It
also generated many clever explanations, and all who saw it agreed
that "Shakespeare must have been a kind good-natured character
and of a very playful disposition."[29]

---

26 *Miscellaneous Papers,* A3ᵛ-A4ʳ.
27 *The Fourth Forger: William Ireland and the Shakespeare Papers* (New York: Macmillan, 1939), 32.
28 *Miscellaneous Papers,* B1ᵛ.
29 *Confessions,* 74.

A few days later William presented his father with another picture, an old watercolor drawing on paper that William had found in Butcher Row, showing a bearded Dutchman on one side, a young man richly dressed in Jacobean style on the other. The picture probably was intended as an emblem to contrast the young man's wastefulness with the old man's thrift. William thought that the old man looked a bit like the Shylocks he had seen on stage, and he quickly converted the drawing into another Shakespeare item. Beside the old man he drew a pair of scales. The young man he altered to resemble as much as possible the Droeshout portrait that serves as the frontispiece to the First Folio (1623). In one corner he drew the Shakespeare coat of arms, though with the spear pointing right rather than left, and in the opposite corner he wrote "W.S." and the titles of a few of Shakespeare's plays. The old man was quickly identified as Shylock, the young man as Shakespeare playing Bassanio. Viewers assumed that the picture had hung in the Green Room of the Globe. John Hewlett, who worked at the Common Pleas Office and was an expert on old handwriting, detected the signature of John Hoskins, a 17th-century painter, in the background of the picture.

William's forgeries had shown Shakespeare as Anglican, witty, honest, modest, and the friend of the great, but the playwright's relationship with Anne Hathaway remained a troublesome matter. He had addressed his sonnets to a fair youth and a dark lady, not to his wife; and in his will he left her only his second-best bed. William now proved that Shakespeare was an adoring suitor and thoughtful husband. This effort was abetted, perhaps inspired, by William's purchase of a packet of 16th-century royal patents from a dealer in Clare Market. The seals of such documents were attached not by strips of parchment, as they were in ordinary legal papers, but by bands of red silk. William had been given a lock of hair as a love token. This lock he tied with the old silk and accompanied it with a letter and poem from Shakespeare to his fiancée. On 10 February 1795 Samuel read,

Dearesste Anna
AS thou haste alwaye founde mee toe mye Worde moste trewe
soe shalt thou see I have stryctlye kepte mye promyse I praye

you perfume thys mye poore Locke withe thye balmye Kysses
forre thenne indeede shalle Kynges themmeselves bowe ande
paye homage toe itte I do assure thee no rude hande hathe
knottedde itte thye Willys alone hath done the worke
Neytherre the gyldedde bawble thatte envyronnes the heade of
Majestye noe norre honourres moste weyghtye wulde give
mee halfe the joye as didde thysse mye lyttle worke forre thee
The feelinge thatte dydde neareste approache untoe itte was
thatte which commethe nygheste untoe God meeke ande
Gentle Charytye forre thatte Virrtue O Anna doe I love doe I
cheryshe thee inne mye hearte forre thou arte ass a talle
Cedarre stretchynge forthe its branches ande succourynge
smaller Plants fromme nyppynge Winneterre orr the boyster-
ouse Wyndes Farewelle toe Morrowe bye tymes I wille see thee
tille thenne Adewe sweete Love   Thyne everre

                                  Wm Shakspeare[30]

Shakespeare included a poem with this letter to "Anna
Hatherrewaye." It begins,

Is there inne heavenne aught more rare
Thanne thou sweete Nymphe of Avon fayre
Is there onne Earthe a manne more trewe
Thanne Willy Shakspeare is toe you

and ends

Synce thenne norre forretune deathe norre Age
Canne faythfulle Willys love asswage
Thenne doe I live and dye forre you
Thy Willye syncere ande moste trewe[31]

James Boaden, editor of the *Oracle* and at first a strong supporter of the authenticity of the Shakespeare papers, thought the
letter "distinguished by the utmost delicacy of passion and poetical spirit,"[32] and Samuel must have been pleased to note that
Shakespeare was thinking of Anne and his letter when he later

30 *Miscellaneous Papers*, A2^v.
31 Ibid., A3^r.
32 In Mair, 42.

wrote in *3 Henry VI,* V, ii, 11–15,

> Thus yields the Cedar to the Ax's edge
> Whose arms gave shelter to the princely eagle,
> Under whose shade the ramping lion slept,
> Whose top branch overpeered Jove's spreading tree,
> And kept low shrubs from winter's pow'rful wind.

At the end of his life William Ireland's Shakespeare was equally devoted. In 1611 he supposedly composed a lengthy deed of trust to John Heminges, in which he made generous provision for Anne:

> Firste untoe mye deare Wife I doe orderr as folowithe thatt she bee payde withinne oune monthe afterre mye dethe the somme of oune hondrythe and fowre score Pounds fromm the moneys whyche be nowe laynge onn Accompte of the Globe Theatre inn the hands of Master John Hemynge **Alsoe** I doe give herr mye suyte of greye Vellvett edged with Silverr tog^r withe mye lyttlle Cedarr Trunke in wyche there bee three Ryngs oune lyttell payntyng of myselfe in a silver Case & sevenn letters wrotten to her before oure Marryage these I doe beg herr toe keepe safe if everr she dydd love me[33]

The same deed awarded the manuscripts of many of Shakespeare's plays to various people, thus demonstrating that Shakespeare was a dedicated artist concerned with the fate of his work. William mentioned *Vortigern* here among Shakespeare's works, thus legitimizing his creation.

The absence of any books known to have been in Shakespeare's library puzzled Ireland's contemporaries. Since manufacturing provenance was quick and undemanding, William-Henry set out to fill this lacuna. In the London bookstalls and shops, particularly those of Benjamin White and Son at Horace's Head in Fleet Street and William Otridge in the Strand, William "discovered" about eighty titles that had belonged to the playwright. Each of them bore Shakespeare's signature on the title

---

33   *Miscellaneous Papers,* C3^v–C4^r.

page, and many of the books contained notes. Among these was a copy of Johann Carion's *Chronicles* (1550), which William embellished with annotations for the reigns of the kings treated in Shakespeare's plays. He found Edmund Spenser's *Faerie Queene* (1590 and 1596), which he enriched with notes; one visitor to Norfolk Street offered to pay sixty pounds for the two volumes. For that price one could in the 1790's buy ten First Folios. A tract dealing with the execution of Guy Fawkes, who in 1605 attempted to blow up the royal family and Parliament, carried the following comment by Shakespeare: "That hee hadd beene intreatedd bye hys freynde John Hemynges to attende sayde executyonne, butte thatte he lykedde notte toe beholde syghtes of thatte kynde."[34] Thus Shakespeare's humanity again manifested itself. Finding a second copy of this pamphlet, William wrote on the title-page, "Thys lyttle booke I ha hadde ownce befoure,"[35] thereby giving credibility to the inscription in the other one. In John Foxe's *Book of Martyrs* (1563) is a picture of Bishop Bonner whipping a Protestant in the bishop's garden at Fulham. William hated both the bishop and Queen Mary Tudor, so he had Shakespeare write beside the illustration,

> O Bonnerr! thyne was fylthy witte,
> So harde the breeche of mann to hytte,
>   Norr blush att suche dysplaye:
> Butt thou alle blushynge hadst foreswore,
> Thatte menne myghte blush for thee: threrefoure,
>   Thou took'st thys fylthy waye.
>
> Butte hadste thou beene as breechelesse too,
> Ande I the whipper overr you,
>   Bye Charon and his floode!
> Soe lustilye would I ha' hytte
> Thou shouldste have homage payde mye wytte
>   Bye blushynge redd withe bloode.[36]

---

34 *Confessions*, 197.
35 *Confessions*, 200.
36 *Confessions*, 205–206.

Here was another proof that Shakespeare was not Catholic. William was eager to annotate a copy of Holinshed's *Chronicles* but could not find one with margins wide enough to allow for his comments. Francis Webb, secretary of the College of Heralds, thought the marginalia typical of Shakespeare. Reading them he could "see this immortal poet rise again to life, holding these sacred relics in one hand and hear him say, *These were mine:* at the same time pointing with the other to these important volumes, once his own, informing us that these were his delightful companions in his leisure hours."[37] On 26 April 1795 William presented his father with the manuscript of *The Devile and Rychard*. Kahan believes that William wanted to show that Shakespeare collected not only books but also manuscripts, in this case one that served as a source for *Richard III*.[38]

Carried away by adulation and enthusiasm, William sometimes made extravagant promises of additional material, such as a full-length portrait of Shakespeare or two copies of the First Folio with uncut leaves. He also mentioned the existence of a complete manuscript of one of Shakespeare's plays, though he did not mention the title because, as he later confessed, he was not yet certain which work he was going to copy. The portrait and folios he could not supply, but early in 1795 Samuel acquired a copy of the 1608 quarto of *King Lear,* and William began to transcribe it in his version of Shakespeare's hand.

His was not to be a slavish copy, though. Shakespeare's admirers were troubled by language that seemed to them coarse, burdened with improper innuendo. William would purge *King Lear* of ribaldry and thus lend support to those who argued that the printed texts were tainted with actors' insertions. In his defense it must be said that even bardolators such as Garrick had no qualms about rewriting Shakespeare for the stage, and editors emended texts. Samuel Johnson condemned such editorial license, but he, too, thought that the printed versions had been corrupted, and sometimes in his edition he attributed lines to actors.

---

37 In Grebanier, 105.
38 *Reforging Shakespeare*, 87.

In William's version Shakespeare began his drama with a modest apology to his source. "Iffe fromme Masterre Hollinneshedde I have inne somme lyttle deparretedde fromme hymme butte thatte Libbertye will notte I truste be blamedde bye mye gentle Readerres[.]"[39] This passage indicates the extravagant orthography of the manuscript. Previously generous with letters even beyond Chatterton, in his *Lear* William became a spendthrift. "Unfriended, new adopted" became "Unnefreynnededde newe adoppetedde." "Observation" turned into "Obserrevatyonne," "indignation" into "innedygnatyonne," "answered" into "anneswerredde," "candle" into "cannedelle."[40] Such spelling prompted a writer for the *Telegraph* (14 January 1796) to manufacture an invitation from the bard to Ben Jonson: "Tooo Missteerree Beenjaammiinnee Joohnnssonn, Deeree Sirree, Wille youe doee meee theee favvourree too dinnee wythee mee onnn Friddaye nextte attt twoo off theee clockee too eatee sommee muttonne choppes andd somme poottaattooeesse, I ammm deeerree sirree, Yourre goodde friendde WILLIAME SHAEKSPARE."[41] To heighten the parody, the letter was dated 27 January 1658, decades after Shakespeare's death on 23 April 1616. The misspelling of Shakespeare's name and the misdating mimic flaws in William's fabrications.

William's liberties with spelling paled beside those he took with the text. Where the 1608 quarto reads, "I would divorce me from thy mother's tomb,/Sepulch'ring an adultress," William wrote, "I would divorce thee fromme thy Motherres Wombe/And saye the Motherre was an Adultresse."[42] In II, iii, Edgar says,

> My face I'll grime with filth,
> Blanket my loins, else all my hair with knots,
> And with presented nakedness outface
> The wind and persecution of the sky.

---

39   *Miscellaneous Papers*, D3^r.
40   Grebanier, 115, lists twenty examples of William's bizarre spelling.
41   Quoted in Grebanier, 116.
42   *The First Quarto of King Lear*, ed. Jay L. Halio (Cambridge: Cambridge University Press, 1994), 69; *Miscellaneous Papers*, 68.

"Else" in the quarto was a misreading for "elfe." It was corrected in the Folio, but William changed the word to "twiste" and rewrote part of the rest of the speech to make Edgar state,

> My face Ile grime with filthe
> Blankette mye loynes twisyte alle mye hayre in Knottes
> And inne Adam lyke Nakeddenesse oute face
> The Winde and persecutyonne o the Skye[43]

At the end of the play Kent declines the monarchy in two simple lines: "I have a journey, sir, shortly to go:/My master calls, and I must not say no."[44] Ireland's Kent is more verbose:

> Thanks Sir butte I goe toe thatte unknowne Land
> That Chaynes each Pilgrim faste within its Soyle
> Bye livynge menne mouste shunnd mouste dreadedde
> Stille mye goode masterre thys same Journey tooke
> He calls mee I amme contente ande strayght obeye
> Thenne farewelle Worlde the busye Sceane is done
> Kent livd mouste true Kent dyes mouste lyke a Manne[.][45]

Mair quotes an unnamed reader who praised William's "original" version of the tragedy. "A better Shakespeare rises to our view, which we evidently see in this his own written play of Lear —by comparing which with the printed copies, we shall perceive how it has been deformed by the bold hand of the meddling printer or his devil."[46] In the preface to the *Miscellaneous Papers* Samuel voiced his preference for the manuscript, which

> presents a style, as undressed as it is uniform; and so much so, that the Editor [Samuel Ireland] is thoroughly assured, that whoever will give himself the trouble of collating a few scenes, must, if he has the smallest critical sagacity, be able to pronounce for himself with certainty as to almost every instance,

---

43   *The First Quarto of King Lear*, 65; *Miscellaneous Papers*, 63.
44   *The First Quarto of King Lear*, 129.
45   *Miscellaneous Papers*, 155.
46   Mair, 48.

in which the general style of the Author is departed from and a new one substituted; and that, instead of his simple phraseology, and sentences framed according to their natural order and construction, the obvious general features of his own writings, there will be found at intervals tumor and gaudy trappings, and hardness, and inversion. (xiii-xiv)

Following the path of praise, William intended to "discover" the manuscript of *Hamlet,* or, as he wrote it, *Hamblette.* He quickly tired of the task, limiting himself only to part of act three. As Hamlet and Ophelia wait for "The Mousetrap" to begin, they have the following exchange:

Hamlet: Lady, shall I lie in your lap?
Ophelia: No my lord
Hamlet: I mean, my head upon your lap?
Ophelia: Ay my lord
Hamlet: Do you think I meant country matters?
Ophelia: I think nothing my lord.
Hamlet: That's a fair thought to lie between maids' legs.
Ophelia: What is, my lord?
Hamlet: Nothing.
Ophelia: You are merry my lord.

In William's version the passage is briefer, and most of the innuendo has been removed.

Hamlet: Shalle I lye i youre Lappe swette Ladye
Ophelia: Aye mye Lorde
Hamlet: I meane mye heade onne youre Lappe forre I meante notte Countrye Matterres
Ophelia: You are merrye my Lorde[47]

William's masterstroke, however, was the discovery of an entirely new play by Shakespeare, *Vortigern and Rowena.* He had been searching for a topic, and one day he noticed a copy of John

---

47 *Hamlet, Prince of Denmark,* ed. Philip Edwards (Cambridge: Cambridge University Press, 1985), 157; *Miscellaneous Papers,* 2–3 (X3^v–X4^r).

Hamilton Mortimer's *The Meeting of Vortigern and Rowena* (1779) that his father had made. The picture shows the early English king Vortigern being served wine by Rowena.[48] In Holinshed William found an account of the monarch, and on 26 December 1794 he informed his father that he had found the manuscript of the drama. To explain why the play had lain unknown for two centuries, William forged a series of letters between the printer William Holmes and Shakespeare. Shakespeare was asking more for this work than he had received for the printing of any other because he regarded it as his finest effort. Holmes refused to meet the playwright's price, and on 22 June 1604 Shakespeare wrote to ask Holmes to return both the manuscript and the correspondence regarding it. Thus, William-Henry Ireland could find all of the letters together with the play. William presented *Vortigern* piecemeal, as he composed it. Having never written a play before, he was uncertain as to how long it should be. By chance he consulted one of Shakespeare's longer plays. Hence, the first version of *Vortigern* contained over 2,400 lines. In creating the piece William drew heavily on *Macbeth*, with Edmunda's madness and recovery taken from *King Lear* and the flight of Vortigern's children Pascentius and Flavia based on *As You Like It*. The fool resembles Touchstone in that play. Samuel owned copies of many Elizabethan and Jacobean dramas, and Kahan suggests that William also borrowed from these.

A psychologist might find in *Vortigern* another of William's appeals to his father. The plot presents a reversal of the Oedipus complex, because at the end of the play a rejected child, Vortigern's daughter Flavia, saves her father's life by convincing Aurelius not to kill him, even though Vortigern was responsible for the murder of Aurelius' father. In V, iii, Aurelius' explanation as to why he does not want Vortigern's sons to accompany him into battle may express William's feelings.

For much 'twould have offended righteous Heav'n
If 'gainst their father they had joined with us.

---

48 Kahan points out other possible visual inspirations; see *Reforging Shakespeare*, 76–81.

For here there always is a sacred tie,
Which suffers not a son's uplifted hand,
To strike a father, be he ne'er so vile.
Did he not give him birth, and nourish him?
And when thy direst foe becomes thy slave,
Say, shouldst thou use revenge? No, rather shame him
With pity and all-softening charity;
Then on a golden bed thou lay'st thy soul,
And art on earth a blessed angel.[49]

As one Shakespeare document followed another, Samuel opened his house to all who wanted to see them. Most visitors praised the discoveries. Francis Webb wrote to a Reverend Dr. Jackson,

All great and eminent Geniuses have their characteristic peculiarities and originality of character, which not only *distinguish* them from *all others,* but *make* them *what they are.* These none can rival, none successfully imitate. Of all men and Poets, perhaps Shakespeare had the most of these. He was a peculiar Being—a unique—he stood alone. To imitate him, so as to pass the deceit upon the world, were impossible . . . [the Papers] bear indubitable proofs of his sublime genius, boundless imagination, pregnant wit, and intuitive sagacity into the workings of the human mind, and evolution of the passions. . . . It must be Shakespeare's and Shakespeare's only. It either comes from his pen or from Heaven.[50]

In that same letter Webb declared, "[T]hese papers bear not only the Signature of [Shakespeare's] hand; but the Stamp of his Soul, and the traits of his Genius —his mind is as manifest, as his hand. . . . [The papers] exhibit him full of Friendship, Benevolence, Pity, Gratitude, and Love. The milk of human kindness flows as readily from his Pen, as do his bold & sublime descriptions. —

---

49   *Vortigern, an Historical Tragedy, . . . and Henry the Second, an Historical Drama* (London: J. Barker [et al.], 1799), 66.
50   Mair, 65–66.

Here we see the Man, as well as the Poet."[51] Samuel Parr was equally impressed with the quality of the writing, declaring that the papers "were either written by Shakespeare or the Devil."[52] Mair cites an encomium by an unnamed enthusiast who maintained that the papers were "written by the unerring hand of nature in the character of Heaven, and we read them by the steady light of Truth."[53] Webb, under the name Philalethes, asserted, "[H]ad not Shakspeare's name appeared upon these papers, I should not have hesitated to have ascribed them to him."[54]

Of all the visitors to Norfolk Street, none was more excited by the Shakespeare documents than James Boswell, who came to look at them on 20 February 1795. On that day William presented his father with a letter from Queen Elizabeth to Shakespeare. In the preface to Bernard Lintot's 1710 edition of Shakespeare's sonnets, William Congreve had referred to a letter from King James to Shakespeare. William may have learned of this reference from John Byng. William wanted to show that Queen Elizabeth, too, held the playwright in high regard. Samuel owned a facsimile of a letter from her, so William could copy her hand. She wrote to Shakespeare,

> WEE didde receive your prettye Verses goode Masterre William through the hands off oure Lorde Chamberlayne ande wee doe Complemente thee one theyre greate excellence Wee shalle departe fromme Londonne toe Hamptowne forre the holydayes where wee Shalle expecte thee withe thye beste Actorres thatte thou mayste playe before ourselfe toe amuse usse bee notte slowe butte comme toe usse bye Tuesdaye nexte asse the lorde Leicesterre wille bee withe usse[.]

Shakespeare had written below the queen's signature, "Thys Letterre I dydde receyve fromme mye most gracyouse Ladye Elyzabethe ande I doe requeste itte maye bee kepte withe alle care possyble."[55] The letter was addressed to Shakespeare at the Globe

---

51 In *Refoging Shakespeare*, 146.

52 Mair, 66.

53 Ibid.

54 *Shakspeare's Manuscripts in the Possession of Mr. Ireland, Examined, Respecting the Internal and External Evidences of Their Authenticity* (London: J. Johnson, 1796), 25.

55 *Miscellaneous Papers*, A1^{r}.

Theatre, not built until after Leicester's death. The reference to the verses was intended to authenticate another of William's forgeries, though he never presented these fabricated verses to his father. The spelling once more reveals William's delight in extra consonants in the manner of his hero, Chatterton. The limited punctuation characterizes William's own letters of the period.

After carefully inspecting this letter, and perhaps the other Shakespeare documents on display, Boswell declared, "Well; I shall now die contented, since I have lived to witness the present day." Then, kneeling before part of the collection he added, "I now kiss the invaluable relics of our bard: and thanks to God that I have lived to see them!"[56] Boswell died, presumably content, less than three months later, on 19 May 1795.

From the beginning a few dissented from the almost universal praise. Edmond Malone, the leading Shakespeare scholar of the age, suspecting their authenticity, did not care to honor them with a visit, and he wanted time to study them. However, his requests to inspect them at a neutral site or at his own house were rejected. After visiting 8 Norfolk Street, Joseph Ritson called the papers " a parcel of forgeries, studiously & ably calculated to deceive the public."[57] In a letter to Samuel Ireland dated 13 February 1795, Thomas Caldecott of the Middle Temple condemned the poetry for its lack of imagination and its metrical deficiencies, though he did not deny the papers' authenticity. Another early doubter, Henry Bate Dudley, editor of the *Morning Herald,* attacked the papers on 17 February 1795:

> The SHAKESPEARE *discoveries,* said to have been made by the son of Mr. IRELAND of Norfolk Street, are the Tragedy of LEAR, and another entitled VORTIGERN and ROWE-NA, now first brought to light, both in the Bard's own handwriting. In the same chest are said to have been also found an antique MELANGE of *love-letters! professions of faith! billets*

---

56 *Confessions,* 96.
57 Letter to George Paton of Edinburgh, quoted in Samuel Schoenbaum, *Shakespeare's Lives,* 2nd ed. (Oxford: Clarendon Press, 1991), 150.

doux! locks of hair! and *family receipts!*—The only danger as to *faith in the discovery* seems to be from the indiscretion of *protesting too much.*[58]

A week later, on 25 February, an impressive array of believers responded by issuing a statement endorsing the papers. Among the signers were Boswell and Parr; classical scholar and fellow of Trinity College, Cambridge, John Tweddell; Thomas Burgess, who later became Bishop of Salisbury; John Byng, an antiquary who had bought part of Shakespeare's chair at the Birthplace; James Bindley, a member of the Society of Antiquaries; Richard Valpy, headmaster of Reading School, who in 1803 adapted Shakespeare's *King John* for performance at Covent Garden; Herbert Croft, whose *Love and Madness* had helped inspire the forgeries; the Duke of Somerset; Isaac Heard, Garter of Arms; Heard's secretary Francis Webb; the Earl of Lauderdale; Baron Kinnaird; and Henry James Pye, poet laureate.

While delighted to have the Shakespeare papers, Samuel was not satisfied with his son's account of their origin. He was eager to communicate directly with "Mr. H.," the name William bestowed on the generous donor.[59] On 31 January 1795 Samuel gave his son a letter to Mr. H., asking whether he, Samuel, might refer to the papers in the preface to his forthcoming *Picturesque Views on the Upper, or Warwickshire Avon.* In responding, William seized the opportunity to try to earn his father's respect. After praising Samuel's introduction, Mr. H. continued,

> It may appear strange that a young man like myself should have thus formed a friendship for one he has so little knowl-edge of, but I do assure you Dr. sir without flattery he is a young man after my own heart in whom I would confide and even consult on the nicest affair. . . . Pray excuse my familiar-ity but I cannot write otherwise to the father of one whom I esteem.[60]

---

58   Mair, 59; Kahan 162.
59   In *Love and Madness* Herbert Croft regularly referred to the murderer James Hackman as Mr. H. Croft's book may thus have suggested to William-Henry the name of the owner of the Shakespeare papers.
60   Mair, 89.

In another letter Mr. H. assured Samuel that William "never utters a syllable unbecoming a dutiful and loving son. O Mr. I.— pray look upon yourself, happy in having a son *who if he lives* must make futurity amazed."[61] The correspondence also allowed William to address his father freely, even to oppose him. William wanted to act in *Vortigern,* a wish he conveyed in a letter from Mr. H. Samuel objected to his son's long hair. Mr. H. assured Samuel that Shakespeare, too, wore his hair long and added that such a style was "manly."[62]

Samuel decided to publish the Shakespeare papers and sought Mr. H.'s view on the matter. William, fearing exposure, resisted. Visitors to Norfolk Street had little opportunity to study the texts, and they could be impressed with the antique-looking script, paper, or parchment. Sometimes in heating his ink William had singed the pages. He thus inadvertently lent further credibility to his productions. In the early 18th century the herald and antiquarian John Warburton gathered some rare Elizabethan and Jacobean plays, which his maid, Elizabeth, used to line pie-tins; and she otherwise destroyed much of his collection. It was believed that Warburton owned manuscripts belonging to Shakespeare, and William hinted that the papers he produced had come from that source. Pages darkened by flame would link the papers to the pie-loving herald. No one noted the contradiction between this provenance and the assertion that the papers had been in Mr. H.'s family for centuries. Examined in cold print, the Shakespeare material might provoke more criticism.

However, after repeated importunities, William could resist no longer. At dinner he told his father that Mr. H. warned him that he was publishing at his own risk. On 4 March 1795 Samuel issued a prospectus of his projected volume, to be published in folio to match the edition of Shakespeare then in press. The cost was the large sum of four guineas, two months' wages for a laborer, but a subscription carried with it the privilege of viewing the papers at Norfolk Street on Monday, Wednesday, and Friday

---

61   Grebanier, 156.
62   Ibid., 90.

between noon and 3:00 P.M. Anyone dissatisfied with his bargain after seeing the originals would have his money cheerfully refunded. Among the 122 subscribers were James Boswell, the aged actor Charles Macklin, the actress Dorothea Jordan, Scottish antiquary George Chalmers, Samuel Parr, Warren Hastings, Richard Brinsley Sheridan, Robert Southey, the Duke of Leeds, and James, Earl of Charlemont; Malone would address his attack on the papers to the earl. Samuel Ireland had 368 copies printed. In addition to the 122 sold to subscribers ten were given away and six sent to the copyright libraries of Great Britain. The rest were destroyed after William's confession of forgery in 1796. Samuel recorded in his diary for 5 July 1796 that he lost £400 on this enterprise.[63]

In the spring of 1795 a visitor wondered aloud what would happen if a descendant of Shakespeare should claim the papers. To deal with this concern William produced a deed of gift between Shakespeare and a William Ireland. By a happy coincidence, a haberdasher named William Ireland rented part of the Blackfriars property that Shakespeare bought in 1613. William gave the haberdasher his own middle name, even though middle names were not used in the early 17th century. According to this deed,

> onne or abowte the thyrde daye of the laste monethe beyng the monethe of Auguste havynge withe mye goode freynde Masterre William Henrye Irelande ande otherres taene boate neare untowe myne house afowresayde wee dydd purpose goynge upp Thames butte those thatte were soe toe connducte us beynge muche toe merrye throughe Lyquorre theye didd upsette oure fowresayde bayrge alle butte myeselfe savedd themselves bye swimmyng for though the Waterre was deepe yette owre beynge close nygh toe shore made itte lyttel dyffyculte for themm knowinge the fowresayde Arte Masterre William henrye Irelande notte seeynge mee dydd aske for mee butte oune of the Companye dydd answerre thatte I was drownynge onn the whyche he pulledd off hys Jerrekynne and Jumpedd inn afterre mee withe muche paynes he draggedd mee forthe I beynge then nearelye deade and soe he dydd save

---

63   *Reforging Shakespeare*, 119.

mye life and for the whyche Service I doe herebye give hym as folowithe!!![64]

What followed was a list of plays: *Henry IV, Henry V, King John, King Lear,* and *Henry III,* as well as ten pounds. The deed was dated 20 October 1604. William assured his father that Mr. H. had determined that he, William, was a direct descendant of his namesake and so entitled to the manuscripts he had found. William presented this deed of gift to his father on 12 June 1795.

Throughout 1795 Samuel corresponded with Mr. H. in an effort to learn his identity and have him come forward to confirm the authenticity of the papers. In one letter he appealed,

> Sir, I submit the business to your mature consideration, and request that you will determine on something that may terminate the anxiety of all parties—I beg to inform you that my situation as to future advantages is likewise at stake as I have now a work ready to lay before the public that has cost me a considerable sum of money, which I dare not bring forward on account of the odium I now labour under from being possessed of the Shakespeare MSS. in so ambiguous and mysterious a manner as to render their authenticity totally [? ?].[65]

To distract Samuel, William on 12 June 1795 told his father that Mr. H. had found in a chest in his country house a 15th-century illuminated manuscript showing Henry V knighting an Ireland. The manuscript had remained in the Ireland family for over a century, being endorsed by William Henry Ireland, Shakespeare's friend, in 1567. William had planned to produce the grant of arms with Henry V's signature, but he could not locate a facsimile of the king's hand, and he feared detection if he invented a sample of the king's penmanship.

William's ruse merely made his father more importunate. He now wanted to meet Mr. H. *and* secure the coat of arms. Instead of complying, Mr. H. promised Samuel a curious writing desk and

---

64 *Miscellaneous Papers,* B2^r–B2^v.
65 Mair, 93.

wrote to assure him of his son's genius. Mr. H. informed Samuel that William was writing a play about William the Conqueror and included a specimen of William's poetry. According to Mr. H., "No *man* but your *son* ever wrote like *Shakespeare*. This is bold, I confess, but it is true. . . . The more I see of him the more I am amazed. If your *son* is not a second Shakespeare I am not a *man*."[66]

Samuel was pleased to learn of his son's ability, but he still wanted to meet Mr. H. In November William presented his father with the "Deed of Trust to John Hemynge," the chief purpose of which was to suggest why Mr. H. had refused to reveal himself. Heminges was charged with distributing Shakespeare's manuscripts and with caring for "thatt Chylde of whom wee have spokenn butt who muste nott be named here."[67] Mr. H. was perhaps a descendant of this illegitimate child and did not want to come forth. Perhaps he was a descendant of Heminges and did not want to publicize the fact that his ancestor had not carried out Shakespeare's wishes. Even if Heminges had executed faithfully his office of executor, Mr. H. may not have wanted to be linked to one who followed so lowly an occupation as that of actor. Whether or not Samuel was satisfied by the deed, Mr. H. did not appear, and the Shakespeare papers were published on 24 December 1795, dated 1796.

On 18 November Samuel and William visited the Duke of Clarence and his mistress, the actress Dorothea Jordan. This visit was followed by another to the Prince of Wales. On the morning of 28 December 1795,[68] as Samuel was about to set off for Carlton House to meet the future George IV, Albany Wallis approached him with a new, and authentic, Shakespearean document that contained John Heminges' real signature, which looked nothing like the version William had manufactured. Samuel went to Carlton House, where the prince reserved judgment on the papers but showed great interest and complimented Samuel on his discoveries. Returning home, Samuel questioned William when the young

---

66   Mair, 97–98.
67   *Miscellaneous Papers,* D1ᵛ.
68   Kahan notes that the *True Briton* gives the date as 31 December (*Reforging Shakespeare,* 234, n.22).

man arrived from Bingley's office and showed him Wallis's genuine signature. William replied that he must consult Mr. H. at once. Hastening to Bingley's office, he executed a receipt signed by Heminges and returned to Wallis, who agreed that the new example was much like the signature he had found. William told Wallis that Mr H. had given him this new document and had explained that there were in fact two John Hemingeses, tall John Heminges of the Globe, whose signature Wallis owned, and short John Heminges of the Curtain. To add further support to his latest forgery, over the next several days William produced several more signatures by the tall John Heminges.

One threat had been thus averted, but another loomed. As soon as *Vortigern* had been discovered, both London theaters asked to stage it even before seeing the text. Because of his friendship with Linley and Sheridan, Samuel allowed Drury Lane to present the piece. Sheridan came to Norfolk Street to read the manuscript. Sheridan did not share the age's idolatry of Shakespeare, but even he found *Vortigern* disappointing. The poetry was halting, and Sheridan at one point broke off his reading to declare, "There are certainly some bold ideas, but they are crude and undigested. It is very odd: one would be led to think that Shakespeare must have been very young when he wrote the play. As to the doubting whether it really be his or not, who can possibly look at the papers and not believe them ancient?"[69]

Negotiations over compensation grew protracted and acrimonious. Sheridan wanted to pay only a percentage of the receipts. Samuel wanted five hundred pounds and a portion of the receipts. Through the mediation of Wallis they agreed in September 1795 that Samuel would receive two hundred fifty pounds and half the profits of the first forty nights of the play's run. Samuel retained the copyright, and the publisher J. Barker offered Samuel a thousand guineas for the right to publish the play on the afternoon *Vortigern* opened. Samuel, fearing that printing the text would keep audiences away from the theater, rejected the proposal.

---

69   In Mair, 121.

Sheridan had agreed to produce *Vortigern* before Christmas, 1795, but he procrastinated. The year ended without the staging of the work.

Samuel had hoped that the production of *Vortigern* would precede publication of the papers because he feared that once in print the documents would provoke questions of authenticity that would reduce the profitability of the play. Samuel's concerns were legitimate, but the delay was not exclusively Sheridan's fault. The original version of *Vortigern* was too long for performance, and the whole Ireland family embarked on abridgement. Having reduced the piece to 1807 lines, they submitted it to John Larpent, Licenser of Plays, in February 1796.[70] Larpent required other changes, including the rewriting of the regicide scene. Louis XVI had lost his head only a few years earlier, and Larpent was ever vigilant against Jacobin tendencies. The text did not reach its final acting form until early March 1796.

Meanwhile, in December 1795 William announced that he had found a new and better play by Shakespeare, *Henry the Second,* which William had composed in ten weeks. At this point he was planning a series of history plays covering the reigns Shakespeare had neglected. The deed of trust to Heminge had already mentioned *Henry III* as well as *Vortigern,* thus preparing the way for another work. *Henry II* came from a second trunk that William had located. It supposedly contained full manuscripts of *Richard II* and *Henry V,* partial manuscripts of *King John* (62 leaves), *Othello* (49 leaves), *Richard III* (37 leaves), *Timon of Athens* (37 leaves), *Julius Caesar* (27 leaves), and *Henry IV* (14 leaves). Previously unknown works in manuscript in the trunk included, in addition to *Henry II,* verses to Queen Elizabeth, Sir Francis Drake, Sir Walter Raleigh, and Lord Howard, and the text of Shakespeare's autobiography. This capacious container also held more books from Shakespeare's library, a deed showing that Shakespeare was a partner in the Curtain Theatre, two drawings of the Globe Theatre on

---

70 Under the Licensing Act of 1737, in force until 1966, all plays had to be approved by the Licenser before being staged. No such restraint existed for published versions, which often restored the cuts the Licenser had made.

parchment, a full-length oil portrait of Shakespeare, and a miniature of Shakespeare set in silver.[71]

As William had feared, though, publication of the papers led to new doubts. On 30 December 1795 the *Tomahawk,* which on 4 November had hailed the discovery of *Vortigern,* attacked Samuel in verse: "Ireland, Ireland, tell to me,/Who wrote Shakespeare's writings?—THEE![72] The January 1796 issue of the *Monthly Mirror* printed in capital letters: "THE WHOLE IS A GROSS AND IMPUDENT IMPOSITION, AN INSULT TO THE CHARACTER OF OUR IMMORTAL BARD, AND A LIBEL ON THE TASTE AND UNDERSTANDING OF THE NATION!!"[73] The author of this charge was James Boaden, editor of the *Oracle,* who had written much in praise of the documents. However, early in 1796 he attacked them in *A Letter to George Steevens, Esq. Containing a Critical Examination of the Papers of Shakspeare.*

Francis Webb replied with *Shakspeare's Manuscripts, in the Possession of Mr. Ireland, Examined, Respecting the Internal and External Evidences of Their Authenticity* (London: J. Johnson, 1796). Here he maintained that "no human wisdom, cunning, art or deceit, if they could be united, are equal to the task of such an imposture" (12). John Wyatt joined the fray by comparing Boaden's comments earlier with those he was now expressing.[74] Dramatist and theater historian Walley Chamberlain Oulton supported the papers in *Vortigern under Consideration* (London: Printed for H. Lowndes,1796), and Samuel drew up a second certificate of belief. While some of the signers of the first statement again subscribed, other names were absent. Pye and Parr declined to endorse the material, as did the three peers who had stated their belief in the authenticity of the documents a year earlier. As

---

71 *Reforging Shakespeare,* 91–92.

72 In Grebanier, 191. Critics of the papers, sharing Samuel's opinion of his son's abilities, assumed that Samuel, not William, was the author.

73 Ibid., 187.

74 *A Comparative Review of the Opinions of Mr. James Boaden (Editor of the Oracle) in February, March and April, 1795; and of James Boaden, Esq . . . in February 1796, Relative to the Shakespeare MSS* (London: Printed for G. Sael, 1796). The work, published anonymously, has also been attributed to Matthew Wyatt.

Grebanier comments, "The new Believers were men of no great consequence."[75]

Nor were matters going well at Drury Lane. Sheridan hesitated to spend money on new sets for a play he disliked. John Philip Kemble, part owner of the theater and the actor who was to take the title role, had no confidence in the piece. He went so far as to propose opening the play on April Fool's Day. Sheridan compelled Kemble to wait until 2 April, but did not stop him from staging Prince Hoare's farce *My Grandmother* as the after-piece. This work deals with a foolish art lover (meant by Kemble to suggest Samuel Ireland) who cannot distinguish a young girl from her dead ancestor. Nor would Sheridan agree to advertise *Vortigern* as Shakespeare's. Instead, it was listed without author. Claiming illness, Sarah Siddons, Kemble's sister, withdrew from the role of the queen, Edmunda, a week before the play was to open, and Mrs. Palmer chose not to undertake the fair Rowena. Siddons actually was ill, but earlier in March she had written to Hester Thrale Piozzi, "All sensible persons are convinced that 'Vortigern' is a most audacious imposter. If he be not I can only say that Shakespeare's writings are more unequal than those of any other man." [76] Samuel had chosen most of the actors, but he left some roles to be filled by Kemble, who purposely miscast them. Pye had agreed to write the prologue, which he did, but in so lukewarm a tone that Samuel asked Francis Webb to pen another. Webb's version, delivered on 29 January 1796, did not satisfy Samuel either, and he turned to Sir James Bland Burgess. His was the prologue spoken on opening night.[77]

On 31 March, two days before the play opened, Edmond Malone published his long-awaited attack on the papers, *An Inquiry into the Authenticity of Certain Miscellaneous Papers and*

---

75   Grebanier, 203.
76   In Grebanier, 201.
77   Kahan observes that Pye was hoping to having his *Henry II* produced at Drury Lane. Knowing Kemble's attitude towards *Vortigern*, Pye did not want to antagonize a man who held in his hands the fate of Pye's own work. This same concern may explain why Pye kept his name off the second certificate of belief *(Reforging Shakespeare*, 172).

Legal Instruments . . . (London: T. Cadell, Jun. and W. Davies, 1796). He had delayed publication until it would attract the most attention, and the five hundred copies of the first edition sold out in two days.[78] Malone examined every aspect of the papers: orthography, phraseology, dating, handwriting. He began by stating, "Not a single paper or deed in this extraordinary volume was written or executed by the person to whom it is ascribed" (23). Of the letter from Elizabeth to Shakespeare he wrote, "I will venture to assert, without the smallest apprehension of being refuted, that the spelling in this letter, as well as in all the other papers, is not only not the orthography of Elizabeth, or of her time, but is for the most part the orthography of no age whatsoever" (33), and he condemned "the absurd manner in which almost every word is over-laden with both consonants and vowels" (34).

Elizabeth's letter had been addressed to Shakespeare at the Globe, not built until a decade after Leicester's death, and referred to her being at Hampton Court with Leicester. The last time the two were together there was 8 December 1585, when Shakespeare was twenty-one, well before he was known as a playwright. Malone even faulted William's copying of the queen's signature: it was too small; it was slanted rather than upright; the forms of the capital "E," the "a," "b," and the "R" were wrong.

William always had the playwright sign himself "Shakspeare," but in all known authentic signatures the spelling was "Shakspere." John Heminges always spelt his name with a final "s," omitted in the Ireland specimens. A receipt to John Lowin for two shillings for performing before Leicester ignored the fact that Lowin was twelve when Leicester died in 1588, and Lowin did not join Shakespeare and Burbage until after 1603. Southampton's handwriting in his letter to Shakespeare did not match that in two authentic letters from the earl.

The deed of gift from Shakespeare to William Henry Ireland states that in 1604 Shakespeare was living in Blackfriars. Malone

---

78   Kahan quotes Malone's statement to Joseph Farington that the *Inquiry* was ready on 20 January 1796. Kahan maintains, correctly, that Malone was waiting to publish his attack to coincide with the opening of *Vortigern (Reforging Shakespeare*, 168–169).

doubted that Shakespeare ever lived there. He certainly had no reason to reside there in 1604, since the King's Men did not acquire the Blackfriars Theatre until 1608. The document is dated "2 James," whereas until the 18th century the Latin form of the monarch's name was used. The deed should therefore have read "2 Jacobi" or "2 Jac." William's first forgery, the lease to Michael Fraser and his wife, refers to "his two Messuages or tenements abutting close to the Globe theatre by Black Fryers London."[79] Malone pointed out that the Globe was on the other side of the Thames from Blackfriars and so could not abut the property in question.

Malone, who had trained as a lawyer, summarily condemned all the legal documents: "One finds it difficult to say in what circumstance the fabricator of them displays the most ignorance; whether his spelling is worse than his phraseology, or the incongruity of his fictions with the history and manners of the time be more observable than either. Even his law is all false" (271). He concluded his attack on the papers,

> In the course of this inquiry it has been shewn that the artificer or artificers of this clumsy and daring fraud, whatever other qualifications they may possess, know nothing of the history of Shakspeare, nothing of the history of the Stage, or the history of the English Language. It has been proved, that there is no external evidence whatsoever that can give any credibility to the manuscripts, which have been now examined, or even entitled them to a serious consideration. (352–353)

Without time to compose a response, Samuel hastily prepared a flier that he distributed at the door of the playhouse urging a fair hearing for *Vortigern:*

> A *malevolent* and *impotent* attack on the SHAKSPEARE MSS. having appeared, on the *EVE* of representation of the play of *Vortigern,* evidently intended to injure the interest of the Proprietor of the MSS., Mr. Ireland feels it impossible, within

---

79 *Miscellaneous Papers,* C2ʳ.

the short space of time that intervenes between the publishing and the representation, to produce an answer to the most illiberal and unfounded assertions in Mr. Malone's enquiry. He is therefore induced to request that the Play of *Vortigern* may be heard with that *candour* that has ever distinguished a *British audience*.[80]

Even before the publication of Malone's *Inquiry*, Samuel had feared that the play would not be judged impartially. On 22 March 1796 he wrote to the Prince of Wales to seek his support. The prince declined to act, but his brother the Duke of Clarence attended because his mistress, Mrs. Jordan, was appearing in the piece. On 27 March, Francis Webb urged Samuel to delay the opening because of a conspiracy against *Vortigern*, but Samuel would not or could not postpone the premier.

At 6:30 P.M. on 2 April 1796 the play opened to a full house of 2,500. *The Times* for 4 April stated that as many more failed to secure tickets, and, according to the *Telegraph* for 7 April, the "house was the fullest ever known." The prologue was interrupted by hostile jeers because it was poorly delivered, but applauded when John Whitfield reached the end of the poem, which again appealed for a fair hearing:

> From deep oblivion snatch'd, this play appears:
> It claims respect, since Shakespeare's name it bears;
> That name, the source of wonder and delight,
> To a fair hearing has at least a right.
> We ask no more—with you the judgment lies;
> No forgeries escape your piercing eyes!
> Unbias'd then pronounce your dread decree,
> Alike from prejudice and favour free.[81]

The curtain rose to applause as act one began, and the first two acts went well. Dorothea Jordan, playing Vortigern's daughter, Flavia, kept reassuring William, who hid in the Green Room,

---

80   *Reforging Shakespeare*, 178–179.
81   *Vortigern*, xi.

too nervous to join his father in his box. Charles Dignum as Second Baron raised a laugh in the third act, but trouble did not begin until act four, when the Saxon Horsus, played by John Phillimore, died. Phillimore had fallen too close to the edge of the stage, so when the heavy drop curtain descended it lay athwart his body and left his legs exposed to the audience. Instead of lying quietly, he groaned and thrashed about until he extricated himself. Kemble then gave the play its death blow in the fifth act. In a tolerable apostrophe to death, William had written,

> O! then thou dost ope wide thy hideous jaws,
> And with rude laughter, and fantastic tricks,
> Thou clap'st thy rattling fingers to thy sides;
> And when this solemn mockery is ended,
> With icy hand thou tak'st him by the feet,
> And upward so, till thou dost reach the heart,
> And wrap him in the cloak of lasting night.[82]

Reaching the line about this solemn mockery, Kemble spoke it in a sepulchral voice that incited ten minutes of laughter; and when that subsided he repeated the line in a voice more sepulchral still. Once the audience quieted, Kemble asked that the rest of the play be heard. The work ended with applause, and Mrs. Jordan was applauded for her epilogue. But when William Barrymore announced *Vortigern* for the next night, he was met with hoots and catcalls. Kemble finally had to come forward to say that Drury Lane would stage *The School for Scandal* instead.

Samuel's profit for the one night was £102 13s. 3d., thirty pounds of which he gave to William. Together with the sixty pounds Samuel had given William from Sheridan's two hundred fifty pound advance, this was the total amount William received for his forgeries.

The failure of *Vortigern* raised still more questions about the authenticity of the Shakespeare papers. On 9 April 1796 Samuel appealed for information to William's friend Montague Talbot,

---

82 *Vortigern*, 64.

who, in one version of William's story, had made the initial discovery. Talbot remained loyal to William but agreed to sign an
affidavit stating that he, William, and Mr. H. were the only parties
privy to the papers' origin. Since the oath maintained that Mr. H.
existed, William rejected this proposal.

Samuel's friends rallied to him and organized a committee of
twenty-four to treat with Mr. H. Mr. H. agreed to meet with two
of the committee members, but they declined the distinction. He
then said that he would meet with Albany Wallis. On 17 May
Samuel watched from across the street to see the mysterious
stranger enter Wallis's house. He saw only William go in and then
come out. William had confessed, but Wallis urged him to keep the
truth concealed. Even after William publicly acknowledged his
guilt, Wallis refused to confirm the young man's statements. He
did, however, help William draft an advertisement that they inserted in various London newspapers:

> In justice to my father, and to remove the Reproach under
> which he has Innocently fallen respecting the papers publish'd
> by him as the MSS. of Shakspeare, I do solemnly declare that
> they were given to him by me, as the genuine productions
> of Shakspere, and that he was and is at this Moment totally
> unacquainted with the source from whence they came or with
> any Circumstance concerning them save what he was told
> by myself and which he has declared in the preface to his
> Publication. With this firm belief and Conviction of their
> Authenticity, founded on the Credit he gave to me and my
> Assurances, they were laid before the World. This will be
> further confirm'd when at some future period it may be judged
> expedient to disclose the means by which they were obtained.[83]

William signed the statement, which was witnessed by Wallis
and his clerk, Thomas Trowsdale, on 24 May 1796. William's suggestions to his father that the papers were spurious and that he was
their author met with Samuel's confirmed disbelief.

---

83   In *Reforging Shakespeare*, 192.

Mair believes that "after the failure of *Vortigern* William began to lose control of his fancies."[84] William certainly began to invent curious tales and to behave strangely. He abandoned his desk at Bingley's, breaking his indentures. He told his father that a mysterious gentleman, a friend of Mr. H., had promised him an estate worth three hundred pounds a year. William rented a carriage and horses but told his sister Jane that these were gifts from the gentleman. He had shown *Henry the Second* to Thomas Harris, who said he would stage it the next season. William reported that Harris had seen *William the Conqueror*, a play that William never finished, and on the strength of that piece had agreed to pay William seven hundred pounds a year in exchange for two plays a season. When Samuel asked Harris about the arrangement, Harris suggested that William had gone mad.

In early May the Irelands vacationed in the country, William riding a horse he had hired but which he said had been lent him by the gentleman. He told his mother that he was to marry a wealthy seventeen-year-old named Miss Shaw, whose family lived in Harley Street. When Samuel's inquiries turned up no Shaw in Harley Street, William changed the name to Shard. Such a family did live in Harley Street but had no daughter.

Back in London, William spent what remained of his ninety pounds driving about with a groom in attendance. Late in May Samuel went to Sunning for a holiday, and on Saturday, 4 June, Jane went to visit her sister, Anna Maria Barnard, and her husband, Robert Maitland Barnard, in Lambeth. The next day Samuel wrote to his son pleading for information about the papers. Instead of responding, on 6 June William left his Norfolk Street home, never to return.

On 14 June William, with Wallis' approval, wrote to his father confessing that he had composed all the documents and plays. For a moment Samuel seemed to believe his son. He wrote back,

> Let your talent be what it may—who do you think will ever sanction you, or associate with you after showing an ability for

---

84   Mair, 196.

such gross and deliberate impositions on the public, and through the medium of your own father. Impositions of such a nature to the well-being of society that the Law holds out certain death as a reward first when detected. The subject is too horrid for reflection, I shall leave you to your own thoughts on the occasion.

Samuel then protested William's taking his own books with him, books William had sold to support himself but not to pay his debts. Samuel concluded the letter, "I have not words to express the high indignation I feel at yr. unnatural Conduct—words or reproaches are now all vain. You have left me with a load of misery and have, I fear, about you a load of infamy that you will find perhaps more difficulty than I shall in getting rid of."[85]

Samuel quickly changed his mind about the possibility of his son's authorship. The next day he wrote again, telling William that if he insisted on claiming that he had written the papers, "Your character . . . will be blasted, that no person will admit you into their house, nor can you anywhere be trusted. Therefore, do not suffer yourself from vanity or any other motive to adhere to any such confession."[86] William replied that he would write a pamphlet setting forth the truth.

On 4 July 1796 William married an Alice Crudge at St. James Church, Clerkenwell.[87] That summer he set off for Wales with Wallis, but William soon left the lawyer, borrowing five guineas from Mrs. Wallis. He went to Gloucester and thence to Bristol, Chatterton's birthplace, where he visited St. Mary Redcliff, the purported source of many of Chatterton's Rowley documents, and called on the poet's sister to listen to stories about his hero. By autumn he was back in London, where on 29 October Frederick Reynolds' *Fortune's Fool* opened at Covent Garden. The play satirizes Samuel Ireland as Sir Bamber Blackletter, who thinks of marrying Miss Union because she owns the manuscript of

---

85   In Mair, 209–210.
86   Ibid., 210.
87   Mair and Kahan give the date as 4 June, Grebanier as 4 July.

"Trickarinda," an unpublished poem by Chaucer in the poet's own hand. She keeps this work in a trunk that recalls the document-laden chests of Chatterton and Ireland. Chaucer's poem reads in part,

> On yon green bank where Trickarinda sleeps
> The wind laughs round her, and the water weeps!
> And lo! a monk all hollow'd from the cloyster
> Grey as the morn and white as any oyster.[88]

Before committing matrimony, Sir Bamber discovers that Chaucer's handwriting and Miss Union's are the same, and the hoax is exposed.

Samuel and William met on 12 December at Wallis' house. William noted that he needed money. He also insisted that he was the author of the Shakespeare papers and that he would publish that fact, as he did a few days later in *An Authentic Account of the Shaksperian Manuscripts*, a work so popular that all copies quickly vanished. Though it initially sold for a shilling, William had to pay 18s. 6d. to get a copy a few years later. The pamphlet did not succeed in clearing his father's name. The *Monthly Mirror*, the *True Briton*, the *Morning Chronicle*, and the *Gentleman's Magazine* all found in the puerile style of William's pamphlet evidence that the young man could not be the author of the forgeries. In December 1796 Samuel published *Mr. Ireland's Vindication of his Conduct Respecting the Publication of the Supposed Shakspeare MSS.*, in which he insisted that the documents were authentic, and in 1797 he followed this work with *An Investigation of Mr. Malone's Claim to the Character of Scholar or Critic, Being an Examination of His Inquiry into the Authenticity of the Shakspeare MSS.*

On 3 January 1797 William wrote to his father to apologize for deceiving him and to ask for help in finding a post. The letter reveals William's long-held suspicions: "If you are *really* my father, I appeal to your feelings as a Parent, if not, I am the more indebted to you for the Care of my youthful Education etc."[89]

---

88 In Grebanier, 262.
89 In Mair, 219.

On 31 March 1797 Samuel and William met again at Wallis', where they quarreled over the authorship of the papers. This was the last time that father and son saw each other. Somehow William scraped together the money to open a circulating library at 1 Princes Place, Kensington, in 1798. Part of his income derived from the sale of copies of his forgeries, which remained in demand. The British Library owns a copy of *Henry the Second* made at the request of one of William's customers. William wrote to Samuel to ask for books for his enterprise, but Samuel never replied, and thus their correspondence ended. On his deathbed in July 1800 Samuel forgave his son and bequeathed him a watch and twenty pounds. As for the Shakespeare papers, Samuel went to his grave believing in them. In 1799 he published *Vortigern . . . and Henry the Second,* in the preface to which he attacked Malone and declared,

> Neither the index-lore, or the alphabetical, lexicographical, labours of this sagacious discoverer, or his congenial fellows or associates, nor any declaration since made from a quarter once domestic to the Editor, through which something like genuine information might naturally have been expected, can induce him to believe that great part of the mass of papers in his possession are the fabrication of any individual, or set of men of the present day. (v)

Despite, or perhaps because of, the controversy over the Shakespeare papers, they proved the most valuable of Samuel's possessions when his property was sold at auction by Leigh, Sotheby & Son, York Street, Covent Garden, beginning Thursday, 7 May 1801 and continuing through Friday, 15 May, Sunday excepted. Samuel's print of Vortigern and Rowena sold for 13s. 6d. His copy of the 1640 edition of Shakespeare's poems brought £2 6s. Samuel's annotated copy of Malone's *Inquiry* went for £5 5s. The last item sold was "The Complete Collection of Shakspearian Papers." Malone attempted to buy them for £120, but they sold for £130. The dramatist William Thomas Moncrieff later acquired them. They passed into the hands of Shakespeare scholar Clement Mansfield Ingleby. In 1877 Ingleby donated the documents to the Shakespeare Memorial Library, Birmingham, where they were destroyed in a fire in 1879.

William spent the rest of his life as a writer, publishing sixty-seven original titles, as well as translations from and into French. He left another twenty-three works unpublished. In 1799 he produced the Gothic novel *The Abbess*. This was followed by *Rimualdo; or, the Castle of Badajos* (1800). *The Woman of Feeling* appeared in 1804, *Gondez, the Monk. A Romance of the Thirteenth Century* in 1805, and *The Catholic, an Historical Romance* in 1807. In 1801 William tried to interest a London theater in his blank verse drama *Mutius Scaevola, or The Roman Patriot,* but neither Covent Garden nor Drury Lane wanted to deal with him. The next year he was able to indulge his love of the stage when Princess Elizabeth engaged him to oversee a series of interludes for the birthday celebration of George III. William even wrote two pieces himself. His efforts were warmly applauded, but the princess paid him only five pounds, which he returned as insufficient compensation. In that same year he published the Chattertonian poem *A Ballade Written on the Feastynge and Merrimentes of Easter Maunday Laste Paste,* and his 1803 collection of poems, *Rhapsodies,* begins with "Elegiac Lines to the Memory of Thomas Chatterton." The book includes "The Bastard," "The Bastard's Complaint," and "Reply to the Bastard's Complaint," indicating William's continuing concerns about his legitimacy.

The fate of Alice Crudge is unknown, but in 1804 William married the widow of Captain Paget Bayly. Perhaps spurred by the desire to earn money or to clear his name, in 1805 William published his *Confessions,* with a full account of his forgeries and a plea for forgiveness. Yet in that same year he manufactured another hoax, *Effusions of Love from Chastelar to Mary, Queen of Scotland,* supposedly a translation "from a Gallic Manuscript in the Scotch College at Paris."[90] In 1807 his anonymous *Stultifera Navis, or the Modern Ship of Fools* attacked, among other fools, book collectors and antiquarians. In a note to his lines about these last he commented, "Among the impostors of this nature should not be omit-

---

90   Grebanier, 294.

ted the Rowleian Chatterton, and the Shaksperian Ireland, whose memories will live as long as old chests and old manuscripts stand on record."[91] Again he was linking himself to his old hero.

William's prolific output did not yield prosperity. From January to 27 July 1811 he was imprisoned for debt at York. Dorothea Jordan sent him five pounds there. An 1812 work, *Neglected Genius,* once more returned to the fate of Chatterton and included imitations of the Rowley documents. In 1814 William, his wife, and two daughters went to France, where they remained until 1823. Dorothea also moved to France in 1815, and William loyally attended her funeral at St. Cloud in 1816. In 1821 he published what he claimed was Napoleon's will, and in 1829 his *King of Holland* appeared under Napolean's name.

Back in England, William in 1824 ran into his early supporter and then opponent James Boaden. That all was not forgiven was clear from Boaden's greeting: "You must be aware, Sir, of the enormous crime you committed against the divinity of Shakespeare. Why, the act, Sir, was nothing short of sacrilege! It was precisely the same thing as taking the holy chalice from the altar and ___ therein."[92]

One of William's last publications was a reissue of *Vortigern* (London: J. Thomas, 1832). In the preface he justly lamented that he had suffered "thirty-six years incessant persecution and obloquy, for the commission of an act only to please a parent, and which, in reality, has injured no one but its author" (vii). Another of his late works was *The Great Illegitimates, the Public and Private Life of that Celebrated Actress, Mrs. Jordan* (1832). William IV, formerly the Duke of Clarence and Mrs. Jordan's lover, paid to suppress the account of the ten children he had fathered by Dorothea. To the last, Ireland was standing up for bastards and for Mrs. Jordan. He died at his home in Sussex Place, St. George's-in-the-Fields, on 17 April 1835 and was buried at St. George-the-Martyr, Southwark, a week later, on 24 April, one day after the anniversary of Shakespeare's death.

---

91   In Grebanier, 295.
92   In Sergeant, 289–290.

On 22 October 1997 *Vortigern* was revived at the Bridewell in Chancery Lane, London, near the office where William created the play while serving his apprenticeship. Among those financing the production were dramatist Alan Ayckbourne and Shakespearean actor extraordinaire Kenneth Branagh. The play ran through 19 November to enthusiastic crowds, though all the reviews were bad. The ghost of William-Henry Ireland must have smirked.

John Payne Collier

V

Shakespearean Forgery 102:
John Payne Collier

*A*s a Shakespearean forger William-Henry Ireland (ch. 4) possessed much vigor but little art. John Payne Collier had both. One of the two leading Shakespeare scholars of the nineteenth century—James Orchard Halliwell was his only rival—he made important contributions to the study of Elizabethan and Jacobean drama. His reprints of rare works made primary sources readily available, his 1842–1844 edition of Shakespeare was the best until the Cambridge version appeared in the 1860's, and his edition of Spenser set the standard for nearly half a century. Because of Collier we have a good idea of the contents of Coleridge's 1811 lectures about Shakespeare and Milton. He was a leading member of the Camden and Percy Societies; the Shakespeare Society (1840–1853) would not have existed without him.

Yet, as Hamlet observed,

[O]ft it chances in particular men,
That for some vicious mole of nature in them . . .
      that these men,
Carrying I say the stamp of one defect,
Being nature's livery or fortune's star,
His virtues else be they as pure as grace,
As infinite as man may undergo,
Shall in the general censure take corruption
From that particular fault. (*Hamlet*, I, iv, 22–35)

Collier's vicious mole of nature was an inability to resist making his legitimate discoveries even more startling by spicing them with spurious additions. This failing manifested itself before he was thirty, and it persisted throughout a life of ninety-four years.

The motivations for his actions were various. Money was one. When Collier's grandfather, a London pharmacist and a silent partner in the firm of John Devaynes, Apothecary to the Queen's Household, retired in 1785, he gave each of his two sons £10,000. The next year Collier's father, John Dyer Collier, married Jane Payne, who brought with her another £7,000. John Dyer Collier invested this money in the Spanish merino wool trade, and his business initially prospered. However, by the time John Payne Collier was born in New Broad Street, London, on 11 January 1789, the Collier fortunes were declining. A collapse in wool prices compelled the family to move to Leeds in a vain effort to save the business. Bankrupt, the Colliers then settled for a time at Thames Ditton, near Hampton Court, where John Dyer read law. His fortunes improved when he became manager of a soap factory belonging to Jane's brother-in-law William Field, but John Dyer quarreled with William over profits. In the summer of 1798 John Dyer Collier left the soap factory and converted his savings into a 250-acre farm at Abridge, Essex, where in three years he bankrupted himself a second time.[1]

In 1801 the family returned to London, and John Dyer began editing the Whig *Monthly Register* and at the same time writing for the Tory *Oracle and Daily Advertiser.* In 1804 he joined the staff of the London *Times* as a law reporter at £200 a year; later he assumed other duties with the newspaper before moving to the *Morning Chronicle* in 1809. Together with John Payne Collier, John Dyer established an early version of the Associated Press, supplying provincial journals with news, and the family fortunes rebounded. Even so, Collier was never rich, and scholarship paid no better in the 19th century than at any other time. Until late in life, John Payne Collier earned most of his money from journalism, but the additional income from his editions and scholarly works was welcome. The more revelations he could offer, the more likely publishers were to print and the public to buy his works.

---

1   Arthur Freeman and Janet Ing Freeman have kindly informed me that the bankruptcy was reported in the London *Times* of 3 May 1802.

Because of the Colliers' financial difficulties, John Payne Collier never attended school. A precocious student, he learned to read when he was three, and his father, who had been educated at the excellent Charterhouse (1771-1776), taught him Latin, Greek, and shorthand; German he learned from a boarder and close family friend, Henry Crabb Robinson. John Payne Collier was always sensitive to his lack of formal education. In his journal for 19 November 1873 he wrote, "I never became a good scholar. To this day I am very ignorant."[2] Making discoveries that eluded such scholars as Edmond Malone or James Orchard Halliwell could compensate for this lack of schooling. As Joseph Crosby wrote to Joseph Parker Norris on 30 October 1877, "I often have fancied that that weakness of his—to *find* something no one expected, & so to show his research—was the source of much of his trouble with the 'Corr. Fo. 1632.'"[3] Kenneth Muir suggested that yet another motive may have been the desire to fool other scholars "and thereby [demonstrate] his superiority."[4]

At the age of seventeen (1806) John Payne Collier joined his father at the *Times* as a Parliamentary reporter, and about this time the young man secured a reader's ticket at the British Museum and admission to the library of the Society of Antiquaries and to the king's library. Collier also began collecting books. One of his earliest purchases was a Third Folio (1664) of Shakespeare's plays. On the fly-leaf of this volume Collier later wrote, "I fancied it the first Edition and a great prize, and what pleasure I had in making up its deficiencies. I was then grossly ignorant, and was only beginning what I wish I had never begun."[5] Another early acquisition, from Thomas Rodd, Sr., then at 2 Great Newport Street,[6] was the 1567

2 In Dewey Ganzel, *Fortune and Men's Eyes: The Career of John Payne Collier* (New York: Oxford University Press, 1982), 17.

3 *One Touch of Shakespeare: Letters of Joseph Crosby to Joseph Parker Norris, 1875–1878,* ed. John W. Velz and Frances N. Teague (Washington, D.C.: Folger Shakespeare Library, 1986), 260. "Corr Fo. 1632" refers to the Perkins Folio discussed later in this chapter.

4 Review of Dewey Ganzel's *Fortune and Men's Eyes, Sewanee Review* 92 (1984): 273.

5 Samuel Schoenbaum, *Shakespeare's Lives,* 2nd ed. (Oxford: Clarendon Press, 1991), 246.

6 Rodd later moved his book store to 9 Great Newport Street.

(fifth) edition of Wilson's *Art of Logic*, first published in 1551. From this work Collier learned that *Ralph Roister Doister* had been written by Nicholas Udall. Such purchases reveal Collier's early interest in the English Renaissance, an interest that may owe something to Charles Lamb, who in 1808 published *Specimens of English Dramatic Poets, Who Lived about the Time of Shakspeare.* Lamb was a friend of both Collier and Collier's parents.

Like Lamb, too, Collier became a lover of the theater at a young age. In *An Old Man's Diary, Forty Years Ago* (London: Thomas Richards, 1871-1872) he recorded under 7 March 1832, "I was present when a boy at the first appearance of [Charles] Mathews and [John] Liston in London—Mathews as *Jabel* in 'The Jew' in 1803, at the Haymarket; and Liston in 1805 as *Sheepface* in 'The Village Lawyer,' also at the Haymarket" (I, 41).[7]

In 1809 Collier succeeded his father at the *Times,* and on 31 July 1811 he began to read law desultorily at the Middle Temple. The subject was hardly congenial, as is evident from a sonnet Collier wrote in 1815:

> Farewell, I oft have said, to verse and song!
> Farewell, each noble, each harmonious line,
> That which men call, and justly call, divine,
> Thou hast consumed my youthful hours too long.
> And come, ye graver studies of the mind,
> The endless labyrinths of tangled law:
> Within your intricacies I must wind;
> From you the means of living I must draw.
> To live by tangling error, making flaw!
> Oh, base invention of our modern wit,
> An insult vile to ethereal soul!
> Often as thus I said or thought of it,
> My heart has spurn'd the melancholy dole,
> And Smil'd at want, than in such wealth to roll.[8]

---

7   *The Jew,* by Richard Cumberland, premiered in 1794, William Macready's *The Village Lawyer* in 1787.

8   Quoted in John Whitehead, *This Solemn Mockery: The Art of Literary Forgery* (London: Arlington Books, 1973), 94.

Preferable to him were the lectures on Shakespeare and Milton that Samuel Taylor Coleridge delivered between Monday, 18 November 1811 and 27 January 1812 at the London Philosophical Society, Scot's Corporation Hall, Crane Court, off Fetter Lane. Collier took careful notes, which he published in 1854 and 1856. In 1817, when Coleridge was preparing another set of lectures on Shakespeare, both Charles Lamb and William Wordsworth wrote to Collier to request his support. Collier again attended and recorded the lectures, thus preserving Coleridge's observations. In the *Times* for 20 May 1816 an unsigned article on Coleridge's "Christabel" appeared. Oskar Wellens argued that Collier wrote this piece, which was one of the few favorable reviews. According to Wellens, Collier was "one of the first reviewers who did not fall back upon Augustan standards when judging contemporary works."[9]

By this time Collier had already embarked on his career of literary fabrication. While vacationing at Margate, he wrote an unsigned article on Punch and Judy puppet shows for the *Morning Chronicle,* in which he gives details of a curious performance that includes Punch's flight to Spain, "his arrest and torture by officers of the Inquisition, and his escape from a prison cell 'by means of a golden key.'"[10] This performance existed only in the mind of Collier. He would include this information in his edition of *Punch and Judy* in 1828 without acknowledging himself as the source, and in that edition he would give the date of the letter as 22 September 1813, exactly a year after the piece in fact appeared.

After Napoleon's exile to Elba, Collier went to Paris, where he secured a pass to the Louvre. During his three weeks in the French capital he visited the museum daily. Years later he wrote in *An Old Man's Diary,* "I look back upon this expedition to Paris as one of the luckiest events of my life; and in questions of art in sculpture and painting, I plume myself no little upon my taste and judgment, thus improved" (I, 48).

9   "John Payne Collier: The Man Behind the Unsigned *Times* Review of 'Christabel' (1816)," *The Wordsworth Circle* 13 (Spring 1982): 68-71, 69.
10   Arthur Freeman and Janet Ing Freeman, "Scholarship, Forgery, and Fictive Invention: John Payne Collier Before 1831," *The Library,* 6th ser., 15 (March 1993), 1–23, 12.

In the spring of 1816 John Dyer Collier bought the failing *Critical Review,* which he kept alive for another fourteen months. John Payne Collier wrote at least forty-seven reviews for his father,[11] and he contributed a regular column entitled "Bibliotheca Antiqua" about old books. In his second essay in this series, published in June 1816, he claimed that he had discovered a new poem by Thomas Churchyard in a copy of *A True Discourse Historical,* in which Churchyard laments the deaths of Sir John Norris and Sir Philip Sidney. Collier published one version of the piece in *The Critical Review,* another in *Archaeologica* in 1852. Collier's own copy of the 1816 article is preserved in the British Library (shelf mark 836.f.26), complete with the alterations he introduced in the later printing. Collier always considered himself a poet, and throughout his life he passed off his work as that of others. The Churchyard piece was but the first of many.

On 20 August 1816 Collier married Mary Louisa Pycroft, a distant relation,[12] at Putney Church. Two years later, under the pseudonym "Amicus Curiae," he began a series of essays on lawyers and the law. First published in *The Examiner* in the fall of 1818, these were collected the following year under the title *Criticisms of the Bar; Including Strictures on the Principal Counsel Practicing in the Courts of King's Bench, Common Pleas, Chancery, and Exchequer* (London: W. Simpkin and R. Marshall, 1819). This was not a work designed to endear him to the profession for which he was supposedly preparing himself, since he had little good to say about any of his prospective colleagues. Collier wrote that Mr. Marryat was "lamentably wanting in all kinds of general information, and ignorant even of the higher branches of his own pursuit. . . . He is one of the most clumsy, negligent speakers that ever opened his lips. . . . Of wit or humor Mr. Marryat has not a particle" (33–43). Sir Arthur Piggot "seems to want a logical head" (90). Robert Peel, then already in Parliament and later to become

---

11   Oskar Wellens, "The Colliers of London: Early Advocates of Wordsworth, Lamb, Coleridge, and Other Romantics," *Bulletin of Research in the Humanities* 86 (1983): 105–127.

12   Arthur Freeman and Janet Ing's Freeman's research has found that she was the youngest child of the older sister (Frances London Pycroft) of John Payne Collier's maternal grandmother (Jane London Payne).

Prime Minister, he called "a young man of overrated abilities, . . . who will never do better than he has done, nor attain a higher rank than that of a debater" (172). In another essay he wrote that "Mr. [John] Bell is a remarkable instance of success in spite of an absence of all those qualifications usually considered requisite in an Advocate, except industry, and a memory of peculiar retentiveness" (272). In addition to singling out many individuals, Collier condemned lawyers in general as "everlastingly on the watch not to improve themselves by imitating excellence, but to degrade others by exaggerating defects and disseminating failures" (167). He also condemned lawyers for their greed: "the love of gain there is the principally operating motive" (162). Collier later repented this indiscreet publication, writing on a fly-leaf of his own copy, "Foolish, flippant, and fatal to my prospects, if I ever had any."

The work does show his wide reading. The essay on Sir Samuel Romilly concludes with a quotation from Samuel Daniel's *Philotus*. His sketch of Mr. Wetherell begins with lines from John Gower's *Confessio Amantis* and includes references from John Marston's *The Scourge of Villanie*. The piece on Henry Peter Brougham quotes George Chapman's *Conspiracie and Tragedie of Charles Duke of Byron*. Milton and Shakespeare are cited repeatedly.

Collier gave further evidence of his scholarship the next year with his *Poetical Decameron,* ten imaginary dialogues about Elizabethan and Jacobean literature among Bourne (Collier), Elliot (Henry Crabb Robinson), and Morton (Thomas Amyot). Here Collier identified Barnaby Riche's "Apolonius and Silla" (1581) as a source for Shakespeare's *Twelfth Night*. In 1806 Octavius Gilchrist had made the same discovery and informed the Shakespeare scholar Edmond Malone in a letter, but Collier almost certainly arrived at his discovery independently and was the first to publish this fact. Unable to remain content with this major contribution to scholarship, he also proposed, without a shred of evidence, that Thomas Nashe was the author of the anonymous *A Yorkshire Tragedy,* sometimes attributed to Shakespeare.

The Poetical Decameron earned Collier £200, part of which he used for the private publication of his Spenserian *The Poet's Pilgrimage,* which appeared anonymously in 1822. Lamb and

Robinson praised the work,[13] prompting Collier to issue a second edition, with his name on the title page, in 1825. Collier later stated that he had composed the work in his youth between 1808 and 1814, but he also remained proud of the poem. On 12 August 1879 he wrote to Joseph Woodfall Ebsworth, "I thought, & think, that I never wrote anything else that was half as good—yet nobody cares a fig about it, but its poor old Author. . . . It is good: it is of its kind, highly meritorious and imaginative. It is good, let who will say the contrary, and by it I will live & die."[14] Collier rarely published poetry again under his own name, but he repeatedly "discovered" Elizabethan ballads that he included in his scholarly works.

In 1823 Collier left the *Times* for the *Morning Chronicle*;[15] he claimed that the rift occurred over a loan that was not repaid him. Two years later the publisher Septimus Prowett engaged Collier to edit his twelve-volume reissue of Robert Dodsley's 18th-century *A Select Collection of Old Plays*. In his 1825 edition of *Gammer Gurton's Needle* for this series, Collier identified *Ralph Roister Doister* as the earliest English comedy and Nicholas Udall as its author. To the series Collier added works by Nashe, Thomas Lodge, Robert Greene, and George Peele, increasing interest in these contemporaries of Shakespeare. A new edition of Peele appeared in 1828, of Greene in 1831, inspired at least in part by Collier. Collier also persuaded Prowett to publish five other early pieces not included in the twelve-volume set: Anthony Munday's *The Downfall of Robert, Earl of Huntingdon,* Munday and Henry Chettle's *The Death of Robert, Earl of Huntingdon,* Thomas Hughes's *The Misfortunes of Arthur,* Nathaniel Field's *A Woman Is a Weathercock, A Comedy,* and *Amends for Ladies, A Comedy.* The first three appeared in 1828, the latter two in 1829.

In 1828 Collier edited *Punch and Judy,* with illustrations by George Cruikshank. In his scholarly apparatus Collier included his

---

13 According to Collier's *Old Man's Diary* Wordsworth also admired the poem; the Freemans are skeptical of this claim.

14 Quoted in Giles E. Dawson, "John Payne Collier's Great Forgery," *Studies in Bibliography* 24 (1971): 1–26, 17.

15 Collier had previously worked for the *Morning Chronicle* between 1813 and 1815.

1812 letter cited above and two poems, "Punch's Pranks" and "Sonnet to Punch." The former he claimed had been "extracted from a curious collection of comic and serious pieces of the kind, in print and in manuscript, with the figures 1791, 1792, and 1793 in various parts of it, as the times, probably, when the individual who made it obtained the copies he transcribed."[16] "Sonnet to Punch" Collier attributed to George Gordon, Lord Byron, whom Collier disliked. Both pieces were by Collier.

Also in 1828 Thomas Amyot introduced Collier to Robert Peel, then Home Secretary. Peel, who apparently held no grudge against his one-time critic, gave Collier access to the documents in the State Paper Office. In 1830 Amyot and Francis Douce sponsored Collier for membership in the Society of Antiquaries; Collier became a fellow on 9 December 1830. In 1847 Collier would become the society's treasurer, and in 1849 its vice president.

Collier was called to the bar on 6 February 1829, but he never practiced. Instead he continued to write for the *Morning Chronicle* from noon until the early hours of the morning. Then, after a few hours' sleep, he would pursue his scholarly interests until mid-day. He was working on a history of early English drama, and in 1830 Amyot introduced him to William Spencer Cavendish, 6th Duke of Devonshire. In 1821 the duke had paid £2,000 for the actor John Philip Kemble's extensive collection of printed plays. Devonshire's collection nicely supplemented the Garrick books at the British Museum, and the duke generously gave Collier free access to his library. He even brought his drama collection from the country to Devonshire House in London to facilitate Collier's researches.

In the spring of 1830 Amyot also introduced Collier to John Allen, Master of the College of God's Gift, Dulwich, established by the great Elizabethan actor Edward Alleyn. Among the treasures housed here were Alleyn's papers and the diary of theatrical entrepreneur and owner of the Rose Theatre Philip Henslowe; Henslowe's diary is one of the most important records of Elizabethan theater history. It lists performances at the Rose between 1592 and 1597, revenues from those plays, loans and

---

16   Quoted in Freeman and Freeman, 11.

payments to actors and playwrights, and the cost of costumes and props. In 1840 Collier would borrow the diary and take it home for his research. Sometime in the early 1830's Collier and Amyot made an important acquisition of their own, paying either £180 or £400—Collier's accounts vary—for the John Larpent collection of manuscript plays, now at the Huntington Library. Larpent had been the licenser of plays from 1778 to 1824, and his collection included not only plays written between 1737 and 1824 but also letters and memoranda relating to performances. In 1853 Collier joined with Amyot's widow to sell the Larpent Collection to Francis Egerton, Lord Ellesmere. Ellesmere's library would be purchased in its entirety by the great American collector Henry Huntington.

The History of English Dramatic Poetry to the Time of Shakespeare; and Annals of the Stage to the Restoration was published by John Murray of London in three volumes in 1831. Collier received £300 for the work. Dewey Ganzel called it "a milestone in literary historiography. It is not too much to say that the systematic study of English drama as a genre began with its publication," and Samuel Schoenbaum described it as "a monument of early nineteenth-century scholarship."[17] Among the Harleian manuscripts collected by the first and second Earls of Oxford in the early 18th century and acquired by the British Museum Collier found the diary of the 17th-century lawyer John Manningham. A devotee of the theater, Manningham recorded seeing a performance of Shakespeare's *Twelfth Night* at the Middle Temple in 1602. Collier's discovery thus helped date the play. He also found two previously unknown masques by Ben Jonson, *The Masque of Blackness* and *The Masque of Queens.*

Such legitimate finds did not suffice for Collier. Ballads were his Cleopatra, which he could not resist. Here he composed one dealing with the riot at the Cockpit in 1617 and referring to Shakespeare's *Troilus and Cressida.* He chastised Edmond Malone, who had used Henslowe's diary, for failing to credit Anthony

---

17 Ganzel, 43; Samuel Schoenbaum, *Shakespeare's Lives,* 247.

Munday with helping to write the play *Cardinal Wolsey* and added, "That he was concerned in Cardinal Wolsey, we have under his own hand, as he signs, as follows, a receipt for money on account of it" (III, 90). The facsimile signature looks nothing like Munday's and was Collier's creation. Collier provided a facsimile of Henry Chettle's signature revealing him as co-author with Michael Drayton and Thomas Dekker of *The Famous Wars of Henry I;* again, the signature is by Collier (III, 419-420). He quoted an entry from Henslowe's diary, "pd vnto Thomas dickers the 20 of desembr 1597 for adycyons to ffostus twentie shellinges and fyve shellinges more for a prolog to Marloes tambelan so in all J saye payde twentye five shillinges" (III, 113). This is the clearest evidence available that Christopher Marlowe wrote *Tamburlaine,* but it was written into Henslowe's diary by Collier and then cited by him. In the State Paper Office he found a petition from the Lord Chamberlain's Men to the Privy Council asking for permission to continue using the Blackfriars Theater, "which hath beene for manie yeares used and occupied for the playing of tragedies, commedies, histories, enterludes, and playes" (I, 299). Collier was convinced that Shakespeare had used the Blackfriars Theatre for decades before its acquisition by the King's Men in 1608, and he manufactured various documents, including this one, to prove his theory. The name of Shakespeare appears fifth on the list of petitioners, reflecting his importance. This item had the additional significance of being "seven years anterior to the date of any other authentic record, which contains the name of our great dramatist" (ibid.). Collier dates the document 1596, though it refers to the Globe Theatre, which was not built until 1599. Collier's manuscript continuation of the annals from 1660 to 1723 is at Harvard. The text contains many ballads that Collier attributed to that period but which are his own creations.

At the urging of Thomas Amyot, Collier dedicated the *History* to the 6th Duke of Devonshire, who was also the Lord Chamberlain. The duke showed his appreciation by giving Collier £100 and sponsoring him for admission to the Garrick Club. In February 1832 the duke engaged Collier for £100 a year to serve as his librarian and literary adviser, though Collier was never in the duke's official employ. Still, Collier secured many rarities for the duke, including a manuscript of John Bale's *Kynge Johan* (which Collier edited for the Camden Society in 1838), one of three known copies of *A Knack to Knowe a Knave* (1594), John Heywood's *A Merry Play between the Pardoner, the Friar, the Curate and Neighbour Pratt* (1533), and *A Yorkshire Tragedy* (1608).[18] As Lord Chamberlain the duke appointed the licenser of plays, a post then held by an aging and ill George Colman. If Collier could persuade Colman to retire, the duke said, the job was his. Colman refused to resign, and Collier never secured this lucrative position.

The quasi-official post of Devonshire's librarian occupied little of Collier's time. After the death of the book collector Richard Heber in 1833, Collier was engaged to help catalogue the early printed English books in Heber's massive library prior to their dispersal at auction. Between 1835 and 1837 he produced another eight books. Five of these were editions of medieval English miracle plays. A sixth was *A Catalogue, Bibliographical and Critical, of Early English Literature; Forming a Portion of the Library at Bridgewater House* (1837). Privately printed in an edition of fifty copies, it served as the basis of Collier's 1865 *Bibliographical and Critical Account of the Rarest Books in the English Language*. This collection belonged to Lord Francis Gower, who became Lord Francis Egerton in 1833 and Earl of Ellesmere in 1847. The political diarist Charles Greville had introduced Collier to the lord, who gave Collier free range of his extensive holdings. Egerton was a descendant of the First Lord Ellesmere, who had been Queen Elizabeth's Keeper of the Great Seal and James I's Lord Chancellor. It was largely from his research in the Egerton library that Collier composed *New Facts Regarding the Life of Shakespeare* (London: T. Rodd, 1835), addressed to Thomas Amyot; *New*

---

18   In July 1832 Collier paid £30 to William Stevenson Fitch for the manuscript of *Kynge Johan;* Fitch probably had stolen this item from the Ipswich Corporation chest. Fitch apparently kept four leaves, though almost all the text on these pages had been canceled by Bale. In 1848 Fitch surrendered to Collier two of the missing leaves. They belonged to the Duke of Devonshire, but Collier kept them. Only after his death did Collier's son John Pycroft Collier return the leaves to the 7th duke (July 1884). See Janet Ing Freeman, *The Postmaster of Ipswich* (London: The Book Collector, 1997), 100–109.

Particulars Regarding the Works of Shakespeare (London: T. Rodd, 1836), addressed to the Reverend Alexander Dyce, editor of the works of various Elizabethan and Jacobean dramatists; and *Farther Particulars Regarding Shakespeare and His Works* (London: T. Rodd, 1839) in the form of a letter to another Shakespeare scholar, the Reverend Joseph Hunter.

According to one document that Collier found among the Bridgewater papers and published in *New Facts,* Shakespeare was already a shareholder in Burbage's acting company in 1589, though he was listed fifteenth. William Kempe's name appears directly below Shakespeare's, even though Kempe was not acting with Burbage in 1589, and Richard Burbage was listed second despite his being only nineteen years old. All were sharers "in the blacke Fryers playehouse" (11); here, then, was another document supporting Collier's belief that Shakespeare and company were performing there well before 1608. According to another document, which Collier assigned to 1608, Shakespeare and Richard Burbage both now owned four shares in the Blackfriars Theatre, and these shares were worth £933 6s. 8d. The paper valued Shakespeare's other property at the Blackfriars at £500 (22–23). Collier had composed both of these items.

In that same year Henry Wriothesley, 3rd Earl of Southampton, supposedly wrote to Lord Ellesmere urging him to support Shakespeare and Burbage against complaints by the Corporation of London. Southampton first writes of Burbage, then turns his attention to the playwright, who, he says,

> is no whitt lesse deserving favor, and my especiall friende, till of late an actor of good account in the cumpanie, now a sharer in the same, and writer of some of our best English playes, which as your Lordship knoweth were most singularly liked of Quene Elizabeth, when the cumpanie was called vppon to performe before her Matie at Court at Christmas and Shrovetide. His most gracious Matie King James alsoe, since his coming to the crowne, hath extended his royall favour to the companie in divers waies and at sundrie tymes. This other hath to name William Shakespeare, and they are both of one countie, and indeede almost of one towne. (33)

The letter is signed "H.S." One would think that unless Lord Ellesmere had been living under a rock he would be familiar with the King's Men and would have heard of William Shakespeare, the most important playwright in the country. The signature H.[enry] S.[outhampton] is unique among Southampton's letters, and Burbage was almost certainly born in London, not at Stratford, as the Southampton letter states.

A fourth document, from 4 January 1609, appointed "Robert Daiborne, William Shakespeare, Nathaniel Field and Edward Kirkham from time to time to provide and bring upp a convenient nomber of Children, and them to instruct and exercise in the quality of playing Tragedies Comedies &c. by the name of the Children of the Revells to the Queene, within the Black fryers in our Citie of London or els where within our realme of England" (41). Curiously, another patent of the same date authorizes "Robert Daborne, and Servauntes of the Queen, from time to time, to provide and bring up a convenient number of children to practize in the quality of playing, by the name of the Children of the Revells to the Queene, in White Fryers, London, or any other convenient place where he shall thinke fit."[19] The latter is authentic; the former, the one cited by Collier, was Collier's own forgery.

So, too, was a letter from Samuel Daniel to Lord Ellesmere, thanking him for the post of Master of the Queen's Revels. Daniel observes that he is not the most deserving candidate:

> if M. Draiton, my good friend, had bene chosen, I should not have murmured, for sure I ame he wold have filled it most excellentlie: but it seemeth to myne humble iudgement that one who is the authour of playes now daylie presented on the public stages of London, and the possessor of no small gaines, and moreover him selfe an Actor in the Kings Companie of Comedians, could not with reason pretend to be M^r. of the Queenes MA^TIES Revells, for as much as he wold sometimes be asked to approve and allow of his owne writings. (48–49)

---

19 Nicholas E. S. A. Hamilton, *An Inquiry into the Genuineness of the Manuscript Corrections in Mr. J. Payne Collier's Annotated Shakspere Folio, 1632; and of Certain Shaksperian Documents Likewise Published by Mr. Collier* (London: Richard Bentley, 1860), 79.

Shakespeare thus wanted to be Master of the Queen's Revels, and the document states that Shakespeare was still acting—Collier's letter from Southampton has Shakespeare retiring from playing about 1608—and was immensely popular as a writer.

Though most of *New Facts* is devoted to Shakespeare, Collier inserts a brief epitaph on Richard Burbage by Thomas Middleton:

> Astronomers and star-gazers this year
> Write but of foure Eclipses—five appeare.
> Death interposing Burbage, and their staying
> Hath made a visible Eclipse of playing. (26)

Collier claimed that he found these verses among Richard Heber's papers, but no reference to the piece appears in Collier's *Catalogue of Heber's Collection of Early English Poetry, the Drama, Ancient Ballads, and Broadsides . . .* (1834) or the auction record of the Heber sale. Alexander Dyce included the poem in his 1840 edition of Middleton; when Collier again alluded to these lines in his edition of Shakespeare, he cited Dyce as his source, suggesting that Collier was seeking to hide his initial responsibility for their invention.

New Facts depended on forgeries for its publication. *New Particulars* actually announced an important discovery. While working on his *History* at the Bodleian Library, Oxford, Collier had heard about a manuscript by a contemporary of Shakespeare with notes about performances of Shakespeare's plays. The manuscript was not accessible then, but subsequently William Henry Black, a librarian compiling a catalogue of the Ashmolean collection, found Simon Forman's *Booke of Plaies and Notes Thereof,* with references to *The Winter's Tale, Cymbeline, Macbeth,* and one other Shakespeare play, probably *Richard II.* Had Collier contented himself with reprinting and analyzing Forman's information, he would have made a valuable contribution to the history of Shakespearean performance.

Instead, he added to his little book more information of his own manufacture. Among the Bridgewater papers he claimed he had found record of a payment of £10 "to Burbidge's players for Othello" supposedly acted before the queen in August 1602 at

Harefield, the home of Sir Thomas Egerton (58), a remarkable document indeed, since *Othello* was not completed until 1604. Collier could not resist harping again on his theme of the Blackfriars: "it was played by the company usually performing at the Blackfriars Theatre in the winter, and at the Globe in the spring, summer, and autumn" (57).

The sixty-eight pages of *New Particulars* was eked out with further Collier fabrications. One is a ballad based on *Othello,* and he cites others that he claimed he had found in "a volume of MS. Ballads, collected, as I conjecture, about the date of the Protectorate" (44). The volume (British Library Add. MS 32,380) contained a manuscript of Charles I's *Eikon Basilike,* with enough blank pages for Collier to fill with thirty genuine and spurious 16th-and 17th-century ballads. In addition to the Othello ballad, Collier here published part of another dealing with the death of Christopher Marlowe. Among the Bridgewater House papers Collier found verses that he suggested were part of a masque. Reading the signature as "W: Sh:" (61), he attributed the poetry to Shakespeare.[20]

In *New Particulars* Collier also presented another elegy for Burbage. In 1831 Collier had quoted from an authentic version of this elegy, which had originally been published by Joseph Haslewood in the *Gentleman's Magazine* 95 (June 1825): 497–499. The poem noted four roles that Burbage had played: Hamlet, Hieronimo (*The Spanish Tragedy*), Lear, and Othello. Now Collier printed an expanded version that extended the list to twenty and indicated in some cases how Burbage had acted in them. For example, the new lines say that Othello died "on the bed where lay the corpse of his beloved Desdemona, and did not tumble down upon the floor at a distance, as most of our modern actors represent it" (34). Forman had written in his *Booke of Plaies* that "when Macbeth had murdered the King, the blood on his

---

20 The sixty-two lines of verse date from the early 17th century and are probably by Sir William Skipworth. Collier misread the signature, which is "W: Sk:" See James Knowles, "WS MS," *TLS* 29 April 1988, 472 & 485 and Knowles, "Marston, Skipworth and *The Entertainment at Ashby,*" *English Manuscript Studies 1100–1700* 3 (1992): 137–192. I am grateful to Arthur Freeman and Janet Ing Freeman for calling these references to my attention.

hands could not be washed off by any means" (25). The Burbage elegy speaks of "Tyrant Macbeth, with unwash'd bloody hand" (30). To mask his authorship of these lines, Collier deprecated their poetic qualities. "Bad as these verses must have been originally, they certainly have been made worse by time. The MS., from which I copied them, was written at the latter end of the reign of Charles I., and, besides omissions, errors had no doubt crept in from frequent transcriptions" (31).

One of the spurious ballads that Collier cited in *New Particulars* was "The Enchanted Island, subscribed R. G., possibly Robert Greene, and on the same tale as Shakespeare's *Tempest*" (46). In *Farther Particulars* Collier printed the text of the poem, now declaring that Greene could not have written it. Collier dated it to the Protectorate and stated that Francis Douce had called it " 'one of the most beautiful ballads he had ever read,' and shook his venerable head (as was his wont) with admiring energy and antiquarian enthusiasm at different passages in it; but I am by no means prepared to give it so high a character" (56). Douce was dead in 1839 and so could not contradict Collier's claim. Collier's typical self-deprecation further masked his responsibility for the piece.

In 1840 Collier helped found the Shakespeare Society and the Percy Society. The latter concerned itself with early popular literature and ballads. Collier served as director for both organizations and edited the first publication of each. For the Percy Society he prepared a collection of twenty-five ballads, and for the Shakespeare Society in January 1841 he edited the *Memoirs of Edward Alleyn*, based on his research at the College of God's Gift, Dulwich. Collier here reprinted a letter from Alleyn's wife, which read in part,

> About a weeke a goe there came a youthe who said he was Mr Frauncis Chaloner who would have borrowed x^li to have bought things for * * * and said he was known unto you, and Mr. Shakespeare of the globe, who came * * * said he knewe hym not, onely he herde of hym that he was a roge * * * so he was glade we did not lend him the monney * * * Richard Johnes [went] to seeke and inquire after the fellow, and said

he had lent hym a horse. I feare me he gulled hym, thoughe
he gulled not us. (63)

The actual text of the letter, transcribed by N. E. S. A. Hamilton,
contained no reference to Shakespeare.[21] Though the document
was in poor condition, there was not even space for the text that
Collier said it contained.

On page 13 of the *Memoirs* Collier printed a seventeen-line
poem referring to "Willes newe playe." Collier notes that this item
had eluded the notice of Edmond Malone when he had examined
the diary, for the simple reason that the poem was of Collier's manufacture. Malone also overlooked a list of actors appended to a letter from the Council giving protection to the King's Men.
Malone's oversight is the stranger because he knew of the document itself, but said nothing of the list, which Collier notes is "in
a different hand and in different ink." Shakespeare is listed second,
behind Burbage, as an actor, proving that he was still performing
in 1604 and demonstrating his importance. The "different hand"
is, of course, Collier's. To an assessment list of Southwark in 1609
Collier added Shakespeare's name to prove he was living there, and
his tax was 6d., the highest possible. Again, Malone, who had
examined Alleyn's papers, had failed to uncover this fact. Collier
also reported that in 1612 Alleyn paid £596 for "a considerable
share" of the Blackfriars Theatre (105), money which Collier
thinks might well have been paid to Shakespeare. This transaction
is another of Collier's inventions; no documentary evidence exists
to support Collier's assertion.

After Collier's death, his library was sold at Sotheby's on 7-9
August 1884. Lot 200 was his transcript of Alleyn's diary; it was
purchased by the College of God's Gift at Dulwich for thirty-two
shillings. Sir George Warner examined it there, and on 23 October
1884 he wrote to William Young, one of the governors of the
college,

---

21 *Inquiry*, 92.

Mr. Collier's extracts from Alleyn's Diary are extremely interesting, since they prove, as I think incontestably that the spurious interpolations in the Diary were made by Mr. Collier.
These interpolations . . . are six in number, all of which,
except the last . . . , appear in the extracts interlined. This fact,
of course, taken by itself, might be used as evidence that Mr.
Collier found them in the original Diary already, and copied
them just as they stood. A curious circumstance, however,
shows that they were not written at the same time as the rest
of the contents of the several pages in which they occur, for in
all cases in which the interlined words are in ink there is a "set
off" on the opposite page from these words, and from these
only. . . . I have no doubt that Mr. Collier's method of pro-
cedure was this: having made his extracts, he first interlined
the spurious words in his copy, and then turned to the original Diary and inserted them there: after which he turned over
the leaf in his copy without troubling to assure himself that
the ink had completely dried in the interval. . . . But there is
even stronger evidence against Mr. Collier, for there are in his
extracts interlined words which are not to be found in the
original Diary at all. On page 175 of the Catalogue you will
find a reference to the forgery "saw Romeo," which in the
original has been partially erased as a failure. In the extracts
[i.e., Collier's transcript] (p. 15) the forgery appeared in the
extended form, "and saw Romeo and Juliett," written in pencil. These words have been rubbed out (after the attempt to
transfer them to the Diary was given up), but the impression
made by the pencil can still be seen and read without difficulty.[22]

Collier did not publish any of these interpolations, but he did not
always use his fabrications. They thus became all the more dangerous. Published, they could be identified and dismissed. Left in
manuscript they are like unexploded bombs waiting for some unwary investigator.

In 1841 George Whittaker asked Collier to prepare a new
edition of Shakespeare, and Collier published a pamphlet explain-

---

22   Quoted in Ganzel, 397–398. Ganzel unconvincingly dissents from Warner's
conclusions.

ing the need for such an enterprise (*Reasons for a New Edition of Shakespeare's Works*). Among his arguments was a happy discovery at Bridgewater House of an annotated First Folio (1623) that had belonged to the first Lord Ellesmere. Collier claimed that these manuscript emendations dated from the reign of Charles I. There were only thirty-two, all of them in the comedies; seven were corrections that had appeared in the Second Folio (1632). Another ten had been suggested by 18th-century editors, an odd coincidence for a text supposedly emended before 1650. Curiously, too, at least four of the corrections had been made in pencil, then in ink on top of the other writing. This First Folio probably had belonged to the Egertons since its publication, yet no one in the previous two hundred years had commented on the presence of annotations.

Collier's edition appeared in eight volumes between 1842 and 1844 and earned him five hundred guineas,[23] about twice his annual salary at the *Morning Chronicle*.[24] It included a biography of the playwright that offered new legitimate information. Robert Lemon, Sr. in the State Paper Office had shown Collier a 1592 document naming John Shakespeare, the playwright's father, as one of those not attending Anglican services either because he was Catholic or because he feared being served a writ for debt. Collier had discovered that Robert Arden, Shakespeare's maternal grandfather, had eight daughters. He found evidence of John Shakespeare's illiteracy and of his sale of some of his wife's property at Snitterfield for £4 in 1579; the low sum suggests that he desperately needed money. An inventory of 4 February 1598 shows Shakespeare with eighty bushels of grain in his Stratford house in Chapel Street; only two others in that ward held more, indicating that he was prospering and was enhancing his theatrical income with other dealings. In his biography, Collier included notes by Thomas Greene, town clerk of Stratford, listing Shakespeare's property holdings in Old Stratford and in Welcombe in 1614. As Samuel Schoenbaum observed, "Had Collier satisfied himself with these valid contribu-

---

23   A guinea contained 21 shillings, a pound 20 shillings.
24   In 1836 Collier had become a sub-editor at the newspaper at a salary of £450, but three years later he was demoted to reporter at £260 a year.

tions to knowledge, his place would have been secure in the great tradition of English literary scholarship."[25]

But Collier could not so satisfy himself. He peppered his account with his earlier forgeries, and he added new ones. Here was a ballad recounting Christopher Marlowe's literally breaking his leg while performing at the Curtain, a London theater. Collier also manufactured a document showing that Shakespeare was living in Southwark in 1596.

Collier's edition itself was excellent for its day because he emended conservatively. As he wrote to Henry Crabb Robinson on 6 June 1842, "My endeavour has been . . . to take as little as I can to or upon myself."[26] Like every other 19th-century editor of Shakespeare, he had no idea of a copy-text, of choosing one version of each play as the most reliable and making a change only when such alteration is absolutely necessary to make sense of a passage. His was an eclectic text, taking readings from whichever version seemed best at a particular moment and even substituting his own conjectures upon occasion. Still, he regarded the First Folio, the first collection of Shakespeare's plays, as reliable and authoritative, and he was among the first to appreciate the importance of the early quarto editions of the individual plays. In the 18th century Alexander Pope had emended Shakespeare based on taste, and his successor, Lewis Theobald, had emended based on sense. Both had taken liberties by relying on their own views of those criteria. The Reverend Joseph Hunter, Collier's contemporary, took a similarly cavalier attitude towards the text: "The first and most important duty of an editor is to take care that there is not palmed upon us something as Shakespeare's which he would have disdained to write, or something which, though not absolutely unintelligible and bad, is yet not so good as that which he had actually written. An editor ought to regard himself as the protector of our poetical inheritance."[27] Clement Mansfield Ingleby similarly maintained that

---

25 *Shakespeare's Lives*, 215.
26 In Ganzel, 90.
27 *New Illustrations of the Life, Studies, and Writings of Shakespeare. Supplementary to All the Editions* (London: J.B. Nichols and Son, 1845), v.

we possess no authoritative text at all; and, of course, the door is open to legitimate conjecture as to the readings to be adopted, wherever the defective state of the text of the quartos or first folio renders emendation expedient. Let it be understood that a text shall be held to be defective, so long as the sense, if any, which it conveys is not such as it is probable a man like Shakspere would have put into the mouth of the speaker on the particular occasion in question. . . . It will thus be evident to my readers that a very wide latitude is allowed to conjecture.[28]

Collier, on the other hand, argued that the editor should not seek to improve Shakespeare, and his edition was the better for his restraint.

In addition to his continuing work for the *Morning Chronicle* and his edition of Shakespeare, Collier published a total of forty titles between 1840 and 1850. Ten of these were for the Percy Society, and he prepared twice that number for the Shakespeare Society. For the latter in 1843 he edited *A Collection of Original Documents Illustrative of the Life and Times of Edward Alleyn, and of the Early English Stage and Drama* from the papers at Dulwich, and two years later the Shakespeare Society published another important document from the Alleyn collection, *The Diary of Philip Henslowe*. When Walter Wilson Greg edited the diary in 1904, he found sixteen additions in Collier's hand. Some of these Collier had discussed in his *History of English Dramatic Poetry;* others he presented for the first time now. None dealt directly with Shakespeare, but all introduced new information about the Elizabethan stage. One entry showed that on 14 May 1597 Thomas Nashe was working on *The Isle of Dogs*. On 14 January 1602 Henslowe paid forty shillings to Henry Chettle and Thomas Heywood for a play entitled *Like Quits Like*. Collier commented, "It is just possible that this may have been a play on the same story as Measure for Measure, near the end of which this line occurs: *'Like doth quit like,* and Measure still for Measure.' The success of

---

28   *A Complete View of the Shakspere Controversy* (London: Nattali and Bond, 1861), 19–20.

Measure for Measure at this date might have produced the rival play" (230). Henslowe had left the name of the play blank, and Malone's transcription confirms the gap. Finding the space, Collier inserted his invented title and stated that Henslowe had later "clumsily filled in" the space. Collier similarly supplied the title for another play for which Chettle was paid on 7 and 9 September 1602, *Robin Goodfellowe*. Collier even had the audacity to comment that "Malone takes no notice of these remarkable entries" (239).

Collier not only added information but also made at least two erasures. One was a minor alteration of "10 day" to "1 day" regarding *A Knack to Know a Knave*, an inexplicable emendation. The other is, however, significant. Henslowe listed *"Joronymo"* as a new play on 7 January 1597. Collier believed this a revival of Thomas Kyd's *Spanish Tragedy* and so removed the "ne," i. e., new, that Henslowe had written at the beginning of the entry.

In 1847 Collier finally was freed from journalism. Francis Egerton, Earl of Ellesmere, was named chairman of a royal commission created to examine the British Museum, and Egerton named Collier as his secretary at a salary of £300 a year. Collier hoped that the commission would recommend the creation of a Keeper of English Books, a post ideal for him and one that would insure his financial future. Unhappily, Collier clashed with Antonio Panizzi, then Keeper of Printed Books and later to become head of the British Museum, over the question of cataloguing. Collier favored a new printed finding list with limited bibliographical information to replace the previous edition that had appeared nearly forty years earlier (1819). Panizzi wanted to continue working on a more detailed manuscript catalogue. Panizzi won the argument; no new printed finding list was undertaken until 1881. The conflict eliminated any chance of Collier's receiving a Museum post.

In the late 1840's Collier continued to produce valuable but sometimes tainted publications. In 1848 and 1849 he edited the Registers of the Stationers' Company from 1557, when the Stationers' Company was created, to 1587. Between 1861 and 1863 in *Notes and Queries* he published further extracts for the period 1588–1595. The registers record the granting of the privilege to print a particular title and so provide important information about the literary history of the period. Among the titles mentioned were ballads, Collier's particular weakness, and in the two volumes of extracts that he prepared, he inserted thirty-four of his own composition but claimed them as antique. Collier had secured a commonplace book once the property of Joseph Hall. Many of the pages were blank, and these Collier filled with eighty-three ballads. Thirteen were authentic, the rest written by Collier. He probably wrote these as he was working on his extracts; finding titles for which no ballads were extant, he supplied the deficiency and then printed them as his own discoveries. Contrary to his usual deprecating comments about his creations, he praised several of these ballads. He observed that "They will be found to add materially to the attractiveness of the volume, and by their poetry, humour, and spirit, to relieve the dryness of the details which elsewhere it has been necessary to enter" (I, vii–viii). "Beauties fforte" he said "has considerable merit [and] must have been written by no inferior hand." "Life and death" he called "a remarkable and striking relic of the time," and "The Kinges hunt is vpp" he termed "an extremely sprightly performance."[29] The results were good enough to fool later scholars. William Chappell included seven of Collier's ballads in *Popular Music of the Olden Times* (London, 1859), and Norman Ault reprinted three of Collier's poems in *Elizabethan Lyrics* (1949).

Collier had free range of the *Stationers' Registers,* and he used this access to add and change information. In the 1780's William Herbert had made a transcript of the documents, giving evidence against Collier's later fabrications, but when Edward Arber reprinted the Registers (1875–1895), he accepted Collier's forgeries as authentic. Franklin Dickey, in "The Old Man at Work: Forgeries in the *Stationers' Registers,*" *Shakespeare Quarterly* 11 (Winter 1960): 39-47, lists nineteen of these Collier emendations. Collier ascribed the anonymous *An Epitaph on the Lady Anne Lodge* (23 December 1579) to "T. Lodge," who, Collier suggested, might have been related to Sir Thomas Lodge, Lord Mayor of London in 1563.

---

29   In Dawson, 17.

Between the title *A Ballad Entitled Youth Seeing All His Ways So Troublesome . . . Recalleth His Former Follies* and the record of payment, Collier squeezed in "By Greene" and argued that Robert Greene was the author, though he concluded by saying that some other Greene might have been intended. Collier criticized his predecessors for failing to note that John Lyly wrote *Sappho,* since the name clearly appears in the margin, "Though in a hand different from the body of the memorandum," Collier conceded. Collier chided Herbert for misreading the name of the author of *The Praise of Nothing* (27 June 1584). Herbert had recorded "by Edward Da.," probably Edward Daunce. Collier erased the "a" of "Da." and then argued that Dyer was the name intended. Perhaps the most striking of Collier's emendations concerns "a memoriall . . . of the life and deathe of the right honorable and renowned warrior the valient lorde Graye of Wilton deceased." Lord Grey had been the patron of Edmund Spenser, and above the entry for this work Collier wrote in "by E. Spenser" and then crossed out the words but left them legible. Collier would again refer to this entry in his 1862 edition of Spenser.

With no prospect of employment at the British Museum, Collier in March of 1850 retired to Holyport, near Maidenhead, about thirty miles from London. Raising a family of six children and supporting his bibliophilia had left him little money, so that he was compelled to move in with his sister Mary and her husband Robert Proctor. His income was limited to a hundred pound annuity from the Duke of Devonshire, supplemented later that year by another £100 pension that Lord Ellesmere, at Collier's request, secured for him from the British government for his services to literature. Collier's wife also had a small income from family property, but Collier's circumstances were nonetheless straitened.

In an attempt to revive the dying Shakespeare Society, Collier undertook to complete Barron Field's edition of Thomas Heywood (1850–1851) and then prepared an edition of Anthony Munday's *John a Kent and John a Cumber* from a manuscript that Frederic Madden of the British Library had discovered among the family papers of Edward Lloyd-Mostyn. The Munday play was published in 1851. These efforts did not save the Society, which dissolved in 1853.

A little less than two years after retiring to Holyport, Collier announced the discovery of a book that would at first make his fortune and then disgrace him in men's eyes by revealing him as a life-long fabricator of literary evidence. This annotated copy of Shakespeare's Second Folio (1632) would become, in Dewey Ganzel's words, "the most notorious book in Shakespeare criticism and Collier the centre of the most shocking literary scandal of the century."[30]

On 31 January 1852 *The Athenaeum* (#1266) included the following communication by Collier, dated 17 January 1852 from Maidenhead:

> A short time before the death of the late Mr. [Thomas] Rodd of [9 Great] Newport Street, I happened to be in his shop when a considerable parcel of books arrived from the country. He told me that they had been bought for him at an auction,—I think, in Bedfordshire; but I did not look on it as a matter of any importance to observe from whence they came. He unpacked them in my presence; and I cast my eyes on several that did not appear to me very inviting,—as they were entirely out of my line of reading. There were two, however, that attracted my attention:—one being a fine copy of [John] Florio's Italian Dictionary, of the edition of 1611,—and the other a much-thumbed, abused, and imperfect copy of the second folio of Shakespeare of 1632. The first I did not possess,—and the last I was willing to buy, inasmuch as I apprehended it would add some missing leaves to a copy of the same impression which I had had for some time on my shelves. As was his usual course, Mr. Rodd required a very reasonable price for both:—for the first, I remember, I gave 12s.,—and for the last, only 1l. 10s. (142)

The book lacked the title page and the last four leaves. On the front cover of the Shakespeare was written "Tho. Perkins, his Booke"; the volume therefore became known as the Perkins Folio.

Collier went on to say that once he took it home, he found that it did not contain the pages that he needed to perfect his other

---

30   Ganzel, 5.

Second Folio, so he put it on a shelf and did not look at it again until he was preparing to move from London to Maidenhead and selecting which books to take with him.

> Then it was that I for the first time remarked that the folio of 1632 which I had bought from Mr. Rodd contained manuscript alterations of the text as it stood printed in that early edition. These alterations were in an old handwriting—probably not of a later date than the Protectorate,—and applied (as I afterwards found on going through the volume here [i.e., at Maidenhead]) to every play. There was hardly a page without emendations of more or less importance and interest,—and some of them appeared to me highly valuable. The punctuation, on which of course so much of the author's meaning depends, was corrected in, I may say, thousands of places.

Collier argued that these corrections were based in part on better manuscripts than were available to the printers, in part on 17th-century performances, and he cited some of the emendations in this and subsequent articles (7 February and 27 March).

This account is difficult to credit. If Collier wanted this Second Folio to perfect another, would he not have made certain that it would answer that purpose? Since it lacked a title page, how could he be certain without some examination that it was a Second Folio? Would Rodd sell a book without looking through it? And if either Rodd or Collier gave the contents even a cursory glance, how could the notes, which number more than 20,000 and which appear on every page, have escaped detection?

Collier's discovery was convenient. He had wanted to produce a new edition of Shakespeare, a profitable enterprise, but his previous edition had not yet sold out and Whittaker and Company was therefore reluctant to undertake another. Moreover, Henry Norman Hudson, Charles Knight, James Orchard Halliwell, Samuel W. Singer, Alexander Dyce, Richard Grant White, and Howard Staunton were all planning to publish Shakespeare editions of their own, potentially saturating the market. The Perkins Folio threatened their plans and offered an excellent argument for a new Collier edition, just as the much more lightly annotated Bridgewater First Folio had supported his argument for his earlier one.

On Tuesday, 10 February 1852, Collier showed his Folio to the Shakespeare Society, and he exhibited it three times to the Society of Antiquaries. He lent it to Lord Ellesmere, and for a week he left it with his publisher, Whittaker and Company, to stimulate their interest in a new edition of Shakespeare. In this last effort he succeeded beyond his hopes. In January 1853 the firm brought out *Notes and Emendations to the Text of Shakespeare's Plays from Early Manuscript Corrections in a Copy of the Folio, 1632 in the Possession of J. Payne Collier, Esq. F.S.A.* Collier received £120 for the first edition, and another £100 for the second edition that followed in June. In 1853 Whittaker brought out a one-volume Shakespeare, priced at a guinea, without notes but containing the text as corrected by the Perkins Folio; and in 1858 Collier's annotated six-volume edition appeared. To quote Ganzel again, "It was one of the most remarkable publishing coups of the nineteenth century."[31] In December 1853 Collier was able to move into his own house, Riverside, at Maidenhead, and he became something of a celebrity, a role that Henry Crabb Robinson noted that the scholar enjoyed. In his diary for 14 August 1856 Robinson wrote that Collier was receiving "attention, as a man of letters, which he had not when he was the inmate of Robert Proctor. This flatters him as it ought, for he feels he is justly appreciated. He perhaps was never so happy as now."[32] As Ganzel wrote, "After years of uncertain position, he was at last eminent and financially secure."[33]

Those whose editions of Shakespeare were threatened by Collier's discovery fought back. Doubts about Collier's reliability had surfaced as early as 1841. In that year John Wilson Croker had written to Charles Knight about the 1608 Southampton letter that Collier had included in *New Facts* in 1835. "If that letter be genuine," Croker stated, "I must plead guilty to a great want of critical sagacity, for somehow it smacks to me of modern invention, and all my reconsideration of the subject, and some other circumstances which have since struck me, corroborate my doubts. Mr.

---

31   Ganzel, 5.
32   *Henry Crabb Robinson on Books and Their Writers,* 3 vols., ed. Edith J. Morley, (London: Dent, 1938), II, 761.
33   Ganzel, 173.

Collier is, of course, above all suspicion of having any hand in a fabrication."[34] Knight re-examined the letter and found reason to suspect it, but he hesitantly concluded that it was genuine. He used the letter in his 1843 *William Shakspere,* though he would change his mind and omit the document from later editions.

Four years later the Reverend Joseph Hunter, Assistant Keeper of the Public Records, again raised questions about the letter in *New Illustrations of the Life, Studies, and Writings of Shakespeare* (1845). He also questioned the 1589 list of Blackfriars shareholders and the 1608 document detailing the value of Shakespeare's shares in the Blackfriars Theatre. Like Croker, Hunter did not suspect Collier of manufacturing the evidence, only of using poor judgment in accepting the documents as authentic. Hunter believed that the 18th-century Shakespeare scholar and prankster George Steevens had produced the documents to deceive his fellow researchers.

On 3 March 1846 Hunter examined the papers at Bridgewater House, where he found several items in a suspiciously similar handwriting on paper more like that used for books than for correspondence. Blank end-papers from books two hundred years old were available; writing paper of that age would be impossible to find. James Orchard Halliwell also examined the papers, and in 1853 he published a limited edition of *Observations on the Shaksperian Forgeries at Bridgewater House.* Halliwell again accused Collier of nothing more than being misled.

The Perkins Folio prompted sharper attacks. Charles Knight weighed in with *Old Lamps, or New? A Plea for the Original Editions of the Text of Shakspere* (April 1853). Knight's collection of Shakespeare's works, the *Stratford Shakspere,* did not sell well. Samuel Weller Singer, whose edition of Shakespeare was delayed two years because of the bankruptcy and death of his publisher William Pickering, wrote *The Text of Shakespeare Vindicated from the Interpolations and Corruptions Advocated by John Payne Collier, Esq. in His "Notes and Emendations"* (May 1853). Alexander Dyce joined the fray with *A Few Notes on Shakespeare,* and James Orchard Halliwell, who did not get as many subscribers as he had

---

34   In Schoenbaum, 256.

hoped for his *Folio Shakespeare,* attacked the Perkins Folio in the first volume of that edition (May 1853) and followed up his criticism with three privately printed pamphlets, including *Observations on Some of the Manuscript Emendations of the Text of Shakespeare* and the previously cited *Observations on the Shaksperian Forgeries.* In *Curiosities of Modern Shaksperian Criticism* Halliwell raised questions about the letter from Alleyn's wife mentioning Shakespeare and about some of the ballads Collier had published in *Memoirs of Edward Alleyn and in Extracts from the Registers of the Stationers' Company.* Yet even Collier's attackers could not resist the appeal of a Folio supposedly annotated only decades after Shakespeare's death. Singer, Dyce, Richard Grant White and Howard Staunton all used some of these emendations.[35] In Berlin Tycho Mommsen and in Moscow Nikolai Khristoforovich Ketcher relied on the Perkins Folio in preparing new editions of Shakespeare in German (1854) and Russian (1862–1879).

Though all of Collier's competitors criticized his work, none accused him of bad faith until Andrew Edmund Brae's pseudonymous *Literary Cookery with Reference to Matter Attributed to Coleridge and Shakespeare* (1855) by "A Detective." Brae's primary target was Collier's publication in *Notes and Queries,* volume 10 (1, 8, 22 July and 5 and 12 August 1854) of excerpts from Coleridge's 1811–1812 lectures, based on the shorthand notes Collier had taken. Brae went on to argue that the emendations in the Perkins Folio were Collier's.

Collier replied by suing the publisher, John Russell Smith, for libel, and Smith withdrew the pamphlet after only fifteen copies had been sold. The court therefore refused to rule in the suit, but the presiding judge, Collier's friend Lord John Campbell, declared that Collier was "a most honorable" man.[36] In his affidavit dated 8 January 1856, Collier testified that every correction he had published in the two editions of *Notes and Emendations* was

---

35   Singer owned two annotated Folios of his own, a Second and a Third, though he questioned the authority of both their texts and annotations.

36   In Schoenbaum, 260. One wonders whether Campbell, or Collier, detected the echo of Marc Antony's speech about Caesar's assassins, whom Antony calls "honorable men."

to the best of my knowledge and belief, a true and accurate copy of the original manuscript in the said folio copy of 1632; and that I have not, in either of the said editions, to the best of my knowledge and belief, inserted a single word, stop, sign, note, correction, alteration, or emendation of the said original text of Shakespeare, which is not a faithful copy of the said original manuscript, and which I do not believe to have been written, as aforesaid, not long after the publication of the said folio copy of the year 1632.[37]

Collier's claim had seemed to receive unsolicited support in 1853. As the frontispiece to *Notes and Emendations* Collier used a facsimile of a page of the Perkins Folio. In April 1853 John Carrick Moore wrote to Collier that a Francis Charles Parry had seen the facsimile and had remarked that he had owned that very book with all its emendations, having been given the volume around 1806, though he had since lost it. Moore had urged Parry to write Collier, but Parry declined. Collier therefore called on him, without bringing the Perkins Folio, and he paid a second visit, again without the Folio, to secure approval for an article, published in *The Athenaeum* of 4 June 1853, containing Parry's statement of his former ownership of the annotated book.

Doubts nonetheless persisted. The first edition of *Notes and Emendations* included 1,100 corrections. The second edition had added another hundred. In 1856 Collier, defying Brae, published seven of Coleridge's lectures in book form,[38] and he included a 120-page "List of Every Manuscript Note and Emendation in Mr. Collier's Copy of Shakespeare's Works, Folio, 1632," though in the preface he acknowledged that he was citing only the significant changes. This incremental augmentation of emendations seemed

---

37   Quoted in Clement Mansfield Ingleby, *A Complete View of the Shakspere Controversy* (London: Nattali and Bond, 1861), 39–40.

38   Reginald Anthony Foakes, in *Coleridge on Shakespeare: The Text of the Lectures of 1811–12* (Charlottesville: University Press of Virginia, 1971), wrote of this work, "What Collier printed in 1856 in *Seven Lectures on Shakespeare and Milton* was a radically reconstructed version of some parts of his diary and of the lectures Coleridge gave in 1811–12. He said he was adding nothing of his own, but in fact he altered both the Diary and the lecture notes freely" (26).

suspicious. Not only did the quantity of alterations seem to change; so did the content. In *Much Ado about Nothing* II, i, 244–246 Benedict complains that Beatrice was "Huddling jest upon jest with such impossible conveyance upon me that I stood like a man at a mark." *Notes and Emendations* reported that the Old Corrector, as Collier called him, had changed "impossible" to "importable." The 1856 list cited the word as "unportable," and in the 1858 edition based on the Perkins Folio the word was again "importable."

The emendations themselves appeared to derive not from better manuscripts or early performances but rather from 18th- and even 19th-century editors, a curious phenomenon if the handwriting dated from the 1650's. Fourteen of the Old Corrector's changes were identical to those found in the Bridgewater First Folio, and the handwriting was also oddly similar. At least sixty of the Old Corrector's emendations confirmed those Collier had made in his earlier edition, even changes that were not necessary to make sense of a passage. Macbeth asks his physician whether he can "Cleanse the stuff'd bosom of that perilous stuff / Which weighs upon the heart" (*Macbeth,* V, iii, 44-45). Critics who found the repetition of "stuff'd . . . stuff" infelicitous generally altered the adjective, but in 1844 Collier altered the second "stuff" to "grief." Two hundred years earlier, the Old Corrector had done the same. In *Romeo and Juliet,* II, ii, 31, Romeo speaks of the "lazy puffing clouds." Collier preferred "lazy-passing," and so did the Old Corrector. On 17 April 1852 William Nanson Lettsom reported in *The Athenaeum* that William Sidney Walker had proposed an emendation for the inscrutable phrase "Her insuite comming" in *All's Well That Ends Well,* V, iii, 216. Walker suggested "Her infinite cunning," a proposal adopted by the authoritative Riverside Shakespeare. The Old Corrector had made this change, too, but Collier had not cited it in his *Athenaeum* articles when he was trying to point out some of the highlights of the Perkins Folio. It appeared in *Notes and Emendations,* where Collier noted that he had seen the Walker correction.

Walker also proposed an alteration in the line "To be of worth, and worthy estimation" (*Two Gentlemen of Verona,* II, iv, 56). Troubled by the repetition of "worth," he emended the first

"worth" to "wealth." The Perkins Folio includes this change, and
Collier stated that Walker had endorsed this revision. Walker died
in 1846, before Collier supposedly had acquired the Perkins Folio,
and in 1874 Collier charged Walker with stealing some of the Old
Corrector's best suggestions. Was Collier trying to take credit for
others' ideas? Did he have the Perkins Folio longer than he
claimed?

In June 1853 Collier had given the Perkins Folio to the 6th
Duke of Devonshire, a generous gesture towards his long-time
patron. As the duke's quasi-librarian, Collier may have had some
control over access to the book, and some claimed that they had
not been allowed to see it. Sequestered in the duke's Derbyshire
estate of Chatsworth, the volume was removed from prying eyes.
On 17 January 1858 the duke died and was succeeded by his
cousin, also named William Cavendish, who continued his prede-
cessor's largess towards Collier. In May 1859 Sir Frederic Madden,
Keeper of Manuscripts at the British Museum, wrote to the new
duke, asking to inspect the Perkins Folio. On 26 May the volume
arrived at the British Museum, and that night Madden recorded in
his diary, "The manuscript corrections do not satisfy me, and I
observed that the forms of the letters differ very much from each
other, and yet evidently all proceed from the same pen. . . . I cannot believe it to be a genuine hand of the 17th century. . . . Collier
is certainly mistaken in supposing the writing to be nearly as early
as the date of the volume (1632)."[39]

The handwriting became curiouser and curiouser. On 17
June Madden wrote in his diary,

> I noticed today for the first time a great number of pencil
> marks in the margins of the Shakespeare, and in some
> instances, I think I can perceive traces of pencil under the ink,
> which, in that case, must have been subsequently written. The
> importance of this discovery is such that I shall subject the

---

39   In Ganzel, 221–222.

volume to a very searching examination leaf by leaf, to satisfy myself on the subject.[40]

Two days later Madden's suspicions were confirmed:

to my very great surprise I ascertained beyond doubt that a perfectly modern hand has made many hundreds, perhaps thousands of corrections in pencil in the margin, partly for the correction of the punctuation, partly for new readings, and partly to draw attention to passages to be altered. These corrections are most certainly in a modern hand, and from the extraordinary resemblance of the writing to Mr. Collier's own hand (which I am well acquainted with) I am really fearful that we must come to the astounding conclusion that Mr. C. is himself the fabricator of the notes![41]

Madden asked Nevil Story Maskelyne, Keeper of the Mineral Department of the British Museum, to examine the book under a microscope and to analyze the ink. Maskelyne reported that the penciling definitely underlay the ink, and that the ink itself looked odd. In the *Times* for 16 July 1859 he reported that the ink resembled "water-colour paint rather than an ink; it has a remarkable lustre, and the distribution of particles of colouring matter in it seem [sic] unlike that in inks, ancient or modern, that I have yet examined." He even tasted the ink and thought that aspect unusual, too.

Securing permission from the Duke of Devonshire to conduct further experiments, Maskelyne noted that the ink

proves to be a paint removable, with the exception of a slight stain, by mere water, while, on the other hand, its colouring matter resists the action of chymical agents which rapidly

---

40   Ibid., 227–228.
41   Ibid., 228. Both Ganzel and Anthony Grafton, *Forgers and Critics: Creativity and Deception in Western Scholarship* (Princeton: Princeton University Press, 1990), p. 40, argue that Madden forged the pencil marks. This view is not widely held, and it does not explain how pencil marks also appear in the Bridgewater Folio. Occam's razor cuts through this attempted defense of Collier.

change inks, ancient or modern, whose colour is due to iron. In some places, indeed, this paint seems to have become mixed, accidentally or otherwise, with ordinary ink, but its prevailing character is that of a paint formed perhaps of sepia, or of sepia mixed with a little India ink.

Using electron microprobe analysis, David C. Jenkins found that the ink in the Perkins Folio does indeed contain iron, but not as much as might be expected. Jenkins thought that his studies neither vindicated nor condemned Collier.[42] Collier owned formulas for ink and could easily have created a product that would mimic older substances. Moreover, as Maskelyne himself stated, enough other evidence challenged the supposed age of the emendations.

But what about Parry's statement that he had owned the Perkins Folio fifty years earlier and it had then contained many annotations? On 13 July 1859 Parry, then aged seventy-eight, went to the British Museum, where he looked at the Perkins Folio and denied ever having seen it before. Collier had never claimed that he had shown the book to Parry in either of his two visits, but now on 20 July 1859 Collier in the *Times* mentioned a third trip to see Parry. This time he had the Perkins Folio with him. He had met Parry in the road, and, after a cursory survey, Parry had identified the book as the one he had formerly possessed. On 1 August 1859 the *Times* published Parry's reply. He recalled the meeting with Collier in the road and some of their conversation, "but I have not the slightest recollection that the volume of *Shakespeare* was under his arm, or of my having asserted that 'it was my book.' "He concluded, however, "I may be wrong, and Mr. Collier may be right" about events six years earlier.

On 13 August 1859 the Reverend Dr. Henry Wellesley, Principal of New Inn Hall, Oxford, wrote to Collier that he recalled the annotated Folio:

---

42 "The Search for the J. P. Collier Ink Syndrome," *Literary Research* 13 (Spring/Summer 1988): 95–122.

Sir,—Although I do not recollect the precise date, I remember some years ago being in the shop of Thomas Rodd, on one occasion when a case of books from the country had just been opened. One of those books was an imperfect folio Shakespeare with an abundance of manuscript notes in the margin. He observed to me that it was of little value to collectors as a copy, and that the price was thirty shillings. I should have taken it myself, but, as he stated that he had put it by for another customer, I did not continue to examine it, nor did I think any more about it, until I heard afterwards that it had been found to possess great literary curiosity and value.[43]

Wellesley's letter would have been more exculpatory had Collier not claimed in 1852 and 1853 that he had taken the volume home with him, and in *Mr. J. Payne Collier's Reply to Mr. N. E. S. A. Hamilton's "Inquiry" into the Imputed Shakespeare Forgeries* that was published on 16 March 1860 he noted that he usually did not leave books with Rodd to be delivered. In *The Athenaeum* for 18 February 1860 Collier sought to reconcile these varying accounts by saying that he bought the book but did not pick it up until later in the day. Madden invited Wellesley to examine the Perkins Folio in London, which Wellesley did. Wellesley then wrote to Madden that this was the same book he had seen in Rodd's shop.

Or was it? On 1 January 1847 Rodd had advertised a Second Folio lacking a title page and four leaves at the end, in soiled condition. This volume has the same defects as the Perkins Folio, but the catalogue entry made no mention of notes in the margins. Clement Mansfield Ingleby advertised for the owner of that book, and William Warner came forward to say that in 1846 he had sold that copy to Rodd, who had been interested in it for its hand-written annotations, which he knew would appeal to a particular customer. Warner even recalled that the name Perkins had been writ-

---

43   Quoted in Herman Merivale, "Art. VII.," *Edinburgh Review 111* (April 1860): 233–251, 245.

ten on the title page or fly leaf. Was this the Perkins Folio? Warner might have erred about the placement of the name, but if Collier had bought the book as soon as it had come from the country, it never would have appeared in a catalogue.

On 7 July 1859 the *Times* published a letter from Collier in which he declared that he would not argue in print the authenticity of the Perkins Folio. In fact he defended himself again in the *Times* for 20 July, in *The Athenaeum* for 18 February 1860, and in his *Reply* the following month. His opponents, however, were more convincing. Nicholas E. S. A. Hamilton, Assistant Keeper of Manuscripts at the British Museum, produced a devastating indictment not only of the Perkins Folio but of a series of forgeries going back to Collier's *History of English Dramatic Poetry*,[44] and Ingleby detailed the case against Collier's Folio in *A Complete View of the Shakspere Controversy* (London: Nattali and Bond, 1861). In 1985 John W. Velz reported that a substantial number of the Perkins Folio emendations match those made in the 18th century by Styan Thirlby in his copies of Lewis Theobald's and William Warburton's editions of Shakespeare. These sets had passed into the hands of Richard Heber, part of whose library Collier had catalogued in the early 1830s when he was perhaps already thinking about editing Shakespeare.[45]

A less resolute man might have been deterred by detection, but Collier continued, in the words of Joseph Crosby, to be "lucky at finding."[46] In his 1860 *Reply to Mr. N. E. S. A. Hamilton's "Inquiry" into the Imputed Shakespeare Forgeries,* composed while he was working on an edition of Edmund Spenser, Collier announced that he had found a 1611 folio copy of Spenser's works that had belonged to Spenser's younger contemporary poet Michael Drayton. And yes, in red pencil Drayton had emended the text of *The Faerie Queene* in some sixty places. Collier's 1862 edition of Spenser incorporated about half of these. The rest Collier

---

44 *An Inquiry into the Genuineness of the Manuscript Corrections in Mr. J. Payne Collier's Annotated Shakspere, Folio, 1632* (London: Bentley, 1860).

45 "The Collier Controversy Redivivus," *Shakespeare Quarterly* 36 (Spring 1985): 106–115.

46 *One Touch of Shakespeare: Letters of Joseph Crosby to Joseph Parker Norris, 1875–1878,* 117.

discussed but dismissed, and they are all cited in the standard Variorum Spenser published by Johns Hopkins University Press (1932–1956).[47]

In 1862 Collier made yet another discovery as he was preparing a reprint of the unique Lambeth copy of *The Trueth of the Most Wicked and Secret Murthering of Iohn Brewen* (1592). Collier wrote in *Notes and Queries* 1, 3rd ser. (29 March 1862): 241:

> We may doubt whether this tract was ever "allowed to be printed" and the only copy we have seen of it was that actually sent to the pubic authorities for approbation. It is a great curiosity in another respect, because on the title-page is written the name of the publisher John Kyd (so spelt) [actually "Iho Kyde"] and at the end of it the name of Thomas Kydde (so spelt) [in fact "Tho. Kydde"] the author—Thomas Kydde being no other than the distinguished dramatic poet and precursor of Shakespeare, the writer of *The Spanish Tragedy, Jeromino, Cornelia,* and other theatrical productions. It is by inference that we suppose him to have been the author of the remarkable production under consideration. And that the publisher of it was his brother, or some near relation.

In his 1863 reprint of the work Collier stated that the signature was not Kyd's but a licenser's. Since no Kyd signatures were known in 1863, Collier had no way to be certain whose the writing was. However, he was clever enough to recognize that a Kyd signature might surface, as it has since. The writing looks nothing like Kyd's, much like Collier's. Also curious is the fact that when Samuel Roffey Maitland catalogued the Lambeth library in 1845, he noted no name on the pamphlet.[48]

Collier's energy did not flag as he aged. Between 1862 and 1870 he edited ninety-four rare titles in nine subscription series. His nephew Frederick Ouvry, a lawyer, helped underwrite these limited editions, the subscription fees failing to cover their cost. *Broadside Black-letter Ballads, Printed in the Sixteenth and*

---

47   See Arthur Freeman's review of Ganzel's *Fortune and Men's Eyes, TLS* 22 April 1983, 392.

48   See Robert Mark Gorrell, "John Payne Collier and *The Murder of Iohn Brewen,*" *Modern Language Notes* 57 (1942): 441–444.

Seventeenth Centuries (1868) and *Twenty-five Old Ballads and Songs from Manuscripts in the Possession of John Payne Collier* (1869) gave Collier further opportunities to publish his own compositions as antique. In 1874 he privately published *Trilogy. Conversations Between Three Friends on the Emendations of Shakespeare's Text Contained in Mr Collier's Corrected Folio, 1632,* in which he defended the authenticity of the Perkins Folio. Yet when he issued a third edition of Shakespeare in forty-two fascicles (1875–1878), limited to fifty-eight copies, he silently dropped most of the textual changes he had printed in 1858. He included *Edward III,* which he had argued was by Shakespeare and had edited in 1874. The play is now regarded by many scholars as Shakespeare's and is included in the second (1998) edition of the Riverside Shakespeare. Collier's edition also contained *Two Noble Kinsmen, A Yorkshire Tragedy,* and *Mucedorus.* In 1875 he announced yet another find, a folio that had belonged to John Milton and containing no fewer than 1,500 of his annotations. In 1879 he reissued his *History of English Dramatic Poetry* with all his former fabrications included.

In the manuscript diary that Collier began in the last decade of his life, he admitted to himself that he had erred. Under the date 21 November 1877 he recorded, "It is my own fault and folly that I am not now *justly* considered the first and best emendator of Shakespeare."[49] On 14 May 1882 he was still more contrite: "I am bitterly sad and most sincerely grieved that in every way I am such a despicable offender. I am ashamed of almost every act of my life. . . . My repentance is bitter and sincere."[50] Collier died the next year, on 17 September 1883, at his home of Riverside, Maidenhead. The following August Sotheby's sold Collier's extensive library, which realized £2,105 16s.

In his review of Dewey Ganzel's book on Collier, Arthur Freeman listed Collier's virtues:

> [He] was one of the most eminent Shakespearian editors
> of the nineteenth century. . . . Perhaps if one includes the

---

49 In Ganzel, 382.
50 In Schoenbaum, 266; Ganzel, 394–395.

traditionally contiguous fields of Tudor and Stuart drama, poetry and popular literature, he was the most eminent of them all . . . As a publicist of the Shakespearian past he added formidably both to the refinement of scholarship and to the spread of its appeal, to the extent that in his mid-career even the popular press . . . covered such matters in astonishing detail. He was a minor poet . . . an untiring administrator of the antiquarian publications societies of the 1830s onward, a library adviser and agent of collectors.[51]

His legacy, however, does not lie with these achievements. Rather, as Richard D. Altick lamented in *The Scholar Adventurers* (New York: Macmillan, 1950),

In his time Collier worked through tons of manuscripts and annotated old books in the private libraries of his blue-blooded patrons, in Dulwich College, in government archives, and in the large collection which he himself amassed in the course of a long and acquisitive career. . . . No single page of this material can be free from suspicion. Even if Collier did not quote from it in his printed works, he may have tampered with it simply out of his queer urge to amplify history for his private delectation. (159)

---

51 *Times Literary Supplement,* 22 April 1983, 392.

George Gordon Byron

VI

George Gordon Byron, Forger of Romantics

𝒪n the summer of 1843, John Murray III, son of the
friend and publisher of the Romantic poet George
Gordon, Lord Byron, received a letter dated 1 July
from America. The letter read in part,

> If I omit an apology for addressing you, let me hope that a
> son of the late Lord Byron, whose esteem and friendship you
> possessed in so eminent a degree, may without apprehension
> appeal to your kindness, and succeed perhaps in conciliating
> your good graces. You will, no doubt, be startled by these
> news—but of the birth of a son to Lord Byron he, himself,
> remained ignorant till a short time before his premature death
> in Greece, and to the world at large family considerations have
> always kept this fact secret. If I disclose it now to a friend of
> the late Lord B., it is because my embarrassing circumstances
> compel me to do so.[1]

According to the author of this letter, who signed himself
Icodad Geo. G. Byron, when Lord Byron visited Spain for the first
time in 1809, the poet fell in love with a Countess de Luna and
secretly married her. From this union George Gordon Byron was
born in 1810, but his mother kept both the marriage and the child
a secret because she was too proud to pursue her errant husband.
Despite the countess' Catholicism, her son was raised as a
Protestant; he was educated in Switzerland and then in Paris. When
he was seventeen, he returned to Spain to visit his mother's grave.

---

1   Quoted in Theodore G. Ehrsam, *Major Byron: The Incredible Career of a Literary
    Forger* (New York: Charles S. Boesen; London: John Murray, 1951), p. 13.
    John Murray II died on 27 June 1843; the letter probably was intended for him.

Left only her diamonds, he began a version of Childe Harold's pil-grimage. According to a letter that Byron[2] sent on 17 June 1844 to Sir Robert Peel, who had attended Harrow with Byron's putative father, Byron visited "all the places which Lord Byron's residence had rendered sacred to me. From his tomb I wandered to Missolonghi [where the poet died in 1824]. . . . For several years I roved over the Orient; from the City of the Sultan to the Cataracts of the Nile; from Mount Ararat to the Mouth of the Ganges."[3] Byron returned to England, where, he said, he secured the rank of major of a regiment of sepoys in the East India service,[4] and he later supposedly held an official post in Persia.

In 1841 Byron came to America, where he lived in Virginia, New York City, and Cleveland before settling in Pennsylvania. Reaching the nub of his letter to Murray, Byron reported that he had bought a farm

> in the immediate neighbourhood of Wilkes Barre, in the clas-sic valley of Wyoming, . . . situated on the Susquehanna River. The farm consists of 250 acres of the richest land, is well improved—and would, in the course of 6 or 7 years pay for itself. But having paid only the first installment of the pur-chase money (3000 Dollars), and the second being due on the 15th August I am at a loss to imagine how I shall be able to make this payment[5]

unless Murray lent him the money. Byron also asked Murray for a copy of Lord Byron's autograph as a memento, a request indicat-ing that Byron was already thinking of forgery. Over the next sev-eral years he would become, according to Richard D. Altick, "the second most mischievous Victorian literary forger," surpassed only by John Payne Collier.[6]

---

2   In an effort to avoid confusion, I call the forger Byron, the poet Lord Byron. Byron also assumed the name of de Gibler and Mr. Memoir, but since he is best known as Byron, I have chosen to retain that sobriquet.
3   Quoted in Ehrsam, 10–11.
4   Byron variously styled himself major or colonel.
5   In Ehrsam, 11–12.
6   *The Scholar Adventurers* (New York: Macmillan, 1950), 161.

Murray having sent neither money nor signature, on 13 January 1844 Byron sailed for England aboard the *Susquehanna*. From London he solicited funds from Murray; from the current Lord Byron;[7] from the poet's daughter, Augusta Ada, Countess of Lovelace; Byron's friend Sir John Cam Hobhouse; and Byron's half-sister, Augusta Leigh. To Robert Peel he wrote on 17 June 1844 to introduce himself as Lord Byron's son and to ask for a loan to pay for his farm, which had migrated to "the Hudson River, near Sing Sing, 32 miles from New York." The price had risen to $12,500, which Byron hoped Peel might help him secure from a member of the poet's family or from "some capitalist."[8] That Byron was becoming known in London is evident from a letter that Elizabeth, Lady Holland, wrote to her son in 1844:

> There is a sharp man who writes to all of Lord Byron's friends, representing himself as his son, the issue of an amour Ld. B. is said to have had with a Spanish lady of rank at Cadiz. The existence of such a being was never notified to Lord Byron till shortly before his death: the letter did not reach its destination till after his death. The man begins by asking a loan of £900, & to Lord C—: upon his refusal begs for £9.[9]

These efforts to raise money proved unavailing, but *audentis fortuna iuvat* —fortune aids the daring. By chance or, more likely, by design, Byron had moved into the house where John Wright was living, or, more precisely, dying: Wright died on 25 February 1844. Wright had assisted Murray in producing *The Works of Lord Byron* (London: Murray, 1832-1836) and was working on a book about Lord Byron at the time of his death. Hence he had in his possession many of the poet's actual papers and copies of others. By purchase or gift Byron secured these papers, even though they legally belonged to Murray; these materials would soon prove useful to Byron.

---

7 George Anson Byron, the poet's first cousin.
8 In Ehrsam, 12.
9 Ibid., 18–19.

Wright also had worked for Shelley's friend, the bookseller-publisher Thomas Hookham, so Wright may have also had papers relating to this writer. From March 1817 to February 1818 the Shelleys lived at Marlow, and when they departed hurriedly, they left behind many letters. Some of these were seized and sold by Rubert Madocks, as compensation for the Shelleys' debt to him. Madocks did not immediately sell all the papers, though; as late as 1858 he still had some.[10] Byron probably visited him some time in 1844 or 1845 and secured at least sixteen letters from Shelley to his second wife Mary Godwin Shelley, four from Mary to Shelley, three by Mary Godwin Shelley's half sister Fanny Imlay to the Shelleys, one by William Godwin, the poet's father-in-law, to Shelley, and one by Pynson Wilmot Longdill, Shelley's lawyer, to Shelley.

As indicated by a letter from Mary Shelley, by 28 October 1845 Byron was negotiating with her to sell his Shelley letters.[11] At the same time, he offered to return without charge those she herself had written, assuming that these had little market value. Mary did not wish to deal directly with Byron and so asked Hookham to handle this affair. Acting for her, on 10 November 1845 Hookham paid Byron £30 for a set of letters, and she agreed to pay £1 each for any additional letters by Shelley. Byron sold her at least two further caches of correspondence before September 1846, when she learned that he was keeping copies of all these materials and was threatening to publish them. Mary secured an injunction against Byron to prevent publication, and she reported him to the Society of Guardians for the Protection of Trade Against Swindlers and Sharpers, which included his name in its circular of 6 October 1846.

---

10   See Charles S. Middleton, *Shelley and His Writings*, 2 vols. (London: T. C. Newby, 1858), I, v.

11   *The Letters of Mary Wollstonecraft Shelley*, 3 vols., ed. Betty T. Bennett (Baltimore: Johns Hopkins University Press, 1980-1988), III, 245. Mary writes to Hookham, "From what Mr. Finch said I hoped to fine [find] a line from you telling me what you thought of the man who called on you & the letters in his possession. Can they be any among those lost with other things in Paris in 1814—I should like to know what you think about the matter. He did not call today. Does he want the letters bought of him—or what?"

While dealing with Mary Shelley, Byron was pursuing his plan to publish a work about his supposed father. To this end he wrote to anyone who might have manuscript material. Typical of the letters he sent is one to George Loddy, dated 4 February 1846:

> Sir,
>
> I will not venture to offer an apology for intruding upon you—permit me to hope that the motive will serve as an excuse. Being about publishing a work relating to the late Lord Byron, I should be under great obligations to you, if you would be good enough to supply me with copies of such autograph matter as you may be possessed of. You will easily conceive how anxious I must be to obtain information that will throw additional light on the genius and character of the poet, when I tell you (*in confidence*) I am the son of Lord Byron.—I should be happy to be permitted to see your *Byronian Collection.*[12]

Loddy, like most of those receiving Byron's request, complied. On 19 March 1846 Byron wrote to thank Loddy for the copies of the letters Loddy had sent. Loddy had trouble reading a few words in one of the letters, and Byron asked whether Loddy might trace these. Instead, Loddy sent the original, which Byron copied and returned.

In June 1846 Byron wrote to Joseph Severn, artist friend of John Keats who had been with the latter when he died in Rome, asking for an autograph of the poet. Severn, as was his wont in responding to such requests, tore off part of a Keats manuscript in his possession, in this case stanzas eight and eleven of "Isabella, or The Pot of Basil,"[13] and sent the verses to Byron. Byron copied stanza eleven, omitting the original seventh line (which Keats had crossed through) and adding Keats's signature, a curious feature to appear in the middle of a poem. Believing the holograph genuine, in 1847 Captain Montagu Montagu, a collector of Keats material,

---

12 Quoted in Robert Metcalf Smith, *The Shelley Legend* (New York: Scribner's, 1945), 51.

13 Because the manuscript is written on both sides of the sheet, stanza 11 is on the verso of stanza 8.

bought this forgery at auction and later gave it to the Bodleian Library, Oxford.

Throughout 1847 Byron gathered material for his book. Early in the year he printed a prospectus that he included in his requests for manuscripts. This prospectus promised that

> In January, 1848, will be published in 3 Vols.
> Royal 8vo.
> Price Three Guineas.
> "BYRON AND THE BYRONS,"
> A Supplemental Biography of the Late
> George Gordon Noel, Lord Byron.
> with
> A History of the Byron Family From
> The Conquest Downwards,
> by
> George Byron, Esq.,

> Including between six and seven hundred unpublished letters and poems of Lord Byron, illustrated by numerous plates and woodcuts (from original drawings made on the spot), with portraits of the earlier branches of the Byrons.

> In addition to the interesting and hitherto inaccessible portion of Lord Byron's correspondence contained in these volumes, the History of the Family will be found scarcely less attractive from the number of romantic episodes with which it is interspersed. . . .

> The whole of the above matter has been derived from the most authentic sources, and under circumstances peculiarly favourable to the Editor, who has spared neither pains nor research in the execution of his task. Whatever may be its demerits of arrangement, he feels confident that the intrinsic importance of the work will render it acceptable to the public.[14]

---

14   In Ehrsam, 41–42.

On 30 March 1846 Byron claimed that he had 250 letters; by the time he issued his prospectus less than a year later he reported having between six and seven hundred, and on the eve of publication in March 1848 he raised that figure to a thousand. In *The Inedited Works of Lord Byron* (New York: Byron and Martin, 1849) Byron wrote, apparently without exaggeration,

> With the exception of one or two solitary and churlish refusals, I received nothing but courtesy in reply to my applications to those who had been in communication at any periods of their lives with the late Lord Byron. In most cases copies of letters and documents were sent to me; or, where withheld, reasons, which it became not me to question, were assigned, so courteously worded, that personally I could not but feel gratified.[15]

Among those who courteously refused to aid Byron was John Fitzgibbon, second Earl of Clare, who, like Peel, had been a schoolmate of the poet. Lord Clare alerted Augusta Leigh to the projected publication, and she, in turn, informed Murray. Perhaps one of them complained to the Society of Guardians for the Protection of Trade, which again took notice of Byron in its circular of 24 June 1847, warning its members that Byron "pretends to be a near relative of the late Lord Byron, and has been offering to different publishers, a collection of Ms. poems, Letters, &c., which he says are in the autograph of the poet. Their genuineness is, however, disputed."[16]

By January 1848 Byron had secured a publisher, W. S. Orr and Company. He hoped that Augusta might still endorse his project and therefore wrote to her for permission to claim that in preparing his work he had had "the free use of all the Poet's own manuscripts in the possession of his Sister, the Honble. Mrs. Leigh."[17] He also hoped that she would allow him to dedicate the work to her. When she did not reply, he sent her some uncorrected proofs of his book. She turned over these papers to Sir John

---

15   Ibid., p. 43.
16   Ibid., 47.
17   Ibid.

Cam Hobhouse, and he in turn consulted his lawyers, Jenkyns and Phelps. Sometime in March 1848 they wrote to Byron, "Mrs. L.[eigh] cannot but disapprove of a Publication which professes to have been compiled from the free use of MSS. to which you have never had access; and you cannot therefore be surprised at her declining the Honor of having it dedicated to herself."[18]

Undeterred, Byron moved ahead with his planned book. *Douglas Jerrold's Weekly Newspaper* for 11 March 1848 carried an advertisement stating,

> The valuable unpublished materials which the editor has been enabled to amass, in tracking the footsteps of Lord Byron, through all his pilgrimages, consist of about one thousand letters; *The Ravenna Journal* of the year 1821-2 enriched with copious notes by the late Sir W.[alter] Scott; numerous unpublished poems including the suppressed portions of his printed works; and a mass of Anecdotes and Reminiscences of Lord Byron by the Countess [Teresa] Guiccioli, Mrs. P. B. Shelley and Miss Bristowe; by Archdeacon Spencer, Sir Humphrey Davy, Messrs. Horace Smith, John Taylor, Trelawny, Gordon, Captain Boldero, and others. To these he is kindly permitted to add numerous letters addressed to Lord Byron by his most familiar friends, and the free use of all the Poet's own manuscripts, in the possession of his sister, the Honble. Mrs. Leigh.

The *Athenaeum* for 18 March promised that Part I of *The Inedited Works of Lord Byron* would appear at the end of the month, but in the following issue W. S. Orr and Company announced that it was withdrawing from the project.[19] Whatever materials it had relating to Byron's book it returned to John Murray. This same issue of the *Athenaeum* declared,

> [W]e have full authority for stating that the Hon. Mrs. Leigh has never permitted this "George Gordon Byron, Esq." who calls himself the son of her illustrious brother, even to see,

18 Ibid., 48.
19 *Athenaeum* 1065 (25 March 1848): 305.

much less to make "free use of all the poet's own manuscripts" in her possession,—and that her solicitor has written
to him, stating rather disagreeable views of theirs on the
subject.[20]

The *Athenaeum* for 1 April published a letter from Jenkyns
and Phelps, dated 24 March 1848, denying that Byron was the
poet's son or that he had had "any access whatever to any MS in
the possession of . . . Mrs. Leigh," nor had any other members of
Lord Byron's family assisted in his research.[21]

Unable to publish, Byron sought to profit from his research
in another way. In the summer of 1848 a young woman
approached the publisher William White, offering him two unpublished letters by Lord Byron. Although White had never bought a
manuscript for himself before, he did so now. The woman soon
returned with two more letters apparently in Lord Byron's hand,
thus arousing White's curiosity. To his question as to how she had
secured these letters she replied that they belonged to

> her elder sister, who resided at St. John's Wood—that they
> had been left her by their father, a deceased surgeon, who had
> been an autograph collector, especially of the MSS. of these
> poets—having made a point of laying his hands upon all he
> could, of their unpublished productions. She also said that he
> knew [William] Fletcher, Byron's valet,—had attended him
> professionally, on his deathbed—and that Fletcher had given
> him some books, which Lord Byron, when he died in Greece,
> had left to him.[22]

She informed White that her sister was selling the letters only
because their agent had absconded with some funds that they
needed to live, but the sister, who, being an invalid, could not
come to White herself, was disposing of the letters most reluctant-

---

20 Ibid., 318.
21 *Athenaeum* 1066 (1 April 1848): 341.
22 William White, *The Calumnies of the "Athenaeum" Journal Exposed. Mr. White's
    Letter to Mr. Murray, on the Subject of the Byron, Shelley, and Keats MSS.*
    (London: William White, 1852), 6.

ly. Hence, she was selling only a few at a time, hoping that more money would arrive before she had parted with them all. Also, she thought that she could receive more by selling individual letters. than by selling everything in one lot. The woman was indeed representing someone else, but this person was not her sister. Rather, she was acting for her husband, George Gordon Byron, and she was selling as originals copies he had made of the poet's letters.

That White was not the only victim of Byron's forgeries is evident from the Charles Hodges sale that began at the rooms of Puttick and Simpson's on 16 December 1848. Hodges had assembled a remarkable collection of autographs: the *Athenaeum* called it the best to come on the market since the John L. Anderson auction (Robert Harding Evans, 13 February 1833).[23] Lots 116-119 consisted of letters supposedly written in the hand of Lord Byron. Lot 116 was addressed to Robert Charles Dallas; it had previously been published twice. Lot 117 was written to Shelley from Pisa on 19 May 1822. According to the excerpt in Hodges' sale catalogue, Lord Byron here observed,

> The Quaterlyers have attacked me. You see what it is to throw pearls before swine. However, it is fit that I should pay the penalty of spoiling the herd, as no man has contributed more than me, in my earlier compositions, to produce that exaggerated and false taste—it is a fit retribution that any really classical production should be viewed as these plays have been treated.[24]

This letter, now in the Gardner Museum, Boston, is a close approximation to an authentic composition that Lord Byron sent to Shelley on 20 May 1820, the last paragraph of which begins,

> The only literary news that I have heard of the plays—(con-

---

23 *Athenaeum* 1104 (23 December 1848): 1297–1298, which erroneously assigns the sale to 1834. Among Anderson's treasures were letters by Martin Luther, Philip Melanchthon, John Calvin, John Milton, Corneille, Racine, Copernicus, Descartes, Isaac Newton, Michaelangelo, and Rembrandt.
24 Quoted in Ehrsam, 53.

trary to your friendly augury) is that the Edinburgh R[eview] has attacked them all three—as well as it could.—I have not seen the article.—Murray writes discouragingly—and says "that nothing published this year has made the least impression" including I presume what he has published on my account also.—You see what it is to throw pearls to Swine— — as long as I wrote the exaggerated nonsense which has corrupted the public taste—they applauded to the very echo— and now that I have really composed within these three or four years some things which should "not willingly be let die"—the whole herd snort and grumble and return to wallow in their mire.—However it is fit that I should pay the penalty of spoiling them—as no man has contributed more than me in my earlier compositions to produce that exaggerated & false taste—it is a fit retribution that anything [like a?] classical production should be received as these plays have been treated.—— 25

The forgery sold for £2 2s. to John Young, a collector of autograph material. In 1907 it appeared in the catalogue of an American dealer priced at $100, and two years later the same dealer was asking $125 for it.

Lot 118, dated 20 March 1822, was addressed to a W. H. Reinganum. This may have been authentic; Leslie A. Marchand includes it in his edition of Lord Byron's letters, though he notes that a letter of the same date addressed to Major P. Byron is a Byron forgery. Lot 119, which brought £2 14s., was addressed to Shelley from Pisa on 24 April 1822 and informs him of the death of Lord Byron's natural daughter Allegra in the convent of Bagna Cavallo. The forged version includes the last line of the actual letter that Lord Byron sent to Shelley on 23 April 1822, "Death has done his work," and contains echoes of a letter from Lord Byron

---

25 *In the Wind's Eye: Byron's Letters and Journals,* vol 9, 1821–1822, ed. Leslie A. Marchand, (Cambridge, Mass.: The Belknap Press of Harvard University Press, 1979), 161. Marchand identifies the quoted words as coming from John Milton's *The Reason of Church Government,* Book 2. The authentic letter is in the Carl H. Pforzheimer Library.

26 Ehrsam quotes the sale catalogue entry for this letter on p. 54. The authentic letter to Shelley appears in *In the Wind's Eye,* 147–148, that to Murray on p. 146–147.

to John Murray of 22 April.[26]

Lot 390 was an eight-line fragment of Keats's "Isabella" signed by the author. This item, which brought 9s., was a Byron forgery derived from Severn's authentic manuscript. Lots 724–731 consisted of seven letters by Shelley and one manuscript. The bookseller Edward Evans, bidding for Mary Shelley, bought lots 724–725 and 729–731. The first of these, dated 3 September 1812, was forged by Byron from a letter that Henry St. John, Viscount Bolingbroke, wrote to Jonathan Swift. Evans paid £1 11s. for it. Lot 725, which cost £1 17s., was addressed to "Dear Hezekiah," Byron's invented middle name for Edward Fergus Graham, whom Byron called John Hezekiah Graham. Frederick L. Jones's edition of *The Letters of Percy Bysshe Shelley* (Oxford: Clarendon Press, 1964) includes two letters from Shelley to Graham written in August 1810, but neither matches the catalogue description of the Hodges piece. Through Evans, Mary also secured a letter to "Ed Graham," two supposedly written to Mary herself and another lacking the addressee's name. The first of these letters to Mary was forged at least in part from an authentic piece dated 4 November 1814, and the letter without name of recipient and dated 12 January 1817 was copied from one sent by Shelley's lawyer, Longdill, on 5 August 1817 and secured by Byron from Madocks at Marlow. Evans paid £4 4s. for this letter.

The most expensive (£6 6s.) and most interesting item was lot 731, dated 11 January 1817. It contains the information that "I have just heard from Godwin that he has evidence that Harriet was unfaithful to me *four months* before I left England with you."[27] Harriet is Harriet Westbrook, whom Shelley married and by whom he had two children before he met and fell in love with Mary Godwin. Shelley, who believed in free love, asked Harriet to live with Mary and him, an arrangement she rejected. On 15 December 1816 Shelley received a letter from Thomas Hookham informing him that Harriet had drowned herself. Byron did forge at least one copy of this letter of 11 January 1817, but the one sold at the

---

27   *The Letters of Percy Bysshe Shelley*, ed. Frederick L. Jones, 2 vols. (Oxford: Clarendon Press, 1964), I, 380. *The Athenaeum* 1104 (23 December 1848): 1298 objected to the sale of this letter while Mary was still alive.

Hodges auction may have been the original.

The great collector Sir Thomas Phillipps paid £3 10s. for lot 726, a letter addressed to Graham and dated 9 February 1812. Phillipps also paid £2 for an undated letter to Graham. Both were Byron forgeries. Captain Montagu Montagu, collector of Keats and Shelley manuscripts, bought "An Ode to Music" for £2. The forged text derives from the authentic Shelley poem entitled "An Ode Written October, 1819, Before the Spaniards Had Recovered Their Liberty."

On 14 January 1849 Byron wrote to Samuel Leigh Sotheby from Paris, "Me voilà since 5 or 6 weeks in this Pandemonium— The total want of the *nervus rerum gerundarum* drove me and my family from London—it is true. I left it *sans regret,* for my existence in England was indeed the very counterpart of Dante's Inferno, with the only exception of the *exit*—[28]

The French interlude must have been brief, because Mrs. Byron continued to offer White letters by Lord Byron. White decided to sell at least some of these to John Murray, who examined them for about two hours before agreeing to pay £123 7s. 6d. for forty-seven (28 April 1849). The average price per letter was thus £2 12s. 6d. Since White paid between £1 and 35s. for each, the bookseller made a tidy profit on the sale.

After exhausting the Lord Byron letters in her possession, the lady, whose name White still did not know, began offering letters by Shelley. White informed Edward Moxon, who had published Mary Shelley's posthumous editions of her husband's works. Moxon told White about the letters that had been left at Marlow and of Byron's subsequent securing these materials. White assured Moxon that these letters had no connection with Byron. Moxon then recommended that White contact Mary Shelley. In response to White's communication, Mary sent Thomas Hookham with an angry letter accusing White of trying to extort money from her.

The mysterious woman was bringing other manuscripts to White as well. Some of these White consigned to Puttick and

---

28   In Ehrsam, 61.

Simpson's to be sold at auction. On the eve of the sale William
Rowsell, a bookseller in Great Queen Street, visited White and
informed him that a Mr. Byron had bought one of the titles sched-
uled to appear in the Puttick and Simpson's sale but had neglected to pay for it. White, having now heard the name of Byron mentioned twice, questioned the mysterious lady on her next visit. She
confessed to being Byron's wife and revealed the "true" source of
the letters. Her husband

> had traveled all over England, France, Italy, and Switzerland,
> to collect autographs and relics of his father, from persons he
> knew to possess them;— . . . he had purchased a great many
> of the letters of Mr. Hodges, of Frankfort, and of Mr. [John]
> Wright, a gentleman connected with the "Quarterly Review"
> . . . the Shelley letters had been collected in various ways;
> some, . . . from the Marlow Box, and from various quarters.[29]

Byron himself, back from France, gave White written assurance
that the letters were genuine.

On 9 July 1849 Puttick and Simpson's sold the collection of
George Morgan Smith. The auction included two letters by Keats
and ten by Shelley that White had purchased from Mrs. Byron and
now was selling. According to the *Athenaeum*, these were the first
two holograph Keats letters to come on the market.[30] One Keats
letter, to "William" (for Benjamin Robert) Haydon, was bought in
by White for £2 15s., the minimum price White was willing to
accept. For £2 17s. Captain Montagu Montagu bought the other,
addressed to William Spencer[31] from Inverary and dated 18 July
1818. Montagu's purchase is now at the Bodleian. Richard
Monckton Milnes included this piece in his edition of Keats's letters,[32] but it is a forgery: Keats actually wrote to Benjamin Bailey
from Inverary on 18 July 1818, but not to Spencer.

Lots 430-439 of the George Morgan Smith sale consisted of

---

29 *The Calumnies of the "Athenaeum" Journal Exposed*, 12.
30 *Athenaeum* 1133 (14 July 1849): 719.
31 William Robert Spencer, a minor poet, corresponded with Lord Byron, but no
    letters from Keats to Spencer are known.
32 *The Life and Letters of John Keats* (London: E. Moxon, 1867), 27-28.

White's Shelley letters. Samuel Leigh Sotheby thought that White wanted to see how much they would fetch on the open market, and again White placed a reserve, in this case £2 5s., on each item. Eight of the letters did not reach that sum and so were bought in by White. Francis Nathaniel, Lord Conyngham, paid £2 8s. for one of the forgeries (lot 431), and a Mr. Holt paid £2 10s. for lot 438.

In July 1849 Byron, his wife, and two children sailed to New York aboard the *Gladiator*. They did not pay for their passage, Byron telling the captain that he was working for the publishing firm of Appleton, which would cover the family's expenses. The ship reached America on 10 August, and the next day the captain went to the Appleton offices for his fare. Appleton denied any knowledge of Byron.

Byron had come to America to publish *The Inedited Works of Lord Byron*. On 8 September he advertised in the New York *Evening Post* that Part I would appear on 1 October. Two days later the *New York Herald* carried a longer announcement describing the projected work:

> A quarter of a century has passed since the death of Lord Byron, and twenty years have elapsed since Mr. [Thomas] Moore's admirable Notices of the Poet appeared. During that period death has been busy with those, out of regard to whom Mr. Moore was induced to omit passages in the published correspondence, as given in the seventeen-volume edition of Lord Byron's works. These passages will now be restored, the editor feeling assured that the public will uphold him in what he looks upon as a sacred duty, the rescuing the memory of Lord Byron from the many unjust aspersions cast upon his character, either from interested motives, or from the mere gratification of envy, hatred, and malice. (3)

Hiram Fuller of the New York *Evening Mirror* refused to carry Byron's notice. Aware of the controversy that had prevented Byron from publishing in England, Fuller instead attacked Byron in his newspaper on 15 September and again on the 19th, calling

33   New York *Evening Mirror,* 19 September 1849, p. 2.

him "an arrant humbug."[33] Byron replied by suing Fuller for $5,000 for libel. Fuller ran this story on 22 September, mentioning the still unpaid captain of the *Gladiator.*

1 October came and went without sign of *The Inedited Works,* but Byron continued to advertise, promising publication on 4 November. He had found a co-publisher, Robert Martin, who had already put out *The Byron Gallery of Highly Finished Engravings* earlier that year. On 6 November the long-promised first installment of what was supposed to be a twenty-part series appeared. The forty-eight page pamphlet cost twenty-five cents. Byron stated that he had composed the work to vindicate his father, and he again declared that he would include much new material, some of which would "altogether remove the charge of infidelity" from the poet.[34] If Lord Byron was in fact married to Byron's mother, though, the poet would have been at least a bigamist, a point Byron did not discuss. *The Inedited Works* began with an account of *Childe Harold's Pilgrimage,* and Byron included seven authentic letters that had never before appeared in print. Three others came from obscure published sources, revealing the extent of the editor's research. The *American Review* for December 1849 praised Byron's effort, writing, "The edition is exquisitely printed, the part of the editor in the first number, the only one as yet published, is well, not to say elegantly written, and the notices of Byron's life and conduct are extremely interesting, placing him in a light very favorable to humanity, and satisfactory to those who admire his genius."[35]

Part II appeared in December 1849 or January 1850. Beginning on page 49, it ended on page 96 in mid-sentence. In this installment Byron included two poems that had appeared in *Fraser's Magazine* in 1833, one satirizing Samuel Rogers and the other the Reverend George Frederick Nott, both men in fact friends of the poet. Neither piece was by Lord Byron. According to Samuel Leigh Sotheby, these two parts of *The Inedited Works of Lord Byron* constituted all that had been set in type by W. S. Orr

---

34   *The Inedited Works of Lord Byron,* p. 3.
35   10: 658.

and Company. The manuscript material had been returned to John Murray, so with the appearance of Part II, the publication ceased.[36] On 5 December 1849 the Superior Court of New York ruled against Byron in his libel suit, and Fuller proceeded to sue Byron for court costs.[37] Unable to publish and facing trial, Byron and his family left America for England.

Byron's forgeries continued to enter the London market even in his absence. At the William Mitchell auction on 17 December 1849 Puttick and Simpson's sold a one-page letter from Shelley to Mary together with an undated letter by Mary herself. The latter was authentic, but the Shelley letter was not. A Mr. Bain secured this lot for 9s. A larger quantity of spurious letters were about to become available as well because White decided to sell the manuscripts he had secured from Mrs. Byron. He sent these to Sotheby's house in August 1850, where they remained unexamined until January 1851, when Sotheby began cataloguing them.

As Sotheby read over the Shelley letters, he noted that some sounded very like those he had seen at the Hodges sale. The auctioneer questioned White, who assured him that the materials in the earlier sale were copies. Sotheby was still worried by the cleanliness of White's letters and by the fact that all were written in the same color ink even though they were composed at so many different times. Yet even the knowledge that White had secured these materials from Byron, twice listed by the Society of Guardians for the Protection of Trade, did not deter Sotheby from proceeding with their sale on 12 May 1851, along with the important collection of autographs gathered by John Wilks, M. P. for Boston, Lincolnshire.

Lots 1167–1203 of that auction consisted of thirty-five letters by Shelley and two manuscripts. The major purchaser was Edward Moxon, who secured twenty-three letters (lots 1167–1189), for which he paid between £1 and £4 each, spending a total of £115 4s. 6d. Edward Evans paid £3 5s. for a letter supposedly written by Shelley to Lord Byron on 4 September 1821. This forgery is now

---

36 *Principia Typographica* (London: McDowall, 1858), II, 112–113.
37 *Evening Mirror,* 5 December 1849, p. 2; 10 December, p. 2.

in the Pierpont Morgan Library.

Lots 1193–1203, eleven letters from Shelley to Mary, were purchased en bloc by Hookham for £57 15s., who insisted that they not be separated. Hookham was acting for Sir Percy and Lady Shelley, Mary Shelley having died on 1 February 1851.[38] Lot 1198 derived from an authentic letter dated 4 November 1851. Lot 1199 was another copy of the famous letter of 11 January 1817, here misdated 1816. One version had already appeared in the Hodges' sale. Lot 1201 is dated 15 (for 16) December 1816; it informs Mary of Harriet Westbrook's death. This, too, was based on an actual letter but was itself a forgery, as were, indeed, all the Shelley letters in the sale. Byron made at least one other copy of this 16 December letter, which he sold to Sir Robert Peel around 1850, and it now is held by Lehigh University, which purchased it from A. S. W. Rosenbach as a forgery for its Shelley collection. Rosenbach had acquired it in 1914 in the purchase of the playwright Harry Smith's Sentimental Library, which consisted of important association copies of books and manuscripts. Smith had published the letter as authentic in the catalogue of his library (1914).[39] The contents of three other letters, dated 12 December 1816, 13 January 1817, and 12 January 1818, are probably Byron creations; no version of Shelley's letters bearing these dates appears in Frederick L. Jones' edition.

Lots 1160-1166 consisted of Byron forgeries of six letters by Keats and one manuscript poem. The first sold for £1 5s. to "T," who also secured lot 1161 for £1 16s. This letter (lot 1161) is addressed to "William" Haydon from Carisbrooke and dated 20 April 1817. It reads in part, "Me voila settled in the 'Isle spoilt by the Milatary,' sic docet an inscription on the window of the room where I slept at Newport."[40] On 17 April 1817 Keats actually

---

38 Sotheby may have delayed the auction until after her death, since the sale included letters to her. Perhaps he recalled the objections raised when such letters had been sold in 1848.

39 Ehrsam, 125–128. According to Robert Metcalf Smith in *The Shelley Legend*, the Smith-Lehigh letter is not the one sold to Peel but yet another forged copy (pp. 98–99).

40 In Ehrsam, 81. "Me voila" recalls the letter that Byron sent Sotheby from Paris in 1849.

wrote to John Hamilton Reynolds, "In the room where I slept at Newport I found this on the Window 'O Isle spoilt by the Milatary.'"[41] The next lot was secured by Richard Monckton Milnes for £2 14s. In this letter from Oxford and written to William Spencer[42] in September 1817, Keats supposedly wrote, "In his own peculiar empire, Wordsworth stands pre-eminent. But however great an admirer of Wordsworth's poetry I may be, I cannot submit to the imputation of having suffered my originality, whatever it is, to have been marred by its influence."[43] Keats was at Oxford in September 1817, and the sentiments are Keatsian; but the letter itself is spurious. Milnes also paid £2 14s. for lot 1163, a three-page letter to "W." Haydon dated 20 November 1817 expressing admiration for Dante. Keats several times in his letters praises the Italian poet, but in his standard edition of Keats's letters Hyder Edward Rollins includes none dated 20 November 1817. "T." paid £1 10s. for another letter to "W." Haydon, this one dated 29 January 1818; Rollins' edition contains no letter with that date. Evans bought the final Keats letter in the sale, dated 8 December 1818 from Wentworth Place and addressed to Richard Woodhouse. On 10 December 1818 Keats did write to Woodhouse, but the authentic letter differs from Byron's fabrication. Lot 1166 consisted of a 112-line poem supposedly in the hand of Keats. Milnes paid £1 16s. for this forgery. Milnes included the two spurious letters in 1867 when he revised his 1848 *The Life and Letters of John Keats,* and in his edition of Keats's poems he included the 112-line poem he had bought. Milnes also printed what he called a "Sonnet of Doubtful Authenticity" in *The Poetical Works of John Keats.* Byron produced two forgeries of this poem by Laman Blanchard, who killed himself on 15 February 1845. To one copy, in Blanchard's hand, Byron added Keats's signature. John Howard Birss in 1933 declared, "The signature is judged by close students of Keats's holograph to be authentic," indicating again how good a forger Byron was.[44] Byron also copied

---

41 *The Letters of John Keats* 1814–1821, 2 vols., ed. Hyder Edward Rollins (Cambridge, Mass.: Harvard University Press, 1958), II, 132.
42 See note 31.
43 In Ehrsam, 81.
44 "A Sonnet Wrongly Ascribed to Keats," *Notes and Queries* 164 (3 June 1933): 388.

out the entire sonnet in his imitation of Keats's handwriting and added Keats's signature; it is this copy that Milnes owned and used in his edition.

Thirty-six lots contained books that had supposedly belonged to Lord Byron. All but two of these bore Lord Byron's signature, and nearly all included his annotations. Item 1129, the first edition of cantos III-V of *Don Juan,* carried the following note on the fly-leaf:

> The publisher is requested to re-print (provided the occasion should occur) from *this* copy, as the one most carefully gone over by the author . . . with all due deference to those superior persons, the publisher and the printer, that they will in future, *less* misspell—mistake—and misevery thing— The humbled MS. of their humble servant.—Oct. 26 1821.[45]

Lot 1140 was a two-volume edition of James Macpherson's *Ossian* dated 1806. In this work the forger had written a forty-two line version of Ossian's famous "Address to the Sun" from "Carthon." The bookseller Henry Bohn paid £3 3s. for the work. In November 1872 Richard Edgcumbe paid £21 for the set. He then took his purchase to John Murray, who identified the annotations as spurious. Edgcumbe returned the set, but Charles Sumner paid twenty guineas for the Macpherson volumes and bequeathed them to Harvard University, where they remain. For decades scholars accepted the poem as genuine; both Ernest H. Coleridge in 1904 and Paul Elmore More in 1905 included it in their editions of Lord Byron's works; P. H. Churchman published an article about it in *Modern Language Notes* of January 1908.[46]

Even more fascinating was lot 1128, a copy of the second edition of *English Bards and Scotch Reviewers.* On the half-title Lord Byron purportedly wrote, "Byron—Athens—At Theodora Marci's—January 1810—Sun shining *Grecianly*—Lemon trees in

45   In Ehrsam, 83.
46   "Espronceda, Byron and Ossian," *Modern Language Notes* 23 (Jan. 1908): 13–16.

front of the house full of fruit—damn the book!—Give me nature and two eyes opposite—."[47] In January 1810 Lord Byron was in fact staying with Theodora Marci and was in love with her eldest daughter, Teresa, aged fourteen, to whom he addressed his poem beginning "Maid of Athens, ere we part,/ Give, oh, give me back my heart!" Evans paid £1 1s. for the volume, but when he tried to sell it the next year at auction it was withdrawn as a forgery. In 1909 Sydney Cockerell acquired the book from H. T. Wake. The bibliographer Thomas James Wise offered Cockerell £100 for the book, but Cockerell refused to sell it until he had authenticated the inscription. When Cockerell discovered the truth, he gave the book to Wise, and it passed to the British Museum with the rest of the Ashley Library after Wise's death. Altogether Henry Bohn bought eight lots of these books, a Mr. Cunningham seven, and Richard Monckton Milnes six. Milnes had the distinction of paying the highest price for one of these, £6 15s. for lot 1133. Excluded from the sale was a copy of Samuel Rogers' *The Pleasures of Memory* (1801). Sotheby returned the book to White because it contained an inscription insulting to Rogers, who was still alive. In 1855 White gave the book back to Sotheby, who donated it, together with a letter forged by Byron, to the British Museum on 26 May 1856.

In February 1852 Moxon published *The Letters of Percy Bysshe Shelley, with an Introductory Essay by Robert Browning.* The volume consisted of the twenty-three letters Moxon had acquired at auction and two he secured elsewhere. Browning, who wrote the introduction from Paris, did not see the letters, but Moxon sent him copies. Browning began his introduction by observing that this collection "will prove an acceptable addition to the body of correspondence, the value of which towards a right understanding of its author's purpose and work, may be said to exceed that of any similar contribution exhibiting the worldly relations of a poet whose genius has operated by a different law."[48] Later in this piece Browning asserted:

---

47 In Ehrsam, 86.
48 *The Complete Works of Robert Browning with Variant Readings & Annotations* (Athens, Ohio: Ohio University Press, 1981), V, 137.

The value [of Moxon's letters] I take to consist in a most truthful conformity of the Correspondence, in its limited degree, with the moral and intellectual character of the writer as displayed in the highest manifestations of his genius. . . . Regarded in themselves, and as the substantive productions of a man, their importance would be slight. But they possess interest beyond their limits, in confirming the evidence just dwelt on, of the poetical mood of Shelley being only the intensification of his habitual mood; the same tongue only speaking, for want of the special excitement to sing. The very first letter, as one instance for all, strikes the key-note of the predominating sentiment of Shelley throughout his whole life—his sympathy with the oppressed.[49]

Browning's choice of his example was fortunate because at least part of this first letter, "To the Editor of the Statesman, London," is authentic; Byron copied this section from the *Westminster Review* for April 1841. Of the twenty-five letters, only two were fully genuine in the sense that they were copied entirely from Shelley's originals, though even these were in Byron's hand. Four others had nothing of Shelley at all, and the rest were composites of Shelley's words and the work of others. Robert Metcalf Smith, who made the most comprehensive study of these forgeries, noted that Moxon's Letter XVII, for example, addressed to "J. H." Graham, includes material from Shelley's *Essays, Letters from Abroad,* edited by Mary Shelley and published in 1840, and from two different issues of the *Monthly Magazine* (1 October 1818 and 1 November 1820); the last line is by the forger himself. Letter XX is addressed to "G. D. Marlow," the name invented by Byron from the place where the Shelleys had lived in 1817-1818. This piece, too, is a composite of Shelley's words and an essay that Byron found in the *Monthly Magazine* (1 April 1821).[50]

Byron had read Shelley's authentic correspondence carefully, dating the letters from the places the poet was living at the moment. He also convincingly copied Shelley's hand. Mary

---

49   Ibid., 145–146.
50   *The Shelley Legend,* 60.

Shelley was apparently fooled; Sir Percy and Lady Jane Shelley certainly were, as was Moxon. In *Shelley Memorials: From Authentic Sources* (London: Smith, Elder and Co., 1859) Lady Jane Shelley, who edited the volume, wrote,

> The art of forging letters purporting to be relics of men of literary celebrity, and therefore apparently possessing a commercial value, has been brought to a rare perfection by those who have made Mr. Shelley's handwriting the object of their imitation. Within the last fourteen years, on no less than three occasions, have forged letters been presented to our family for purchase. In December [for May], 1851, Sir Percy Shelley and the late Mr. Moxon bought several letters, all of which proved to be forgeries, though, on the most careful inspection, we could scarcely detect any difference between these and the originals; for some were exact copies of documents in our possession. The watermark on the paper was generally, though not always, the mark appropriate to the date; and the amount of ingenuity exercised was most extraordinary. (v-vi)[51]

In "A Talk over Autographs" George Birkbeck Hill reported an incident confirming Byron's imitative talents:

> Many years ago, one of the great London auctioneers—either Christie or Sotheby, I forget which—asked [an old friend of Hill] and old John Murray, the poet's [Lord Byron] publisher, to call at his office, as he had a curiosity to show them. "Here," he said, when they came in, "are some genuine letters of Byron's, and here are forgeries of them. We must not mix them, for if we do we shall never be able to separate them."[52]

George Frederic Lees noted that Byron had also captured Shelley's sentiments and tone. Lees observed that Browning "was deceived, not on account of the fairly close resemblance between the forger's handwriting and that of Shelley [since Browning never

---

51 The three occasions refer to the three lots offered to and secured by Mary Shelley in 1845–1846.

52 *Atlantic Monthly* 75 (April 1895): 445–457, 447.

saw the actual letters], but because of the spirit of truth which runs through all these amazing documents."[53]

To add still more verisimilitude to his efforts, Byron even forged postmarks, but here his efforts were less convincing. The *Athenaeum* for 6 March 1852 commented, "Where 'Ravenna' on a genuine letter was in small sharp type—in the [forged] Shelley letter it was in a large uncertain type;—and in the letters from Venice the postmark . . . was stamped in an *Italic*, and not as in [Byron's] Shelley specimens in a Roman letter!"[54] The article nonetheless went on to praise Byron's abilities:

> There has been of late years, as we are assured, a most sys-
> tematic and wholesale forgery of letters purporting to be writ-
> ten by Byron, Shelley, and Keats,—that these forgeries carry
> upon them such marks of genuineness as have deceived the
> entire body of London collectors,—that they are executed
> with a skill to which the forgeries of Chatterton and Ireland
> can lay no claim,—that they have sold at public auctions and
> by the hands of booksellers, to collectors of experience and
> rank,—and that the imposition has extended to a large collec-
> tion of books bearing not only the signature of Lord Byron,
> but notes by him in many of their pages—the matter of the
> letters being selected with a thorough knowledge of Byron's
> life and feelings, and the whole of the books chosen with the
> minutest knowledge of his tastes and peculiarities.[55]

As the date of the *Athenaeum* exposure indicates, the forgeries did not long go undetected despite Byron's skill. Chance played its part in the quick revelation of the hoax. Moxon sent a copy of his publication to Alfred, Lord Tennyson, the poet laureate, who was entertaining Francis Turner Palgrave when the volume arrived. Looking through it, Palgrave recognized a passage in one of Shelley's letters that had been written by Palgrave's father, Sir Francis Palgrave, and published in the *Quarterly Review* in

---

53 "Recollections of an Anglo-Parisian Bibliophile III—The Great Shelley Forgery,"
   The Bookman 83 (October 1932):, 31-37, 33.
54 *Athenaeum* 1271 (6 March 1852): 279.
55 Ibid.

September 1840.[56] On 23 February 1852 Sir Francis Palgrave wrote to Moxon, "It is a duty I owe both to you and to myself to inform you that in the letters just brought out by you and ascribed to Mr. Shelley there is one, viz. that dated Florence, which is cribbed from an article by me published in the Q[uarterly] R[eview] (Vol. CXL). Even a misprint is ignorantly preserved by the fabricator of the correspondence."[57] Even without this chance discovery, the forgeries would soon have been detected. A letter in the *Literary Gazette* for 28 February 1852 questioned their authenticity, and the *Athenaeum* article noted borrowings from the *Monthly Magazine* of 1818 and 1819 and from the *Edinburgh Literary Almanac* for 1826. Once Moxon examined the postmarks, he became convinced that the letters were spurious, and he suppressed his edition.

Murray now doubted his purchases, too; on 12 March he wrote to White, who had already responded to criticism in the *Athenaeum* with a pamphlet in the guise of a letter to Murray. Dated 11 March and published on the sixteenth, it stated that both Murray and Moxon had been acquainted with the source of the letters. Murray immediately replied to this public defense with a published letter of his own, dated 17 March, which appeared in the *Literary Gazette* 1835 (20 March 1852): 279:

> I have received from you a *printed* letter, beginning "Dear Murray," relating to certain forged letters of Shelley and Byron which have been sold by you at different times.
>
> As you have thus publicly appealed to me, I am compelled to contradict your statement that I knew "as much of the history of these letters as yourself." I knew nothing of the connexion of the person calling himself George Byron with them; or I should certainly have hesitated to buy them. I cannot account for your conduct in concealing from me all mention of his name, until the week before last, when I called on you to tell you that I had ascertained that they were forgeries.

White's pamphlet letter was attacked in the *Athenaeum* and the *Examiner.* The latter agreed that White had been deceived, but

---

56 The lines Byron copied appear on pages 315–319 and 327–328
(The Shelley Legend, 60).

57 *The Shelley Legend,* 57.

it faulted him for failing to notify Moxon and Murray once he had learned the actual source of the letters.[58] After months of procrastinating, White reimbursed Murray and Moxon for the cost of the letters, though he did not compensate the latter for the loss he had sustained in having to recall his edition of the forgeries. On 4 March 1853 White gave the forty-seven Byron letters and twenty-three Shelley letters to the British Museum. Even then he was not convinced that all were spurious. "Should you have leisure to look them over I think you will agree with me in the difficulty of believing that all of these letters are forgeries," he wrote to Sir Henry Ellis, principal librarian of the British Museum."[59]

Curiously, Milnes, Evans, and the Shelleys never returned the forgeries they acquired, perhaps because, as George Birkbeck Hill's anecdote indicates, they could not distinguish the authentic letters from Byron's copies. That is certainly the case with the 16 December 1816 letter. In 1867 Spencer Shelley, son of Sir John Shelley (of the senior branch of the family) received the authentic version of this letter, though with Byron's addition of a spurious Shelley signature; Mary Shelley had bought a forged copy that had passed into the collection of Sir Percy and Lady Jane Shelley. Spencer Shelley sent a transcript of the genuine letter to Lady Jane and asked whether she wanted the original. She replied that it was a forgery. Harry Buxton Forman bought the letter from Spencer Shelley's widow for £21 in 1908, and Thomas James Wise secured the letter in trade from Forman. This letter later went to the British Museum with the rest of Wise's library. Lady Shelley also apparently mistook a Byron forgery of the 11 January 1817 letter from Shelley to Mary as the original and rejected the original as a fake, even though in this case she had both letters in her possession.

Exposure of the forgeries forced the Byrons to leave England for America, where he seems to have served for a time in the Union army. In 1862 the family settled in New York City. In 1869 Byron published a series of six articles about Lord Byron and Shelley in *The Albion, a Weekly Journal of Literature, Art, Politics,*

---

58   *Examiner* 2303 (20 March 1852): 181.
59   In Ehrsam, 95.

Finance, and News. The first, published on 27 February 1869, claimed to be "Reminiscences of Lord Byron, By his Valet, Now Living in the United States." The valet was the Swedish Paul James Lindberg, whom Lord Byron engaged at Genoa, and the article consisted of a letter from Lindberg to Byron (the forger) and various anecdotes Lindberg had related to him. They included the information that

> Lord Byron was superstitious. He believed in supernatural appearances, in apparitions, in presentiments, in omens and dreams. A drawer of horoscopes had predicted that his twenty-seventh or thirty-seventh year would be fatal to him, and he could not get the prediction out of his head. Friday was always a black day in his calendar. He was struck with terror when he remembered that he had embarked for Greece, at Genoa, on a Friday; he once dismissed a tailor at Geneva, who brought him home a new habit on that day.[60]

The article was Byron's invention.

Byron's second contribution to *The Albion* appeared a week later, on 6 March. It purported to provide five unpublished letters from Lord Byron to Thomas Moore. All five had been printed in *The Keepsake* for 1830, and none had been addressed to Moore. *The Albion* for 13 March carried Byron's "An Unpublished Poem by Lord Byron on Samuel Rogers, With Notes" (pp. 127-128). The poem had appeared at least twice before, once in *Fraser's Magazine* for September 1830 and again in the second and final part of Byron's *The Inedited Works of Lord Byron*. It was no more by Lord Byron this time than it had been before. "A Second Unpublished Poem by Lord Byron," entitled "Woman and the Moon" constituted the fourth contribution (20 March 1869). The ninety-six line piece apparently is the work of the forger. "An Unpublished Poem by Percy Bysshe Shelley" entitled "The Calm" appeared on page 141 of *The Albion* for 27 March 1869. The piece was composed by Byron, as was the final item in this series, an "Unpublished Epistle from Lord Byron to John Murray," which begins,

---

60 *The Albion* 47 (27 February 1869): 99–100, 100.

A Turkish Tale I shall unfold,
A sweeter tale was never told;
But then the facts, I must allow,
Are, in the East not common now;
Tho' in the "olden time" the scene
My *Giaour* describes had often been.
What is the cause? Perhaps the fair
Are now more cautious than they were;
Perhaps the Christians not so bold,
So enterprising as of old.
No matter what the cause may be,
It is a subject fit for me.[61]

Later that year Byron went to Europe, where he attempted to persuade Teresa Guiccioli, Lord Byron's last mistress, that he was the poet's son. She was not convinced, but she found him appealing. On 27 August she wrote to Emma Fagnani, "I have seen Colonel Byron often; he is really an excellent man. He is not the son of the illustrious Byron, but by his goodness he deserves to be."[62] Guiccioli had published *My Recollections of Lord Byron* in French in 1868 and in English in 1869. In July of 1869 *Blackwood's Magazine* favorably reviewed the work. Harriet Beecher Stowe responded with "The True Story of Lady Byron's Life," which appeared in September simultaneously in the *Atlantic Monthly* in America and in *Macmillan's Magazine* in England. Stowe's article attacked Guiccioli, so to curry favor with Lord Byron's former lover Byron collected articles critical of Stowe. A letter signed "B." appeared in the London *Morning Post* praising Guiccioli and attacking Stowe. Byron may have been the author of that piece. Guiccioli appreciated his support. On 7 November she wrote again to Fagnani, "He is an excellent man and I will see him gladly when I return to Paris."[63] Even after he sent her some of his unpaid hotel bills (which she refused to pay) she described him to Fagnani as "a good man in spite of his being an *adventurer*."[64]

---

61 *The Albion* 47 (27 March 1869): 170.
62 In Ehrsam, 110.
63 Ibid.
64 Ibid., 111.

In November Byron went to England to meet with Ralph Gordon King-Milbanke, Lord Wentworth, Lord Byron's grandson, who rejected Byron's claim of kinship. While in England Byron may have met Henry Schultes Schultess-Young, whose aunt, Julia Puddicombe, owned some letters by Lord Byron. Schultess-Young set about collecting as many letters by Lord Byron as he could find, and on 6 March 1872 Richard Bentley agreed to publish 750 copies of the *The Unpublished Letters of Lord Byron*. After the books had been printed and bound, but before they were distributed to booksellers, Bentley discovered that at least some of the contents had appeared in Thomas Moore's *The Life of Lord Byron, with His Letters and Journals*, first published in 1838 and frequently reprinted by the Murrays. Bentley therefore wrote angrily to Schultess-Young,

> You expressly told me that the letters were all new and unpublished. I should not think for a moment of publishing any letters which have appeared before, and the fact of copyright having just expired of any letters published by Mr. Murray would be no inducement to me to publish the letters. . . . I have desired the printers to suspend proceedings.[65]

All but ten copies were destroyed. Bentley sent one of these ten to John Doran, then editor of the *Athenaeum*. After Doran's death, his library was sold by Sotheby's; and the Schultess-Young book was acquired by the bookseller Bertram Dobell. According to a note in the *Bookman* (1 [October 1891]: 20) Dobell advertised the volume in a catalogue, and Harry Buxton Forman paid four guineas for it. Responding to a question about the volume, in 1891 Dobell commented, "As to the genuineness of the letters, the opinion I formed after a careful reading was that they were undoubtedly [Lord] Byron's own, for only another Byron could have forged them."[66] In his essay on "The Character of Lord Byron" that was to have served as the preface to the *Unpublished Letters*, Schultess-

---

65 Ibid., 152.
66 "Byron Volume," *Notes and Queries* 12, 7th ser. (14 November 1891): 389–390, 389.

Young cited a forged letter from Keats; and Schultess-Young also included other Byron's forgeries, among them the forty-seven letters that White had sold to Murray and sixteen letters addressed to "L—," whom Schultess-Young identified as Laura. Thomas James Wise, who acquired the Schultess-Young book from Forman, was initially convinced that these letters were authentic:

> [T]here are so many features in the letters, & in the manner in which they are dealt with, which I cannot imagine the most experienced and skillful manipulator to have accomplished— far less a youthful amateur such as Schultess-Young. Is it possible that so youthful a rogue (for rogue he must have been if the documents are spurious) could have introduced so much realism into the letters? Could any young man of 20, could any man, have invented phrases so absolutely Byronic as the two I have printed? Who save Byron himself would have written the sardonic "a bastard Byron is better than no Byron . . ." ?[67]

After corresponding with John Murray V (grandson of the Murray who bought the Lord Byron forgeries) and Richard Bentley (son of the Richard Bentley who suppressed the Schultess-Young volume), Wise concluded that the letters to Laura were "based on genuine originals crudely and improperly edited."[68]

---

67 In Ehrsam, 155. Ehrsam notes that the remark about the bastard Byron, which appears in the letter to L— dated 29 February 1813, echoes comments that the forger Byron used in his letters. Thus to John Murray on 1 July 1843 Byron stated, "I am a Byron—the bar sinister notwithstanding—Civil law cannot change nature" (Ehrsam, 163). Wise printed extracts from the letters to L— in the first volume of *The Ashley Library* (London: Printed for Private Circulation Only, 1922), I, 165. Combining passages from three of the letters to L— as if they were all from one, the first of the two extracts as Wise printed it reads,
> "I do not understand your letter, but only know that I love you, and you know I shall never marry you, for which you have reason to be thankful. I wonder whom I shall espouse, for I must take up the conjugal cross some day, and perpetuate the name of Byron better than by my rhymes. . . . When I leave England I will not forget the things you ask for, and regret that you cannot accompany me, which is impossible, not for the sake of my character but yours. . . . The child is dead. I do not regret it, though a bastard Byron is better than no Byron".

Because of the date of the letter, the dead child cannot be Allegra. Presumably it was the child of Byron and L—.

68 Ibid.

Yet some of the material in these letters must have been invented. One letter, for example, dated 3 October 1811, refers to a copy of *Childe Harold,* the first part of which was not published until 1812. Another is dated from Venice on 10 November 1816, the day before Lord Byron reached that city. Marchand includes none of these pieces addressed to L— in his standard edition of Lord Byron's letters. The likely manufacturer of these spurious documents was not Schultess-Young but rather Byron.

Schultess-Young and Wise were not the only ones deceived by the letters to L— . The American book dealer Ernest Dressel North secured a copy of the Schultess-Young work, which he sold to the New York City publishers Covici and Friede in the spring of 1929. They asked the Shelley scholar Walter Edwin Peck to prepare an edition of the letters to L—. Peck believed them authentic, as did the Lord Byron specialist Earle C. Smith, who assured Peck, "I have read them through and make no doubt of their authenticity if I may judge from their tone. Certainly they are too characteristically Byronic in so many passages—I mean in such intimate touches as the forger generally misses—for me to have the slightest hesitancy in accepting them."[69] Covici and Friede published the letters, together with another Byron forgery addressed to "Mary," in a limited edition on Dutch Pannekoek paper in May 1930.[70]

Leaving behind a flurry of unpaid bills, the Byrons in 1870 once more returned to New York City. To support themselves, Mrs. Byron worked as a maid; and Byron continued to sell books with Lord Byron's annotations. He also published occasional articles based on manuscript material in his possession and generally of his own manufacture. Until his death in London on 4 June 1882 he continued to insist on being the poet's son; Ehrsam reports that "his dishes, silverplate, and stationery, all carried the Byron marking."[71] Robert Metcalf Smith quotes a passage in the *American Antiquarian* 4 (March 1886): 330 describing Byron in his later years:

---

69 Ibid., 163.
70 *Seventeen Letters of George Noel Gordon Lord Byron to an Unknown Lady, 1811–1817.*
71 Ehrsam, 113.

He used to wear a semi-military uniform with spurs, and carried a lady's riding whip in his hand. . . . He posed at various times, as a litterateur, a journalist, a diplomatist, a Government agent, an officer of the British army in the East Indies, a British naval officer, an officer of the United States Army, a mining prospector, a broker, a merchant, a spy, an agent for cotton claims, a commission agent, an Oriental traveler, a representative of European mercantile interests, a bookseller, a patents right agent, a gentleman of means, and an aristocratic exile, expatriated and pensioned on condition that he should never reveal his genealogy.

The same article reported that Byron maintained an office at 40 Broadway, "where he . . . made a show of doing business by exhibiting what he called a patent fish-tail rudder in a trough of water."[72]

In his definitive edition of Lord Byron's letters, Leslie A. Marchand lists 122 Byron forgeries. The number of spurious Shelley and Keats letters that Byron produced is harder to estimate. Frederick L. Jones suggested fifty of the former,[73] with some of these being duplicates and even triplicates. Keats seems to have interested Byron less than the other two; apart from about half a dozen letters and two spurious poems, Byron apparently left Keats alone. While some of Byron's forgeries may remain unidentified and so deceive collectors and scholars, and while some of these forgeries were accepted by late 19th- and early 20th-century scholars, perhaps Byron's most pernicious effect lay in his calling into question the genuine letters that Shelley wrote regarding Harriet Westbrook. She may not have been false to Shelley, but Godwin and Shelley believed that she was. Byron's forgeries of the genuine letters of 16 December 1816 and 11 January 1817 prompted Robert Metcalf Smith to challenge these, together with a few other authentic pieces.

Byron claimed that he wanted to clear the names of Lord Byron and Shelley from aspersions that had been wrongly cast upon

---

72 *The Shelley Legend*, 82–83.
73 "The Shelley Legend" in *An Examination of "The Shelley Legend,"* (Philadelphia: University of Pennsylvania Press, 1951), 87.

them. A reviewer of Moxon's collection of forgeries wrote that

> It seemed . . . as though the letters had been selected, if not
> composed, with the view of illustrating some foregone con-
> clusion, or to be adapted to some text previously chosen at
> random. For instance, we will, without reference to any par-
> ticular letter, presume the writer to have wished to prove
> (what we earnestly hope and trust was the fact) that Shelley,
> spite of his works and professions, had within his breast that
> germ of hope and fidelity which, had he been spared us,
> might have borne goodly fruit.[74]

Yet Byron's primary motive was financial gain. He hoped at
first that he could live on his physical resemblance to Lord Byron
and his claim of being the poet's son that rested on that evidence.[75] Samuel Leigh Sotheby and the historian John Lothrop
Motley accepted his story; Augusta Leigh and Sir John Cam
Hobhouse (who had accompanied Lord Byron on the trip to Spain
during which the poet supposedly met the Countess de Luna)
came to suspect that the story might be true. Such limited accept-
ance could not, however, feed a family that grew to contain six
children, so Byron turned to forgery. That he could hope to make
money from the manuscript materials he manufactured indicates
how public opinion had changed from the 1820's, when Shelley
and Keats found few readers and when Byron lived a virtual exile
from England.[76] By the 1840's all three were recognized as major
authors, worthy of having their poems read—and of having their
letters forged.

---

74 *Tait's Edinburgh Magazine* 19, 2nd ser. (1852): 252.
75 Friends of Major Byron found striking similarities in the hair, eyes, and nose of the
    forger and his alleged father. Hiram Fuller, editor of the New York *Evening Mirror,*
    on the other hand, wrote that "the person claiming to be a 'son of Lord Byron' has
    the look of a sneak and the manners of a Jeremy Diddler." (Quoted in Charles
    Hamilton, *Great Forgers and Famous Fakes* [New York: Crown, 1980], 148.)
76 In 1834 Keats's publisher declared, "The world cares nothing for" Keats. (Quoted
    in Andrew Motion, *Keats* [New York: Farrar, Straus and Giroux, 1998], xii).

LUCAS

VII

Vrain-Denis Lucas, Prince of Forgers

*G*eorge Gordon Byron's forgeries (ch. 6) attest not only to the enhanced reputations of John Keats and Percy Bysshe Shelley in the 1840s and 1850s but also to the increased interest in collecting autographs. The first public auction in England devoted exclusively to autographs was held at Sotheby's on 21 May 1819, when the collection assembled by John Thane was dispersed. William Upcott, one of the premier British autographiles of the early 19th century, reported that at the sale of John Bindley's autographs by the auctioneer Robert Harding Evans on 8 August 1820, "I found many competitors."[1] According to A. N. L. Munby, between 1821 and 1830 ten major auctions contained a large amount of autograph material, and Janet Ing Freeman has identified an eleventh at Sotheby's in 1824. Between 1831 and 1840 the number rose to twenty-two. Twenty-nine such sales were held in the next decade; forty-three between 1851 and 1860, forty-four in the period 1861–1870, and fifty-three between 1871 and 1880.[2]

The same trend is evident in France. As in England, major sales of autographs commenced there about 1820. In the post-Napoleanic period monastic and aristocratic libraries were dispersed. Between 1825 and 1835, 12,000 autograph documents were sold at auction in France. In the next five years, nearly as many, 11,000, went to the block. Fifteen thousand were offered

---

1 Cited in A. N. L. Munby, *The Cult of the Autograph Letter in England* (London: Athlone Press, University of London, 1962), 8.
2 Ibid., 85; Janet Ing Freeman, *The Postmaster of Ipswich* (London: The Book Collector, 1997), 135.

between 1841 and 1845, and from 1846 to 1859 another 32,000 were sold.[3]

Such demand gave opportunities to the unscrupulous to prey on the unwary. In 1864 Louis Marie Paul Vogt, comte d'Hunolstein, issued *Correspondence inédité de Marie Antoinette* (Paris: E. Dentu).[4] The volume contained 132 letters by Marie Antoinette, and the third edition, published later that year, added nineteen more. For these letters Hunolstein had paid £3,400 (about 78,000 francs), but only two of these documents were authentic. Also in 1864 Felix-Sébastien Feuillet de Conches published *Causeries d'un curieux* (conversations of a collector), in which he included two previously unknown letters by Montaigne. Feuillet de Conches was among the most noted of French autograph collectors and was regarded as the supreme authority in the field. Yet even he was deceived: the Montaigne letters were spurious. Feuillet de Conches was also fooled by counterfeit letters of Marie Antoinette. He bought eight from a Parisian grocer who claimed that he had found them in the street during the 1848 Revolution. Feuillet de Conches owned another of the queen's letters that supposedly fell out of her hair when she was executed; the letter was stained with her blood. This manuscript, too, was a fake.

The Montaigne letters that Feuillet de Conches published had been shown to him by his friend the marquis Antoine-Théodore Du Prat. Du Prat was seeking proof of his descent from Cardinal Antoine Du Prat, Chancellor of France under François I. The marquis went to the Letellier genealogical collection but initially found nothing. He then appealed to one of Leteller's employees, Vrain-Denis Lucas, who soon found fifteen letters from the 16th and 17th centuries relating to the chancellor, including the two from Montaigne. All fifteen were the manufacture of Lucas, the most prolific and audacious forger in the annals of literary fabrication. Du Prat, believing these letters authentic, published them in 1865.[5]

---

3   J. A. Farrer, *Literary Forgeries* (London: Longman's, Green, 1907), 215.
4   Unpublished letters of Marie Antoinette.
5   *Glanes et regains, récoltés dans les archives de la maison Du Prat* (Versailles: Beau); gleanings and aftermaths, harvested in the archives of the Du Prat family.

Lucas had come to Paris from Châteaudun in 1852. Born the son of a peasant in 1818, he had received little formal education. Having a taste for letters, he read indefatigably and, like Chatterton and Ireland, secured a post as a law clerk at Chartres. The loan register of the public library at Châteaudun reveals his interest in history and bibliography: items checked out to him include Jean François Dreux de Radier's *Bibliothèque historique, et critique du Poitou* (Paris: Chez Ganeau, 1754);[6] an account of the library assembled by Mazarine (which included a Gutenberg Bible); and the *Bibliothèque des auteurs qui ont écrit l'histoire* (library of authors who have written history). Sometime in the 1840s Lucas temporarily moved to Paris to attend lectures at the Sorbonne. His teachers were Jean Philibert Damiron (1794–1862), whose subject was the history of philosophy and science; Charles Lenormant (1802–1859), professor of history; and Eugène-Nicolas Gérusez, professor of rhetoric and literary history. In his spare moments he wrote poetry "for fun and to pass time," as he stated in the preface to "The Garland of Flora," one of fifteen pieces found in a notebook that Lucas used in the late 1840s.[7] This preface reveals his awareness of the obstacles he faced in seeking to become a man of letters:

> I am quite unlearned;
>
> ***
>
> I swear by all that's holy[,]
> Reader, that in my infancy
> No one, such was my destiny,
> Taught me either Greek or Latin,
> Important matters these
> If one would rhyme with ease,
> And then see his work in print![8]

---

6   Historical and critical library of Poitou.
7   *Prince of Forgers,* trans. Joseph Rosenblum (New Castle, DE: Oak Knoll Press, 1998), 50.
8   Ibid.

When Lucas left Châteaudun permanently in 1852 to seek his fortune in Paris, one of the librarians, the abbot Sonazay, wishing him well, wrote under Lucas' list of borrowings, "The industrious M. Lucas is going to live in Paris. He deserves to succeed. A self-made young man from Lanneray."

Whatever his merits, Lucas could not secure the kind of position he wanted. His love of books, manuscripts, and antiquity took him first to the Imperial Library on rue Richelieu. Although armed with a recommendation addressed to the chief librarian, Lucas was deemed unsuitable because he held no degree. M. Roux, a professor at the college at Chartres and a collector of manuscripts, had been sufficiently impressed with Lucas to recommend him to Roux's friend Auguste Durand, a Parisian bookseller whose shop stood on the rue des Grés. Durand, too, refused to hire Lucas, in this instance because Lucas knew no Latin.

Lucas found employment with the Letellier genealogical collection, which engaged him as an agent to solicit business from families who might want information about their ancestors. From its establishment in 1845, this organization was regarded "as a dispensary from which emerged a mass of false documents forged with amazing skill."[9] Exactly when Lucas began his criminal career is unclear. He may have supplied Roux with spurious autograph documents, and Du Prat may not have been the first of his Parisian clients to persuade him to manufacture evidence of a pedigree. However, by the time the Letellier collection was dispersed in 1858, Lucas had discovered his true calling, and thereafter he worked at it diligently. He would leave his apartment about 11:00 A.M., eat lunch, and then devote the rest of the day to study at one of the Parisian libraries. The library of Sainte-Geneviève banned him after one of the curators found him with a sharp instrument; he was apparently preparing to excise old blank leaves to use for his forgeries.

Sometime in 1861 Lucas called on the geometrician and autographile Michel Chasles, one of the leading mathematicians in France, perhaps the world. Born at Epernon, France, on 15

---

9   Ibid., 51.

November 1793, Chasles entered the École Polytechnique in 1812. Even before graduating, he began to publish, and after leaving school he pursued his mathematical studies independently. In 1837 he published *Aperçu historique sur l'origine et le développement des méthodes en géométrie,* a history of geometry from its beginnings to 1800. Two years later he was elected a corresponding member of the Academy of Sciences, and in 1841 his alma mater appointed him Professor of Mechanics and Geodesy. In 1846 he became the first occupant of the school's chair of modern geometry. In 1851 he was elected a member of the Academy of Sciences. In 1854 the Royal Society (London) named him a foreign member, and in 1865 it would award him the Copley Medal, its highest honor. Two years later he became the first foreign member of the London Mathematical Society.

Why Lucas selected Chasles is unclear, but the choice was inspired. Chasles was eager to acquire rarities, and he felt a kind of kinship with Lucas because the latter had come from Châteaudun, near Chartres, where Chasles had been raised. For 500 francs Chasles purchased a letter from Molière. Lucas soon returned with a letter by Rabelais, then one from Racine, each of which Chasles bought for 200 francs. Translating such sums into modern terms is impossible, but the exorbitance is evident when one considers that the average wage in Paris in 1872 was just under five francs a day. A carpenter in 1870 could expect to earn 6 francs, a mason 5 francs 50 centimes.[10] Chasles, though, was so pleased with his purchases that he insisted that Lucas sell only to him. When Chasles learned that a civil servant named Belley had secured four notes from Lucas, Chasles at once bought them for 200 francs.

Lucas assured Chasles that such items were readily available. Supposedly in the 18th century the Comte de Boisjourdain had assembled an extensive collection of manuscripts, to which Louis XVI had contributed 6,000 items. Forced to emigrate in 1791, the count had died in a shipwreck off the coast of America, and some

---

10   Émile Levasseur, *Histoire des classes ouvrières et de l'industrie en France de 1789 à 1870* (Paris: Arthur Rousseau, 1904), II, 709, 713.

of his papers had suffered water damage. Most, however, had been rescued and were now in the possession of an old man, a relative of the count. The man needed money, so he had engaged Lucas to act as his agent. Lucas received a 25% commission on his sales.

In addition to letters, the count had assembled a valuable library of association copies, books that had belonged to famous people. For example, Lucas sold to Chasles a 1613 edition of Giovanni Mario Verdizotti's *Cento favole bellissime de' più illustri antichi & moderni autori Greci, & Latini* (one hundred most lovely stories by the most illustrious ancient and modern Greek and Latin authors). The volume was stained and lacked both half-title and free end-papers, but on the title page were the words "Ex libris J. de La Fontaine," and on the front pastedown the count had written,

> This book is extremely rare; only one copy is known in a library in Venice, and moreover, this present copy is unique because it belonged to the good-natured La Fontaine and inspired his delightful fables. Also I paid dearly for this volume at an auction. Monsieur the Duke de La Vallière having raised the bidding to 900 livres, I was forced to pay more. Later, monsieur the duke made me several offers in order to acquire the book and I never wanted to let go of it. Its engravings are exceedingly delicate.[11]

La Vallière had been forced to content himself with a first edition of this title (Venice, 1570) in mint condition and bound in blue morocco. When La Vallière's library was sold at auction in 1783 after his death, this first edition fetched 48 francs. Lucas charged Chasles 800 francs for his later printing. When Chasles consulted Jacques Charles Brunet's *Manuel du libraire* (bookseller's guide) and discovered this discrepancy in price, he complained to Lucas. Lucas soon returned with apologies from the old man who employed him; the owner of the book had agreed to compensate Chasles by giving him a dozen letters by Blaise Pascal for only another hundred francs. Chasles readily agreed.

11   *Prince of Forgers*, 25. Louis-César la Baume le Blanc, duc de La Vallière
     (9 October 1708-16 November 1780) was one of the greatest French book
     collectors.

By 1865 Chasles' collection had become internationally famous. In that year the Neopolitan chemist de Lucca suggested that Chasles lend Florence one of his Dante autographs for the six-hundreth anniversary of that poet's birth. Chasles consented, but the piece arrived too late to figure in the festivities. The next year Chasles gave the Royal Academy of Belgium, of which he was a member, two of his fifteen letters from Emperor Charles V to François Rabelais. In one of these, dated 10 September 1542, the emperor writes,

> To Master François Rabelais, learned in all sciences and good letters[.]
>
> Master Rabelais,
>
> You who have a fine and subtle mind, would you be able to gratify me? I have promised 1,000 écus to the person who will discover how to square the circle, and no mathematician has been able to solve this problem. I have thought that you who are ingenious in all matters would be able to satisfy me, and, if you do so, you will be well compensated for so doing. May God come to your aid.[12]

The Belgian archivist Louis Prosper Gachard suspected the letters as soon as he learned of their contents, and became even more convinced of their spuriousness when he looked at them. Chasles, undeterred by Gachard's doubts, lent two other letters to Maximilien Quentin, archivist of the department of Yonne, and Aimé-Alexandre Cherest, a lawyer, when these men were assembling the correspondence of the 18th-century abbot Jean Lebeuf, historian of Paris. These letters were duly published in 1867. The contents were authentic, but the transcription was by Lucas, one from a letter he had found in the Imperial Library, the other from the September 1742 issue of the *Mercure de France* (p. 1915).

On Monday, 8 July 1867, Chasles donated to the Academy of Sciences four letters from the poet Jean de Rotrou. The

---

12   Quoted in French in George Girard, *Le parfait secrétaire des grands hommes* (Paris: Cité des Livres, 1924), 69.

Academy had celebrated its two-hundreth anniversary the previous year,[13] and two of the Rotrou letters, addressed to Cardinal Richelieu, urged him to imitate medieval Toulouse in establishing a literary academy at Paris. In thanking Chasles for this gift, the president of the Academy, Michel-Eugène Chevreul, used the occasion to ask Chasles to share with his fellow members his work on Pascal.

The Boisjourdain collection was particularly rich in Pascal material; by 1869 Chasles would own 2,316 autograph documents from the French philosopher. Reading these letters, Chasles had learned that Pascal, not Newton, had discovered the law of gravity; and Chasles was working on a book to set the record straight. To Chevreul's request Chasles replied that on the following Monday, when the Academy of Sciences held its next meeting, he would be happy to discuss his findings.

On 15 July Chasles donated to the Academy four notes signed by Pascal and two letters from Pascal addressed to the English chemist Robert Boyle. One of these letters contained nothing significant, but the other clearly demonstrated that Pascal had anticipated Newton's discovery by some thirty-five years. Dated 2 September without a year, but presumably like the other from 1652, it read,

> Sir, Among celestial movements, the force operating in direct proportion to the masses and in inverse proportion to the square of the distances [between them] suffices for all, and furnishes the grounds for explaining all these great revolutions that propel the universe. Nothing is so beautiful, from my point of view: but when it comes to sublunary phenomena, to the effects that we see from a shorter distance and the examination of which is easier for us, the attractive force is a Proteus that often changes its shape. Crags and mountains do not exhibit any observable evidence of gravitational attraction. This is because, one may say, these small particular gravitational forces are as it were absorbed by that of the terrestrial

---

13   Begun about 1640 as an informal group of scientists, it was given formal status by Jean-Baptiste Colbert in 1666 as the Académie royale des sciences.

sphere, which is infinitely greater; nevertheless, one gives as an effect of gravitational force the froth that floats on a cup of coffee and proceeds with most perceptible haste towards the side of the vessel. Is that your opinion?[14]

In his address Chasles presented various calculations that were still more surprising because they showed that Pascal had more precise figures for the masses and densities of planets than Newton possessed until 1726, when the third edition of his *Principia* appeared.

At the next session of the Academy the physicist Jean Marie Constant Duhamel noted this oddity, and Hervé-Auguste-Étienne-Albans Faye objected that even with these figures Pascal could not have arrived at the calculations attributed to him because in 1652 Newton had not yet invented the calculus necessary to arrive at Pascal's alleged results. On 29 July the Academy heard letters from Armand-Prosper Faugère, author of various works dealing with Pascal and his family, and Monsieur Bénard of Evreux, who challenged the authenticity of the Pascal letters. Faugère's research had found no evidence of Pascal's interest in astronomy; he also thought the style unworthy of the author of the *Lettres provinciales* (provincial letters). Bénard, like Duhamel, found the calculations anachronistic and suggested that they had been copied from modern works.

Undeterred, Chasles continued to produce documentary support for his position. On 22 July he presented another fifty-three notes and letters from Pascal, including one to Pierre Gassendi dated 24 January 1655. Here Pascal writes,

> I have previously spoken to you about a young English student named Isaac Newton who has submitted to me certain memoirs regarding the calculus of the Infinite, on the treatise of the system of vortexes, and on the equilibrium and weight of liquids, etc., in which memoirs I have found signs of intelligence so clear and so subtle that I have remained astonished, to the point that I could not believe that these works came to me from a young man still a student. Having been reassured

---

14 *Prince of Forgers*, 150 n.1. The original French version is quoted on pp. 149–150.

about this matter by our friend M. Boyle, I have hastened to reply to this young scholar; and since in the most recent letter he wrote to me he has attested to me his desire to make your acquaintance and has asked me to forward to you a letter he intends for you, I am sending it to you and recommend this young scholar as a tender plant that must be cultivated with care for the sake of science. I am also sending you various notes, the fruit of my former observations, that I hope you will find pleasant.[15]

On 29 July Chasles showed that Pascal had begun corresponding with Newton when the latter was twelve years old. In a letter dated 20 May 1654 Pascal wrote to the young Newton, then a student at the grammar school at Grantham,

My young friend,

I have learned with what care you would attempt to initiate yourself into the mathematical and geometric sciences and that you would like to delve intelligently into the works of the late M. [René] Descrates. I am sending you various of his papers that were given to me who was one of his good friends. I am also sending you various mathematical problems that once occupied me regarding the laws of abstraction,[16] in order to exercise your mind. I beg you to send me your thoughts about them. It is not necessary though, my young friend, for you to overstrain your young mind. Work, study, but do so in moderation. That is the best way to acquire knowledge and to profit from what you have gained.[17]

In this same group of letters were some from Newton to Pascal and to Jacques Rohault. Oddly, Newton's mother at one point uses her maiden name, and Newton's French in these letters is better than in those he had previously been known to write.

On 12 August the Academy heard by letter from Sir David Brewster of Edinburgh, one of the body's associate members. Sir

---

15   Girard, 82–83.
16   Lucas's forgeries occasionally exhibit such solecisms.
17   Girard, 81.

David had written a biography of Newton, whose papers were carefully preserved at Hurtsbourne Park, seat of the Earls of Portsmouth. Nowhere was there any mention of Pascal. Chasles thereupon sent Sir David photographs of his letters; these Sir David returned, reaffirming his belief that they were "contemptible forgeries."[18]

These debates in Paris quickly spread beyond the confines of the Academy of Sciences. In Brussels the *Indépendance* reported that Newton had been dethroned, and the mathematician Augustus de Morgan published a defense of Newton in the *Athenaeum* for 17 August 1867.[19] He questioned the correspondence between Pascal and Boyle in 1652, since Boyle published nothing until 1660 and so would not have attracted the attention of the Frenchman so early. De Morgan also challenged as an anachronism the 1652 reference to coffee, a drink unknown in Paris until 1657. This point also troubled Armand-Prosper Faugère, who raised it at the Academy meeting on 16 August.

On 12 September the Academy listened to a letter by Robert Grant, director of the Glasgow Observatory, again questioning the possibility of Pascal's having such accurate figures so early. Grant noted that Pascal's results depended on observations made by James Pound and James Bradley, the elder of whom was not even born until 1669, seven years after Pascal's death. Grant repeated his objections in the London *Times* for 20 September 1867. Chasles replied with more documents. According to these papers even James II and Louis XIV grew concerned when Newton attempted to conceal his indebtedness to Pascal and Descartes, and Newton responded by acknowledging the latter as the greatest genius of the age.

On 7 October Chasles introduced the name of Galileo to the debate, producing letters showing that the Florentine astronomer had been investigating the laws of gravity and had sent some of his calculations to the young Pascal. Among the correspondence were three letters by Galileo dated January, May, and June 1641. These

---

18   *Prince of Forgers*, 12.
19   #2077, pp. 209–210.

were curiosities indeed, since Galileo had been blind since the end of 1637. Also, Galileo referred in 1641 to the satellites of Saturn, the first of which was not discovered by Christian Huygens until March 1655, twelve years after Galileo's death. Grant pointed out these discrepancies in a letter read to the Academy on 11 November, but Chasles produced another hoard of autographs the following week. Twenty letters by Galileo, his pupil Vincenzio Viviani, Boulliau, Giovanni Domenico Cassini, Huygens, and others agreed that Galileo was not blind until the last months of his life. Indeed, in his last years he created a telescope through which he could observe the moons of Saturn. This very telescope he sent to Pascal, who gave it to Boulliau and thence it passed to Huygens, who used it to view the ringed planet.

Gilbert Govi of Florence, Father Pietro Angelo Secchi of Rome, the astronomer Harting of Utrecht, and Thomas Henri Martin of Rennes, author of a study of Galileo, all objected that these letters contradicted everything known about Galileo. The very fact that the letters of Galileo were in French revealed their spuriousness, since the Florentine never wrote in that language.

Yet Chasles was not without his champions as well. Louis Adolphe Thiers, historian of Napoleanic France, accepted the proposition that Pascal had discovered the laws of gravity, and on 5 April 1869 the Academy itself endorsed this view through its permanent secretary, who declared,

> An autograph letter from Galileo to Louis XIII, paraphrased by Louis XIV, *in his own hand,* in which the noted astronomer ingenuously explains to the king of France that he is not as completely blind as it is said, but he is careful not to dispel the fortunate misconception, which was providing the protection of the freedom he was being allowed, such a letter appears to me to be an historical document of incomparable worth. . . . The authors of the letters and notices inserted into the most recent number of the *Proceedings* had written without affectation; but nobody could assume the role of placing himself in the position of writing at will from Galileo, from Milton, from Louis XIV, from Cassini, consistent with circumstances always more or less changing and obscure. . . . The other pieces in sufficiently large number that M. Chasles has entered into the

Proceedings, in the course of almost two years, without the
discovery of any inconsistencies that could not have failed to
emerge from forgers, present in a manner no less evident the
moral certainty of their authenticity.[20]

The Academy's position rested not only on the subjective
matter of style but also on chemical analysis. Lucas had told
Chasles that the Boisjourdain collection had nearly perished in a
shipwreck, and the first 1,200 or so pieces that Lucas sold Chasles
were so water-damaged as to be nearly impossible to read. Chasles
took these to a colleague at the Academy, the chemist Sainte-
Claire Deville, to render them more legible. Instead of restoring
the text, Deville's treatment made them completely black. Deville
explained that the papers' previous immersion in water had diffused the sulfate of iron from the ink throughout the pages. Lucas'
story of a shipwreck must therefore have been true. The papers
had indeed been immersed in water, but by Lucas himself in an
effort to support his story. He had not intended to damage them
as much as he had, but his inexperience had worked to his benefit.

Antoine-Jérôme Balard and Jules-Célestine Jamin, two other
chemists of the Academy, had devised a test to distinguish between
old and new ink based on the principle that old ink is harder to
remove from a page when that paper is subjected to an acidic solu-
tion. They found that Chasles' documents resisted the action of
dilute hydrochloric acid, indicating that if the documents had been
forged, they had been produced long ago.

Then there was the matter of the content. Lucas was but
indifferently educated, but how could even the most learned know
so much about 17th-century science? Would not a forger be bound
to reveal himself by anachronisms?

A week after the Academy gave its stamp of approval to
Chasles' documents, an engineer attached to the Paris Observatory,
Paul Émile Breton de Champs, demonstrated that sixteen notes by
Pascal and two fragments from a letter by Galileo, all of which

---

20 *Prince of Forgers,* 16.

Chasles had read before the Academy in 1867, were copies extracted from Alexandre Savérien's *Histoire des philosophes modernes* (Paris: Brunet, 1761–1767; history of modern scientists). Here, then, was the explanation for the accuracy of the forgeries. Lucas invented nothing; he merely copied.

At the next meeting Chasles responded. The letters he had submitted to the Academy were not copies of Savérien's work. On the contrary: Savérien had quoted these very letters. To prove his contention Chasles brought forth three more letters demonstrating that Montesquieu had secured for Savérien access to the library of Madame de Pompadour, rich in manuscript material, and that Savérien had borrowed and transcribed material from that store.

Why then, asked Breton de Champs, did Savérien not report Pascal's discovery of the law of gravity? Why did he say nothing about Galileo's observing a moon of Saturn? On 26 April Chasles brought forth more documents to answer these objections. Savérien was a Newtonian, a friend of Voltaire, and tactless. Madame de Pompadour therefore quickly banished him from her door, so he remained unaware of the full contents of her collection.

Over the course of four sessions of the Academy in June and July 1869, Urbain Jean Joseph Le Verrier summarized the case against the documents, but Chasles was prepared to defend them. In the midst of Le Verrier's disquisition, though, Chasles received some disquieting news. In May he had sent a photograph of a Galileo letter to Florence for authentication. Dated 5 November 1639, it would, if genuine, demonstrate that Galileo was not blind at that date; it would also show that Galileo wrote in French. On 12 July the Academy heard the report from Florence: the handwriting was not Galileo's, and the text had come from Engenio Alberti's 1856 edition of Galileo's works. Undaunted, Chasles replied that he had sent the wrong copy, but the verdict on the second one he sent was the same.

On 13 September 1869 Chasles conceded that the documents might not be authentic. Even then he was unwilling or unable to admit that Lucas had forged them:

> If one considers that they match so well with others, from all periods up to the last century, and treat so many different

subjects, one cannot believe that they are the work of one person, one forger, who, among other considerations, knows neither Latin, nor Italian, nor the slightest bit of mathematics or the other sciences with which a considerable portion of these documents deal. A mystery remains to be solved, and until it is, nothing can be concluded with certainty.[21]

This partial concession displeased Chasles' colleagues, who maintained that Chasles continued to challenge the reputations of Newton and Huygens. Chasles replied at the next session that while he regarded the origins of the documents unresolved, he could not rely on them to impugn the honor of either scientist.

Lucas had been arrested on 9 September on the complaint of Chasles. Chasles was not concerned that Lucas had sold him forged documents. At this stage Chasles could still not believe that Lucas even knew that the autographs were fakes. Rather, Lucas had failed to deliver some three thousand autograph documents that he had promised, and Chasles was afraid that Lucas was about to abscond with these precious papers and sell them abroad. When Lucas was apprehended, no such documents were discovered because Lucas had not yet manufactured them. One telling letter, not quite finished, was discovered in his possession; it was an attempt to explain why Newton's first and second editions of the *Principia* contained figures less accurate than those that Pascal had reported decades earlier. Dated 22 November 1688, the year after Newton published the first edition of his *Principia*, it read,

> Sir, I have read in times past certain manuscript fragments of your book dealing with the mathematical principles of natural philosophy [science] with all the care I was able. I once again read them recently, in order to tell you my feelings, as you asked me to do. As far as I am concerned, the work is perfect. You know precisely how to organize and how to use the materials that M. Pascal furnished you while, of course, adding to these much of your own. While this is obvious, I nevertheless

---

21   *Prince of Forgers,* 19–20.

regret one thing and allow me to make this confession, that is to say, forgive my outspokenness in making it to you, which is that you have tried too hard to dissimulate. You cannot be unaware that there remain traces of the writings of P(ascal) and G(alileo). I want to admit to you fully that I am aware of some of these writings; I have compared them with your work, and I have had definite proof that you must have had copies of these. There can be no doubt, and I regret one thing, which is that in seeking to dissemble you have used certain calculations, that you have included certain figures, that, from my viewpoint, are not as precise as those found in the writings in question. That is why, sir, if you ever reprint this work, I urge you to pay attention to these calculations, relating to the distance between planets, etc., etc. I do not say to you . . .[22]

Because Lucas was arrested before he could finish this letter, the designated signer remains a mystery.

At a former Lucas residence more incriminating evidence was found. This material included copies of autographs extracted from the *Isographie des hommes célèbres; ou Collection de facsimilés de lettres autographes et de signatures* (Paris: A. Mesnier, 1828-1830), a collection of facsimile signatures and autograph letters; old paper; and volumes of Louis Moreri's *Le grand dictoinaire historique* and of the periodical *Mercure de France*, all lacking end-papers. These works had provided text for Lucas's forgeries and the blank pages on which he wrote them.

Once Chasles recognized the truth, that his documents were spurious, he prosecuted Lucas for fraud. Lucas maintained that while he had indeed created some of the documents that he sold to Chasles, the authentic items he had included were worth at least as much as he had charged for everything he had delivered. The court appointed two investigators to prepare a report. Henri Bordier, a lawyer formerly associated with the national archives, had helped investigate the thefts of Guglielmo Libri some three decades earlier. Libri, appointed to inspect French libraries to pre-

---

22 *Prince of Forgers*, 20–21.

serve their treasures, instead stole a large quantity of valuable materials and then fled to England in 1848 just before he was to be arrested. Libri not only stole books and manuscripts but also doctored them to enhance their value, and in 1867 his name was bandied about unjustly as the genius behind Lucas' forgeries.[23] Émile Mabille, Bordier's fellow investigator, was employed in the Department of Manuscripts of the Imperial Library. Their report, *Une fabrique de faux autographes, ou récit de l'affair Vrain Lucas* (Paris: Léon Techener, 1870), provides the fullest account of Lucas' activities and reveals the full extent of his industry.[24]

On 28 October 1867 Chasles had submitted to the Academy of Sciences a list of documents that he then owned relating to the Pascal controversy, and over the next two years, as his collection grew, he introduced new items into the Academy's *Proceedings.* By September, 1869, the documents presented at the weekly meetings of the Academy totaled 381. Impressive as these figures were, they proved to be a small sampling of the riches Chasles possessed. The Academy saw eighty letters and notes from Pascal; as already noted, Chasles owned some 2,000 supposedly in his hand. Twenty-nine autograph documents by Newton passed before the eyes of the Academy; Chasles' library contained 622. Galileo is represented in the *Proceedings* by twenty entries, but Chasles owned more than 3,000 bearing his signature.

Even these constituted less than 20% of the documents that Lucas sold to Chasles over the course of nine years at a sum of something over 140,000 francs. Though Lucas began with French authors of the 17th and 18th centuries, his success emboldened him. In time he moved farther into the past, creating letters by Gregory of Tours, Pepin the Short, Alcuin, and Charlemagne. Although he knew only modern French, Lucas also composed documents by Sappho, Alexander the Great, Julius Caesar, Cleopatra, Saint Matthew, Maecenas, Vercingetorix; hardly an important figure from history escaped him. All wrote in French; all

---

23   In an ironic twist of history, Chasles was chosen to fill the seat in the Academy of Sciences vacated by Libri.

24   *Prince of Forgers,* cited repeatedly in this chapter, is an English translation of this report, to which the translator has added related documents.

wrote on paper, much of it bearing a fleur-de-lis watermark. By September 1869 Chasles had bought 27,345 forgeries. In addition, Lucas sold him seventy-four virtually worthless authentic documents from the 16th, 17th, and 18th centuries, of which twenty-two were embellished with spurious notes giving them a noteworthy provenance, and 105 fairly common books similarly sophisticated to make them appear valuable.

To explain the seeming anomaly of ancient Greek writers communicating in French, Lucas produced letters such as the following from Charlemagne to Alcuin:

> Most learned and dearly beloved Alcuin, I rather think just as you told me that long ago the Celtic Language, which appears to be the mother of all languages, was better known among all the people of the earth and that Pythagorus, Plato, Aristotle, etc., etc. not only knew it but also taught it[. T]his is what is evident from the various documents that you have sent me and that I return to you. These documents are letters from these same Pythagorus, Plato, Aristotle and also the king Alexander of Macedon and of learned travelers, geographers, and historians and also mathematicians who have[,] taken together[,] traversed the two ends of the world. . . . I charge you to preserve these writings as precious objects and to make accurate copies for me.[25]

Curious as such a view may seem, Lucas was not its inventor. In his 1769 *Origine des premières sociétés* Poinsinet de Sivry argued that the Celts were the inventors of letters. Even the ancient Hebrews were Celts. "Eden," for example, was a Celtic word. Lucas may well have read this work. He makes Archimedes express a similar sentiment in a letter to Hieron: "According to my way of thinking, the languages that today vary among all the countries of the world must have been formed from the wreckage of the primal language, which seems to be the Celtic, which appears to be the one used by Moses, who must be regarded as the most ancient

---

25   *Prince of Forgers*, 35.

author known to us in the course of time."[26] Saint Jerome informs Sulpicius Severus that among the letters being returned to him is one from Jesus himself proving that the Celtic or Gallic language was the first to be created by the descendants of Noah. One cannot doubt, Jerome continues, that Greek and Latin derived from it, and Jesus assures his disciples that Greek, Latin, and the German languages borrowed "an infinity of words" from the Celtic.[27] Poinsinet de Sivry had made this same argument.

This French inclination to self-glorification had troubled Dante,[28] and in the 18th and early 19th centuries the popularity of Ossian in France owed much to French identification with the spurious Celtic bard and his Celtic language that rivaled Homer and his Greek epics in antiquity and excellence. In *Le Rhin* (1841) Victor Hugo declared, "At the present time, the French spirit comes to replace the old soul of every nation. The greatest intelligence of today, representing for the whole universe politics, literature, science, and art, all belong to France, and France offers them to civilization." Hugo also maintained that French literature was not merely the best but the only literature.

Lucas was thus testifying to a widely held belief, at least among Frenchmen, in the primacy of the French language, French letters, French science, and of France itself. Plato writes to Euthymenes of traveling to Gaul to learn from the Druids. Alexander urges Aristotle to do the same "for the good of my people, because you are not unaware of the esteem I have for that nation that I consider as being that which has brought the light [of learning] into the world."[29] Cleopatra writes to Julius Caesar that she intends to send their son, Caesarion, to Marseilles to study, eschewing Alexandria, Athens, and Rome. Had she lived about a century later she might have chosen Lyons, where, Flavius Josephus informs Pliny the Elder, the emperor Caligula in the year 40 established a literary festival. Pliny the Younger assures his Gallic friend, the poet Sentius Augurinus, that he is pleased to learn of the state

---

26   Girard, 34.
27   Girard, 46.
28   See the *Inferno*, XXIX, 123.
29   *Prince of Forgers*, 32.

of science and letters in Gaul in the year 113. He wonders whether the methods of Pythagoras, who had himself praised the Gauls of his day, are still remembered in France. Lucas forged to make money, but he apparently shared the patriotism of his countrymen, a patriotism that reached an apogee under Louis-Napolean and culminated in the disasters of Mexico and Verdun. One is reminded of Samuel Johnson's definition of patrotism as the last refuge of the scoundrel.

How could one account for the existence of documents dating back to the 7th century B.C.? According to the letters Lucas created, Charlemagne urged Alcuin to preserve these letters at Tours. In the 16th century King François I and Margaret d'Angoulème urged Rabelais to gather as many of these as he · could. Rabelais' documents had passed into the hands of Nicolas Joseph Foucault. Chasles thus could choose among fictions. Perhaps these letters had been transcribed and partially translated into modern French by Rabelais. If he preferred, Chasles could regard the documents as antique.

Lucas devoted little effort to duplicating handwritings, even of those people whose letters were available or whose signatures were reproduced in the *Isographie*. Neither did he attempt to imitate scripts. Instead, he merely produced letters that looked old. Julius Caesar writes in a curious blend of hands smacking of 9th-century Carolingian semi-uncial and the still later bâtarde. Nor did Lucas know Old French well enough to use it for an entire letter. Gregory of Tours, Charlemagne, Alcuin, Heloise, Abelard use the occasional antiquated form of a word: "ay" for "ai" (I have); "doulx amy" for "doux ami" (sweet friend); "escrivez" for "écrivez" (write). Even when he copied a story from the history of Gregory of Tours, Lucas chose a version that had been translated into modern French rather than the original text.

The spurious nature of the letters seems to declare itself on every page. Lucas' lawyer, Horace Helbronner, argued that Chasles' gullibility placed him beyond the protection of the law. The physical appearance of the letters, their quantity, their curious tendency to allude to each other over the centuries, all smacked of forgery. Their very numbers were against them. No letters of Shakespeare were known, yet Chasles bought 145, together with notes, stories, and sonnets purportedly in Shakespeare's hand. Newton's papers had been preserved by his descendants; Lucas still produced hundreds of others.

Chasles believed in the letters because he wanted them to be authentic. As the bookseller and author Larry McMurtrie observed regarding the purchase of documents forged by the Texan C. Dorman David,

> The willingness to believe, contra the dictates of reason, is evidently too human and too powerful to be readily overridden, even in supposedly rationalist professions. . . . It goes with an urge to be larger, to have more, to exceed the ordinary. . . . The urge to collect—or, more basically, to acquire—is deeply atavistic and almost always overrides rationality. Few of those afflicted with the need to acquire want to slow things down by asking awkward questions when the chance to get something [extraordinary] comes along.[30]

Challenged by his colleagues on some point, Chasles would consult Lucas, who then would discover documents answering those objections. Pascal lacked the mathematical tools to make his calculations? Here was a letter showing that Newton had provided them. Galileo anachronistically referred to a moon of Saturn? Here was a document proving that the Florentine astronomer had seen that moon. And if the letters of the 17th and 18th centuries were authentic, how could Chasles doubt earlier autographs? Moreover, in the mass of correspondence, involving hundreds of people writing to hundreds of others, Lucas rarely confused chronology, and he often drew on reliable sources to manufacture his forgeries. Indeed, some of his forgeries were transcriptions of authentic works. It was his reliance on the best scientific studies that contributed to his downfall, since these did not record the earlier, less accurate calculations of Newton's first edition of the *Principia*.

Lucas was tried in February 1870. In his defense he insisted that the authentic documents he had sold Chasles were worth at

---

30   Introduction to W. Thomas Taylor, *Texfake: An Account of the Theft and Forgery of Early Texas Printed Documents* (Austin, Texas: W. Thomas Taylor, 1991), xviii.

least 140,000 francs. Bordier and Mabille placed their value at 500 francs at most. Lucas also argued that he had harmed no one:

> If to arrive at my goal I have taken a roundabout way, if I have used artifice to gain attention and to pique public interest, it was in order to remind [people] of historical facts forgotten and even unknown by the majority of scholars. . . .

> I taught while amusing. The proof is that during the entire time that the discussion at the Academy of Sciences lasted, many people paid attention to the sessions and became interested in what was going to be read there. . . . Never has M. Chasles been more heeded.[31]

The jury might have sentenced Lucas to five years in prison and fined him 3,000 francs. Instead, it sent him to jail for two years and limited the fine to 500 francs. Chasles received no restitution for the tens of thousands of francs that he had wasted. What became of Lucas after his trial is uncertain, though a rumor claims that upon his release from prison he returned to the only occupation he knew—forging. Chasles continued to enjoy his colleagues' respect, and after his death on 18 December 1880 he was eulogized by the mathematician and permanent secretary of the Academy of Sciences Joseph-Louis-François Bertrand as one of the glories of France.

At the Bibliothèque nationale are housed the more than 27,000 forgeries that Lucas produced. They remain fascinating witnesses to the curious encounter between the prince of forgers and the man whom R. Tucker, writing in *Nature,* called "a prince of geometers."[32]

---

31   *Prince of Forgers,* 71.
32   *Nature* 23 (6 January 1881): 225–227; 225.

TRANSLATION:

2.—*Challenge of Julius Caesar to Vercingetorix*

Julius Caesar to the leader of the Gauls.
I am sending to you a friend of mine who will tell you the purpose
of my voyage; I wish to cover with my soldiers the land where you
were born. It is pointless for you to wish to prevent me. You are
brave, I know, but I will be so as well if the gods wish, so surrender
to me your arms or prepare yourself for combat. This VI of the
Kalends of July.

Julius Caesar

On the back.

This is the challenge that Julius Caesar sent to Vercingetorix,
leader of the Gauls.

Facsimile of an original Lucas forgery with translation
courtesy *Prince of Forger.*

Thomas James Wise

VIII

Thomas James Wise:
The Adventure of
the Unscrupulous Bibliographer

he Dictionary of National Biography describes Thomas James Wise as "book-collector, bibliographer, editor, and forger," to which should be added bookseller, publisher, pirate, and thief. An astute and aggressive buyer of books, he was among the first to pursue 19th-century authors, building virtually complete collections of William Wordsworth; Samuel Taylor Coleridge; Percy Bysshe Shelley; George Gordon, Lord Byron; Walter Savage Landor; the Brownings; Algernon Charles Swinburne; Dante Gabriel Rossetti; and William Morris. At the same time, he did not ignore earlier British literature. His library held every play by Ben Jonson from *Every Man in His Humour* (London: Walter Burre, 1601) to *The Widow* (London: Humphrey Moseley, 1652) and extensive holdings in John Milton, John Dryden, Alexander Pope, Matthew Prior, and John Gay. His bibliographies, tainted though they sometimes are with his own fabrications, were among the earliest to demonstrate the connection between literary history and such technical matters as variant title pages and the presence of canceled leaves. Wise helped build other important collections, most notably that of John Henry Wrenn, which now enriches the University of Texas; and his approximately 250 privately printed works, while issued for profit, made previously inaccessible works available, and, in the case of Joseph Conrad, provided the author with much-needed money. At the same time, Wise, together with Harry Buxton Forman, created about a hundred spurious or pirated first editions that sought to confuse collectors and literary historians. So egregious were these fabrications that Wilfred Partington called Wise, perhaps with excusable hyperbole, "[T]he secret Emperor and Grand Lama of Forgers."[1] Even worse were Wise's thefts from the British Museum of about three hundred leaves from pre-Restoration drama. Many of those leaves are now lost; and even when they have been recovered in Wise's own books or those he sold, the violated volumes' bibliographic integrity can never be restored.

The eldest child of Thomas and Julia Victoria (Dauncey) Wise, Thomas James Wise was born at 52 Wrotham Road, Gravesend, Kent, on 7 October 1859. Wise's grandfather, also named Thomas, was a prosperous silversmith in Clerkenwell, who left each of his two sons, Thomas and Joshua, an income of £50 a year. Wise's father, who married Julia Victoria Dauncey in 1858, variously described himself as "Manufacturing Jeweller" (1859), "Pencil Case Maker" (1862), "Independent" (1864), and "Tobacconist." Wise called him a "Manufacturing Traveler." In 1860 the family moved to London, living at 37 Devonshire Road (now Axminster Road), Holloway. Though not rich, Wise's father must have been moderately successful, because at his death in 1902 he left to his third wife an estate worth £2,362. Although Wise's younger brother Herbert Athol claimed that because of delicate health the future bibliographer was educated at home, the young Wise probably attended the local schools. Wise's formal education ended in 1875, when he joined the firm of Herman Rubeck and Co., London, dealers in essential oils (oils extracted from plants) used in perfumes and flavorings. He remained with the firm at least until 1912, rising from junior clerk to cashier and office manager.

Wise recalled that he began collecting in 1877 with the purchase of first editions of Shelley's *The Cenci* (Italy: Printed for C. and J. Ollier, 1819) and Thomas Moore's *The Epicurean* (London: Rees, Orme, Brown, and Green, 1827), paying £1 for the pair. According to Wise, "From the joy of owning and reading these two books, there sprang the question, 'Why not go right on until I possess for my use and pleasure, a perfect copy of the first and other important editions of all the works of the great English poets

---

1 *Forging Ahead: The True Story of the Upward Progress of Thomas James Wise* (New York: G. P. Putnam's Sons, 1939), 5.

and dramatists?' So the resolution was made."[2] However, Wise also told Augustus Muir, "I am a bibliographer by choice and intention. I simply drifted into book collecting because books and MSS formed the tools necessary for my job — and so tools had to be acquired."[3]

Whether bibliophily or bibliography came first, the two grew together for Wise. Bibliography was just emerging as a serious discipline in the 1870s and 1880s with the work of Frederick James Furnivall, Richard Garnett, Richard Herne Shepherd, Harry Buxton Forman, and Robert Alfred Potts. These men met at Potts's house, and Wise joined them as the junior member of the group.

On the salary of a junior clerk, perhaps £4 a week, Wise could not initially afford many rarities. To save money he walked to and from work, and he sought his books in the inexpensive shops and outdoor bookstalls along Farrington Road, Fleet Street, and the Strand. He also visited the antiquarian shops in the more expensive western end of London; here he noted prices, studied condition, and added to his bibliographic knowledge.

Wise began collecting Robert Browning in 1880 with the purchase of the newly issued second series of *Dramatic Idylls* (London: Smith, Elder, 1880). In 1881 Wise joined the Browning Society at its founding, becoming the organization's secretary. His mother died in that year, and in 1882 his father married Hannah Waldock. The family moved to 127 Devonshire Road, where Wise had a room fitted out as a library by Jones Brothers of Holloway.[4]

In 1884, despite his limited earnings, Wise paid £45 for a first edition of Shelley's *Adonais* (Pisa: From the Types of Didot, 1821), then a record price, and £40 to the Glasgow firm of Kerr & Richardson for two other Shelley first editions. When Wise later

---

2   Quoted in Nicolas Barker and John Collins, *A Sequel to "An Enquiry into Certain Nineteenth Century Pamphlets" by John Carter and Graham Pollard* (London: Scolar Press, 1983), 46.

3   "A Treasure-House of Books: Mr. Thomas J. Wise and the Ashley Library," *Strand* 80 (Sept. 1930): 280-288, 288 .

4   Hannah Waldock died in 1896. Two years later the elder Wise married Jeannie Carden, who died in 1909.

found a first edition of *Adonais* that Shelley had presented to Jane
(Claire) Clairmont, Wise sold his first copy of the work for £200.
Claire Clairmont (1798–1879) was the step-sister of Shelly's second wife, Mary Godwin Shelley and accompanied the couple when
they fled England for the Continent. Claire was the mother of
Lord Byron's daughter Allegra and may have been Percy Shelley's
lover also.

Wise's quest for books prompted him to seek out the descendants of early 19th-century literary figures. In 1886 he met the
daughter of Leigh Hunt, and from her he secured the copy of
Shelley's *Epipsychidion* (London: C. and J. Ollier, 1821) that the
poet had given Hunt. In 1887 he secured the manuscript of
Shelley's *Hellas* (London: Charles and James Ollier, 1822) from
the son of Sir John Bowring, who had received the manuscript
from Mary Shelley, the poet's second wife. For £36 he secured one
of seven known copies of the suppressed *Oedipus Tyrannus*
(London: Published for the Author, by J. Johnston, 1820) from
Lieutenant-Colonel Charles Call, son-in-law of Shelley's friend
Edward John Trelawny, to whom Shelley had given this book.
Wise was a pioneer in the collecting of Shelley. As he commented,
"During the first 20 years of my search for Shelleyana, I met with
no opposition I was unable to defeat, and Mr [Frederick Robert]
Halsey of New York became my first serious and successful com-
petitor."[5] In 1903 Halsey defeated Wise for one of only two
known copies of *Proposals for an Association of Those Philanthropists
Who Convinced of the Inadequacy of the Moral and Political State of
Ireland . . . Are Willing to Unite to Accomplish Its Regeneration*
(Dublin: I. Eaton, 1812). Halsey paid £530 for it, and Wise never
secured a copy. Still, Wise acquired many important and rare
Shelley titles. For example, in 1890 he paid Richard Garnett £42
for one of the three known copies of Shelley's *A Refutation of
Deism* (London: Printed by Schulze and Dean, 1814), and at one
time or another he owned all three known copies of *Original
Poetry by Victor and Cazire* (Worthing: Printed by C. and W.

---

5   *Forging Ahead*, 54.

Phillips, for the Authors, 1810), i.e., Percy Bysshe and Elizabeth Shelley.[6]

At the urging of the linguist Henry Sweet (the model for Professor Henry Higgins in George Bernard Shaw's *Pygmalion*), in 1886 Frederick James Furnivall, founder of the Browning Society, created the Shelley Society; Shelley had been a friend of Furnivall's father. Wise, already a noted Shelley collector, was placed in charge of the society's publication program. This he pursued so vigorously, issuing thirty-three publications in seven years, that by 1892 the organization was bankrupt. Wise's association with the Shelley and Browning Societies introduced him to people who advanced his collecting and his bibliographic knowledge, such as the Reverend Stopford Brooke, who encouraged Wise to collect Wordsworth. Another person whom Wise met through the Shelley Society, though they had been corresponding since 1882, was Harry Buxton Forman, a civil servant and respected scholar of Keats and Shelley. The two first met in 1886 and soon afterwards began their joint piracies and fabrications of spurious first editions.

The inspiration for these fakes may have been the Browning Society's issuing a type facsimile of Robert Browning's very rare first publication, *Pauline* (London: Saunders & Otley, 1833). Only about a dozen copies of the original exist. Wise oversaw the reprinting, which was executed by Richard Clay & Sons, who would print virtually all of the Wise-Forman forgeries. In April of 1886 Wise also oversaw the first of the Shelley Society's publications, a type-facsimile of *Adonais*, followed that year by *Hellas* and *Alastor*, all executed again by Richard Clay & Sons. In supervising these reprintings Wise learned much about bibliographical details such as missing commas, extra spaces, alternate title pages, and canceled leaves. This knowledge would bear fruit in his bibliographies and his fabrications.

---

6   In a letter to Wilfred Partington, Wise stated that he paid £155 when the first known copy surfaced in 1898. Wise wrote to Wrenn that he had paid £255 for that work. When a better copy appeared five years later Wise paid £600 for it, selling the first copy to John Henry Wrenn. Then a third copy, a presentation copy to William Wellesley, 4th Earl of Mornington, Shelley's schoolmate, appeared on the market. Wise bought it for £600 and sold his other copy to Henry E. Huntington.

Forman also issued a type-facsimile in 1886. He had acquired a copy of Byron's rare first book, *Fugitive Pieces* (Newark: Printed by S. and J. Rudge, 1806). Of this work only three copies are known, and one of these is imperfect. Forman paid £70 for the work, then issued his facsimile, the sales of which paid for his original. Wise and Forman may have recognized that such productions offered a way of making money to finance their book buying.

In 1887 Wise and Forman produced their first joint venture, a Shelley piracy. Edward Dowden had published his *Life of Percy Bysshe Shelley* (London: K. Paul, Trench) in 1886 and had included in it some previously unpublished poems that dealt with the poet's love for his first wife, Harriet Westbrook. Wise and Forman extracted these pieces and published them as *Poems and Sonnets,* supposedly edited by a Charles Alfred Seymour of the Philadelphia Historical Society, and bearing the false imprint, "Philadelphia: Printed for Private Circulation Only, 1887." In *The Ashley Library* and *A Shelley Library* Wise claimed that

> Dowden, [William Michael] Rossetti, Forman, and other friends were with me in my desire to have these poems in a convenient form. But Lady Shelley expressed dissent (as she did with most projects connected with Shelley not originating directly with herself) although she held no interest whatever in the copyright of the verses. To avoid discussion with her Ladyship the name of Charles Alfred Seymour was invented, and Philadelphia was selected as the nominal place of printing.[7]

Despite Wise's claim, Dowden at least was not involved in this project, which was undertaken to make money for Wise and Forman from the sale of a Shelley "first edition." In response to Wise's gift of a copy of *Poems and Sonnets* Dowden expressed his thinly veiled anger at Wise's action:

> You are very good to give me (on behalf of "Mr. Charles Alfred Seymour") the beautiful quarto. When a gentleman of

---

7   *The Ashley Library* (London: Printed for Private Circulation Only, 1924), V, 100.

the road makes you stand and deliver, and then courteously hands you back your purse, you can do no less than make a bow and say that he has the manners of a Prince. And so I feel to that amiable member of the Phila. Hist. Soc. He has done his work with the greatest care and correctness as far as I can see, and I hope you will greet him from me in the words of Shelley in his Homeric hymn which tells of the light-fingered doings of the first of pirates.[8]

Wise had already prepared but not yet printed another false imprint for Shelley's *Letters . . . to Elizabeth Hitchner* (1890, 2 vols.). Henry James Slack of Forest Row, Sussex, allowed William Michael Rossetti to transcribe the originals in his possession to include in an anthology that never appeared. Wise borrowed the transcript from Rossetti, prepared a false title page (New York, 1886), and published the work in a limited edition, printed by Richard Clay & Sons. Between 1889 and 1894 Wise issued five other volumes of Shelley's correspondence; they bear no publisher's or printer's imprint, though the last two carry Wise's library device.

By 1888 Wise and Forman had begun to vary piracy with a little forgery.[9] Choosing short 19th-century works that for the most part had not appeared individually in book form, they created spurious first editions. Their productions could not be compared with authentic first editions because none existed, thus making detection of their frauds difficult. In early 1888 Wise sent Swinburne a copy of *Cleopatra* bearing the imprint "London: John Camden Hotten, Picadilly. 1866" but actually printed by Richard Clay & Sons in late 1887 or 1888. Wise claimed to have paid seven guineas for it, which is true if one applies the cost to the entire run of thirty to fifty copies. If he was hoping that Swinburne's response would lend authenticity to the fabrication he was disappointed. On 27 April 1888 Swinburne replied, "I am quite certain, quite positive, that I never set eyes on the booklet before, nor heard of its existence."[10]

---

8   Quoted in Barker and Collins, 133–134.
9   The spurious Dante Gabriel Rossetti *Verses,* containing "At the Fall of the Leaf" and "After the French Liberation of Italy," may date from late 1887.
10 In Barker and Collins, 134.

Probably the next Wise-Forman fabrication was Elizabeth Barrett Browning's *The Runaway Slave,* supposedly printed by Edward Moxon (London) in 1849 but manufactured by Richard Clay & Sons in 1888. Wise told Robert Browning about the work, but the response was once more disappointing. On 1 August 1888 Browning wrote, "I never heard of a separate [English] publication, and am pretty certain such a circumstance never happened. I fear this must be a fabricated affair." Confronted with the actual pamphlet, Browning relented:

> I daresay the fact has been that, on the publication of the Poem in America, the American friends (in London) who had been instrumental in obtaining it, wrote to the Authoress (in Florence) for leave to reprint it in England, and that she of course gave her consent. . . . The respectability of the Publisher and Printer is a guarantee that nothing surreptitious had been done.[11]

Proof sheets of Wise-Forman fabrications exist only for *Cleopatra* and *The Runaway Slave,* suggesting that these were apprentice efforts.

Algernon Charles Swinburne had arranged for the printing of six copies of *Siena* (1868) to secure copyright, and Wise attempted to imitate this edition. The facsimile was sufficiently different to attract attention. In 1894 John Herbert Slater's *Early Editions: A Bibliographical Survey of the Works of Modern Authors* (London: K. Paul, Trench, Trübner) condemned this "pirated reprint" (294). Wise replied in May 1894 in his review of Slater's book, "The 'masterly pirated reprints' of 'Siena' described on p. 294 is a creation of the author's fancy, these 'forged copies' being none other than examples of the first published edition of the pamphlet."[12] The first appearance of the Wise fabrication at auction dates from

---

11   In John Collins, *The Two Forgers: A Biography of Harry Buxton Forman & Thomas James Wise* (New Castle, Del.: Oak Knoll Press, 1992), 90.

12   Quoted in *An Enquiry into the Nature of Certain Nineteenth Century Pamphlets* (London: Constable; New York: Scribner, 1934; 2nd ed., edited by Nicolas Barker and John Collins (London: Scolar Press, 1983), 113. All references to *An Enquiry* are from the second edition.

1889, indicating that it was another early effort. By 1896 Wise, while taking no responsibility for the publication, labeled it as the "second—or spurious—edition."

Swinburne's *Dead Love* ("London: W. Parker and Son, 1864") was produced in 1890. Wise and Forman took their text from the October 1862 *Once a Week*.[13] Swinburne denied the existence of any separate publication, and the firm of W. Parker and Son had ceased operation in 1863. The piece first appeared at auction in 1907, when it sold for £3 15s. At the January 1929 Jerome Kern sale a copy fetched $60, and a year later a copy sold at auction for $120.

Another early fabrication was Alfred, Lord Tennyson's *Idylls of the Hearth* ("London: Edward Moxon & Co., Dover Street. 1869"),[14] which Wise created by removing the title page from authentic copies of *Enoch Arden,* substituting a spurious title page, and having all copies bound to mask the alteration. In at least some copies Wise used the final blank of the authentic publication to create his spurious title page. Tennyson had in fact considered using Wise's title, and this was the title that appeared in the early proofs.

To gain respectability for their fabrications, Wise and Forman placed them in the British Museum, some through gift, others through purchase. The pamphlets would then be catalogued as legitimate. On 16 August 1888 Wise, acting through E. Schlengemann, a co-worker at Herman Rubeck & Co., sold a copy of *The Runaway Slave* to the British Museum for £5, and on 23 October a copy of George Eliot's *Brother and Sister* ("London: For Private Circulation Only, 1869" but a Wise-Forman fake) for three guineas. Perhaps this income helped pay for Wise's 1888 purchase of a first edition of Robert Browning's *Pauline*. Wise paid Fred Hutt of Clements Inn £22 10s. for the work, again showing Wise's understanding of the rare book market. In 1894 another copy sold for £325. In 1889 the British Museum bought

---

13 7: 432–434.
14 On 20 May 1890 the British Museum paid five guineas to Otto Rubeck for a copy. The fabrication may have been produced as early as 1888. The University of Texas owns three proof sheets of the title page. These proof sheets suggest that *Idylls* was an early fabrication.

a copy of *Cleopatra* for £5 5s. two Ruskin fabrications for two guineas each, and Matthew Arnold's *St. Brandon* ("London: E. W. & A. Skipworth. 1867," but another Wise-Forman fabrication) again for two guineas. The vendor was Otto Rubeck, son of Wise's employer.

Though these figures may seem low, they were moderately expensive for the time; pre-Restoration drama, for example, was selling for about the same prices. Even at two guineas a pamphlet, an edition of thirty would yield a handsome profit, since production would cost about £7. But Wise and Forman were aiming at higher profits still. The initial sale or gift to the British Museum would establish a work's authenticity; then Wise and Forman could raise their prices. For example, on 10 December 1888 Sotheby's (London) auctioned a copy of the Wise-Forman *Agatha* ("London: Trubner & Co., 60 Paternoster Row. 1869") by George Eliot, which Forman bought for £10 5s. Selling the pamphlet at auction provided still another means of creating an air of legitimacy, and paying a high price for one copy would establish the value of the others that Wise and Forman would release on the market.

Yet another way of validating forgeries was through listings in bibliographies, a device Wise would use repeatedly. In November 1889 the second part of James P. Smart's and Wise's *A Complete Bibliography of the Writings in Prose and Verse of John Ruskin* appeared; in it Wise inserted a description of *The National Gallery* ("London: 1852"), a Wise-Forman fabrication. Wise here observed that *The National Gallery* "was probably printed only for private distribution, as Messrs. Smith, Elder & Co. have no record of any copies having been offered for sale by them."[15] This observation would forestall suspicion should anyone examine the purported publisher's records. Similarly, in *Elizabeth Barrett Browning and Her Scarcer Books* (1896) Forman gave his imprimatur to *The Runaway Slave*.

Money was an important motive for these forgeries: Wise and Forman may have earned as much as £50,000 from their fabrications. Another motive was prestige. Like John Payne Collier, Wise

---

15   Quoted in Barker and Collins, 135.

established a reputation for bibliographic knowledge by "discovering" and describing works otherwise unknown. Thus, on 16 February 1897 Wise wrote to Edmund Gosse, "I wonder you did not know of [Swinburne's] 'The Devil's Due.' It only shows how very circumstantial is the knowledge of even the best of us when such trifles as the minute points of Bibliography are in question." Wise goes on to say, "I knew of the tract years ago: or rather I had heard that such a tract was set up in type, for until a month ago I had never been able to see a copy."[16] Wise had not seen a copy because it had not existed as a separate publication until Wise and Forman created it in 1896 or January 1897. In this letter Wise claimed that Fairfax Murray had first called his attention to the work. In the preface to *A Swinburne Library* (London: Privately Printed, 1925, p. x), Wise credited the discovery to Frederick James Furnivall.

Wise's questionable activities did not go unnoticed. On 11 January 1888 Bertram Dobell, a learned dealer who sold books to Wise and Forman, and who was a member of the Browning and Shelley Societies, wrote in his diary, "Wise is still proceeding on his wild career of reprinting or pirating Browning, Shelley, Swinburne, &c."[17]

At the same time that Wise was engaged in manufacturing spurious first editions, he was also creating for collectors limited edition reprints of 19th-century works such as Edward Fitzgerald's *Rubaiyat* (1887) and William Morris' *Letters on Socialism* (1894). Already by 1889 he had produced about fifty such pamphlets.

On 12 July 1890 Wise married Selima Fanny Smith, daughter of Frederick Smith, a salesman.[18] She was twenty-two, ten years Wise's junior. The couple settled in 52 Ashley Road in north London. Though Wise lived here for only about six years, the street provided the name for his library; the name was suggested by two of Wise's neighbors, Clement King Shorter, a fellow bibliophile and editor of the *Illustrated London News,* and William Robertson Nicoll, editor of *The Bookman.* In 1893 Frederick Colin Tilney

16 In Barker and Collins, 229–230.
17 Ibid., 48.
18 Wise probably met her at the Camden Road Baptist Church.

designed a bookplate and trademark for the Ashley Library; Tilney also supplied the decorations for Wise's most notorious forgery, the "Reading, 1847" edition of Elizabeth Barrett Browning's *Sonnets [from the Portuguese]*, released in 1894 but manufactured perhaps as early as 1890.

In 1890 Wise and Forman definitely produced four spurious pamphlets of Swinburne, two Ruskins, two by William Morris, three Robert Brownings, and one each by Matthew Arnold, Tennyson, Dante Gabriel Rossetti, and William Makepeace Thackeray. Only three fabrications date from 1891: two Swinburnes and a Charles Dickens. The figure rose to seven in 1892: two Ruskins, one Swinburne, one Matthew Arnold, a George Meredith, and two Tennysons. The next year saw the production of a spurious Swinburne and another Arnold.[19]

The year 1892 brought two important people into Wise's life. The first was the fourteen-year old Herbert Gorfin. Herman Rubeck relocated to 59 Mark Lane, London, in that year and hired Gorfin as office boy. Even as a teenager Gorfin helped Wise with his book-selling, and he would become a leading purveyor, perhaps unwittingly, of Wise's fabrications.

An even more profitable association began that year when the Chicago publisher and bibliophile W. Irving Way introduced his fellow Chicagoan and collector John Henry Wrenn to Wise, who gave Wrenn a tour of the already impressive Ashley Library. In 1893 the two began a correspondence that ended only with Wrenn's death in 1911. According to Wise, Wrenn was worth £1,000 a year to him. Wise was able to exploit the American in a variety of ways while at the same time helping him build an impressive collection of English literature. About 80% of Wrenn's library came from Wise, and Wrenn's collection mirrors Wise's, which in turn was modeled on the Rowfant Library assembled by Frederick Locker-Lampson, who created a collection of the masterpieces of English literature from Chaucer to Swinburne. By the time Wise began collecting, certain

---

19   William B. Todd's "A Handlist of Thomas J. Wise" in *Thomas J. Wise Centenary Studies,* ed. William B. Todd (Austin: University of Texas Press, 1959), 80–122 is a useful but incomplete guide to the year by year production of the Wise-Forman fabrications.

authors, particularly Shakespeare, were beyond his purse, but to the extent possible Wise followed his model.

In April 1897 Wise sold Wrenn a first edition of Milton's *Paradise Lost* (London: Printed and Sold by Peter Parker, Robert Boulter, and Matthias Walker, 1668) for £70, a fine volume though not the first issue Wise claimed it was. In that year Wise also sold Wrenn a copy of Tennyson's *Idylls of the Hearth,* a Wise creation. Wrenn's interest in Tennyson probably encouraged Wise and Forman to manufacture first editions of that poet. Tennyson's death in 1892, the year Wise and Wrenn met, reduced the risk of such productions. Wise was able to sell Wrenn a copy of *The Last Tournament* ("London, 1871") for £28 10s., or about four times the cost of the entire edition printed by Richard Clay & Sons. The Wise-Forman *Morte D'Arthur* ("London: Edward Moxon, Dover Street, MDCCCXLII") cost Wrenn £40 in 1899. Between 1897 and 1907 Wise and Forman made about £900 through the sale of some seventy-five fabrications to Wrenn.

Wise also sold Wrenn his more legitimate privately printed pamphlets, and he profited through other bookselling. In 1902 a copy of Thomas Dekker's *Wonder of a Kingdom* (London: Printed by Robert Raworth, for Nicholas Vavasour, 1636) sold at auction for £4. Wise sold a copy to Wrenn in 1903 for £25. James Shirley's *Triumph of Peace* (London: William Cooke, 1633) brought £5 at auction in 1902, or half of what Wise charged Wrenn for a copy that year. One way that Wise profited by his sales to Wrenn was by purchasing imperfect copies of works and then completing them by stealing leaves from British Museum copies. Wise stole between 200 and 300 leaves from the British Museum, sixty of which he used in books he sold to Wrenn. Another eighty-nine were inserted in Wise's own books, and still others served to perfect other works that Wise then sold. In 1905 Wise sold a perfect copy of Ben Jonson's *The Case Is Alterd* (London: Printed for Bartholomew Sutton and William Barrenger, 1609) to Wrenn for $500; it includes seven leaves stolen from two British Museum copies. At Sotheby's on 9 December 1902 Pickering bought a copy of Thomas Nabbes's *The Bride* (London: Laurence Blaikelocke, 1640) lacking leaves B2 and B3. On 17 April 1903 Wise sold this copy to Wrenn, but it had been perfected. The British Museum copy now lacks leaves B2 and B3, as well as F3, H3, and I2.

Wise exploited Wrenn in another way also. Wrenn sent a copy of William Davenant's *The Witts* (London: Richard Meighen, 1636) to Wise for binding. Wise exchanged three inferior leaves of his own copy for the better leaves in Wrenn's. Wise bought the Rowfant Library copy of Thomas Nash's *Summer's Last Will and Testament* (London: Walter Burre, 1600) for Wrenn, but before sending it to America he exchanged twelve leaves from his copy for the better ones in the Rowfant volume. In calculating the thousand pounds a year Wrenn was worth to him, Wise may have included the Continental holidays on which the American took Wise each year, paying all expenses except tips, and Wise may have added in profits from other Americans to whom Wrenn introduced Wise. John Alden Spoor of Chicago was probably among them; Spoor's library contained an even larger number of Wise-Forman fabrications that Wrenn's.

Wise began contributing to *The Bookman* in 1892, and the next year he undertook the "Notes on Recent Book Sales" section. Although Wise had published little as yet, he already had a reputation as a bibliographer, as indicated by Nicoll's May 1893 announcement of Wise's column:

> Our readers will learn with great pleasure that Mr. Thomas J. Wise, the well-known collector and bibliographer, has undertaken the editorship of our "Notes on Recent Book Sales." . . . [He] will add, out of the fullness of his knowledge and experience, such comments as will be interesting to all readers and particularly valuable to book buyers and booksellers.

The column became yet another means of promoting faked first editions, but it also encouraged the collecting of 19th-century authors.

With the demise of the Shelley and Browning Societies in 1892, Wise turned his energies to the Society of Archivists and Autograph Collectors. Its chief purpose was to publish monographs on scripts of selected authors, "giving hints for guidance in the detection of forgeries." The society published nine volumes. Wise contributed the monographs on Charlotte Brontë and Charles Dickens, and he edited five others between 1893 and 1898. During this period Wise also edited Edmund Spenser's *Faerie Queene* (1894–1897) and John Ruskin's *Harbours of England* (1895) for the London publisher George Allen.

In the *Fortnightly Review* for March 1894 William Roberts, a traditionalist, criticized the vogue for modern firsts:

> Time was when the craze existed in a perfectly rational form, and when the first editions in demand were books of importance and books with both histories and reputations, whilst their collectors were scholars and men of judgment. Now every little volume of drivelling verse becomes an object of more or less hazardous speculation, and the book market itself a stock exchange in miniature.[20]

Wise replied in *The Bookman* for April and May 1894, in his response touting Matthew Arnold's *Saint Brandan* and *Geist's Grave*, William Morris' *Sir Galahad* and *Hapless Love*, Ruskin's *The Scythian Guest* and *The Queen's Gardens*, Dante Gabriel Rossetti's *Verses* and *Sister Helen*, Tennyson's *Lucretius*, Robert Browning's *Gold Hair*, George Eliot's *Agatha*, and Swinburne's *Siena*, all of these Wise-Forman fabrications.

In his review of John Herbert Slater's *Early Editions: A Bibliographical Survey of the Works of Modern Authors*, Wise in the *Bookman* for May 1894 again promoted *Gold Hair*, which Slater accepted as legitimate and valued at £5. "*Gold Hair*," Wise wrote, "is a privately printed pamphlet of the greatest rarity, and the sale of no copy has ever been recorded by Browning specialists. There would be no difficulty in finding buyers for a half a dozen copies at *Twice* the £5 at which it is here reported to be 'selling.' "[21] Wise quoted a price of £42 for his spurious *The Scythian Guest* and chided Slater for failing to include the work in his bibliography. This high price may have been based on the John Rylands Library (Manchester) 1892 purchase of *The Scythian Guest*, together with

---

20   "The First Edition Mania," 61:347–354, 347.
21   In Collins, 115.

a copy on vellum of Wise's acknowledged private printing of Ruskin's *Two Letters Concerning Notes on the Construction of Sheepfolds* (1890), for £63. At its first auction appearance *The Scythian Guest* (Sotheby's, 10 June 1903), bound in morocco, fetched £10 5s. Slater's bibliography reflects contemporary collecting interests. Wise and Forman understood their market: of the thirty-two authors listed, thirteen are represented in the Wise-Forman fabrications. As John Carter and Graham Pollard wrote in 1934, the forgeries are "a faithful reflection of the collecting taste of the modern school of 1885–1895" and so demonstrate an astute sense of literary history, literary taste, and bibliography.[22]

Carter and Pollard, booksellers themselves, noted the demand for rare pamphlets around the turn of the century. Hence,

> Those whose business it is to supply such demands naturally ransacked their stock for anything of the kind which they might unearth, and there were eager buyers, both trade and private, for anything offered; without too much regard, perhaps, to its provenance. There were, it is true, a fair number of pamphlet issues in the output of the fashionable authors of the moment: but, as these really were rare, there were not nearly enough. If only some others could be discovered, what pleasure and what profit would be provided for all concerned![23]

Just as public demand for autographs created the environment conducive to the fabrications of George Gordon Byron and Vrain-Denis Lucas, so the rage for modern first editions, especially in limited private printings, helped call forth Wise's productions. In 1894 those released were Elizabeth Barrett Browning's *Sonnets from the Portuguese,* two Swinburnes, a Ruskin, a Robert Louis Stevenson, and another by Elizabeth Barrett Browning, bringing the total number of spurious works to about forty.

In 1895 Wise's friendship with Clement Shorter proved profitable when Shorter and Robertson Nicoll traced Charlotte Brontë's husband, the Reverend Arthur Bell Nicholls, to Banagher,

---

22   *An Enquiry into the Nature of Certain Nineteenth Century Pamphlets,* 113.
23   Ibid., 108.

Ireland. Shorter and Wise paid £400 for copyrights and a collection of manuscripts and letters, including the juvenile tales of Angria. Wise bought most of the material from Shorter, and later he secured additional Brontë items from Nicoll through Forman. To finance these purchases Wise published some of the material in his characteristic pamphlets, but he also sold some of the manuscripts, thus dispersing the Angria collection. From Shorter Wise also secured other important letters. The two regularly visited London bookshops together and then lunched. Instead of paying the bill, Shorter would give Wise a letter from Thomas Hardy, George Meredith, or some other writer he knew.

In the year of the Charlotte Brontë purchase, Wise published an expanded version of *The Ashley Library: A List of Books Printed for Private Circulation,* first issued two years earlier. Another, still larger list appeared in 1897. In the 1895 catalogue Wise claimed that

> the following list is printed as a Record, not by way of adver-
> tisement. Books printed in short numbers for private circula-
> tion become so rapidly and entirely absorbed, that it is
> exceedingly difficult to obtain information regarding them
> when such is required for bibliographical or other purposes.
> Hence the necessity for the recent catalogue.

In fact Wise was using the catalogue to advertise his private publications, particularly letters by Shelley and Ruskin.

In 1895, too, Wise's wife left him; a divorce was granted him in 1897. Wise left Ashley Road in 1896 and moved to 15 George's Road (now Priory Terrace), Kilburn, London. Wise forgeries in 1896 included Tennyson's *The Last Tournament, Morte D'Arthur,* and *The Promise of May,* and five Swinburne fabrications.

Wise's new address put him closer to Forman, and together they edited *Literary Anecdotes of the Nineteenth Century* (1895–1896), which they used to lend legitimacy to their spurious first editions. In the second volume of *Literary Anecdotes,* published in December 1896, Wise wrote,

> It is said that concurrently with its appearance in the columns
> of *The Examiner, The Devil's Due* was printed in pamphlet
> form for private distribution but was rigidly suppressed in

consequence of the unexpected result of the action for libel brought by Mr. Robert Buchanan against Mr. P. A. Taylor, M. P., the Proprietor of *The Examiner*. If such a pamphlet does exist it must be of the utmost rarity, as no copy is known to the Editors of *Literary Anecdotes,* who have instituted a lengthy search in the hopes of finding a stray example.[24]

Then, as noted earlier, in February 1897 Wise reported to Sir Edmund Gosse that he had located a copy, but the owner was asking the exorbitant sum of £15 15s. In 1899 Wise "located" a copy for Wrenn. Supposedly it belonged to Joseph Howell of Cambridge, and Wise sold it to Wrenn for £12 10s. After Swinburne died in 1909 and his executor Theodore Watts-Dunton in 1914, Wise in *A Bibliography of the Writings in Prose and Verse of Algernon Charles Swinburne* (London: Printed by Ricahrd Clay & Sons, 1919–1920) was able to revise his history to say that in 1897 Watts-Dunton had sold him a copy for £21 and then, in 1900, had located a cache of fifteen others that he sold to Wise for three guineas each. How Wise was able to sell Wrenn a copy in 1899 is unexplained in this account, and Joseph Howell vanishes from the story. Wise even manufactured a presentation copy to Watts-Dunton from Swinburne by inserting an inscribed piece of paper into a copy bound by Robert Riviere. The inscription and Wise's Swinburne bibliography validated the fabrication.

Wise's anecdotal abilities thus rivaled his skill in producing first editions. In 1901 he informed Wrenn of the purchase of Thackeray's *A Leaf out of a Sketch Book* ("London: Emily Faithfull & Co., Victoria Press, 1861"). Wise claimed that the copy had belonged to George Dolby, Charles Dickens' secretary during Dickens' American tour, and that Thackeray had given it either to Dickens or Dolby. In fact, Wise had produced the pamphlet about 1899.

Forman's name was left off the title page of *Literary Anecdotes,* prompting an angry response in which Forman accused Wise of unethical behavior in failing to note the number of copies

---

24   *Literary Anecdotes of the Nineteenth Century* (London: Hodder & Stroughton, 1896), II, 355.

being printed of a limited edition of Ruskin's letters. Wise wrote back on the letter, "And we print 'Last Tournament' in 1896, and want 'some one to think' it was printed in 1871! *The moral position is exactly the same!*"[25] This letter came into the possession of the American collector Carl Pforzheimer and confirmed the guilt of Wise and Forman in producing the faked first editions.

In 1896 Wise, as always claiming that he was acting only as a friend and intermediary, began selling to another American, William Harris Arnold. Although Wise also sold to Robert Alfred Potts, Alfred Crampon, and others in England, he preferred American customers because in general they were less inquisitive regarding Wise's fabrications. Arnold, like Wrenn, collected Tennyson. In *Ventures in Book Collecting* (New York: Charles Scribner's Sons, 1923) Arnold wrote, "Through the kind offices of my new, but now dear old, friend, the distinguished collector and bibliographer, Thomas J. Wise, . . . I obtained one Tennyson rarity after another, most of which at the time were unknown to American collectors" (14). As in the case of Wise's sales to Wrenn, many of these items were legitimate, such as *The Victim* (Canford Manor, Dorsetshire: Author, 1867), rare examples of Tennyson's habit of printing a few copies of a poem before making final revisions for actual publication. Wise did, however, have the unfortunate propensity to identify authors' proofs as independent first editions, even though printed from the same setting of type as the copies sold to the public.[26] Wise also sold Arnold the fabricated *The Falcon* ($350), *The Promise of May* ($330), and *Lucretius* ($25) as well as the "Reading, 1847" *Sonnets* ($115), *The Runaway Slave* ($30), and *Gold Hair* ($13.60). The *Sonnets* was a double forgery, since it bore a false inscription indicating that the pamphlet was a gift from Mary Russell Mitford, who supposedly oversaw its publication, to the author Charles Kingsley. Yet Arnold did not lose money in his dealings with Wise. When his books were sold at auction in November 1924, all but *The Runaway Slave* brought more than Arnold had paid for the Wise productions. The

---

25 In Collins, 131.
26 See Roger C. Lewis, *Thomas James Wise and the Trial Book Fallacy* (Aldershot, Eng.: Scolar Press, 1995).

Sonnets did especially well, fetching $440, nearly four times what Arnold had paid.

In 1897 Wise and Forman manufactured eleven fakes, including five Tennysons. In this year Wise also published bibliographies of Swinburne and Robert Browning, which listed his fabrications. As Partington notes, these bibliographies "advanced his reputation as a bibliographer and a collector; they also publicized his forgeries and piracies, and assisted his bookselling." Yet Partington conceded that "with all their faults [they remain] unmatchable as the performance of one man. There is nothing like them for range of interest in the vast literature of literature."[27]

Among the pamphlets Wise and Forman produced in 1898 or 1899 was the aptly named *The Story of a Lie*. Robert Louis Stevenson had first published this work in *The New Quarterly Magazine* for October 1879 (pp. 307–355). Wise's fabrication bears the imprint "London: Hayley & Jackson, Little Queen Street, W.C., 1882." No such establishment existed. When William Francis Prideaux was preparing his Stevenson bibliography, Wise invited him to visit and showed him his copy of *The Story of a Lie*. Wise may even have given Prideaux a copy of his own. In his 1903 bibliography, Prideaux duly listed it. Here he echoed Wise's story that the work had been printed but never published, and that most of the copies had been destroyed.

In 1900 Wise married Frances Louise Greenhalgh; she was twenty-five, he forty-one. The couple occupied 23 Downside Crescent, Hampstead. In 1910 they moved to 25 Heath Park, their final address. Between 1900 and 1903 Wise and Forman produced another dozen forgeries, six of them Tennysons. According to John Collins, by 1903 sales of these pamphlets had yielded about £900 in England and twice that in America.

Wise sold his fabrications privately to individuals and through auction, but he also disposed of them through unwitting booksellers. His first victim was J. E. Cornish of Manchester, but James E. Evans and Walter T. Spencer of London also bought from Wise. In 1904 Spencer created a fake first edition of *Dead Love* from

27 *Forging Ahead*, 125, 174.

Wise's forgery. Wise exposed Spencer and wrote, "The whole thing proves once more that, easy as it appears to be to fabricate reprints of rare books, it is in actual practice absolutely impossible to do so in such a manner that detection cannot follow the result."[28]

This statement was supported by the comments of Sir Edward Tyas Cook and Alexander Wedderburn in their 39-volume edition of the works of John Ruskin. In 1903 they challenged *Leoni: A Legend of Italy* ("London: 1868") and *The Scythian Guest* ("MDCCCXLIX[,] Printed for the Author"), and in 1904 they labeled *The National Gallery* ("London: 1852") "a fake." Of *The Queen's Gardens* ("Manchester: Printed in Aid of the St. Andrews Schools Fund, 1864") they wrote in volume 18 of their edition,

> This pamphlet, which figures in dealers' language as "of the extremist scarcity" is — like the separate issues of *Leoni* . . . and *The National Gallery* . . . what is known in the trade as a "fake." It purports to have been "printed in aid of the St. Andrew's School Fund"; in which case the issue would obviously not have been limited to a few copies; yet until 1893 no copy of it ever came to light. It bears the imprint of a firm which now at any rate is "not known" by the Post Office. . . . [T]he pamphlet is not what it purports to be, but is a clumsy "fake." The person who put it upon the market, not knowing that Ruskin had revised the lecture in 1871, had this "original edition of the utmost scarcity," set up from the later edition.[29]

Cook and Weddenburn did not, however, accuse Wise, and their comments were buried in the notes to their extensive edition.

Others also expressed doubts. Bertram Dobell's 1888 diary entry has already been noted. A decade later George D. Smith, the leading bookseller in New York, perhaps in America, raised questions about Wise's fabrications. In *Prices Current of Books* he cautioned,

---

28 Quoted in Collins, 161.
29 *The Works of John Ruskin,* 39 vols. (London: G. Allen, 1903-1912), XVIII (1905), 14–15.

> There is an uneasy feeling among collectors on this side regarding the numerous little privately printed pamphlets by celebrated modern authors which are being offered from England. Grave suspicions are entertained that some of these are being manufactured—but that these suspicions are well grounded, cannot be said. One thing is certain, however, the rarity of these ephemera has been much exaggerated.[30]

Three years later, in *The Literary Collector* for March 1901, Smith was still more critical: "It is significant that all these high-priced and 'rare' privately printed items are of the pamphlet variety and of modern date—few being over 20pp. and of an earlier date than 1865. They are easy of fabrication and we believe them to have been fabricated."[31] Smith did not blame Wise, by now a well-respected bibliographer and collector, and Smith's warnings went unheeded.

Wise may have been more alarmed by them than anyone else. In a letter to Wrenn, Wise sought to allay any concerns of his valuable client, dismissing Smith's statements as "absurd nonsense talked, or written, by a second rate New York bookseller, who cannot get copies of the rarer Tennyson pieces, and so tries to put his customers off them by crying 'sour grapes,' and asserting that they have been reprinted."[32] In the entry for "Bibliography" in the 1910 *Encyclopaedia Britannica* (11th ed.), noted bibliographer A. W. Pollard again raised questions about the 19th-century pamphlets, but again virtually no one paid attention.

By 1904 Wise and Forman had abandoned their forgeries. Forman was earning £1,000 a year, and in 1905 Wise joined in a prosperous partnership with Otto Portman Rubeck, the son of his employer, in an essential oils distillery that they called W. A. Smith & Co., though he continued to supplement his income through the publication of properly dated, if sometimes pirated, pamphlets and the sale of books to Wrenn, Arnold, and others.

---

30 Quoted in Barker and Collins, 158.
31 John Carter, "Thomas J. Wise in Perspective," in *Thomas J. Wise Centenary Studies*, 3–19, 5n.
32 *Letters of Thomas J. Wise to John Henry Wrenn: A Further Inquiry into the Guilt of Certain Nineteenth-Century Forgers*, ed. Fannie E. Ratchford (New York: Knopf, 1944), 208–209.

Wise's friendship with Clement Shorter once more enriched the Ashley Library in 1904, when the two men bought all the unpublished manuscripts of George Borrow from the writer's widow. Between 1913 and 1914 Wise published forty-four pamphlets containing much of this material, and all were then listed as first editions in Wise's 1914 bibliography of Borrow.

Wise's increased prosperity is evident in his book-buying. In August 1905 he bought a large segment of Frederick Locker-Lampson's Rowfant Library, which had inspired his own collecting interests, and in September 1905 he paid Forman £350 for Shelley's *Queen Mab* (London: P. B. Shelley, 1813). Only 250 copies were printed, and far fewer entered circulation. Many of these were mutilated by Shelley, who removed the imprint and dedication leaf to protect those associated with this radical work. Wise also bought heavily from Bernard Quaritch. Among his acquisitions between 1905 and 1908 were one of only two known copies of Ben Jonson's *Volpone* (London: T. Thorpe, 1607, £60) to contain the verses of Nathan Field, and Jonson's *The Alchemist* (London: W.[alter] Burre, 1612, £39). Other purchases during this period include Samuel Daniel's *The First Foure Bookes of the Civile Wars* (London: Simon Waterson, 1595, £25), George Chapman's *The Conspiracie and Tragedie of Charles Duke of Byron* (London: T. Thorpe, 1608, £20), Thomas Nash's *Have with You to Saffron Walden* (London: Printed by John Danter, 1596, £99) and *Lenten Stuff* (Printed for N. L.[ing] and C. B.[urbie], 1599, £111), and John Marston's *The Malcontent* (London: William Aspley, 1604, £70). One of his most expensive purchases from Quaritch was John Lyly's *The Woman in the Moone* (London: W. Jones, 1597), for which he paid £264.

Between 1905 and 1908 Wise issued the first catalogue of the Ashley Library. The two large quarto volumes describe about seven hundred items and include some two hundred illustrations. Wise reproduced title pages of some of his forgeries, but always from copies in other collections to enhance their appearance of authenticity and to divert suspicion.

Wise had long been an admirer, collector, and fabricator of Swinburne's books. In *A Swinburne Library* (1925) Wise wrote, "Three hundred and sixty-five days were included in the year

1886. One of these days was a red-letter day for me . . . it was with a thrill of delight that I was one day informed by Miss Mathilde Blind that she had asked and obtained permission to bring me to *The Pines*," where Swinburne was living with Theodore Watts-Dunton. After Swinburne died on 10 April 1909, leaving all his property to Watts-Dunton, Wise bought most of Swinburne's papers, including all the unpublished material, and some copyrights. Wise paid £3,000 for the manuscripts. He also bought some of Swinburne's Elizabethan books. Wise resold fifty of the manuscripts to Frank T. Sabin, a London bookseller, for £3,213. Others he sold to collectors including Wrenn and William K. Bixby of Saint Louis. To the publisher William Heinemann he sold the publishing rights to the new material (£900), and he privately printed seventy-six pamphlets. Wilfred Partington estimates that Wise made about £10,000 from his Swinburne purchases. Between 1909 and the death of Watts-Dunton in 1914 Wise bought additional books and manuscripts from The Pines.

By 1909 Wise had resolved to dissociate himself from all but the most profitable of his forgeries. Between 23 November 1909 and May 1912 he sold most of his stock, some nine hundred copies of about twenty titles, for £400 to Herbert Gorfin, who in 1912 established himself as a bookseller in Charing Cross Road. Wise retained his copies of the "Reading 1847" *Sonnets*, the most expensive of the fabrications, and six other titles but allowed Gorfin to sell them on commission.[33]

World War I created lower prices for books and higher prices for essential oils. Though Wise left Herman Rubeck in 1912, he remained active in his partnership with Otto Rubeck at least until 1920. During this period Wise continued to build his collection, publish limited editions, and produce bibliographies: of Coleridge

---

33 The other six were Tennyson's *The Sailor Boy* ("London: Emily Faithfull & Co., Victoria Press, 1861"), *A Welcome to Alexandria* ("London: Henry S. King & Co., 1874"), *The Falcon* ("London: Printed for the Author, 1879"), *The Cup* ("London: Printed for the Author, 1881"), and *The Promise of May* ("London: Printed for the Author, 1882"), as well as Thackeray's *A Leaf out of a Sketch Book* ("London: Emily Faithfull & Co., Victoria Press, 1861"). See Carter and Pollard's *An Enquiry*, p. 376.

in 1913, Borrow in 1914, Wordsworth in 1916, the Brontës in 1917, Elizabeth Barrett Browning in 1918, all based largely on his own holdings. In his limited editions Wise did not always scrupulously observe the laws of copyright. For example, in 1912 he published thirty copies of Dante Gabriel Rossetti's *Jan Van Hunks*, even though the copyright belonged to Theodore Watts-Dunton. In 1909 Wise had purchased Rossetti's manuscript of the work, but not the copyright, from Watts-Dunton. Wise also distorted the bibliographic record to enhance the value of his private printings. To increase the value of his legitimately produced thirty copies of Stevenson's *The Hanging Judge,* he denied the authenticity of the 1887 private printing when copies began surfacing.[34] Contrary to his common practice of elevating proofs to the level of first editions, he dismissed copies of the 1887 edition as proofs. In a 1929 letter to Stevenson biographer Sir Graham Balfour he went so far as to stigmatize copies of the 1887 printing as forgeries: "So many copies have been offered for sale from time to time that I am very suspicious of them. I have a strong idea that they have been fraudulently reprinted and that most of them are merely reprints."[35] Balfour wrote to R. and R. Clark, the Edinburgh publishers responsible for the 1887 edition, and learned the truth.

Towards the end of World War I Richard Curle, who was collecting Joseph Conrad, interested Wise in this writer. On 2 October 1918 Conrad wrote to Wise,

> Though I suppose John Quinn would like to have [the typescript and manuscript of *The Rescue*] and indeed may be said to have a moral claim on it, I will, if you at all care for it, reserve it for you, so that you should have the very last as well as the very first of the conception and execution of *The Rescue*. The two texts side by side may form a literary curiosity showing the modification of my judgment, of my taste, and also of my style during the 20 years covering almost the whole writing period of my life.[36]

34   No one had known of the 1887 edition when Wise published his in 1914.
35   Quoted in Roger C. Lewis, 220.
36   In Georges Jean-Aubry, *Joseph Conrad: Life and Letters* (Garden City, New York: Doubleday, Page, 1927), II, 209.

Quinn, a New York lawyer and collector who had become a patron of Conrad, was supposed to have first refusal of Conrad's manuscripts. Conrad later excused his action by saying, "I sold the typed first draft of *A.[rrow]* of *G.[old]* and also the incomplete MS. of *Rescue* (completed in type) to Mr. Wise because I wanted the money at once for a specific purpose."[37] Conrad continued to sell his postwar typescripts (he essentially ceased writing drafts by hand) to Wise rather than to Quinn, and Wise paid handsomely. In 1920 he gave Conrad £100 for the corrected typescript of Conrad's unproduced play *Laughing Anne* and £150 for the typescript of the stage version of *The Secret Agent*. In 1921 he paid £100 for the original draft and first typescript of *Job* and £200 in 1922 for the corrected typescript of *The Rover*. For Conrad's 8,500 word introduction to Thomas Beer's *Stephen Crane: A Study in American Letters* (New York: A. A. Knopf, 1923) Wise paid £110 in 1923. Wise and Clement Shorter also issued limited editions of Conrad's short pieces, sharing the profits with the author. In 1919 alone Conrad earned £200 from the sale of these works. By 1921, when Wise issued the second edition of his Conrad bibliography, Wise had produced at least twenty private Conrad publications. These pieces, which cost Wise less than £2 each, sold for at least ten times that sum, earning him a large profit. Moreover, though Wise claimed that each pamphlet was limited to only twenty-five copies, he had extra proofs produced. These he labeled as trial copies and later sold them at a premium to collectors.

In the 1920s Wise was at the apogee of his career. In 1922, the year he was elected president of the Bibliographical Society, the first two volumes of the alphabetically-arranged catalogue of his Ashley Library appeared. The introduction to each of the eleven volumes of the Ashley Library catalogue was written by a prominent bookman. Richard Curle wrote the introduction to volume one, giving an overview of the collection. Curle called Wise's "easily the foremost Private Library in England" and then explained why it merited that title:

---

37 In B. L. Reid, *The Man from New York: John Quinn and His Friends* (New York: Oxford University Press, 1968), 382.

Mr. Wise's aim, throughout the forty-and-more years during which he has been collecting books, has been to form a Library of the first editions of the famous English poets and dramatists, in perfect state, from Elizabethan times until the present. And what strikes one so forcibly is the extraordinary success which he has achieved. . . . I would not like to hazard a guess as to the number of celebrated authors of whose first editions Mr. Wise's collections are the finest, not alone in private hands but in existence, and as to the number of them which are here either absolutely or virtually complete; but in this double sense I would mention the names of Nashe, Ben Jonson (the plays), Shirley, Milton (poetry and tracts), Ford, Davenant, Chapman (the plays), Waller, Dryden, Pope, Prior, Gay, Wordsworth, Coleridge, Shelley, Keats, Byron, Landor, Tennyson, the Brownings, Arnold, the Brontës, Borrow, Morris, D. G. Rossetti, and Swinburne. To read the entries in this Catalogue under these names . . . is to all intents and purposes the same as reading their complete bibliographies.[38]

Curle also called the Ashley Library catalogue "a permanent and priceless addition to our knowledge of the authors of whose books they treat." David Nichol Smith echoed this sentiment in his introduction to volume eight (1926) of the catalogue:

We may . . . say that the completion of these eight volumes with their wealth of detail, their scrupulous accuracy, and their generous supply of reproductions, is an event of real significance in the steady progress of English scholarship. . . . The whole section on Pope is a contribution of great importance to our knowledge of the poet.[39]

In these volumes as in his other bibliographies Wise sought to describe a book as precisely as possible, including the collation (leaves and gatherings), but also to explain why a book assumed its particular physical state. He discussed typographical errors, variant title pages, gaps in page numbers in volumes without missing text.

---

38 *The Ashley Library* (London: Printed for Private Circulation Only, 1922), I, vii.
39 *The Ashley Library* (London: Printed for Private Circulation Only, 1926), VIII, viii–x.

Wise also provided the personal background of his books and their literary history, the personal as well as the technical side of bibliography.

The library, which continued to grow even as the catalogues were issued and which ultimately contained between 5,000 and 7,000 volumes, included over three hundred manuscripts and thousands of autograph letters. At least thirty-seven volumes were unique; another eighteen existed in only two copies, and fifty-eight items were not in the British Museum. Wise owned the only known perfect copies of *Gammer Gurton's Needle* (London: Thomas Colwell, 1575) by "Mr. S.," probably the schoolmaster William Stevenson, Thomas Dekker's *Wonderful Yeare* (London: Printed by Thomas Creede, 1603), Matthew Prior's *Pindarique on His Majesty's Birthday* (London: John Amery, 1690), John Gay's *To a Lady on Her Passion for Old China* (London: J. Tonson, 1725) and "Molly Mogg," a 1726 broadside, Coleridge's *Remarks . . . on Sir Robert Peel's Bill* (London: Printed by W. Clowes, 1818), and Edward Fitzgerald's *Translations into Verse from Comedies of Molière and Casamire Delavigne* (Paris: A. E. W. Galiguari, 1829); the only uncut copies of John Marston's *Wonder of Women* (London: I. Windet, 1606), John Dryden's *MacFlecknoe* (London: D. Green, 1682), and Thomas Gray's extremely rare *Ode on a Distant Prospect of Eton College* (London: Printed for R. Dodsley, 1747); and the tallest known copy of Milton's *Comus* (London: H. Robinson, 1637).

The extent of Wise's holdings of various authors' works is as impressive as these individual treasures. Sixty-four pages of volume four of the Ashley Library catalogue are devoted to the works of Alexander Pope; Wise is still cited as an authority on this author. Wise's holdings begin with the first edition, first issue of *An Essay on Criticism* (London: Printed for W. Lewis, 1711) and Bernard Lintot's *Miscellaneous Poems and Translations* (London: Lintot, 1712), which contains the first appearance of *The Rape of the Lock* in two cantos, later expanded to five. Wise owned one of two known copies of the two-page leaflet *The Court Ballad* (London: Printed for R. Burleigh, 1716); the other copy is in the Wrenn Library at the University of Texas. Wise also sought to untangle the complicated publication history of the 1728 *Dunciad,* a task that continues to bedevil bibliographers.

The Wordsworth holdings exhibit similar completeness. These begin with Wordsworth's first two books, *An Evening Walk* and *Descriptive Sketches,* both published by J. Johnson of London in 1793. The former is a presentation copy to Joseph Cottle of Bristol, who published the first issue of Wordsworth's *Lyrical Ballads* in 1798. Wise owned a copy of this landmark in English literature. Also in Wise's library was the seventy-three-page manuscript of *The Waggoner* (London: Hurst, Rees, Orne, and Brown, 1819), transcribed by Sarah Hutchinson, the poet's sister-in-law, and corrected by Wordsworth himself between 1806 and publication in 1819. Gordon Wordsworth, the poet's grandson, gave Wise this manuscript in 1924, along with the manuscript of Dorothy Wordsworth's "The Mother's Return," first published in the 1815 edition of Wordsworth's poems, and the manuscript of "At Vallombroso" written in 1840 or 1841 and first published in 1842. This Wordsworth collection shows Wise at his best and worst. He achieved virtual completeness, and he demonstrated a clear understanding of these works, including the complicated bibliographical history of the 1798 *Lyrical Ballads.* Yet not content with so much, he manufactured a spurious issue of *Lyrical Ballads* by creating a false canceled leaf to give his library another unique item, in the process misleading other collectors. He also included in his Wordsworth listings the pamphlet *To the Queen* ("Printed for the Author by R. Braithwaite and Son, Kendal, 1846"), one of his own fabrications.

Wise's holdings of Coleridge and Shelley rival his Wordsworth collection. One of the treasures relating to the former is the Reverend James Boyer's *Liber Aureus,* a manuscript notebook with sixty-five compositions by his students at Christ's Hospital. Coleridge contributed twelve compositions, five poems and seven prose pieces. Also included here is Charles Lamb's "Mille Viae Mortis" dated 1789, the earliest known Lamb manuscript. Wise's list of Shelley's works covers sixty-one pages. Not only are the holdings once more virtually complete, but many of the volumes have important associations. Wise's *Queen Mab* contains corrections in the poet's hand. His copy of *A Refutation of Deism* (London: Printed for Schulze and Dean, 1814) was

Shelley's own. His *Adonais* had belonged to Shelley's friend Thomas Love Peacock.

John O'London's Weekly for 28 March 1931 carried a description of this incomparable library:

> In an unpretentious house in a quiet tree-lined road at Hampstead reposes one of the most remarkable libraries in the world. It is known as the Ashley Library, and has been accumulated during a lifetime of painstaking research and unflagging enthusiasm by the eminent bibliographer, Mr. Thomas J. Wise. . . . The library is a big square room, a peaceful sanctuary from the ceaseless flux of the world without. Glossy walnut panelling, glass fronted bookcases hide its walls. Here are two comfortable settees, there a writing desk. A broad window looks out on to a trim garden. Here is the arm chair in which Conrad used to sit, there the famous bust of [Robert] Browning carved by his son, which formerly stood in the poet's own home.

Actually the collection overflowed from this room into the rest of the house.

Honors continued to arrive. In 1924 Wise was elected Honorary Fellow of Worcester College, Oxford, and two years later the university awarded him an honorary M.A. In 1927 the Roxburghe Club, England's oldest and most distinguished organization of book collectors, made Wise a member. Booksellers are not admitted to the club, but Wise assured the members, "No man has ever regarded his books in a less mercenary manner than I have throughout my life."[40] Two years later Wise wrote to Richard Curle, who acted as his American agent: "In a few days I will try and send you some further letters of [George Bernard] Shaw, &c. It is not worth while, I think, to send you my ordinary Shaw books worth about £5 or so each. . . . Three of the excessively rare 'Trial Books' . . . are not signed by G. B. S. so they might go. But I would not part with them unless I got a really large price for them."[41]

---

40   In Collins, 229.
41   In Barker and Collins, 58–59.

The American collector A. Edward Newton observed in 1934 that Wise had become "almost a national figure,"[42] respected for his learning and his library that seemed to admit only the finest copies of great literature but that he willingly shared with anyone who asked to use it. In that same year, though, two young book-sellers, John Carter and Graham Pollard, published *An Enquiry into the Nature of Certain XIXth Century Pamphlets.* The title echoes Edmond Malone's 1796 *An Inquiry into the Authenticity of Certain Miscellaneous Papers and Legal Instruments,* which exposed the Shakespearean forgeries of William-Henry Ireland, and perhaps Nicholas E. S. A. Hamilton's *An Inquiry into the Genuineness of the Manuscript Corrections in Mr. J. Payne Collier's Annotated Shakspere, Folio, 1632* (1860) attacking Collier's fabrications. As already noted, Bertram Dobell had known of Wise's fabrications from their inception, and over the years some of Wise's faked first editions had been condemned. Still, Carter and Pollard were the first to apply new techniques of paper and typographical analysis to some fifty publications, proving them spurious, and, without directly accusing Wise of creating them, clearly implicating him in their manufacture.

Like others in the trade, Carter and Pollard were particularly suspicious of the so-called Reading edition of Elizabeth Barrett Browning's *Sonnets,* the most expensive of the Wise-Forman fabrications. As Carter and Pollard wrote, "During the past few years a vague rumor has been circulating, with a gradually increasing frequency and volume, that the privately printed first edition of Mrs. Browning's 'Sonnets from the Portuguese' (*Sonnets* by E. B. B., Reading, 1847) was not all that it pretended to be. . . . To establish the authenticity or otherwise of this book was therefore our first task."[43] Carter and Pollard began by considering the suspicious origins of the pamphlet. There were no presentation copies (unusual for privately printed works), no record of ownership before about 1900, no mention of the Reading *Sonnets* in the letters of Mary Russell Mitford or the Brownings, no copies in old bindings, no copy in Robert Browning's own library. Wise

---

42 Collins, 253.
43 *An Enquiry,* 3, 6.

claimed that Elizabeth had shown the poems to Robert at Pisa in 1847, and that Robert had urged their publication, which was undertaken by their friend Mary Russell Mitford in England. Yet in a letter to Leigh Hunt of 6 October 1857, which Wise himself had owned, Robert Browning noted that he had first learned of the existence of these sonnets in 1849 at Bagni di Lucca.

Looking at the typeface of the Reading *Sonnets,* Stanley Morison, designer of the famous Times New Roman font and an expert in the field of typography, was surprised to see that the letters "j" and "f" lacked kerns, overhanging bits of type that tend to break. By the 1880s these fragile fragments had been eliminated from typefaces, but a book printed in 1847 should contain letters with kerns. In April 1933 Carter secured a bit of paper from the Widener Library (Harvard) copy of the Reading *Sonnets.* Analysis found chemical wood pulp, not used in England until 1874, twenty-seven years after the supposed publication of the pamphlet.

In examining *Alaric at Rome. A Prize Poem, by Matthew Arnold. A Type-Facsimile Reprint of the Original Edition Published at Rugby in 1840* (London: Printed for Private Circulation Only, 1893) edited by Wise, Carter and Pollard recognized the type used in the Reading *Sonnets* and the other suspected pamphlets. *Alaric* had been printed by Richard Clay & Sons. From Herbert Gorfin they learned that Wise was the source of the *Sonnets.* As Carter and Pollard examined other pamphlets dated as early as 1842, they discovered no auction records for them prior to 1889, nor had the British Museum acquired any copies before 1888. Though printed for private circulation and hence purportedly intended as gifts, all but one lacked an inscription from the author. Many had first been "discovered" and then sold by Wise.

In October 1933 Pollard confronted Wise with his findings; Wise could not explain away the evidence. He tried to bribe Gorfin to accuse Forman of the forgeries,[44] and attempted to persuade

---

44   Forman had died on 15 June 1917. Forman had been as guilty as Wise, but Forman's reputation was unassailable, and Wise's accusations further convinced the public of his own culpability.

Cecil Clay to deny his firm's association with the pamphlets. When these efforts failed, he sought to suppress publication of *An Enquiry*,[45] and when that attempt also proved unsuccessful he enlisted Frederick Page, an editor at the Oxford University Press, to publish over Wise's signature a defense of the *Sonnets* (*Times Literary Supplement*, 24 May 1934, 380).[46] The letter claimed that H. Buxton Forman was the source of the *Sonnets,* a charge Wise repeated in a 30 June interview published in the *Daily Herald,* where he claimed that all the doubtful pamphlets began with Forman.

The *Enquiry* appeared on 2 July 1934. It did not directly accuse Wise of fabricating the pamphlets, since all the evidence was circumstantial. Carl Pforzheimer did not show Carter and Pollard the incriminating letter regarding *The Last Tournament* until 28 March 1935, and he refused to allow its publication for another decade. Still, *An Enquiry* proved a devastating indictment. Condemning some fifty pamphlets—more fabrications have since been revealed—the book declared,

> Mr. Wise, by his credulity, by his vanity in his own possessions, by his dogmatism, by abuse of his eminence in the bibliographical world, has dealt a blow to the prestige of an honourable science, the repercussions of which will be long and widely felt. . . . In the whole history of book collecting, there has been no such wholesale and successful perpetration of fraud as that which we owe to this anonymous forger. It has been converted into an equally unparalleled blow to the bibliography and literary criticism of the Victorian period by the shocking negligence of Mr. Wise. (141)

In the 12 July 1934 *Times Literary Supplement* (p. 492) Wise defended himself, blaming Forman and Richard Herne Shepherd (a minor forger unconnected with any of the condemned pamphlets) for the fabrications.

A week later Gorfin replied in the same publication:

---

45 A. Edward Newton, who had written the introduction to the sixth volume of *The Ashley Library* (London: Printed for Private Circulation Only, 1925), also sought to block publication of *An Enquiry*.

46 "Mrs. Browning's 'Sonnets' 1847."

Sir,—Mr. Wise states in a letter in your issue of July 12, that he got his copies of those pamphlets which are shown in Messrs. Carter and Pollard's book to be forged, from H. Buxton Forman. Among other material, I was selling these regularly on commission for Mr. Wise from 1898 onwards, and I purchased from him what I understood to be the entire remainder in 1909–1911. In all our many transactions this connexion of the pamphlets with H. Buxton Forman was never mentioned, even by implication; and the suggestion that he was the source from which they came was only made to me, by Mr. Wise himself, on October 14, 1933—two days after Mr. Pollard had visited him and explained that they were forgeries. Mr. Wise had previously given me a totally different account of their origin.[47]

In the 23 August 1934 issue of the *Times Literary Supplement,* Oliver Sylvain Baliol Brett, Viscount Escher, called upon Wise to defend himself and the condemned publications:

Those of us who have bought the forged pamphlets for large sums of money cannot consent to leave the matter where it is.

Mr. Wise has said in an interview that "a large proportion of the books are genuine." It is only fair that Mr. Wise should tell us collectors which are the genuine ones and why. . . . It is clear from [*An Enquiry*] that Mr. Wise played a great part in the distribution of the forged pamphlets, and therefore must be more anxious than any to pursue the enquiry.

We collectors have been accustomed to look upon Mr. Wise as an expert bibliographer. . . . [H]e has stated that on a more careful reading of Mr. Carter and Mr. Pollard's book, he will have something further to say. A considerable time has elapsed, and the collectors who have followed Mr. Wise have a right to know how they stand in the matter. (577)

Wise's American supporters also urged him to tell his side of the story. Charles F. Heartman, one of the country's leading book-

---

47 *Times Literary Supplement,* 19 July 1934, 511. Wise gave Gorfin four hundred pounds to destroy the remaining pamphlets. The sum was exactly what Gorfin had paid twenty years earlier for Wise's stock of fabrications.

sellers and the editor of the *American Book Collector,* wrote in the August-September 1934 issue of his magazine, "I still believe in him" (V, 272). Heartman offered to publish Wise's response to Carter and Pollard, an invitation Wise initially accepted. As he had in the past, Wise here accused the long-dead Forman of being responsible for any spurious pamphlets. Understanding that publication of this piece would prompt Carter and Pollard to produce more evidence against him, Wise withdrew the article before it could appear in print. In the October 1934 issue of the *American Book Collector* Heartman declared his conviction of Wise's guilt. "On the strength of written and properly signed statements I have convinced myself that Messrs. Carter and Pollard have positive proof to connect Mr. Wise with the origin of these [condemned] pamphlets. . . . [I]t seems now that Mr. Wise has written the third chapter in the book, of which Mr. Ireland wrote the first, and Mr. Collier, the second" (V, 311).

New York bookseller Gabriel Wells took longer to reach that view. Wells conceded that the pamphlets were recent fabrications, but he maintained in *The Carter-Pollard Disclosures* (Garden City, New York: Doubleday, Doran & Co., 1934) that Wise's "intense love for books, his genuine solicitude for integrity in collecting, and his zeal in building up his own monumental library, would hardly have allowed the growth in him of any parasitic impulses. Nor in fact was he commercially inclined, except incidentally" (6–7). By 1938 Wells, too, recognized Wise's responsibility for the spurious pamphlets.

Instead of defending himself, Wise resigned from the Roxburghe Club on 10 December 1934, giving ill health as his reason. He retreated into silence, and on his deathbed he said only, "It's all too complicated to go into now."[48]

Wise died at his home on 13 May 1937, leaving an estate worth about £138,000, not including his library, on which he said he had spent about £40,000 and that was worth at least £100,000 in 1937. Among those hoping to secure that library was the

---

48 In Barker and Collins, 59.

Philadelphia bookseller A. S. W. Rosenbach, who telegraphed Wise's widow offering to buy the collection in its entirety, but Wise's will gave the British Museum first refusal. Noted bibliographer Seymour de Ricci supported the purchase, writing to Wilfred Partington,

> The British Museum numerically is rich beyond praises. But there are hardly a dozen of their English first editions which can compare in condition with the Wise copies. Many valuable "firsts" in the Museum are in the sad condition of St. Peter's statue in the Vatican, slowly destroyed by the kisses of admiring worshippers. To add the whole of the Wise Library to the British Museum would be to give the Keepers of that Institution exactly what they need the most: books they might save from the hands of Twentieth Century readers for the benefit of the year 2,000.[49]

De Ricci did not suspect that the sad condition of some of those firsts was the result of Wise's extractions.

The British Museum agreed to buy Wise's library for £66,000, payable over ten years, and Mrs. Wise added the Ashley Library bookcases. The British Museum assumed that it was getting all the volumes listed in the Ashley Library catalogues, but about two hundred items had vanished. Fourteen of these were Wise fabrications, but other missing items included eight Conrad manuscripts, four of Swinburne, two by Hardy, ten 17th-century first editions including two Drydens, two Shadwells, and William Congreve's tragedy *The Mourning Bride* (London: Jacob Tonson, 1697). The most desirable of the missing works is John Keats and Fanny Brawne's copy of Henry Francis Cary's translation of Dante, *The Vision; or, Hell, Purgatory, and Paradise* (London: Printed for Taylor and Hessey, 1814; 3 vols.) On the blank end fly-leaf of the first volume Keats wrote his sonnet "A Dream after Reading Dante's Episode of Paulo and Francesca," almost certainly the first complete draft of the poem, since on the front fly-leaf and back board are two false starts. Keats gave the set to Fanny Brawne in

---

49   Quoted in Partington, 129–130.

1819, and on another fly-leaf of the first volume she copied his last sonnet, "Bright star, would I were steadfast as thou art." A. Edward Newton went book-hunting with Wise when the American collector visited London, and Wise sold the set to him. At Newton's sale (1941) these volumes fetched $7,000. Yale acquired the set about 1960. Vincent Giroud, Curator of Modern Books and Manuscripts at the Beinecke Library, Yale University, reports that "the case containing the three volumes [also] bears the bookplate of Hannah D. Rabinowitz."[50]

On 1 April 1959 the University of Texas, the home of the Wrenn Library, commemorated the centenary of Wise's birth. John Carter summed up the enigma that was Thomas James Wise:

> Wise's faults were many and gross and despicable. . . . He was guilty of the systematic and cynical perversion of bibliographical truth for his own aggrandizement and his own profit. He was capable of every effrontery in the manipulation of evidence. . . . He was not above swindling his best customer [Wrenn], a generous, simple, honourable man who for twenty years believed him a friend. He was vulgar, arrogant, and pretentious, a liar, a bully, and a thief.
>
> But . . . Wise was beyond dispute a great collector; . . . and he was also a great forger. . . . The nineteenth-century pamphlet forgeries were ethically reprehensible, bibliographically deplorable, and economically distressing. But their maker was an artist.[51]

The passage of time has allowed for a more balanced view of Wise. Wise had been such a respected authority that the Carter-Pollard disclosures eclipsed all his other achievements. Lucifer had become the Prince of Darkness. A fair assessment must acknowledge that Wise's library enriched the British nation. He pioneered the interest in modern authors and helped build important collections. Wrenn's is the most notable example, but he also helped Newton, William Harris Arnold, and others on both sides of the Atlantic. His very fabrications have become collectible. Take Wise for all and all, in spite of his faults he was a great bookman.

---

50 Personal communication.
51 "Thomas J. Wise in Perspective," 17–19.

Mark William Hoffman

IX

Making History:
A Tale of Hofmann

*O*n June 1978 a mysterious stranger wearing Temple clothing, the sign of a devout Mormon, called on Sandra and Jerald Tanner at 1350 South West Temple in Salt Lake City. The Tanners were not likely people for a religious Mormon to visit: their Utah Lighthouse Ministry regularly published critiques of the history and beliefs of the Church of Jesus Christ of Latter-day Saints. The Tanners were so inimical to mainstream Mormons that their visitor refused to give his name. "My family would be embarrassed that I am associated in any way with the Tanners," he told them.[1] Yet he was not only associating with them but also offering them a photocopy of a secret Mormon ritual, the Second Anointing Ceremony.

This ceremony is performed only by the head of the Church, the Prophet, and is administered only to the Prophet's two counselors and the Twelve Apostles, in other words, the highest ranking Church leaders. The Second Anointing guarantees these men exaltation in the Celestial Kingdom after death. All other Mormons must wait until the Last Judgment to learn their fate. As Robert Lindsey wrote, the ceremony "was a secret ticket to heaven, a case of rank having its privileges."[2]

No text of the ritual was known, and the visitor's document had not been meant for circulation. In the upper left-hand corner was stamped "SALT LAKE TEMPLE," and opposite the stamp, on the upper right-hand corner, was written in partially erased pencil,

---

1 Quoted in Steven Naifeh and Gregory White Smith, *The Mormon Murders: A True Story of Greed, Forgery, Deceit, and Death* (New York: Weidenfeld & Nicolson, 1988), 83.

2 *A Gathering of Saints: A True Story of Money, Murder and Deceit* (New York: Simon and Schuster, 1988), 298.

"Destroy this copy." The page was dated "c. 1912."[3] The visitor claimed that the document had belonged to his grandfather. The Church sought to hide not just the text of this elitist ceremony but its very existence. Why, then, was a seemingly devout Mormon showing this paper to the Tanners? With their newsletter, the Salt Lake *Messenger,* and their stream of anti-Mormon publications, they would surely disseminate this discovery and so embarrass the Church. In fact, the Tanners did not publish the Second Anointing Ceremony. Though they believed the text was authentic, they were hesitant to print anything about it without further verification. They simply filed away the photocopy.

In October of 1979 Mark William Hofmann, a twenty-five year old senior at Utah State University in Logan, approached A. Jeff Simmonds, curator of special collections and archives at the Utah State library. Born on 7 December 1954, Hofmann had enrolled at Utah State after completing a two-year mission in England.[4] Simmonds knew Hofmann well from the latter's frequent visits to special collections. Hofmann now offered Simmonds a copy of the Second Anointing Ceremony. It bore the stamp of the Salt Lake Temple, and in the upper right-hand corner in partially erased pencil were the words, "Destroy this copy." It was dated "c. 1912." Simmonds bought the document for the library for $60.

Shortly after selling Simmonds the Second Anointing Ceremony, Hofmann showed him another controversial discovery. Here was a letter sent from Montrose, Iowa, on 23 June 1844, by Joseph Smith, Jr., the founder and first Prophet of the Mormon Church, to Maria and Sarah Lawrence. "I take opportunity this morning," Smith wrote,

> to communicate to you two some of the peepings of my heart; for you know my thoughts for you & for the City & people that I love. God bless & protect you all! Amen. I dare not linger in Nauvoo Our enimies shall not cease their infernal howling until they have drunk my lifes blood. I do not know

---

3   Linda Sillitoe and Allen D. Roberts, *Salamander: The Story of the Mormon Forgery Murders* (Salt Lake City: Signature Books, 1988), 227.

4   Young Mormon men are expected to undertake a two-year mission to seek converts.

what I shall do, or where I shall go, but if possible I will try to interview with President Tyler. . . . I want for you to tarry in Cincinnati untill you hear from me. Keep all things treasured up in your breasts. burn this letter as you read it. I close in hast. Do not dispare. Pray for me as I bleed my heart for you.[5]

Smith had fled Nauvoo after a warrant was sworn out for his arrest for ordering the destruction of an opposition press. Smith was killed on 27 June 1844.

Jerald Tanner noted that certain phrases in the Lawrence letter echo those in a letter of 18 August 1842 that Smith wrote to Bishop Newel K. Whitney, Whitney's wife Elizabeth Ann, and their daughter Sarah Ann Whitney, Smith's polygamous wife of twenty-two days. Smith urged the Whitneys to burn the letter as soon as they had read it, but to keep its contents "locked in your breasts." Other expressions recall a letter Smith wrote to his first wife, Emma, on 23 June 1844. He told Emma, "I do not know where I shall go, or what I shall do, but shall if possible endeavor to get to the city of Washington." Smith suggested Cincinnati as a possible place to meet Emma, and he urged her, "Do not dispair."[6]

While even orthodox Mormon historians acknowledge Smith's polygamy, Hofmann's discovery called attention to one of the Prophet's less savory unions. Maria and Sarah Lawrence were teenage sisters, and Smith had been appointed their legal guardian. Along with his brother Hiram and William Law, Joseph Smith, Jr. was also an executor of their estate. Law twice found Smith "in a compromising position" with the nineteen-year-old Maria and sued Smith for adultery. Hofmann's letter added evidence to Smith's marriage to the two women.

When the Church encountered such damaging documents, it tended to acquire and then hide them. Particularly sensitive items might be stored in the vault of the First Presidency,[7] thus allowing

---

5   Quoted in Jerald Tanner, *Tracking the White Salamander,* 3rd ed. (Salt Lake City: Utah Lighthouse Ministry, 1987), 110. Naifeh and Smith assign Hofmann's presentation of this document to 1982. Sillitoe and Roberts think he produced it in 1978–1979, and Tanner, too, thinks it was an early "find."

6   Tanner, 111.

7   The First Presidency consists of the Prophet and his two counselors.

the Church to deny the existence of a document in the archives. Simmonds was not interested in the Lawrence letter, though. "I think it's a forgery," he told Hofmann. Simmonds suggested that the document had been created in the 19th century by an opponent of the Mormon Church seeking to prove that Smith was a polygamist.[8] The Church did acquire the letter later, either by gift from Hofmann or by purchase.

Simmonds was more responsive to Hofmann's next discovery. In 1827, after allegedly receiving from the angel Moroni the golden plates containing the Book of Mormon, Joseph Smith, Jr. began dictating the text to his wife Emma. Martin Harris, a neighboring well-to-do farmer impressed with Smith's account of the discovery of the plates, became his second scribe. Despite his belief in the plates' divine origin, Harris wanted to see them. Smith, however, refused to show them to anyone. Even Smith did not look at them when he dictated their contents. Rather, he kept them wrapped up or in a chest. With the concealed plates nearby, he buried his head in his hat, into which he placed two stones, his "Urim and Thummim," that allowed him to see the plates and to translate their "reformed" Egyptian characters into English. This feat was all the more miraculous because Jean François Champollion's deciphering of the Rosetta stone was not available in English until 1837, nearly a decade after Smith had "translated" the plates.[9]

Martin at length insisted on seeing at least a transcript of the characters incised on the plates. He would take this copy to the greatest scholars in the country, and, if they endorsed the translation, he would pay to have the Book of Mormon printed. In the spring of 1828 Smith provided a sample transcription, which Harris took to Samuel L. Mitchell, vice-president of Rutgers Medical College and a recognized polymath. Mitchell directed Harris to Charles Anthon, professor of Greek and Latin at Columbia College, New York City. According to Harris, Anthon could not read the

---

8   Sillitoe and Roberts, 233–234.

9   Champollion's work made possible the deciphering of Egyptian hieroglyphics. He published his discovery in the pamphlet *Lettre à M. Dacier . . . relative à l'alphabet des hiéroglyphes phonétiques . . .* (Paris: Firman Didot, 1822). John Wilkinson's *Manners and Customs of the Ancient Egyptians* (London: John Murray, 1837) made the Frenchman's findings accessible to Anglophones.

characters but concurred that they were reformed Egyptian, as Smith had said. Harris returned from his journey satisfied that the Book of Mormon was authentic, and he mortgaged his farm to pay for the first printing of 3,000 copies of the book.

After the Book of Mormon was published and Anthon learned that he supposedly had endorsed it, he wrote a vigorous denial to Eber D. Howe (17 February 1834), which Howe published in his anti-Mormon *Mormonism Unvailed: or, A Faithful Account of That Singular Imposition and Delusion, from Its Rise to the Present Time* (Painesville, Ohio: Author, 1834, 270–272). There Anthon stated that the Book of Mormon was intended as "a hoax upon the learned [or] a scheme to cheat [Harris] of his money." In that same letter Anthon described the transcript he had seen. It

> consisted of all kinds of crooked characters disposed in columns, and had evidently been prepared by some person who had before him at the time a book containing various alphabets. Greek and Hebrew letters, crosses and flourishes, Roman letters inverted or placed sideways, were arranged in perpendicular columns, and the whole ended in a crude delineation of a circle divided into various compartments, decked with various strange marks, and evidently copied after the Mexican calendar by [Alexander von] Humboldt, but copied in such a way as not to betray the source whence it was derived.[10]

The Reorganized Church of Jesus Christ of Latter-day Saints, founded by Mormons who refused to follow Brigham Young to Utah and whose headquarters are in Independence, Missouri, owned a copy of the Anthon Transcipt that Martin Harris had made and given to David Whitmer, another friend of Smith and an early Mormon convert. The Reorganized Church's copy did not, however, match Anthon's description. The symbols were arranged in horizontal rows rather than in vertical columns, and the circular Aztec zodiac sign was absent.

10 Quoted in Fawn M. Brodie, *No Man Knows My History: The Life of Joseph Smith the Mormon Prophet* (New York: Knopf, 1945), 51–52.

On 17 April 1980 Hofmann, carrying a Bible and a piece of paper, rushed into Simmonds' office. Hofmann related that in March he had bought a 1668 Bible printed at Cambridge, England, from a Salt Lake City businessman, who in turn had secured the book in the 1950s at Carthage, Illinois. Joseph Smith, Jr. had been killed at Carthage, and some of his descendants still lived there. What had first interested Hofmann about the Bible was the fact that the Book of Amos, missing from the printed text, had been supplied in manuscript. At the end of the handwritten sheets was the name Samuel Smith. Both Joseph Smith, Jr.'s grandfather and great-grandfather were named Samuel, as was one of his brothers. Hofmann said that while looking through the Bible just yesterday, he had noticed that two pages at Proverbs 91 were stuck together. Prying them apart, he found an old piece of paper glued to the book. This he extracted. The paper was glued shut but he could see Joseph Smith, Jr.'s, signature.

Excited, Simmonds tried to unseal the paper with toluene. Next he tried scraping the black goo that held the page shut. Finally, with Hofmann's permission, Simmonds carefully sliced through the adhesive. He saw strange characters arranged in columns, culminating in an Aztec zodiacal circle. Lest any doubt remain as to the nature of this document, the back carried an endorsement: "These caracters were dilligently coppied by my own hand from the plates of gold and given to Martin Harris who took them to New York Citty but the learned could not translate it because the Lord would not open it to them in fulfilment of the prophecy of Isaih within the 29th chapter and 11th verse."[11] The statement was signed by Joseph Smith, Jr. Simmonds felt certain that here was the original Anthon Transcript.

Hofmann next took the Bible and paper to the Church's Institute of Religion on the Utah State University campus. Danel W. Bachman looked at the document briefly and then called Dean Jessee, a member of the Church's Historical Department based in Salt Lake City. Jessee was the leading authority of Joseph Smith's

---

11   In Tanner, 72. *Isaiah* 29:11 states, "And the vision of all is become unto you as the words of a book that is sealed, which men deliver unto one that is learned, saying, Read this, I pray thee: and he saith, I cannot, for it is sealed."

handwriting. When Hofmann had shown Jessee his letter from Smith to the Lawrences, Jessee had dismissed it as a forgery at worst, a later copy of an authentic letter at best. On Friday, 18 April 1980, Jessee looked at the Anthon Transcript and thought that it probably was a genuine Smith holograph. By 21 April he was certain it was. That afternoon Hofmann met with Church Prophet and President Spencer W. Kimball, Kimball's two counselors, and the Apostles Gordon B. Hinckley and Boyd R. Packer, the Mormon equivalent of an audience with the pope and the College of Cardinals. Hinckley suggested that Hofmann leave the Bible and paper with the Church for authentication. Even though Kimball indicated that the process could take as long as two years, Hofmann agreed.

In fact, less that two weeks later the Church was hailing the discovery. Jessee held a news conference on 28 April to declare his confidence in the transcript's authenticity. In the 1 May 1980 Provo (Utah) *Herald,* Richard L. Anderson of Brigham Young University compared the transcript to the Dead Sea Scrolls because Hofmann's document confirmed the truth of the Book of Mormon in the same way that the scrolls from Qumran supported Biblical texts. Dr. Hugh Nibley in that same issue of the newspaper asserted that the transcript had to be authentic because no one could have imitated the characters. He said that he recognized at least two dozen as part of the demotic Egyptian alphabet.

Barry Fell, marine biologist, linguist, director of the National Decipherment Center, and president of the Epigraphic Society, went even farther than Nibley. Having seen a published version of Hofmann's document, Fell translated it:

> Revelation of Nephi: I have written these things. . . .
> I, Nephi, a son born of sagacious parents . . . in series 19 of Ancient Alphabets . . . have transcribed this:
> Zedekiah in Judah had just begun his reign
> My father, Lehi, was of Salem, the Holy City Most Sacred (The 19th cipher still I write) It happened that a tornado occurred. Brilliant lightning flashed overhead. . . .

Fell concluded,

> The decipherment leads to me believe that there must once have existed, and may yet exist, an ancient book entitled the

Revelation of Nefi, dealing at its outset with some events at the beginning of the reign of King Zedekiah in 597–596 B.C., and that an Arabic version of this book, or a fragment of it, was known to exist as late as the 12th or 13th century A.D., when some unidentified scribe cited passages from it. The cited passages somehow served as a model for an illiterate copy that was made in ink on paper, apparently about the year 1828. Somehow this illiterate copy found its way to Logan, Utah.[12]

According to the Book of Mormon, Lehi had taken his family, including his son Nephi, from Jerusalem to the New World at the beginning of the reign of King Zedekiah. Fell's translation was thus consistent with Smith's text.

On 3 May the Church newspaper, the *Deseret News,* carried an article about the discovery, complete with a photograph of the document and of Hofmann's meeting with Church leaders. The paper reported excitedly,

> A handwritten sheet of paper with characters supposedly copied directly from the gold plates in 1828, and also bearing other writing and the signature of Joseph Smith, has been found in an old Bible by a Utah State University student.
>
> This would make it the oldest known Mormon document as well as the earliest sample of the Prophet's handwriting. His earliest known writing previously dated to 1831.[13]

The July 1980 *Ensign,* the Church's magazine, carried color photographs of the transcript, an article on the authenticity of the document, and an interview with Hofmann, in which he credited his wife, Doralee Olds Hofmann, with first noticing the paper inside the Bible.[14] According to the interview, both Hofmann and his wife believed that so important a document should belong to the Church.

In the summer of 1980 Hofmann went to Illinois with his parents. His mother, Lucille Sears Hofmann, wanted to attend a

---

12   Lindsey, 70–71.
13   Tanner, 72.
14   The Hofmanns had married in the Salt Lake Temple on 14 September 1979.

celebration in Nauvoo honoring women in the Mormon Church, and Hofmann used the opportunity to establish the provenance of his Bible. He knew that in the 1950s Mary Hancock, the granddaughter of Joseph Smith, Jr.,'s sister, Catherine, had operated an antique shop at Carthage. On 27 June Hofmann called on Hancock's daughter Dorothy Dean to ask for any information she might have about the Bible he had purchased from a Mr. White in Salt Lake City. He had even brought the Bible with him for her to identify. Dean did not recognize the book, nor did she think that her mother would sell the family Bible. However, she agreed to check the store's records. The next day she called the Hofmanns at their motel. She had found that on 13 August 1954 a "relative to Ansel White from California" had made an unnamed purchase for six dollars. "That must be it," Hofmann remarked, and Dean concurred.[15]

On 13 October 1980 Hofmann gave the Church an affidavit, signed by Dean and himself, tracing the Bible's provenance from the Smith family to Mr. White to Hofmann. Tests had verified the handwriting and the age of the ink and paper. In exchange for the transcript and Bible, Hofmann received an 1850 five-dollar Mormon gold coin, a first edition of the Book of Mormon lacking a title-page, and several examples of early Mormon paper currency. Altogether these items were worth about $20,000. When Hofmann had decided in the spring of 1980 to drop out of college and abandon plans of attending medical school, friends had expressed doubts. He had replied that he could make a living selling antiquarian documents. Apparently he was correct.

After leaving Utah State, Hofmann and his wife moved to the Salt Lake City suburb of Sandy. He became a frequent visitor to the Mormon archives run by Donald T. Schmidt. He also began associating with collectors and historians. Early in 1981 he spoke with Buddy Youngreen, a Provo collector of Joseph Smith material, about the question of Joseph Smith, Jr.'s successor. The Reorganized Church claimed that Smith had named his son as the next Prophet, whereas the Utah-based Church recognized Brigham

15 Lindsey, 72.

Young as Smith's rightful heir. On 12 February 1981 Hofmann called Mormon historian Michael Marquardt to ask where Joseph Smith had been on 17 January 1844. Marquardt checked and reported that Smith had been home in Nauvoo on that day.

In that same month Hofmann borrowed $10,000 from Salt Lake City coin dealer Alvin Rust to buy a collection of papers that had belonged to Thomas Bullock, one of Smith's secretaries and for seventeen years the Church Historian for Brigham Young. Hofmann told Rust that an Alan Lee Bullock of Coalville, Utah was prepared to sell these documents. On 16 February Hofmann showed Schmidt a photocopy of one of the documents that he had just acquired.

As Hofmann looked on, Schmidt read,

> Blessed of the Lord is my son Joseph, who is called the third, — for the Lord knows the integrity of his heart, and loves him, because of his faith, and righteous desires. And, for this cause, has the Lord raised him up;—that the promises made to the fathers might be fulfilled, even the anointing of the progenitor shall be upon the head of my son, and his seed after him, from generation to generation. For he shall be my successor to the Presidency of the High Priesthood: a Seer, and a Revelator, and a Prophet, unto the Church; which appointment belongeth to him by blessing, and also by right.[16]

Though little in the hand of Thomas Bullock was known, the blessing appeared to be in his writing. The document also carried the endorsement "Joseph Smith 3 blessing" in Smith's own script. Apparently, the Reorganized Church had been right in refusing to follow Brigham Young and instead to name Joseph Smith III their Prophet in 1860. Hofmann offered Schmidt the original for $5,000, but Schmidt was not interested.

"I think that the Reorganized Church might possibly trade a Book of Commandments for it," Hofmann suggested.

The first edition of the Book of Commandments is the rarest of Mormon religious works. While it was being printed in Missouri in 1833, a mob attacked and destroyed the press. Mormons res-

---

16 Transcribed from photocopy of original in Tanner, 80.

cued a few sets of unbound sheets, but most of the print run was lost. A copy in 1981 could be worth as much as $40,000.

"If you think you can get a Book of Commandments for [the blessing] then you ought to try," Schmidt coolly replied.[17]

Hoping that Dean Jessee would be more responsive, Hofmann showed him the photocopy under the guise of seeking authentication (23 February 1981). Hofmann wondered whether Smith might himself have recorded the blessing in the Book of the Law of the Lord, Joseph Smith, Jr.'s diary and record of Church-related documents and revelations. This large leather-bound volume was kept in the vault of the First Presidency, and only Francis M. Gibbons, secretary to the First Presidency, had a key. Gibbons checked but found no record of the blessing; nor did Jessee show any interest in buying Hofmann's document.

Hofmann therefore called the Reorganized Church on 24 February. The archivist with whom he spoke was excited about the discovery. Soon the assistant commissioner of history for the Reorganized Church called Hofmann and asked him to read the text of the blessing over the phone. Richard P. Howard, historian of the Reorganized Church, now spoke to Hofmann: Howard would fly to Salt Lake City on 2 March to look at the original. If it proved genuine, Howard would acquire it for the Reorganized Church in exchange for a copy of the Book of Commandments.

The Salt Lake City Church meanwhile was having second thoughts about the document. On 27 February Jessee asked to see the original. The Blessing proceeded up the hierarchy until it reached N. Eldon Tanner of the First Presidency, who decided to buy the item if possible. On Sunday, 1 March, Don Schmidt spoke with Hofmann, who agreed to meet with him at 8:00 AM the next day, just before Hofmann was to see Howard. At that 8:00 A.M. meeting, Hofmann agreed to let the Church buy the blessing. Hofmann then visited Howard, who left Salt Lake City with the impression that on 17 March Hofmann would bring the blessing to Independence, Missouri for authentication. Howard was therefore surprised and angry to learn on 6 March that the other

---

17 In Richard E. Turley, Jr., *Victims: The LDS Church and the Mark Hofmann Case* (Urbana: University of Illinois Press, 1992), 42.

Mormon Church had acquired the document. Hofmann received a first edition of the Book of Mormon with title page, an 1860 Mormon gold coin, the pattern used to make that coin, and four other pieces of Mormon currency; these items were together worth something over $20,000.

Howard protested to both Schmidt and Hofmann. On 19 March the Church agreed to turn over the blessing to Howard in exchange for the Book of Commandments. Hofmann had been right about the value of the document. Perhaps he had nonetheless decided to renege on his agreement with Howard because he did not want to wait for payment until the Reorganized Church had completed its tests of the paper, ink, and handwriting. Perhaps he wanted to maintain the good will of the Salt Lake City Church in case he found other Mormon documents. The Salt Lake City Church did, after all, have a lot more money than its mid-western cousin.

Later in March Schmidt bought from Hofmann four "White Notes," handwritten currency created by the Mormons in 1849. While the production of these notes was recorded in Mormon histories, no one had ever seen any examples in modern times. Consisting of one note each of fifty cents, a dollar, two dollars and five dollars, all of Hofmann's examples were executed in the hand of Thomas Bullock. The White Notes bore a seal showing the twelve Mormon Apostles, identical to the seal on some of the printed Mormon money Hofmann had received from the Church. The White Notes had come from the same collection that had supplied the Joseph Smith III blessing. Schmidt traded Hofmann about $20,000 in material for these supposedly unique items. In fact, Hofmann had found eight White Notes, and he sold the other four to Alvin Rust for $12,000. Later he located nine more, which Rust bought for $27,000.

Rust was an authority on early Mormon money, as was Hofmann. In the preface to *Mormon and Utah Coin and Currency* (Salt Lake City: Rust Rare Coin Company, 1984) Rust thanked Hofmann for his assistance with the book. Hofmann also helped Harry F. Campbell prepare *Campbell's Tokens of Utah* (Salt Lake City: Campbell, 1980; 3rd ed., 1987). Rust later bought from Hofmann two sets of notes issued by the Spanish Forks Co-operative, a 19th-century Mormon Utopian community; Rust paid $2,500 for one set, $1,500 for the other. These, too, were supposedly unique, but in 1982 Schmidt bought from Hofmann another set of the notes issued in 1867. In 1984 Hofmann sold Rust a complete set of Deseret paper money issued in 1858. One series contained notes of $1, $2, $10, $20, $50, and $100, the other consisted of notes for $1, $2, $3, and $20. Rust had never seen any denominations larger than $3. Rust paid Hofmann $35,000 for the notes. In October 1985 Curt Bench of Deseret Book also bought a set of these notes from Hofmann for $18,000 and resold them to Phoenix dentist Richard Marks, a collector of Mormon material, for $35,000.

On 4 September 1981 Hofmann visited Gordon B. Hinckley, recently elevated from Apostle to Second Counselor in the First Presidency. Hofmann placed on his desk a five-paragraph letter from Thomas Bullock to Brigham Young dated 27 January 1865. The letter read in part,

> I have only the kindest regards for you, and for brother G.[eorge] A. Smith. Altho' I must confess that I felt insulted at being turned out, without advance notice, nor warning; and this after nearly 17 years of faithful employment. I have never said that you are not the right man to head the Church, and if any man says otherwise, he is a *liar;* I believe that you have never pretended to anything that did not belong to you. Mr. Smith (Young Joseph) has forfeited any claim which he ever had to successorship, but *I do not believe* that this gives you licence to destroy every remnant of the blessing which he received from his Father, those promises *must* be fulfilled by some future generation.
>
> I will not, nay I can not, surrender that blessing, knowing what its certain fate will be if returned, even at the peril of my own livelihood and standing. I regret the necessity of disobeying your instructions, altho' I believe that you understand my feeling of loyalty towards brother Joseph, as well as towards yourself.[18]

18　Turley, 61.

Here was additional confirmation that the blessing was authentic. Not wanting this letter to fall into the wrong hands, Hofmann was giving it to the Church. Hinckley happily accepted the gift, which he promptly placed in the Church's Holy of Holies, the vault of the First Presidency.

Scientific testing of the blessing also verified its genuineness. James R. Dibowski, former chief of the Cincinnati Postal Crime Laboratory, and Albert W. Somerford, retired head of the Questioned Documents Laboratory of the Bureau of the Chief Postal Inspector, Washington, D.C., confirmed that the handwriting was authentic and the ink of the proper age. Walter C. McCrone Associates tested the paper. It, too, had been produced in the 19th century. In *The John Whitmer Historical Association Journal,* Brigham Young University professor Dennis Michael Quinn argued for the legitimacy of the document:

> All internal evidences concerning the manuscript blessing of Joseph Smith III, dated 17 January 1844, give conclusive support to its authenticity. Anyone at all familiar with the thousands of official manuscript documents of early Mormonism will immediately recognize that the document is written on paper contemporary with the 1840s, that the text of the blessing is in the extraordinarily distinctive handwriting of Joseph Smith's personal clerk, Thomas Bullock, that the words on the back of the document ("Joseph Smith 3 blessing") bear striking similarity to the handwriting of Joseph Smith, Jr., and that the document was folded and labeled in precisely the manner all one-page documents were filed by the church historian's office in the 1844 period.[19]

In 1982 the Reorganized Church added the blessing to its sacred scriptures.

Hofmann's fame brought him new customers. Brent F. Ashworth, a lawyer for Nature Sunshine Products and a Mormon bishop living in Payson, near Provo, an hour south of Salt Lake City, had assembled an impressive group of American historical

---

19   1 (1981): 12.

documents, including letters by Thomas Jefferson, George Washington, Benjamin Franklin, Abraham Lincoln, and Robert E. Lee. In May 1981 Ashworth called Hofmann to express his interest in adding Mormon materials to his collection. Shortly afterwards Hofmann sold Ashworth a brief letter from Joseph Smith, Jr. to his wife Emma, dated 6 March 1833, for which Ashworth paid $4,000 in cash and $20,000 in documents.

Hofmann issued a catalogue in 1981, listing thirty-five Mormon manuscripts. The most expensive item was a group of papers dealing with the December 1843 trial of Orrin Porter Rockwell, one of Joseph Smith, Jr.'s bodyguards ($9,000).[20] Despite the brevity of the catalogue, Hofmann stated that he had hundreds of items in stock, and he solicited want lists. All items were guaranteed authentic.

On 6 March 1982 Hofmann told Ashworth that he had located an important letter. Signed by Martin Harris though written in a different hand, perhaps that of Harris' son, it was dated 13 January 1873. It was addressed to Walter Conrad, who had written Harris to ask his opinion of Smith and the Book of Mormon. Harris had been one of the three original witnesses to the authenticity of the gold plates, and his testimony appears in the preface to every copy of the Book of Mormon. Though he had not seen the plates, Harris, along with Oliver Cowdery and David Whitmer, had been vouchsafed a vision of them in 1829. Even though Harris had subsequently left the Church, in his 1873 letter he confirmed his earlier declaration regarding the vision and expanded on his previous statement. In his letter to Conrad he said that God had told him, "'I am the Lord,' and . . . the plates were translated by God and not by men, and also that we should bear record of it to all the world."[21]

---

20   Rockwell was suspected of the 1842 murder of the anti-Mormon Missouri governor Lilburn Boggs. Rockwell was not indicted for the crime, but while he was in jail awaiting a grand jury hearing, he attempted to escape. For this offense he was convicted and was sentenced to five-minutes' incarceration. The leniency of the punishment is balanced by his having spent nine months behind bars awaiting the grand jury's finding.

21   Lindsey, 94.

Ashworth wanted the letter. If it was authentic, he would trade Hofmann a letter by Washington, another by Lincoln, and a third by Lee for it. Together these were worth $27,000. In October, Jessee declared the letter genuine.

By then Ashworth had bought another gem from Hofmann. On 29 July 1982 Hofmann showed Ashworth a letter dated 23 January 1829 and written by Lucy Mack Smith, the mother of the Prophet. Hofmann had found it among a group of 19th-century stampless covers, letters bearing postmarks and signatures of post-masters from the period before postage stamps had been intro-duced. Lucy Smith wrote to her sister-in-law: "It is my pleasure to inform you of a great work which the Lord has wrought in our family, for he has made his paths known to Joseph in dreams and it pleased God to show him where he could dig to obtain an ancient record engraven upon plates made of pure gold and this he is able to translate."[22]

Here was confirmation of Joseph Smith, Jr.'s account of his discovery of the gold plates containing the text of the Book of Mormon. The letter went on to discuss the contents of the book, and Lucy Smith mentioned two pieces of information missing from the known text. After translating 116 pages of the Book of Lehi, Smith reluctantly allowed Martin Harris to take the manu-script to show Harris' incredulous wife. These pages disappeared. According to one account, Mrs. Lucy Harris was so angry at her husband's giving money to the Smiths that she threw the pages into the fire. Smith never translated the pages again. He claimed that God had told him that if he did translate them, enemies of the Church would alter the first version and argue that the discrepan-cies between the two texts proved Smith a charlatan. Emma's let-ter explained that according to the Book of Lehi, Lehi and Ishmael, two patriarchs in the Book of Mormon, were brothers-in-law. The letter also declared that Jerusalem fell partly because of a secret evil society. Ashworth was ecstatic. "Mark, this is the great-est thing I've ever seen. This is really marvelous."[23]

---

22   Turley, 64.
23   In Sillitoe and Roberts, 260.

Hofmann suggested that so important a letter should perhaps go to the Church. Ashworth began taking framed documents from his walls and offering them to Hofmann in exchange for the Lucy Smith letter. Onto the pile went an 1857 letter from John Brown, an 1820 letter from Andrew Jackson, a document signed by Benjamin Franklin, a book that had belonged to Solomon Mack, Lucy Smith's father, a first printing of the Thirteenth Amendment. When Ashworth was finished, he had exchanged $33,000 worth of manuscripts and printed rarities for Hofmann's letter. On Tuesday, 24 August 1982, the *New York Times* reported the discovery of the Lucy Mack letter. Dean Jessee had verified the handwriting and noted its importance in showing that the Smith family already regarded the Book of Mormon as scripture, not as a novel that later came to be treated as sacred. If the 116 pages of the Book of Lehi could be found, the Lucy Mack letter could confirm its text, and already on 13 April 1981 Hofmann had said that he had some leads as to its whereabouts.

The same envelope that held the 1873 Harris letter contained a similar response to Conrad from David Whitmer, another of the original three witnesses. Like Harris, Whitmer had left the Mormon Church (1838), but, also like Harris, in 1873 he repeated his early belief in the Book of Mormon. "Anyone who is without prejudice," he wrote in 1873, "can easily learn the Book of Mormon is the word of God if he will earnestly seek the truth."[24] Although Hofmann supposedly had acquired this letter with the one from Harris, he waited until October to offer it to the Church. Hinckley agreed to pay Hofmann's price of $15,000, but Hofmann, claiming he was embarrassed to take that much money from the Church, accepted only $10,000 (20 October 1982).

The next day Hofmann sold Ashworth a half-page manuscript fragment from the Book of Mosiah, part of the Book of Mormon, for $5,000. In 1841 Smith placed the complete manuscript of the Book of Mormon in the cornerstone of the Nauvoo House, then under construction. The building was never finished, and in 1882 Emma Smith's second husband, Lewis Bidamon (a non-Mormon),

---

24   Lindsey, 98.

retrieved what remained of the document, which had suffered from its decades of exposure to dampness. Over the years Bidamon gave away leaves of the manuscript to friends and souvenir hunters, and recipients in turn would give away parts of leaves. Utah businessman Joseph W. Summerhays received a leaf of the Smith manuscript, and in 1884 he gave half of that sheet to a man who later donated his fragment to the University of Utah. Hofmann had located the other half of that leaf and now sold it to Ashworth. Ashworth subsequently paid $25,000 for an entire leaf from the Book of Helaman, another part of the Book of Mormon. Both of Hofmann's discoveries were in an excellent state of preservation.

In an interview with Jeffrey Keller of the Brigham Young University *7th East Press* (September 1982) Hofmann expressed his delight in dealing with such material. "The real reward in the whole business is being able to see things that no one else knows about. It gives me a kick to know that this is original stuff, that no one else on earth has pieced this together or knows what this says. So there's the pleasure. It's like being a detective." Keller hinted at another reward as well, titling his article, "Making a Buck Off Mormon History."[25]

That same month the liberal Mormon *Sunset Review* also ran an interview with Hofmann in which he confirmed Keller's suspicion. "I'm in this for the money," Hofmann stated bluntly. He explained that much of his success came from tracking down descendants of early Mormons. "I have gone door to door in places like Cedar City looking for things rumored to be there," he told the interviewer, Peggy Fleming.[26] Also, he carefully examined stampless covers. Most collectors valued them only for their philatelic interest and cared nothing about their contents. By reading stampless covers from western New York he had located the Lucy Mack Smith letter.[27]

In January 1983 Hofmann's diligence paid off with yet another discovery. Dated from Canandaigua, New York, on 18

---

25   In Sillitoe and Roberts, 267–268.
26   Cedar City is located in southwestern Utah. The 1996 *Rand McNally Road Atlas* gives its population as 13,443.
27   Naifeh and Smith, 108; Lindsey, 98–99.

June 1825, it was the earliest known letter by Joseph Smith, Jr. He was writing to Josiah Stowell, a farmer in Bainbridge, New York, for whom Smith worked briefly.

> Dear Sir:
>
> My father has Shown me your letter informing him and me of your Success in locating the mine as you Suppose but we are of oppinion that Since you cannot ascertain any particulars you Should not dig more untill you first discover if any valluables remain you know this treasure must be guarded by Some clever Spirit and if such is discovered So also is the treasure So do this take a hasel Stick one yard long being new cut and cleave it Just in the middle and lay it asunder on the mine so that both inner parts of the stick may look one right against the other one inch distant and if there is treasure after a while you shall See them draw and join together of themselves.[28]

In 1826 Joseph Smith, Jr. was convicted of defrauding people by claiming to use seer stones and hazel wands to find buried treasure. He was tried again for such activities in 1830. Church apologists asserted that the defendant in these cases was not the Mormon Prophet, but this letter belied such statements. The connection between Joseph Smith, Jr. and money-digging was especially troubling because his claim of finding golden plates and translating them by means of seer stones sounds much like the statements he and others were making at this time about buried treasure.

Hofmann took the letter to G. Homer Durham, head of the Church's Historical Department. Durham consulted Hinckley, who was in effect running the Church, since both people nominally his superiors were old and frail. Hinckley wanted the letter if it was authentic. Hofmann flew to New York, where on 11 January 1983 he showed the manuscript to Charles Hamilton, a documents dealer and author of *Great Forgers and Famous Fakes* (New York: Crown, 1980). Hamilton, who had known Hofmann for

---

28 Tanner, 87.

about a year, was an authority on forgeries: among his accomplishments was the exposure of the Hitler diaries. Hamilton at first dismissed the letter as a fake. "The spelling's too good and the handwriting is stiff and labored—like a man walking, strutting with his chest out. Smith's handwriting is bent over like a man running and leaning forwards."[29]

Hofmann asked Hamilton to reconsider. Noticing Smith's characteristically redundant consonants, Hamilton wavered. The letter was early, predating by ten years any others written by Smith. Penmanship can change in a decade. Hofmann left Hamilton's gallery on West 57th Street with the dealer's imprimatur and an appraisal of $10,000–$15,00 for the letter. Three days later Hinckley, on behalf of the Church, paid Hofmann $15,000 and added the embarrassing document to the contents of the vault of the First Presidency.

In March 1983 Hofmann sold the Church, through Hinckley, the original 1829 contract signed by Joseph Smith, Martin Harris, and printer Egbert B. Grandin of Palmyra for the production of the first edition of the Book of Mormon. The price was $25,000. Soon afterwards Hofmann traded A. Jeff Simmonds a 5" by 7" fragment of the manuscript Book of Mormon for a first edition of the work in Hawaiian.

On a business trip to Missouri, Brent Ashworth visited the archives of the Reorganized Church at Independence. There he saw two letters written by Joseph Smith, Jr. from prison in Carthage the day he died, 27 June 1844. Ashworth was so moved that he asked Hofmann to locate another such letter. Always lucky at finding, Hofmann soon did so. Like the two letters Ashworth had seen, Hofmann's was dated 27 June 1844, and it was addressed to Jonathan Dunham, head of the Nauvoo Legion, the Mormon militia. According to orthodox Mormon history, Smith went to his death like a lamb to the slaughter. Smith's previously known letters from the Carthage jail confirmed this view. On the morning of his death, Smith wrote to his wife Emma, "I want you

---

29   Quoted in Lindsey, 105.

to tell Bro[ther] Dunham to instruct the people to stay at home and attend to their own business and let there be no groups or gatherings together unless by permission of the Gov[ernor]."[30] The Dunham letter that Hofmann had found revealed a less resigned Smith. Here Smith sounded like a caged tiger eager to escape: the Mormon leader ordered Dunham to use as much force as necessary to free him. Rumors of the existence of this letter had long circulated. According to Thomas B. H. Stenhouse's *Rocky Mountain Saints* (New York: Appleton, 1873), Dunham received but ignored Smith's plea. The letter had later been found on a street in Nauvoo, and Dunham had been murdered for disobeying the Prophet's order. Donna Hill's *Joseph Smith, the First Mormon* (New York: Doubleday, 1977) also mentions the letter.

Ashworth offered Hofmann $30,000 for the letter. Oddly, Hofmann instead sold it for $20,000 to Phoenix dentist Richard Marks, perhaps because Marks would pay cash, whereas Ashworth would exchange documents that Hofmann would have to resell to get his money. Ashworth was furious and vowed never to deal with Hofmann again. However, Hofmann had too many tantalizing tidbits; Ashworth soon resumed his weekly Wednesday trips to Salt Lake City, where he and Hofmann would meet and do business at Crossroads Mall. When Dean Jessee published *The Personal Writings of Joseph Smith* (Salt Lake City: Deseret Book, 1984), he included the Dunham letter as well as another from Smith to his brother Hiram dated 25 May 1838. In this document, which Hofmann sold to Schmidt on 29 September 1983, Joseph urges his brother to come west, where he will find buried treasure. The letter to the Lawrence sisters also appeared in that volume, but the Stowell letter did not because Jessee was unaware of its existence.[31]

In late December, after Hofmann had promised Ashworth the Dunham letter but before he had sold it to Marks, Hofmann offered Ashworth another item, a letter written by Martin Harris to William Wines Phelps, a Palmyra newspaper editor. Dated 23

---

30 In *The Personal Writings of Joseph Smith*, ed. Dean C. Jessee (Salt Lake City: Deseret Book, 1984), 611.

31 Jessee's collection also included the Anthon Transcript, the Joseph Smith III Blessing, and the 6 March 1833 letter from Smith to his wife that Ashworth had purchased from Hofmann.

October 1830, it read:

> Dear Sir:
>
> Your letter of yesterday is received & I hasten to answer as fully as I can—Joseph Smith Jr. first come to my notice in the year 1824. In the summer of that year I contracted with his father to build a fence on my property. In the corse of that work I aproach Joseph & ask how it is in a half day you put up what requires your father & 2 brothers a full day working together? He says I have not been with out assistance but can not say more only you better find out. The next day I take the older Smith by the arm & he says Joseph can see any thing he wishes by looking at a stone. Joseph often sees Spirits here with great kettles of coin money. . . . In the fall of the year 1827 I hear Joseph found a gold bible. I take Joseph aside & he says it is true. I found it 4 years ago with my stone but only just got it because of the enchantment. The old spirit come to me 3 times in the same dream and says dig up the gold, but when I take it up the next morning the spirit transfigured himself from a white salamander in the bottom of the hole & struck me 3 times & held the treasure & would not let me have it because I lay it down to cover over the hole when the spirit says do not lay it down. Joseph says when can I have it? The spirit says bring your brother Alvin. Joseph says he is dead, shall I bring what remains? but the spirit is gone. Joseph goes to get the gold bible but the spirit says you did not bring your brother—you can not have it—look to the stone. Joseph looks but can not see who to bring. The spirit says I tricked you again—look to the stone. Joseph looks and sees his wife. On the 22d day of Sept. 1827 they got the gold bible.[32]

Harris went on to speak of the Anthon Transcript and to describe how Smith translated the Book of Mormon from the "short hand Egyptian": "Joseph found some giant silver specticles from the plates. He puts them in an old hat & in the darkness reads the words & in this way it is all translated & written down."[33]

---

32 Lindsey, 118.
33 Ibid., 119.

Hofmann already had tried to sell the Church what became known as the Salamander Letter. Unwilling to appear to be black-mailing his best customer, Hofmann sent Lyn Jacobs to show Hinckley the document. Jacobs dealt in foreign language Mormon material and had become Hofmann's business partner. Jacobs, pretending that he had found the letter, asked Hinckley for a $10 Mormon gold coin, worth as much as $100,000, in exchange for the letter. When Hinckley balked, Jacobs lowered the price to a Book of Commandments, but Hinckley still was not interested. Ashworth, too, refused the letter. He thought it a forgery, and if it was authentic it should belong to the Church.

The letter certainly was controversial enough to appeal to Mormon leaders. Smith had claimed that the golden plates had been guarded by the angel Moroni, not a lizard. Harris further linked Smith with occult money-digging operations as well. Hofmann next offered the document to Don Schmidt. Still claiming that Jacobs owned the letter, Hofmann said that he might be able to buy it for $20,000. The Church was having second thoughts about its earlier refusal to purchase this item, but leaders did not want to acquire it directly. If, however, someone were to buy it and then donate it to the Church, Hinckley or Schmidt could deny purchasing it if asked about the controversial contents.

Shortly after Christmas 1983, G. Homer Durham called Mormon bishop and successful businessman Steven Christensen to say that the Church would appreciate his buying the Salamander Letter and donating it to the Church. On 6 January 1984 Christensen agreed to pay Hofmann $40,000 for the document. As head of Gary Sheet's Coordinated Financial Services and already nearly a millionaire, Christensen could easily afford the cost. He even convinced Sheets, a fellow Mormon, to hire Dean Jessee, Ronald Walker of Brigham Young University, and Brent Metcalfe, a liberal Mormon historian already in Christensen's employ, to research the letter. Christensen would underwrite the publication of a book explaining how this letter, which apparently challenged the very origins of Mormonism, confirmed the orthodox account. Once the research was finished, Christensen would give the letter to the Church. In the interim, as news of the letter's content leaked to the press, Mormon apologists explained that since salamanders were reputed to live in fire, a white salamander would be an apt metaphor for the fiery angel Moroni.

Christensen sent the original letter to document dealer Kenneth Rendell in Newton, Massachusetts, for authentication. Rendell in turn consulted paper expert William G. Krueger of Appleton, Wisconsin, who confirmed the age of the document. Rendell verified the postmark and handwriting, relying on the few known examples of Harris' signature. Albert H. Lyter, a forensic chemist from Raleigh, North Carolina, determined that the ink, like the paper, dated from about 1830.

Despite all this evidence, and despite their rejection of Smith's claim to have received gold plates from an angel, the Tanners suspected that the Salamander Letter was a fake. Ashworth and the Tanners noted that the reference to the salamander closely resembled a comment in Howe's *Mormonism Unvailed*. According to Howe, when Smith opened the box holding the plates, Smith saw a toad, which turned into a man and struck him on the side of the head. The Tanners further recalled that in 1976 Dean Jessee had published Joseph Knight's manuscript account of the discovery of the gold plates. Knight asserted that the spirit instructed Joseph to bring his brother Alvin. Joseph replied that Alvin was dead. The spirit told Smith to consult his seer stone to identify an appropriate partner; Smith saw the image of his wife Emma. The similarity between the two accounts could indicate that both were authentic, but Harris' style in the letter resembled Knight's account, unpublished until 1976. Such cavils went unheeded.

By late 1984 Coordinated Financial Services was heading for bankruptcy. The idea of a book was abandoned, in large part because of Church opposition—the letter was proving hard to reconcile with Mormon doctrine. Hofmann offered to buy back the Salamander Letter for $50,000, and Christensen, who needed money, was eager to accept the proposal. Hofmann said that Yale would purchase the letter. When Christensen consulted Hinckley, the latter replied that the Church still wanted the document. On 12 April 1985 Christensen presented it to the Church.

On 30 November 1984 Hofmann sold Ashworth a Mormon hymnal that had belonged to Emma Smith. The Church had traded the hymnal to Lyn Jacobs for some other material after removing the final leaf, which includes the table of contents. The Church had another copy of the hymnal lacking this page and so used the Emma Smith leaf to perfect its other hymnal. Hofmann bought the Emma Smith hymnal from Jacobs; in its damaged state it was worth about $1,000. By the time Ashworth bought it, the book was again perfect, and Ashworth paid $10,000 for the volume. Curiously, on 1 November 1984 a Mike Hansen had ordered from DeBouzek Engraving and Colorplate Company, located a few blocks east of Temple Square in Salt Lake City, a plate that might be used for printing the table of contents of the Mormon hymnal.

Hofmann's skill at locating the exotic was not limited to Mormon material. He told Kenneth Woolley, millionaire cousin of Hofmann's wife, that he had located a cache of eighteen Daniel Boone documents belonging to one of the frontiersman's descendants living in North Carolina. She was willing to sell them for $70,000, about a third of their value. One letter alone, Hofmann said, was worth $100,000. Dated 1 April 1775 and addressed to Colonel Richard Henderson, Boone's business associate, the letter told of Boone's blazing the Wilderness Road through the Cumberland Gap. The text of the letter had been published in 1830, but the original had disappeared. Woolley invested $50,000. A few weeks later Hofmann reported selling part of the collection and gave Woolley $25,000. Though the Henderson letter did not achieve the price Hofmann had predicted, when it sold at Sotheby's (New York) on 31 October 1985 it set a record for a Boone document, fetching $31,900.

Hofmann learned that the University of Chicago was willing to sell two leaves of the manuscript Book of Mormon for $50,000. Woolley supplied half the purchase price; a week later Hofmann said that he had nearly doubled their investment, selling the leaves for $90,000. He urged Woolley to roll over his money to help Hofmann buy a library that had been assembled by a Dutchman named Oppenheimer. This collection included works by Charles Darwin, Isaac Newton, and Daniel Defoe, as well as 17th-century Shakespeare quartos. The books could be purchased for $238,000. Woolley supplied half the sum. Soon afterwards Hofmann told Woolley that he had sold the lot for $430,000, yielding nearly a $100,000 profit. The success of Hofmann's schemes was surpass-

THE OATH OF A FREEMAN.

I·AB· being (by Gods providence) an Inhabitant, and Freeman, within the iurifdictiō of this Common-wealth, doe freely acknowledge my felfe to bee fubject to the governement thereof; and therefore doe heere fweare, by the great & dreadfull name of the Everliving-God, that I will be true & faithfull to the fame, & will accordingly yield affiftance & fupport therunto, with my perfon & eftate, as in equity I am bound: and will alfo truely indeavour to maintaine and preferve all the libertyes & privilidges thereof, fubmitting my felfe to the wholefome lawes, & ordres made & ftablifhed by the fame; and further, that I will not plot, nor practice any evill againft it, nor confent to any that fhall foe do, butt will timely difcover, & reveall the fame to lawefull authoritee nowe here ftablifhed, for the fpeedie preventing thereof. Moreover, I doe folemnly binde my felfe, in the fight of God, that when I fhalbe called, to give my voyce touching any fuch matter of this ftate, (in which freemen are to deale) I will give my vote & fuffrage as I fhall judge in myne owne confcience may beft conduce & tend to the publick weale of the body, without refpect of perfonnes, or favour of any man. Soe help mee God in the Lord Iefus Chrift.

Facsimile of the Hoffman's original "Oath" forgery.

ing that of Charles Ponzi, who in 1919-1920 had promised investors a 40% return in 90 days.

In September 1984 Shannon Flynn, working for Hofmann, offered Arizona businessman Wilford Cardon a one-third interest in the only known letter signed by Betsy Ross. On 30 October Cardon paid $6,000 for his share in the letter and loaned Flynn another $6,000 so Flynn could buy a share also. In December Flynn sent Cardon a photocopy of the Ross letter they had bought. He suggested that they allow Hofmann to exchange the letter for sixteen promissory notes dated 1852. These were made out to the company of Livingston and Kincaid and bore the name and "X" of Jim Bridger, a famous frontiersman who guided Brigham Young to the Great Salt Lake. No Jim Bridger notes were known to survive; the value of sixteen such documents far exceeded $18,000. Cardon agreed to the trade.

Hofmann sold one Bridger note to Ashworth, claiming it was unique. Ashworth paid $5,000. At their next Wednesday rendezvous at Crossroads Mall, Hofmann reported finding three more. Ashworth bought another for $5,000. Steven Barnett of Cosmic Aeroplane bought two. One he kept; the other he advertised in his April 1985 catalogue as "an incredibly rare and highly desirable autograph." The price was listed as $9,995.00.[34] Deseret Book bought three, and one sold at Sotheby's for $8,602.50.

Such good fortune paled in comparison to Hofmann's next stroke of luck. In March of 1985 Hofmann went to New York to attend an auction at Sotheby's, where he secured a first edition of *Uncle Tom's Cabin* (Boston: John P. Jewett; Cleveland: Jewett, Proctor & Worthington, 1852) for $13,200, using Justin Schiller as his agent. Schiller specialized in children's books, which Hofmann and his wife were collecting. On 13 March, the day after the auction, Hofmann went to Argosy Book Store on East 59th Street, where he spent $51.42 on four prints and a broadside entitled "The Oath of a Freeman." Flying back to Salt Lake City, Hofmann looked through the catalogue of an upcoming Sotheby

---

34   In Tanner, 69.

auction. Lot 32 was John Child's *New England's Jonas Cast Up in London* (London: T. R. and E. M., 1647). The description noted that "the book also provides the earliest reprint of 'The Freeman's Oath,' the first issue of Stephen Daye's Cambridge Press, of which no copy of the original survives."[35] Had Hofmann located the Holy Grail of Americana, the first item printed on the first press in British North America?

On 15 March Hofmann called Schiller to ask whether his might be the long-sought "Oath." Schiller replied that he was not an expert in the field of early American imprints. If Hofmann would send a photocopy, though, Schiller would show it to someone who was.

In late March Hofmann returned to New York for another auction. He brought with him the "Oath" he had bought at Argosy Book Store. Schiller summoned Michael Zinman, a collector of 17th-century American imprints. Zinman had bought the Child volume that Hofmann had seen listed in the Sotheby catalogue. Zinman thought that the paper looked too white. Hofmann replied that it had been attached to a piece of old cardboard like that laundries used for packaging shirts. Perhaps when Hofmann soaked the document to free it, bleach in the cardboard and chemicals in the Salt Lake City water had whitened the broadside. If this was the Stephen Daye "Oath," Hofmann wondered whether it might be worth as much as $30,000. "More than a million dollars," Zinman replied.

The next day Schiller, Zinman, and Hofmann visited the New York Public Library, which conveniently was displaying its copy of the *Bay Psalm Book* (Cambridge: Stephen Daye, 1640), the first book printed in British North America. The type, printer's ornaments, and paper closely matched Hofmann's "Oath." Schiller invited James Gilreath, a specialist in American historical documents at the Library of Congress, to come to New York. Gilreath brought a fluoroscope with him to check for erasures, overprinting, and other signs of forgery. He found none. Might he take the broadside back to Washington for further testing? Hofmann

---

35 Quoted in Naifeh and Smith, 161.

agreed. On 8 April 1985 Hofmann and Schiller put a $1.5 million price tag on the "Oath."

While waiting for this windfall, Hofmann continued to acquire other valuable material. Thomas Wilding, Hofmann's insurance agent and former classmate at Utah State University, had learned of Hofmann's successes and asked him to invest some money for himself, his brother-in-law Sid Jensen, and others. Hofmann happened to know of a valuable book collection that he could buy for $40,000 and sell for considerably more. Wilding's group gave Hofmann $22,500, which Hofmann soon returned, together with a $10,000 profit. Hofmann asked that the group now make a much larger investment. The Pforzheimer Foundation in New York was selling Charles Dickens' manuscript of *The Haunted Man* (1848), the only manuscript of a Dickens Christmas book still in private hands. Schiller and his partner M. Raymond Wapner were the agents; the price was $300,000 plus a 10% commission. Wilding's group invested $160,000. Wilford Cardon also contributed $110,000.[36]

In April 1985 Hofmann approached Alvin Rust with another offer. William E. McLellin had joined the Mormon Church in 1831, becoming an Apostle in 1835. The next year he left the Church but returned in 1837. In 1838 he was declared an apostate for criticizing Joseph Smith, Jr.'s financial speculations. Because he had held so important a position in the Church, rumors arose that he had secured documents embarrassing to Smith and his followers. His diaries and letters also might contain unflattering revelations. Hofmann told Rust that he had found McLellin's papers in New York and could buy them for $185,000. The Church would pay him twice that sum. Rust took out a $150,000 second mortgage on his house.

---

36 Hofmann never sent Schiller the Wilding group's $160,000. Gregory Gilbert kindly wrote to me (31 March 1999), "Eventually Hofmann's creditors [including Schiller] took control of the manuscript, and it was sold to a collector by the name of Richard Manney." Gilbert added that Manney sold his collection at Sotheby's on 11 October 1991, where *The Haunted Man* appeared as lot 93. It fetched $308,000, including the 10% buyer's commission. Heritage Book Shop of Los Angeles was the purchaser. Later that year Heritage sold the manuscript to a private collector for an undisclosed sum.

Given the size of his investment, Rust insisted that his son accompany Hofmann to secure the papers. Gaylen Rust and Hofmann flew to New York, but Hofmann left Gaylen at the Sheraton Centre Hotel on 53rd Street and Seventh Avenue when he went to collect the documents. Returning to the hotel, Hofmann showed Gaylen three post office insurance receipts, each made out for $75,000. The papers had been mailed to Hofmann's house, not to Rust's store. A week later Hofmann informed Rust that the church had bought the McLellin Collection for $300,000. No one was to know about the sale, though, and payment might be delayed.

Despite these successes, the checks that Hofmann gave his investors and creditors sometimes were returned because of insufficient funds. In April of 1985 he borrowed $40,000 from Salt Lake City orthodontist Ralph Bailey. As security he gave Bailey some books, including a first edition *Tom Sawyer* that Twain had given to his friend Joseph Twitchell, a first edition of *Peter Rabbit,* and a first edition of Jack London's *Call of the Wild* bearing an inscription from the author to one of his closest friends: "To Buck and his human friend, Austin Lewis." Lewis's address was stamped inside the volume. Six weeks later Hofmann asked Bailey for another $50,000 to buy ten Joseph Smith, Jr. letters. Lyn Jacobs' library served as collateral.

On 14 June 1985 the Library of Congress returned the "Oath" to Schiller. The paper, ink, and type were consistent with the *Bay Psalm Book.* However, the Library thought the price of $1.5 million was too high, especially in the absence of any provenance beyond an Argosy Book Store sales slip. Schiller and Wapner now offered the "Oath" to the American Antiquarian Society in Worcester, Massachusetts, which has holdings in early American imprints second only to those at the Library of Congress. The American Antiquarian Society began its own examination of the document.

Without even seeing the document, Boston bookseller George T. Goodspeed declared the "Oath" a fraud because it had no provenance. Robert Mathiesen, who examined the "Oath" for the American Antiquarian Society, was suspicious but concluded that if the "Oath" was a forgery, "it [was] a brilliant one, a product of real scholarship created at considerable expense."[37]

As negotiations over the "Oath" continued, Hofmann approached the Church about the McLellin papers. Despite what he had told Rust, the Church had not yet bought the collection, nor had Hofmann. He told Hinckley that he needed $185,000 to purchase the material from a collector in Texas. Hinckley refused to approve the expenditure. Hofmann turned to Wilford Cardon, but Cardon would not act without Hinckley's approval. On 28 June 1985 Hofmann appealed to Steven Christensen. Hofmann said that he had only until 30 June to exercise his option to buy the papers. The anti-Mormons Wesley Walters and George Smith were waiting to pounce at the first opportunity, and the McLellin Collection, Hofmann said, would make the Salamander Letter look like a Mormon Sunday School text. Among the McLellin materials Hofmann had seen some papyrus that Smith had claimed to have translated as the Book of Abraham. In 1967 some fragments had surfaced at the Metropolitan Museum of Art. These had proved to be part of an Egyptian Book of the Dead. Also in the McLellin Collection was proof that Smith had tried to sell the copyright of the Book of Mormon to a Canadian publisher, thus indicating that Smith had written the work to make money. Another item, written by Emma Smith, denied what was known as the "First Vision." Smith in 1832 asserted that in 1820 he had seen God in a vision. Later he added that he had seen Christ as well. According to Emma's letter, he had seen neither. Christensen no longer had any money himself. Recognizing the importance of the McLellin papers, however, Christensen took Hofmann to see Hugh Pinnock, a Church elder who also sat on the board of directors of First Interstate Bank. A call from Pinnock yielded Hofmann an unsecured loan for $185,000. Hofmann told Pinnock and Christensen that he would repay the loan with the money he would receive from the Library of Congress for his "Oath" and then donate the

---

37 In *The Judgment of Experts: Essays and Documents about the Investigation of the Forging of the "Oath of a Freeman,"* ed. James Gilreath (Worcester, Mass.: American Antiquarian Society, 1991), 74.

McLellin papers to the Church. That day Hofmann paid Alvin Rust a substantial portion of the $297,000 he owed him.

Two weeks later, on 12 July 1985, Hofmann showed Pinnock one item from the McLellin Collection, a contract dated 19 January 1822 between Sidney Rigdon and Solomon Spaulding. From the earliest days of Mormonism, critics had claimed that the uneducated Joseph Smith, Jr. could not have created the Book of Mormon. They contended that Rigdon had written it, basing his account on an unpublished novel by Spaulding. Rigdon had given the text to Smith, who pretended to translate it from the golden plates. According to John Spaulding, Solomon's brother, Solomon's "Manuscript Found" dealt with the journey of Jews from Jerusalem to the New World. The Jewish leaders were named Nephi and Lehi. In America the Jews divided into two groups, the Nephites and the Lamanites. Wars arose between these factions, and the burial mounds in the Old Northwest contained the bodies of those who died in their battles. Others attested to John Spaulding's recollection of the manuscript's contents, which sounded much like the Book of Mormon. When the manuscript itself surfaced, it showed fewer similarities than John had claimed. Both texts supposedly had been found buried in the earth, both spoke of a voyage from the Old World to the New, and both asserted that the burial mounds had been erected for dead warriors. Spaulding's account had no religious content, though. Furthermore, Rigdon, who converted to Mormonism in late 1830, after the Book of Mormon had been published, denied any knowledge of Spaulding or his writings until he read Howe's *Mormonism Unvailed* in 1834. The McLellin Collection's contract added fuel to the charge of plagiarism, since Rigdon and Spaulding clearly had known each other. Although the contract was part of the McLellin Collection that the Church was planning to buy, Hofmann sold this document to Steven Barnett of Cosmic Aeroplane for $400 (20 September 1985). Hofmann had asked for $2,000, but Barnett discovered that the Solomon Spaulding who wrote "Manuscript Found" had died in 1816. Hence, only the Rigdon signature was of interest.

For some reason, Hofmann in July 1985 decided to buy back the Jonathan Dunham letter from Richard Marks and sell it to Ashworth. Hofmann asked Deseret Book to make the purchase, which it did for $90,000. With commission and taxes, Hofmann's cost was $116,000. He resold the letter to Ashworth for $19,000 in cash and $41,000 documents, which included three letters that Hofmann had previously sold Ashworth: two letters by Joseph Smith, Jr. and one by Brigham Young.

Hoping to receive $1 million from the American Antiquarian Society for his "Oath," Hofmann and his wife on 8 August made a $5,000 down payment on a $550,000 house. They would pay $200,000 at closing on 15 October and the balance in two annual installments.

On 11 September 1985 Curt Bench of Deseret Book called Hofmann to say that he had found in his safe a Book of Common Prayer with the name of Nathan Harris in front and the address of Kirtland, Ohio, where the Mormons had settled after leaving New York. Perhaps this Nathan Harris was related to Martin Harris. Bench was willing to sell the book, which Deseret Book had owned for over a decade, for $50. Hofmann bought it. A few days later he returned to give Bench a thousand dollars.

"You know that handwriting in the back of the book. I found out it belonged to Martin Harris," Hofmann reported. He had sold the prayer book to the Church for $2,000 and was sharing the profit. Bench only vaguely recalled the writing but was glad to get the money.[38] As Hofmann left the shop, Bench must have thought that while Hofmann's checks might sometimes bounce, he was at bottom an honest man. Hofmann did not sell the prayer book to the Church until 3 October, and he received in exchange Mormon currency worth about $600.

Hofmann's debts continued to mount. Happily, as he informed Thomas Wilding, he had located a second copy of "The Oath of a Freeman." Lyn Jacobs had acquired it about a year ago at a ridiculously low price and so would be willing to part with it for $500,000, a third of its value. He also told Wilding that the manuscript of *The Haunted Man* would be sold on 16 October for $500,000, giving him a substantial return on his $160,000 invest-

---

38 Sillitoe and Roberts, 339.

ment. On 12 September Wilding and Sid Jensen handed $173,870 to Hofmann, who said he was leaving that day for Boston to pick up the "Oath." Hofmann stopped at Deseret Book to pay $100,000 of the $116,000 he owed.

Later that day Wilding and Jensen had second thoughts about their investment. They learned that Hofmann still owed First Interstate Bank $185,000, and that the flight number and departure time Hofmann had given for his flight were false. The next morning they found Hofmann still at home and demanded their money back. All he had left was $18,000, having, he said, sent the balance to Boston already. Wilding and Jensen insisted that Hofmann sign two promissory notes for the $455,155 he owed them. If he did not give them the money by 16 October, he agreed to pay an additional $4,000 a day in penalties.

In mid-September Hofmann called Kenneth Rendell. Hofmann had found a customer seeking a first century A.D. Egyptian papyrus written in hieratic script and containing text from the Book of the Dead. Rendell was surprised at the request; most collectors preferred the more decorative hieroglyphics. Hofmann, however, insisted on the hieratic. On 16 September Rendell sent Hofmann on consignment two samples from an English collection. Hofmann's cost would be $10,500 for the pair. Three days later Hofmann offered Curt Bench of Deseret Book a fragment of papyrus from the McLellin Collection for $40,000.

"I thought that the Church had the McLellin collection," Bench queried.

"Well, this piece is being marketed separately," Hofmann replied.[39]

Bench declined the papyrus. On Sunday, 22 September, Hofmann offered a piece of papyrus to Ashworth for $30,000. Ashworth wavered but finally decided not to buy it. In early October Hofmann sold $38,000 worth of Mormon currency and a Jim Bridger promissory note to Deseret Book, but his finances remained troubled.

---

39   In Sillitoe and Roberts, 340.

On Wednesday, 2 October, Hofmann and Christensen went to see Hugh Pinnock at 10:30 P.M. Hofmann confessed that he would not be receiving any money from the Library of Congress for his "Oath." He also admitted that he had used the McLellin Collection as collateral for a $150,000 loan from Alvin Rust. However, he added that the American Antiquarian Society would be paying him $150,000 for the "Oath of a Freeman." He would then pay Rust, but he still needed a buyer for the McLellin Collection to repay the First Interstate Bank Loan.

Pinnock also had an interest in the repayment of the loan. On 4 October he called Nova Scotia businessman David E. Sorensen. Sorensen did not collect documents, but as a loyal Mormon he was willing to buy the McLellin papers and then donate them to the Church. Sorensen wanted to be certain that the documents were authentic, and Pinnock suggested that Christensen examine them. Hofmann claimed that Rust had the key to the safe-deposit box that held the material; the sale could be completed as soon as Rust returned from a fishing trip.

On 6 October Rendell called Brent Ashworth, one of his good customers, to say that he was planning a trip west late in the month and would stop in Salt Lake City to see Ashworth and Hofmann. Ashworth conveyed the news to Hofmann.

On 11 October Hofmann informed Hinckley of another discovery. In the 1840s three men from Kinderhook, Illinois, had manufactured six bell-shaped copper plates, incised them with meaningless symbols, and buried them in an Indian mound. They then "discovered" the plates in the presence of some Mormons, who took the copper bells to Joseph Smith, Jr. Smith informed them that according to the plates the man interred in the mound was "a descendant of Ham, through the loins of Pharaoh, king of Egypt."[40] Hofmann had found the copper plates and, more embarrassingly, Smith's translation in the hand of Orson Pratt, one of Smith's twelve Apostles. Hinckley expressed no interest in acquiring this material.

---

40 Naifeh and Smith, 218.

Hofmann's debts on that day stood at $1,322,655. He owed Wilding and his group $455,155, a sum about to grow by $4,000 a day. He had managed to pay $20,000 on his First Interstate Loan, but interest and principal outstanding came to $171,000. To Rust he owed $132,000, and he had never sent Schiller the $160,000 Wilding had invested in *The Haunted Man* manuscript. Bailey had received no payment on the $90,000 Hofmann had borrowed from him, and on 15 October the Hofmanns were to close on their half-million-dollar house. On the credit side, the American Antiquarian Society was planning to buy the "Oath of a Freeman," though the offer was for only $250,000; and Sorensen would pay Hofmann $185,000 as soon as Christensen verified the contents of the McLellin Collection.

Perhaps the sale of the collection could be completed that very day, since Rust had returned unexpectedly. Hofmann, however, procrastinated, and the banks would be closed for the Columbus Day holiday on Monday, 14 October. Tuesday, 15 October, would be the day of reckoning. Ahead of that date, Hofmann on 14 October visited Wade Lillywhite of Deseret Book. Hofmann offered him a piece of papyrus from the McLellin Collection for $100,000 and a manuscript page of the Book of Mormon for $20,000. "Come back Wednesday," Lillywhite told him.

Shortly after 8:00 A.M. on 15 October Steve Christensen arrived at his office. In front of his door was a package addressed to him. It had no postage. As he picked it up, it exploded, killing him instantly. At 9:45 A.M. a similar bomb exploded at the home of Christensen's former boss, Gary Sheets, killing Gary's wife, Kathy. The failure of the Sheets-Christensen Coordinated Financial Services had created well over a thousand unhappy investors. Perhaps one of them had been unhappy enough to kill. Sheets and Christensen had both been involved with the Salamander Letter. A fanatical Mormon might have been sufficiently angered by its contents to have planted the bombs.

On the day of the bombings Hofmann went to see Hugh Pinnock. Pinnock was not available, so Hofmann talked to Pinnock's supervisor, Dallin Oaks. Hofmann thought that he might be questioned about the deaths. Should he say anything about the McLellin Collection? He also wondered whether the sale of the collection would be delayed. Oaks saw no connection between the bombings and controversial Mormon documents.

"Why would the police want to question you?" Oaks asked. Had Hofmann been associated with Coordinated Financial Services? Could the bombings be related to documents? "Do you know anyone in your documents business who would enforce his contracts with a bomb?"

"No."

"Well, then, what do you have to worry about? The police probably won't question you, and if they do, just tell them the truth."[41]

The sale of the McLellin Collection could be completed on the 16th, with recently retired Church archivist Don Schmidt replacing Christensen as the examiner. Hofmann agreed to bring the papers at 10:00 the next morning.

The morning of the 16th came and went with no trace of Hofmann. At 2:00 P.M. he parked near Crossroads Mall, expecting to meet Brent Ashworth for their usual Wednesday rendezvous. Ashworth had driven to Salt Lake City on Monday and Tuesday, though, and so did not make the trip that day. At 2:40 Hofmann returned to his Toyota MR-2. Moments later the car exploded, severely injuring Hofmann. Perhaps the bombings were document-related after all.

That evening, in the hospital, Salt Lake City Police Department detective Jim Bell visited Hofmann. He asked the injured man to describe what had happened. Hofmann replied that as he opened his car door, a package fell from the driver's seat. He tried to grab it, but it hit the floor and exploded. Jerry Taylor of the United States Treasury Department's Bureau of Alcohol, Tobacco, and Firearms already had determined that the bomb that injured Hofmann was the same type that had killed Christensen and Sheets. All used gunpowder packed in a pipe and were detonated when a mercury switch was tripped by movement of the package concealing the device. The bomb that killed Christensen had contained

---

41   Quoted in Naifeh and Smith, 236.

cement nails, but that was the only difference. Whoever made the bomb that wounded Hofmann had made the other two. When Bell left the hospital he returned to the remains of Hofmann's car. Taylor was still there. After Bell relayed Hofmann's account, Taylor replied, "If he told you that, he might be your man."[42] The pattern of the explosion and Hofmann's injuries showed that the bomb had not exploded on the floor but rather near the console next to the driver's seat, and that Hofmann had been inside the car, not standing outside, when the blast occurred.

Other evidence linked Hofmann to the bombings. Bruce Passey, a jeweler who worked in the same building as Christensen, saw Hofmann's face on the television news. He recalled seeing Hofmann the day before, wearing a green high school letterman's jacket, riding in the elevator. Hofmann was carrying a package addressed to "Steve Christensen." Inside the trunk of Hofmann's MR-2 was a felt-tipped pen like that used to address the packages that had killed Christensen and Sheets. Investigators also found there a piece of galvanized pipe and some Egyptian papyrus. A search of Hofmann's house yielded a green high school letterman's jacket wadded up in a closet. Aaron Teplick, a thirteen year old who lived close to the Sheets family, recalled seeing a gold Toyota van near the Sheets house the night before Kathy Sheets was killed. Hofmann owned such a vehicle.

During a second search of Hofmann's house, detectives found an envelope bearing the name M. Hansen. An M. Hansen had bought a mercury switch and a D-battery cell-pack from the Radio Shack at Cottonwood Mall in south Salt Lake City on 7 October. The bombs that killed Christensen and Kathy Sheets had used mercury switches and C-cell battery packs. The address that Hansen gave led investigators to a vacant lot near Hofmann's house.

Still, why would Hofmann want to kill Christensen? Hofmann had never even met Kathy Sheets. And why would he put a bomb in his own car? Jim Bell believed that the answers lay in the mate-

---

42   Lindsey, 208.

rials Hofmann had been selling. On 18 October he told detective Kenneth Farnsworth, "These documents are all forgeries, and this case revolves around documents. It's too good to be true. . . . Everybody's out looking for this stuff, and only Mark finds it."[43] Farnsworth was skeptical about Bell's idea. After all, the country's leading experts had validated these works. On Wednesday, 27 November 1985, David Biggs of the Salt Lake County Attorney's office wrote in his journal, "It has now been over a month since the deaths and bombings and nothing seems as clear as it was on 10/16/85 after Hofmann was blown out of his MR-2. I feel that all the pieces of the puzzle are at our fingertips but the placement is askew."[44]

The next day the pieces of the puzzle shifted a bit. The Salt Lake *Tribune* announced on Thanksgiving, 28 November, that the McLellin Collection had been found in Houston, Texas. The owner, Otis Traughber, had never heard of Mark Hofmann. Otis Traughber was the son of John Logan Traughber, Jr. In the 1870s John Traughber, Jr. was working on a book about Mormonism. In the course of his research he spoke to and corresponded with William McLellin. After McLellin died, his widow sent Traughber some of her husband's papers, which had stayed in the Traughber family. In 1908 the supposedly controversial early journals, covering the years 1831–1836, had been purchased by the Church from John Traughber, Jr. for $50 but had not been catalogued.[45]

What remained in Traughber's possession did not treat the early Mormon Church kindly. McLellin denied some of Joseph Smith, Jr.'s revelations, including Smith's claim that John the Baptist had ordained him, that Smith had translated the Book of Abraham from papyrus taken from a mummy, and that the angel Moroni had supplied the "Urim and Thummim," the seer stones Smith used to translate the Book of Mormon. McLellin accused Smith of using the pretext of divine revelation to seduce women and of ordering the murder of opponents. However, the collection

43 In Sillitoe and Roberts, 76.
44 In Lindsey, 254.
45 The Hofmann affair led to the journals' discovery. The journals were published in 1994.

contained no papyrus, no embarrassing letters by members of the Smith family.

If Traughber and the Church owned the McLellin Collection, what was Hofmann offering for $185,000? Where had he obtained the Rigdon-Spaulding contract and the parchment? Might there have been no McLellin Collection for Christensen to verify? Could Hofmann have killed Christensen in an effort to prevent discovery of a fraud?

In December 1985 George Throckmorton, an examiner of documents for the Utah Attorney General's Office, joined the investigation into the bombings. Because so many of Hofmann's discoveries challenged orthodox Mormon history, Throckmorton, himself a Mormon, wanted someone from outside the Church to help with the examination of the manuscripts Hofmann had sold. He summoned William Flynn, a documents analyst for the Arizona State Crime Laboratory at Phoenix. When the two looked at Hofmann's manuscripts under 60-power magnification, they saw signs of cracking in the ink. Documents of the same age that were not connected to Hofmann did not exhibit this characteristic. Throckmorton and Flynn also noticed that the Jonathan Dunham letter written from prison on 27 June 1844 was on paper different from the other two Smith had sent that day. The date on the Rigdon-Spaulding contract had been changed from 1722 to 1822.

Over the Christmas holiday Flynn experimented with inks. Among the items seized at Hofmann's house was a copy of Charles Hamilton's *Great Forgers and Famous Fakes*. Using Hamilton's formula for making gallotannic ink, the kind that had been used since the Middle Ages, and then aging the iron through oxidation with household ammonia (ammonium hydroxide) or sodium hydroxide, Flynn recreated the cracking he had seen in Hofmann's manuscripts.

In January 1986 Gerry D'Elia and Michael George, investigators with the Salt Lake County Attorney's Office, went to New York to ask Charles Hamilton to look again at the Salamander Letter he had authenticated three years earlier. Hamilton at first repeated his confidence in the letter's genuineness. Then he exclaimed, "*You dumb son of a bitch.*"

"Who?" asked George.

"Me," Hamilton replied.[46]

Stampless covers in the early 19th century were folded in such a way that all four sides were closed. The Salamander Letter was open on one side. The seal was off to the side, not in the middle of the letter where it belonged. When D'Elia and George showed Hamilton other letters, supposedly written by Lucy Mack Smith, Martin Harris, and Harris' son, Hamilton noticed striking similarities in the penmanship. Hamilton declared that all the letters were forgeries.

Richard Forbes, like D'Elia and George working with the Salt Lake County Attorney's Office, went from New York to Boston with D'Elia to meet Kenneth Rendell. When he first learned that Hofmann was suspected of forgery, Rendell said that if Hofmann were charged, he, Rendell, would lead a team of experts into court to prove the documents genuine. Now, looking at the letters under ultraviolet light, he saw a strange blue glow. Rendell was not ready to denounce the Salamander Letter, but he thought that at least some of the manuscripts were of recent manufacture.

Michael George meanwhile flew to California to interview Reginald and Frances Magee, who had owned the Nathan Harris Book of Common Prayer until 1973. Reginald Magee was Martin Harris' great-grandson. George showed Frances the prayer book; she instantly declared that no poem in Harris' hand had been found in the book while it had belonged to her. Verne Rounds, who had obtained the prayer book from the Magees and had sold it to Deseret Book in 1974, could not recall any such poem, either. Harris' handwriting in the Book of Common Prayer matched that of the Salamander Letter. If one was a fake, both were.

The district attorney felt that enough evidence had emerged to warrant arresting Hofmann. On 4 February 1986 he was charged with two counts of capital murder and twenty-three counts—later raised to twenty-six—of theft by deception and fraud.

During the interval between 4 February and the preliminary hearing, investigators made new discoveries. Among the reams of paper found at Hofmann's house was a sheet in Hofmann's hand-

---

46   In Lindsey, 286.

writing bearing the name Mike Hansen, an address on 25ᵗʰ Street with no city or state, and a phone number without an area code. After various calls to places in Utah and surrounding states, Jim Bell tried Colorado. A voice answered, "Cocks-Clark Engraving." Claiming to be Mark Hansen, Bell asked for copies of receipts for work the company had done for him. The receptionist said she would be happy to mail him a receipt for the zinc plate he had requested entitled "Deseret Currency."

On 3 March 1986 detectives Kenneth Farnsworth and David Biggs went to Utah Engraving at 231 Emerson Lane, Salt Lake City. Jorgen Olsen, who worked there, had prepared a zinc plate that matched the Jim Bridger promissory notes. The purchaser was Mike Hansen. At DeBouzek Engraving and Colorplate Company detectives learned that on 25 March 1985 an M. Hansen had paid for a zinc plate entitled "The Oath of a Freeman." The text matched Hofmann's discovery at Argosy Book Store. Coincidentally, on 8 March a Mark Harris had ordered a plate with the same title but with a different text, a 19th-century hymn. Although Harris had ordered the plate, Hofmann had written a two-dollar check as partial payment. Hofmann had taken the first version of the "Oath" with him to New York. He had "found" it at Argosy, paid $25, and obtained a receipt to provide provenance. Back in Salt Lake City, he had printed the "Oath" that the American Antiquarian Society would have bought but for the bombings. In December 1984 DeBouzek Engraving had prepared a plate bearing a facsimile of the inscription in Hofmann's copy of *The Call of the Wild*. A stamp bearing Austin Lewis' address had been ordered by a Mark Hansen from the Salt Lake Stamp Company. On the receipt for the stamp, detectives found Hofmann's fingerprint.

The first copy of the "Oath" was still in New York, but Wilding had secured the second copy and was holding it as collateral for the money Hofmann owed. On 11 April 1986 Michael George and Throckmorton examined Wilding's "Oath." Flaws in the printing showed that it had been manufactured from the DeBouzek plate.

Three days later Hofmann's preliminary hearing began to determine whether he should stand trial. On 22 May 1986 he was ordered to be tried for all counts, but in January 1987 he agreed to a plea-bargain whereby he confessed to two counts of second-degree murder and two counts of fraud. He admitted that he had killed Christensen to delay the sale of the McLellin Collection. The bomb that killed Kathy Sheets was intended as a diversion, to link Christensen's death to the failure of Coordinated Financial Services. Hofmann said that the third explosion had been a suicide attempt. Prosecutors suspected that Hofmann had intended the third bomb for Brent Ashworth or Hugh Pinnock.

Ashworth had intervened in an attempt by Hofmann to pass off a spurious Lincoln signature. For $17,500 Hofmann had sold Wade Lillywhite of Deseret Book a copy of the Lincoln-Douglas debates signed by Lincoln. Lillywhite returned the work as questionable. Hofmann then offered it to Steven Barnett at Cosmic Aeroplane for $9,500. When Ashworth heard of the deal he asked Barnett to show him the signature. Ashworth owned a letter signed by Lincoln, and the two signatures did not match. Barnett did not buy Hofmann's book.

More threateningly, Kenneth Rendell would soon be visiting Ashworth, who had paid $225,000 for Hofmann discoveries. Rendell had verified individual items, but suppose he saw Ashworth's entire collection. Might he, like Hamilton, detect similarities in penmanship? Hofmann had been sufficiently worried to try to buy back his forgeries from Ashworth, offering him $250,000 for the Lucy Mack Smith letter and some other items, $500,000 for another eight documents. Hofmann said that he could easily resell these at a profit. Suppose Rendell asked about the papyrus he had sent Hofmann on consignment. Had Hofmann found Ashworth at Crossroads Mall, the dealer could have lured him to the MR-2 with news of some new treasure. Hofmann could have told Ashworth to look inside the package in the car while he himself withdrew under the pretext of getting something from the trunk.

Pinnock's death also had its advantages, since it might well have discouraged the Church from pursuing the purchase of the McLellin Collection that Hofmann could not provide. Over time, Hofmann could have created the 116-page Book of Lehi, which he admitted intending as his crowning achievement. In 1981 he had hired Jeff Salt, a friend from college, to write each word of the Book of Mormon on index cards. Hofmann said that he wanted to study the vocabulary and syntax. With such knowledge he could duplicate Smith's style in producing the missing text. The Church might have paid as much as $25 million for this manuscript, and Hofmann could have said that it had been part of the McLellin Collection.

As part of the plea bargain, Hofmann agreed to explain how he had executed his forgeries. Even before entering his guilty plea on 23 January 1987, Hofmann met with prosecutor Robert Stott and David Biggs from the Salt Lake County Attorney's Office at the home of Hofmann's lawyer, Ron Yengich. Hofmann here explained that before composing the Salamander Letter, he carefully researched Smith's activities, read books about magic, and discussed money-digging with Brent Metcalfe. Once he had gathered his information, Hofmann wrote the letter in about two hours. The handwriting was modeled on the few known Martin Harris signatures. Hofmann even studied the Palmyra, New York postal schedules and postmarks. The Lucy Mack Smith postmark, for example, consisted of a black double-line oval, duplicating those used at Palmyra between 1829 and 1834. The beginning of the Salamander Letter, " Your letter of yesterday is received & I hasten to respond as fully as I can," Hofmann copied from a contemporary example he had found.

Hofmann was interviewed at Utah State Prison between 11 February and 27 May 1987. He told of stealing blank pages from 19th-century books and magazines in the University of Utah library. The 17th-century sheet that he used for "The Oath of a Freeman" had come from the library at Brigham Young University. He had manufactured ink as Flynn had done, though he had used as his manual a volume he had stolen from the Utah State Library rather than Hamilton's *Great Forgers*. He had aged his writing by oxidizing the iron in the iron gallotannic ink using hydrogen peroxide rather than ammonium hydroxide. For the first copy of "The Oath of a Freeman" Hofmann had insured that the ink would pass even carbon-14 dating, and it deceived cyclotron analysis at the University of California at Davis. Hofmann burned 17th-century paper for the lampblack, and the tannin came from the leather of a 17th-century binding boiled in distilled water. These he combined with linseed oil and beeswax. For the second copy of the "Oath" Hofmann was less meticulous; he knew that it would not have withstood close scrutiny.

Hofmann usually undertook his own photography, etching, and printing. He had created the seal of the twelve Apostles for his forged notes from authentic bills he had received in trade from the Church. As his press he used a C-clamp. The items he printed were small: "The Oath of a Freeman," for example, was only 4" x 6." None of his printed forgeries were as large as even half a sheet of paper. The impression of the letters would be uneven, but such poor press-work was consistent with the printing he was imitating. Flaws in alignment of the "Oath," for example, were attributed to Stephen Daye's amateurish failure to lock properly the case holding the type.

While Hofmann had not made the plate for the "Oath," he had photocopied pages from the 1956 facsimile of the *Bay Psalm Book* published by the University of Chicago Press and printed by the Meridan Gravure Company, Meridan, Connecticut. He cut out and arranged individual letters, and sometimes whole words, to produce his text, and then photocopied his mock-up. He used a pen to distort some of the letters so they would not look exactly like those in the psalter, and once he secured the plate he ground down some of the characters and rubbed the plate with steel wool to change its appearance even more.

During his mission to England, Hofmann had bought an old Bible at Bristol. When he decided to create the fake Anthon Transcript, he wrote two sets of the initials "SS" on the verso of the title page to link the Bible to the Smith family and added Samuel Smith's signature (no example of which was known) to the hand-written Book of Amos. He had copied the figures of the transcript itself from a facsimile of the Harris-Whitmer example but had arranged them according to Anthon's description. The Transcript was sealed with Elmer's Glue blackened with the tip of a burnt match. The Betsy Ross letter had been created by adding "Ross" to a letter signed "Betsy." Hofmann had changed the date from 1837 to 1807, but he had not removed the signature of postmaster William B. Smith, who assumed that office in 1834.

Hofmann had initially forged for fame. After the birth of his first son, his primary motivation had become money. Whenever he needed cash, he would "discover" something. Hofmann may have had another motive as well. He had lost his faith at the age of fourteen, but his father, William, so intimidated him that he went on a mission, wore Temple garments, and pretended to accept Mormon beliefs. Shortly before his marriage, Hofmann told his former fiancée, Kate Reid, that despite his lack of faith he had to appear to be a good Mormon to have access to the materials and customers he needed. "Eventually," he said, "the documents I find are going to show people that they believe in a fairytale."[47]

Hofmann did not regard himself as a fabricator. On 27 February 1987 he told prosecutors,

> I believed that the documents that I created could have been a part of Mormon history. I'm speaking specifically, for example, of the magic-related items. The 1825 Stoal [Stowell] Letter, the so-called Salamander Letter. In effect, I guess, the questions I asked myself in deciding on a forgery [—] one of the questions was, what could have been? I had a concept of Church history and I followed that concept.[48]

On 22 April Hofmann repeated his claim of being faithful to fact:

> It is true that I wrote the documents according to how I felt the actual events took place. In other words, I believed that Joseph Smith [Jr.] was involved in folk magic, but the idea there was more to keep it in harmony with what I thought potentially genuine, discoverable type documents may say. In other words, to make it fit the history as accurately as possible so I wouldn't be found out or whatever.[49]

Prosecutors asked whether Hofmann worried that people were "investing sentiment and emotion and belief in these [spurious] documents." Hofmann did not:

---

47 In Sillitoe and Roberts, 231.
48 *Hofmann's Confession: A Photographic Printing of the Transcripts of Salt Lake County Prosecutors' Interviews with Convicted Forger and Murderer Mark Hofmann,* 3 vols. (Salt Lake City: Utah Lighthouse Ministry, 1987), I, 113.
49 Ibid., III, 427.

> My view is, when I forged a document and sold it, . . . I was not cheating that person that I was selling it to because the document would never be detected as being a fraud. . . . My example would be the Mormon Church. . . . To me it is unimportant if Joseph Smith had that [First V]ision or not as long as people believe it. The important thing is that people believe it.[50]

As another example he told of an early bit of counterfeiting. In his youth Hofmann had collected coins. On a dime worth a dollar or two he electroplated a "D" mint mark that made the coin worth over a thousand dollars. A dealer surprised that so young a numismatist should have so valuable a coin sent the item to the Treasury for authentication. The Treasury replied that the coin was genuine. Since the counterfeiting could not be detected, the purchaser would not lose money or the faith invested in the acquisition.

On 28 January 1988 the Utah Board of Pardons sentenced Hofmann to life in prison without the possibility of parole. Two months later Hofmann, speaking with Michael George of the Salt Lake County Attorney's Office, estimated that he had earned about $2 million from his forgeries. These had included works signed by nearly a hundred American and European figures, among them George Washington, John Adams, Daniel Boone, John Brown, John Hancock, Abraham Lincoln, John Milton, Miles Standish, even Button Gwinnett, whose death shortly after he put his name to the Declaration of Independence makes his the most elusive and expensive of all the Signers' autographs. Hofmann had forged so many documents that he could not remember them all. He did recall selling an Emily Dickinson poem that he had composed and to which he had signed her name. A year later the poem was published as a newly discovered work by the Belle of Amherst.

Charles Hamilton, a victim of Hofmann's frauds, described Hofmann as "unquestionably the most skilled forger the country has ever seen. . . . He fooled me—he fooled everybody." Hamilton added that Hofmann's success derived not only from his technical

---

50 Ibid., 407, 425–426.

virtuosity but also from his ability to appear friendly, sincere, and trustworthy. "He packaged himself as a bespeckled, sweet, unobtrusive, hard-working, highly intelligent scholar dedicated to the uncovering of history. Now we know he's more than he appeared to be."[51] Through his fabrications, Hofmann became part of the Mormon history he sought to change.

---

51   *New York Times,* 11 February 1987, A20.

BIBLIOGRAPHY

General Studies

Altick, Richard D *The Scholar Adventurers*. New York: Macmillan, 1950.

Bagnani, Gilbert. "On Fakes and Forgeries." *Phoenix* 14 (1960): 228–244.

Baines, Paul. *The House of Forgery in Eighteenth-Century Britain*. Brookfield, VT: Ashgate, 1999.

Bozeman, Pat, ed. *Forged Documents: Proceedings of the 1989 Houston Conference*. New Castle, DE: Oak Knoll Books, 1990.

Brooke, Christopher Nugent Lawrence. "Approaches to Medieval Forgery." *Journal of the Society of Archivists* 3 (1968): 377–386. Reprinted in Brooke's *Medieval Church and Society: Collected Essays*. London: Sidgwick & Jackson, 1971; New York: New York University Press, 1972: 100–120.

Brown, T. J. "The Detection of Faked Literary MSS." *The Book Collector* 2 (Spring 1953): 6–23.

Chambers, Edmund Kerchever. *The History and Motives of Literary Forgeries, Being the Chancellor's English Essay for 1891*. Oxford: Blackwell; Simpkin, Marshall, 1891.

Constable, Giles. "Forgery and Plagiarism in the Middle Ages." *Archiv für Diplomatik, Schriftgeschichte, Siegel- und Wappenkunde* 29 (1983): 1–41.

Farrer, James Anson. *Literary Forgeries*. London: Longmans, Green, 1907.

Grafton, Anthony. *Forgers and Critics: Creativity and Duplicity in Western Scholarship*. Princeton: Princeton University Press, 1990.

Hamilton, Charles. *Great Forgers and Famous Fakes: The Manuscript Forgers of America and How They Duped the Experts*. New York: Crown, 1980.

_____. *Scribblers and Scoundrels*. New York: P. S. Eriksson, 1968.

Jones, Mark, ed. *Why Fakes Matter: Essays on Problems of Authenticity.* London: British Museum, 1990.

Jones, Mark, Paul Craddock, and Nicholas Barker. *Fake? The Art of Deception.* London: British Museum, 1990.

Lang, Andrew. "Literary Forgeries." In *Books and Bookmen.* London: Longman's, Green, 1892.

McDougall, Curtis D. *Hoaxes.* New York: Macmillan, 1940.

Meyvaert, P. "Medieval Forgers and Modern Scholars: Tests of Ingenuity." In *The Role of the Book in Medieval Culture: Proceedings of the Oxford International Symposium 26 September-1 October 1982.* Edited by Peter Ganz. 2 vols. Turnhout: Brepols, 1986.

Myers, Robin, and Michael Harris, eds. *Fakes and Frauds: Varieties of Deception in Print and Manuscript.* Winchester, England: St Paul's Bibliographies, 1989.

Rhodes, Henry T. F. *The Craft of Forgery.* London: John Murray, 1934.

Sergeant, Philip W. *Liars and Fakers.* London: Hutchinson, 1925.

Thierry, Augustin. *Les grandes mystifications littéraires.* Paris: Plon-Nourrit, 1911.

_____. *Les grandes mystifications littéraires, deuxième série.* Paris: Plon-Nourrit, 1913.

Tout, T. F. "Medieval Forgers and Forgeries." *Bulletin of the John Rylands Library* 5 (April-November 1919): 208–234.

Whitehead, John. *This Solemn Mockery: The Art of Literary Forgery.* London: Arlington Books, 1973.

George Psalmanazar

Farrer, James Anson. "Psalmanazar: The Famous Formosan." In *Literary Forgeries.*

Psalmanazar, George. *An Historical and Geographical Description of Formosa.* London: Dan. Brown [et al.], 1704.

_____. *Memoirs*. London: Printed for the Executrix, 1764; 2nd ed., London: R. Davis [et al.], 1765.

Sergeant, Philip W. "Psalmanazar the Formosan." In *Liars and Fakers*.

Whitehead, John. "History of Formosa." In *This Solemn Mockery*.

James Macpherson

Blair, Hugh. *A Critical Dissertation on the Poems of Ossian, the Son of Fingal*. London: T. Becket and P. A. De Hondt, 1763.

Carnie, Robert Hay. "Macpherson's 'Fragments of Ancient Poetry' and Lord Hailes." *English Studies* 41 (1960): 17–26.

DeGategno, Paul J. *James Macpherson*. Boston: Twayne, 1989.

Gaskill, Howard. "'Ossian' Macpherson: Towards a Rehabilitation." *Comparative Criticism* 8 (1986): 113–146.

_____, ed. *Ossian Revisited*. Edinburgh: Edinburgh University Press, 1991.

_____. "What Did James Macpherson Really Leave on Display at His Publisher's Shop in 1762?" *Scottish Gaelic Studies* 16 (1990): 67–89.

Greenway, John L. "The Gateway to Innocence: Ossian and the Nordic Bard as Myth." *Studies in Eighteenth-Century Culture* 4 (1975): 161–170.

Hamilton, Ian. *The Making of History: A Study of the Literary Forgeries of James Macpherson and Thomas Chatterton in Relation to Eighteenth-Century Ideas of History and Fiction*. Rutherford, NJ: Fairleigh Dickinson University Press, 1986.

Highland Society of Scotland. *Report of the Committee of Enquiry the Highland Society of Scotland Appointed to Enquire into the Nature and Authority of the Poems of Ossian*. Edinburgh: A. Constable [et al.], 1805.

Leneman, Leah. "Ossian and the Enlightenment." *Scotia* 11 (1987): 13–29.

Macpherson, James. *Poems of Ossian*. Edited by Malcolm Laing. 2 vols. Edinburgh: A. Constable, 1805.

_____. *The Poems of Ossian and Related Works*. Edited by Howard Gaskill. Introduction by Fiona Stafford. Edinburgh: Edinburgh University Press, 1996.

Roger, James Cruikshank. *Celtic Manuscripts in Relation to the Macpherson Fraud*. London: E. W. Allen, 1890.

Saunders, Thomas Bailey. *The Life and Letters of James Macpherson*. London: S. Sonnenschein; New York: Macmillan, 1894.

Shaw, William. *An Enquiry into the Authenticity of the Poems Ascribed to Ossian*. London: J. Murray, 1781.

Sher, Richard. " 'Those Scottish Imposters and Their Cabal': Ossian and the Scottish Enlightenment," in *Man and Nature: Proceedings of the Canadian Society for Eighteenth-Century Studies*. Edited by R. L. Emerson et al. London, Ontario: Published for the Society by the Faculty of Education, the University of Western Ontario, 1982.

Smart, John Semple. *James Macpherson: An Episode in Literature*. London: David Nutt, 1905.

Snyder, Edward D. *The Celtic Revival in English Literature, 1760–1780*. Cambridge, MA: Harvard University Press, 1923.

Stafford, Fiona J. "Dr. Johnson and the Ruffian: New Evidence in the Dispute between Samuel Johnson and James Macpherson." *Notes and Queries* 234 (March 1989): 71–77.

_____. *The Sublime Savage: James Macpherson and the Poems of Ossian*. Edinburgh: Edinburgh University Press, 1988.

Stewart, Larry LeRoy. "Ossian in the Polished Age: The Critical Reception of James Macpherson's Ossian." Ph.D. diss., Case Western Reserve University, 1971.

Thomson, Derick. *The Gaelic Sources of Macpherson's "Ossian."* Edinburgh: Oliver and Boyd for the University of Aberdeen, 1952.

Tieghem, Paul van. *Ossian en France*. 2 vols. Paris: F. Rieder, 1917.

_____. "Ossian et l'ossianisme au XVIIIe siècle." In *Le préromantisme: Études d'histoire littéraire européenne*. Paris: Félix Alcan, n.d.

Tombo, Rudolf., Jr. *Ossian in Germany*. New York: Columbia University Press, 1901.

Whitehead, John. "Ossian and Fingal." In *This Solemn Mockery*.

Thomas Chatterton

Browning, Robert. "Essay on Chatterton." Edited by Donald Smalley. In *The Complete Works of Robert Browning with Variant Readings & Annotations*. Athens, Ohio: Ohio University Press, 1971. III, 159–179.

Bryant, Jacob. *Observations upon the Poems of Thomas Rowley in which the Authenticity of Those Poems is Ascertained*. London: T. Payne, 1781.

Chatterton, Thomas. *Poems, Supposed to Have Been Written at Bristol by Thomas Rowley and Others*. Edited by Thomas Tyrwhitt. London: T. Payne and Son, 1777.

_____. *Miscellanies in Prose and Verse*. Edited by John Broughton. London: Fielding and Walker, 1778.

_____. *The Complete Works*. Edited by Donald S. Taylor and Benjamin B. Hoover. 2 vols. Oxford: Clarendon Press, 1971.

Clarke, Sir Ernest. *New Light on Chatterton*. London: Blades, East & Blades, from the [Bibliographical] Society's Transactions, 1916.

Ellinger, Esther Parker. *The Marvelous Boy*. Philadelphia: University of Pennsylvania Press, 1930.

Farrer, James Anson. "The Tragedy of Chatterton." In *Literary Forgeries*.

Forman, Henry Buxton. *Thomas Chatterton and His Latest Editor*. London: Beveridge, 1874.

Haywood, Ian. "Chatterton's Plans for the Publication of the Forgery." *Review of English Studies* NS 36 (February 1985): 58–68.

_____. *The Making of History: A Study of the Literary Forgeries of James Macpherson and Thomas Chatterton in Relation to Eighteenth-Century Ideas of History and Fiction.* Rutherford, NJ: Fairleigh Dickinson University Press, 1986.

Holmes, Richard "Thomas Chatterton: The Case Re-opened." *Cornhill Magazine* 178 (Autumn 1970): 203–251.

Ingram, John Henry. *The True Chatterton.* London: T. Fisher Unwin, 1910.

Kaplan, Louise J. *The Family Romance of the Impostor-Poet Thomas Chatterton.* New York: Atheneum, 1988.

Kelly, Linda. *The Marvelous Boy: The Life and Myth of Thomas Chatterton.* London: Weidenfeld and Nicolson, 1971.

Malone, Edmond. *Cursory Observations on the Poems Attributed to Thomas Rowley.* London: J. Nichols, 1782.

Mathias, Thomas James. *An Essay on the Evidence, External and Internal, Relating to the Poems Attributed to Thomas Rowley.* London: T. Becket, 1783.

Masson, David. *Chatterton: A Biography.* London: Hodder and Stoughton, 1899.

Meyerstein, Edward Harry William. *Life of Thomas Chatterton.* New York: Charles Scribner's Sons, 1930.

Nevill, John Cranstoun. *Thomas Chatterton.* London: F. Muller, 1948.

Russell, Charles Edward. *Thomas Chatterton, the Marvelous Boy.* London: Richards, 1909.

Taylor, Donald S. *Thomas Chatterton's Art: Experiments in Imagined History.* Princeton: Princeton University Press, 1978.

Warton, Thomas. *An Enquiry into the Authenticity of the Poems Attributed to Thomas Rowley.* London: J. Dodsley, 1782.

Whitehead, John. "The Marvelous Boy." In *This Solemn Mockery.*

William-Henry Ireland

Boaden, James. *A Letter to George Steevens, Esq., Containing a Critical Examination of the Papers of Shakspeare* . . . London: Martin and Bain, 1796.

Chalmers, George. *Apology for the Believers in the Shakspeare-Papers.* . . . London: T. Egerton, 1797.

_____. *An Appendix to the Supplemental Apology for the Believers in the Supposititious Shakspeare-Papers.* . . . London: T. Egerton, 1800.

_____. *A Supplemental Apology for the Believers in the Shakspeare-Papers.* . . . London: T. Egerton, 1799.

Fleming, Juliet. "This Solemn Mockery." *Times Literary Supplement,* 31 October 1997, 24.

Grebanier, Bernard. *The Great Shakespeare Forgery.* New York: Norton, 1965.

Halliday, Frank E. "Shakespeare Fabricated." In *The Cult of Shakespeare.* New York: Thomas Yoseloff, 1960.

Hamilton, Charles. "The Boy Forger." In *Scribblers and Scoundrels.*

Haraszti, Zoltán. *The Shakespeare Forgeries of William-Henry Ireland: The Story of a Famous Literary Fraud.* Boson: Trustees of the Public Library, 1934.

Hastings, William T. " 'Shakespeare' Ireland's First Folio." *The Colophon, New Graphic Series* 1 #4 (1940): [75–86].

Ireland, Samuel, ed. *Miscellaneous Papers and Legal Instruments under the Hand and Seal of William Shakspeare.* London: Egerton [et al.], 1796 (for 1795).

_____. *Mr. Ireland's Vindication of His Conduct, Respecting the Publication of the Supposed Shakspeare MSS.* . . . London: Faulder and Robinson, 1796.

Ireland, William-Henry. *An Authentic Account of the Shaksperian Manuscripts &c.* London: J. Debrett, 1796.

_____. *The Confessions of William-Henry Ireland.* . . . London: T. Goddard, 1805.

Jaggard, William. *Shakespearean Frauds.* Stratford-upon-Avon: Shakespeare Press, 1911.

Kahan, Jeffrey. *Reforging Shakespeare: The Story of a Theatrical Scandal.* Bethlehem, PA.: Lehigh University Press, 1998.

Mair, John. *The Fourth Forger: William Ireland and the Shakespeare Papers.* New York: Macmillan, 1939.

Malone, Edmond. *An Inquiry into the Authenticity of Certain Miscellaneous Papers and Legal Instruments.* . . . London: T. Cadell [et al.], 1796.

Oulty, Wally Chamberlain. *Vortigern under Considertaion.* . . . London: H. Lowndes, 1796.

Schoenbaum, Samuel. "The Ireland Forgeries: An Unpublished Contemporary Account." In *Shakespeare and Others.* Washington: Folger Shakespeare Library, 1985.

_____. *Shakespeare's Lives.* Oxford: Oxford University Press, 1970; 2nd ed., 1991.

Sergeant, Philip W. "Young Ireland: An Unappreciated Jester." In *Liars and Fakers.*

Sherbo, Arthur. "The Earliest (?) Critic of the Ireland Shakespeare Forgeries." *Notes and Queries* 35 (December 1988): 498–500.

Webb, Francis [Philalethes, pseud.]. *Shakespeare's Manuscripts, in the Possession of Mr. Ireland, Examined, Respecting the Internal and External Evidences of Their Authenticity.* London: J. Johnson, 1796.

Whitehead, John. "Vortigern and Rowena—The New Shakespeare." In *This Solemn Mockery.*

Wyatt, John. *A Comparative Review of the Opinions of Mr. James Boaden (Editor of the Oracle).* . . . London: G. Sael, 1796.

John Payne Collier

Altick, Richard D. "A Gallery of Inventors I." In *The Scholar Adventuers*.

Arnold, Thomas. "Mr. Collier's Reply." *Fraser's Magazine for Town and Country* 61 (May 1860): 722–738.

_____. "The Old Corrector." *Fraser's Magazine for Town and Country* 61 (February 1860): 176–187.

_____. "The Shakesperian Discovery." *Fraser's Magazine for Town and Country* 61 (January 1860): 53–64.

Brae, Andrew Edward. *Literary Cookery*. London: Smith, 1855.

Chambers, Edmund Kerchever. *William Shakespeare: A Study of Facts and Problems*. 2 vols. Oxford: Clarendon Press, 1930.

Collier, John Payne, ed. *The Diary of Philip Henslowe, from 1591 to 1609*. . . . London: Shakespeare Society, 1845.

_____. "Early Manuscript Emendations of Shakespeare's Text." *Athenaeum* #1266 (31 January 1852): 142–144; #1267 (7 February 1852): 171; #1274 (27 March 1852): 355.

_____, ed. *Extracts from the Registers of the Stationers' Company of Works Entered for Publication between the Years 1557 and 1570*. London: Shakespeare Society, 1848.

_____, ed. *Extracts from the Registers of the Stationers' Company of Works Entered for Publication between the Years 1557 and 1587*. 2 vols. London: Shakespeare Society, 1849.

_____. *Farther Particulars Regarding Shakespeare and His Works. In a Letter to the Rev. Joseph Hunter, F. S. A.* London: Rodd, 1839.

_____. *The History of English Dramatic Poetry to the Time of Shakespeare; and Annals of the Stage to the Restoration*. London: John Murray, 1831; rev. ed., London: Bell, 1879.

_____. *Memoirs of Edward Alleyn, Founder of Dulwich College: Including Some New Particulars Respecting Shakespeare, Ben Jonson, Massinger, Marston, Dekker, &c.* London: Shakespeare Society, 1841.

_____. *Mr. J. Payne Collier's Reply to Mr. N. E. S. A. Hamilton's "Inquiry" into the Imputed Shakespeare Forgeries.* London: Bell & Daldy, 1860.

_____. *New Facts Regarding the Life of Shakespeare. In a Letter to Thomas Amyot, Esq., F. R. S., Treasurer of the Society of Antiquaries.* London: Rodd, 1835.

_____. *New Particulars Regarding the Works of Shakespeare. In a Letter to the Rev. A. Dyce.* London: Rodd, 1836.

_____. *Notes and Emendations to the Text of Shakespeare's Plays, from Early Manuscript Corrections in a Copy of the Folio, 1632 in the Possession of J. Payne Collier.* . . . London: Whittaker, 1853.

_____. *An Old Man's Diary, Forty Years Ago.* 4 vols. London: Printed by T. Richards, 1871-1874.

_____. *Reasons for a New Edition of Shakespeare's Works.* . . . London: Whittaker, 1841; enlarged 1842.

_____. "Shakespearian Discovery." *Times* (London), 7 July 1859, 9; 19 July 1859, 12.

_____. *Trilogy: Conversations between Three Friends on the Emendations of Shakespeare's Text Contained in Mr. Collier's Corrected Folio, 1632, and Employed by Recent Editors of the Poet's Works.* 3 vols. London: Richards, 1874.

Dawson, Giles E. "John Payne Collier's Great Forgery." *Studies in Bibliography* 24 (1971): 1–26.

Dickey, Francis. "The Old Man at Work." *Shakespeare Quarterly* 11 (Winter 1960): 39–47.

Foakes, R. A. Review of *Fortune and Men's Eyes,* by Dewey Ganzel. *Huntington Library Quarterly* 45 (Autumn 1982): 317–324.

Freeman, Arthur. Review of *Fortune and Men's Eyes,* by Dewey Ganzel. *Times Literary Supplement,* 22 April 1983, 392–393.

Freeman, Arthur, and Janet Ing Freeman. "Scholarship, Forgery, and Fictive Invention: John Payne Collier before 1831." *The Library,* 6th ser., 15 (March 1993): 1–23.

Ganzel, Dewey. *Fortune and Men's Eyes: The Career of John Payne Collier.* Oxford: Oxford University Press, 1982.

Gorall, Robert Mark. "John Payne Collier and *The Murder of Iohn Brewen.*" *Modern Language Notes* 57 (1942): 441–444.

Halliday, Frank E. "Shakespeare Incorporated." In *The Cult of Shakespeare.* New York: Thomas Yoseloff, 1960.

Hamilton, Nicholas E. S. A. *Inquiry into the Genuineness of the Manuscript Corrections in Mr. J. Payne Collier's Annotated Shakspere, Folio, 1632* . . . London: Richard Bentley, 1860.

_____. "Shakspearian Discovery." *Times* (London), 2 July 1859, 12.

Hultin, Neil C., and Warren U. Ober. "John Payne Collier, Thomas Crofton Croker, and the Hoby Epitaph." *Neophilologus* 73 (January 1989): 142–149.

Ingleby, Clement Mansfield. *A Complete View of the Shakspere Controversy.* London: Nattali and Bond, 1861.

_____. *The Shakspeare Fabrications.* London: Smith, 1859.

Jaggard, William. *Shakespearean Frauds: The Story of Some Famous Literary and Political Forgeries.* . . . Stratford-upon-Avon: Shakespeare Press, 1911.

Jenkins, David Clay. "Flies in Amber: John Payne Collier's Falsifications of Pope." *Huntington Library Quarterly* 34 (August 1971): 337–353.

_____. "The Search for the J. P. Collier Ink Syndrome." *Literary Research* 13 (Spring/Summer 1988): 95–122.

Jones, G. P. "A Burbage Ballad and John Payne Collier." *Review of English Studies* NS 40 (August 1989): 393–397.

_____. "John Payne Collier's Reputation: Review Article." *Medieval & Renaissance Drama in England: An Annual Gathering of Research, Criticism, and Reviews* 3 (1986): 255–263.

Kaplan, Joel H. "Thomas Middleton's Epitaph on the Death of Richard Burbage, and John Payne Collier." *Papers of the Bibliographical Society of America* 80 (1986): 225–232.

Maskelyne, Nevil Story. "Shakespearian Discovery." *Times* (London), 16 July 1859, 5.

Merivale, Herman. "Art. VII: [The Alleged Shakspeare Forgeries]." *Edinburgh Review* 111 (April 1860): 233–251.

_____. "The Corrector of Shakespeare." *Edinburgh Review* 103 (April 1856): 183–197.

Muir, Kenneth. Review of *Fortune and Men's Eyes*, by Dewey Ganzel. *Sewanee Review* 92 (April-June 1984): 270–273.

Myers, Robin. "Stationers' Company Bibliographies: The First 150 Years: Ames to Arber." In *Pioneers in Bibliography*. Edited by Robin Myers and Michael Harris. Winchester, England: St. Paul's Bibliographies, 1988.

Schoenbaum, Samuel. *Shakespeare's Lives*. Oxford: Oxford University Press, 1970; 2nd ed., 1991.

Singer, Samuel Weller. *The Text of Shakespeare Vindicated from the Interpolations and Corrections Advocated by John Payne Collier, Esq., in His "Notes and Emendations."* London: Pickering, 1853.

Tannenbaum, Samuel A. *Shakspere Forgeries in the Revels Accounts*. New York: Columbia University Press, 1928.

_____. *Shaksperian Scraps and Other Elizabethan Fragments*. New York: Columbia University Press, 1933.

Velz, J. W. "The Collier Controversy Redivivus." *Shakespeare Quarterly* 36 (1985): 106–115.

Wellens, Oskar. "John Payne Collier: The Man behind the Unsigned *Times* Review of 'Christabel' (1816)." *The Wordsworth Circle* 13 (Spring 1982): 68–71.

Whitehead, John. "Librarian Gone Wrong." In *This Solemn Mockery*.

Wood, D. T. B. "The Revels Books: The Writer of the 'Malone Scrap.'" *Review of English Studies* 1 (1925): 72–74.

_____. "The Suspected Revels Books." *Review of English Studies* 1 (1925): 166–172.

Ziegler, Georgiana. "A Victorian Reputation: John Payne Collier and His Contemporaries." *Shakespeare Studies* 17 (1985): 209–234.

George Gordon Byron

Altick, Richard D. "A Gallery of Inventors II." In *The Scholar Adventurers.*

Birss, John Howard. "A Sonnet Wrongly Ascribed to Keats." *Notes and Queries* 164 (3 June 1933): 388.

Byron, George Gordon, Lord. *Byron's Letters and Journals.* Edited by Leslie A. Marchand. 12 vols. Cambridge, MA: Belknap Press of Harvard University Press, 1973–1982.

Chew, Samuel C. *Byron in England, His Fame and After-Fame.* New York: Scribner's, 1924.

Davey, Samuel John. "The Story of the Byron and Shelley Forgeries; with a Notice of Mr. Browning's Essay on Shelley." *The Archivist* 1 (1888): 2–7.

Ehrsam, Theodore G. *Major Byron.* New York: Charles E. Boesen; London: John Murray, 1951.

Farrer, James Anson. "The Forged Letters of Byron and Shelley." In *Literary Forgeries.*

Hamilton, Charles. "Lord Byron's Bastard Son: Major George Byron." In *Great Forgers and Famous Fakes.*

Jones, Frederick L. "The Shelley Legend." *Publications of the Modern Language Association* 61 (1946): 886.

Kessel, Marcel. "A Forged Shelley Letter." *Times Literary Supplement,* 29 May 1937, 412.

Lees, Frederic George. "Recollections of an Anglo-Parisian Bibliophile. III. The Great Shelley Forgery." *Bookman* 83 (October 1932): 31–37.

Mayor, Andrew. "A Suspected Shelley Letter." *Library,* 5th ser., 4 (September 1949): 141–145.

"The 'Pseudo-Byron,' and the Literary Forgeries of Thirty Years Ago." *American Antiquarian* 4 (March 1886): 327–330.

Shelley, Mary Wollstonecraft. *The Letters of Mary W. Shelley.* Edited by Frederick L. Jones. 2 vols. Norman: University of Oklahoma Press, 1944.

Smith, Robert Metcalf. *The Shelley Legend.* New York: Scribner's, 1945.

Sotheby, Samuel Leigh. *Principia Typographia.* 2 vols. London: McDowall, 1858.

White, Newman Ivey, Frederick L. Jones, and Kenneth N. Cameron. *An Examination of "The Shelley Legend."* Philadelphia: Univesity of Pennsylvania Press, 1951.

White, William. *The Calumnies of the "Athenaeum" Journal Exposed. Mr. White's Letter to Mr. Murray, on the Subject of the Byron, Shelley, and Keats MSS.* London: William White, 1852.

Whitehead, John. "Major Byron and the Forged Letters." In *This Solemn Mockery.*

Vrain-Denis Lucas

Bordier, Henri, and Émile Mabille. *Une fabrique de faux autographes, ou récit de l'affaire Vrain Lucas.* Paris: Léon Techener, 1870. Translated by Joseph Rosenblum under the title *The Prince of Forgers.* New Castle, DE: Oak Knoll Books, 1998.

Chasles, Michel. *Sur l'ouvrage de M. Faugère, intitulé "Défense de B. Pascal . . . ."* Paris: Gauthier-Villars, 1868.

Farrer, James Anson. "A French Forger: Vrain-Denis Lucas." In *Literary Forgeries.*

Faugère, Armand-Prosper. *Défense de B. Pascal et accessoirement de Newton, Galileo . . . contre les faux documents présentés par M. Chasles à l'Académie des sciences.* Paris: L. Hachette, 1868.

Girard, Georges, ed. *Le parfait secrétaire des grands hommes, ou les lettres de Sapho, Platon [etc.] mises au jour par Vrain Lucas.* Paris: À la Cité des Livres, 1924.

Whitehead, John. "Two Europeans." In *This Solemn Mockery*.

Thomas James Wise

Altick, Richard D. "The Case of the Curious Bibliographers." In *The Scholar Adventurers*.

Arnold, William Harris. *Ventures in Book Collecting*. New York: Scribner's, 1923.

Barker, Nicolas, and John Collins. *A Sequel to "An Enquiry."* London: Scolar, 1983.

Bratcher, J. T., and Lyle H. Kendall. *A Supplemental Critique of Wise's Swinburne Transactions: Addendum to "An Enquiry."* Austin: Humanities Research Center, University of Texas, 1970.

Carter, John. "Thomas J. Wise." In *Books and Book Collectors*. Cleveland: World, 1957.

Carter, John, and Graham Pollard. *An Enquiry into the Nature of Certain Nineteenth Century Pamphlets*. London: Constable; New York: Scribner's, 1934. Edited and augmented by Nicolas Barker and John Collins. London: Scolar, 1983.

Collins, John. *The Two Forgers: A Biography of Harry Buxton Forman and Thomas James Wise*. New Castle, DE: Oak Knoll Books, 1992.

Foxon, David. *Thomas James Wise and the Pre-Restoration Drama: A Study in Theft and Sophistication*. London: The Bibliographical Society, 1959.

Foxon, David, and William B. Todd. "Thomas J. Wise and the Pre-Restoration Drama: A Supplement." *The Library,* 5th ser., 16 (December 1961): 287–293.

Lewis, Roger C. *Thomas James Wise and the Trial Book Fallacy*. Aldershot, England: Scolar, 1995.

Macdonald, Dwight. "Annals of Crime: The First Editions of T. J. Wise." *The New Yorker* 38 (10 November 1962): 165–205.

Muir, Augustus. "A Treasure-House of Books: Mr. Thomas J. Wise and the Ashley Library." *Strand* 80 (September 1930): 280–288.

Pariser, Sir Maurice. *Catalogue of the Celebrated Collection Formed by Sir Maurice Pariser, of Manchester, of the Notorious Nineteenth Century Pamphlets and Other Important Wiseana Manuscript and Printed.* London: Sotheby, 1967.

Partington, Wilfred. *Forging Ahead.* New York: Putnam's, 1939. Enlarged as *Thomas J. Wise in the Original Cloth.* London: Hale, 1947.

Pedley, Katharine Greenleaf. *Moriarty in the Stacks: The Nefarious Adventures of Thomas J. Wise.* Berkeley, CA: Peacock, 1966.

Ratchford, Fannie E., ed. *Between the Lines: Letters and Memoranda Interchanged by H. Buxton Forman and Thomas J. Wise.* Austin: University of Texas Press, 1945.

Raymond, W. O. "The Forgeries of Wise and Their Aftermath." *Journal of English and Germanic Philology* 44 (July 1945): 229–238.

Nowell-Smith, Simon. "T. J. Wise as Bibliographer." *The Library,* 5th ser., 24 (June 1969): 129–141.

Todd, William B. *Suppressed Commentaries on the Wiseian Forgeries: Addendum to "An Enquiry."* Austin: Humanities Research Center, University of Texas, 1969.

_____, ed. *Thomas J. Wise Centenary Studies.* Austin: University of Texas Press, 1959.

Whitehead, John. "Not So Wise." In *This Solemn Mockery.*

Wise, Thomas James. *Letters of Thomas J. Wise to John Henry Wrenn: A Further Inquiry into the Guilt of Certain Nineteenth-Century Forgers.* Edited by Fannie E. Ratchford. New York: Knopf, 1944.

Mark William Hofmann

Gilreath, James, ed. *The Judgment of Experts: Essays and Documents about the Investigation of the "Oath of a Freeman."* Worcester, MA: American Antiquarian Society, 1991.

Hofmann, Mark William. *Hofmann's Confession: A Photographic Printing of the Transcripts of Salt Lake County Prosecutors'*

Interviews with Convicted Forger and Murderer Mark Hofmann. 3 vols. Salt Lake City: Utah Lighthouse Ministry, 1987.

Lindsey, Robert. *A Gathering of Saints: A True Story of Money, Murder and Deceit.* New York: Simon and Schuster , 1988.

_____. "The Mormons: Growth, Prosperity and Controversy." *New York Times Magazine,* 12 January 1986, 18+;

McLellin, William E. *The Journals of William E. McLellin.* Edited by Jan Shipps and John W. Welch. Provo, Utah: *BYU Studies,* Brigham Young University, 1994.

Naifeh, Steven, and Gregory White Smith. *The Mormon Murders: A True Story of Greed, Forgery, Deceit, and Death.* New York: Weidenfeld & Nicolson, 1988.

Sillitoe, Linda, and Allen D. Roberts. *Salamander: The Story of the Mormon Forgery Murders.* Salt Lake City: Signature Books, 1988.

Tanner, Jerald. *Tracking the White Salamander: The Story of Mark Hofmann, Murder and Forged Mormon Documents.* Salt Lake City: Utah Lighthouse Ministry, 1986; 3rd ed., 1987.

Turley, Richard E., Jr. *Victims: The LDS Church and the Mark Hofmann Case.* Urbana: University of Illinois Press, 1992.

INDEX